Drawn by
Geo. H. Durfee.
Co. K first Reg.
Minn.
Vol $

May 27th
1862

Columbian College

Barrack's
Hill.

BRICKS WITHOUT STRAW

Washington planning the city. (Painting by Garnet Wolseley Jex, M.F.A., 1931.)

ELMER LOUIS KAYSER

BRICKS
WITHOUT STRAW

The Evolution of
George Washington University

*There is no straw given unto thy servants,
and they say to us, Make bricks.* EXODUS 5:16

NEW YORK
APPLETON-CENTURY-CROFTS
EDUCATIONAL DIVISION
MEREDITH CORPORATION

Library of Congress Catalog Card Number 77-110893

PRINTED IN THE UNITED STATES OF AMERICA
390-49615-4

To
ARTHUR HALLETT PAGE IV

Contents

Illustrations

Washington planning the city. *Frontispiece*

These pictures follow page 48

Luther Rice (1783-1836), founder of Columbian College.
An appeal for the contribution of funds toward the construction of the buildings on College Hill.
The original College building on College Hill.
The first building of the Medical Department.
Enoch Reynolds, first Secretary of the Board of Trustees.
Obadiah B. Brown, first President of the Board of Trustees.
Henry Clay, a powerful ally in obtaining a charter for the College.
John C. Calhoun, a strong supporter of the College.
The Marquis de Lafayette, guest of honor at the first Commencement.
President James Monroe, who signed the charter.
William Staughton, D.D., first President, 1821-1827.
Stephen Chapin, D.D., second President, 1828-1841.
Joel Smith Bacon, D.D., third President, 1843-1854.
Joseph Getchell Binney, D.D., fourth President, 1855-1858.
John Withers, Trustee, 1832-1861.
John Quincy Adams, principal creditor of the early College.
A student's account covering all expenses for a term (1825).

These pictures follow page 112

The seal of Columbian College, drawn by James Peale, adopted in 1821.
The College building on College Hill after 1860.

ix

Washington Infirmary, quarters of the Medical Department, 1844-1861.
The Law School, 1865-1884.
Tenth Street, showing Ford's Theatre and the first Medical School.
Tent wards in Columbian College General Hospital.
Columbian College and Carver Barracks, 1864.
A convalescent ward in Columbian College General Hospital.
George Whitefield Samson, D.D., fifth President, 1859-1871.
The Medical School, 1866-1868.
The Law School, 1899-1910.
The Medical School, 1868-1902.
James Clarke Welling, sixth President, 1871-1894.
Samuel Harrison Greene, D.D., acting President, 1894-1895, 1900-1902.
Benaiah Longley Whitman, D.D., seventh President, 1895-1900.
Charles Willis Needham, eighth President, 1902-1910.
William Wilson Corcoran, principal benefactor of the University in the
    late nineteenth century.

These pictures follow page 176

"The Original Thirteen," Columbian College, 1899-1900.
The University building, 1884-1910.
The three buildings of the Medical School, 1921.
The football squad of 1908.
Fifteenth Street, showing the University building in the right center.
The College of Veterinary Medicine, 1908-1918.
Charles Herbert Stockton, ninth President, 1910-1918.
William Miller Collier, tenth President, 1918-1921.
Howard Lincoln Hodgkins, President pro tempore, 1921-1923.
William Mather Lewis, eleventh President, 1923-1927.
2023 G Street, 1912-1938, the first building occupied when the University
    was relocated in the West End.
Woodhull House, 1912, later the office of President Hodgkins.
Porter House, 1912, later the office of President Collier.
Quigley's Pharmacy, 1912.
Patterson House, 1912, later the office of President Lewis.
New Masonic Temple, home of the Law School, 1910-1921.
School of Pharmacy, 1906-1919.

These pictures follow page 240

The Law School, 1921-1925.
"The Tin Tabernacle" at the time of its completion in 1924.
Woodhull House, Registrar's Office, the Easby houses, Lisner Hall, *c.* 1932.
The Hall of Government, Woodhull House, Alexander Graham Bell Hall, Lisner Library, Gilbert Stuart Hall, the office of the President, residences used as offices, and Stockton Hall.
Corcoran Hall, 1924.
The Jacob Burns Law Library, 1968, and Stockton Hall, 1925.
Convocation in honor of H.M. Albert, King of the Belgians, 1919.
Delegates to the inauguration of University President William Mather Lewis at the White House, 1923.
Convocation in honor of the Rt. Hon. Ramsay MacDonald, Prime Minister of Great Britain, 1929.
Convocation in honor of H.M. Prajadhipok, King of Siam, 1931.
University Hospital, 1948.
Cloyd Heck Marvin, twelfth President, 1927-1959.
Oswald Symister Colclough, Acting President, 1959-1961, 1964-1965.
Thomas Henry Carroll, thirteenth President, 1961-1964.
Lloyd Hartman Elliott, fourteenth President, 1965-
Warwick Memorial, 1954.
Lisner Auditorium, 1946.

These pictures follow page 304

University Yard, Gilbert Stuart Hall, 1936; Lisner Library, 1939; Alexander Graham Bell Hall, 1935.
Hall of Government, 1938.
Hattie M. Strong Residence Hall for Women, 1936.
Meyer Pavilion, the University Hospital, 1968.
James Monroe Hall, 1951.
Thurston Hall, 1964.
Winter Convocation of 1929 at which President and Mrs. Calvin Coolidge received honorary degrees.
Commencement of 1946 at which President Harry S. Truman received an honorary degree and Margaret Truman her degree in course.

Preface

This book is not a history of the schools, colleges, and divisions, but of George Washington University itself. Unfortunately, most of the history of these academic units is left untouched, except insofar as it concerns the larger institution itself. Particularly it is to be regretted that even the names of many significant figures do not appear in a book already formidable in size.

What might have been an expanded summary appears as the first chapter. In it the purpose of the volume is stated quite fully. The material shows specifically the ways by which a church-related liberal arts college evolved into an independent urban university, ways that are described in the narrative chapters which follow Chapter 1. The early history of the University was truly a matter of "bricks without straw," of maintaining and expanding an institution faced constantly with financial difficulties and valiantly paying off recurring debts, but having to wait well over a century before it accumulated the means for growth.

This history is presented in terms of broad concepts, rather than in terms of the overall administration of the individual presidents. It is a *topic* as it involves presidents that is stressed, rather than the presidents themselves and their action in relation to that topic. Thus one aspect of the University's history—early finances, for example—may involve more than one of its presidents, and the same presidents may appear also in another chapter dealing with the early growth of the University. For this reason there is no separate indication of the names and terms of office of the various presidents, as such, within the chapters. A chronological list covering this information appears on page 344.

It is not an official history in the usual sense. No part of it has been submitted for criticism or approval to any officer of the University or to any person other than members of the Historian's staff. For what appears, the author is alone responsible, and any statement which is made and not documented is based on his personal knowledge and experience during an association with the University for more than half a century.

In the course of the preparation of the book, obligations have been incurred to many people and institutions. The vast resources of the city of Washington, with its many libraries and collections of historical material, have been generously drawn upon, and the value of the material itself has been greatly enhanced by the courtesy and efficiency of their staffs in making their holdings so readily available.

A special debt of gratitude is due Doctor Davis C. Wooley, the Executive Secretary of the Historical Commission of the Southern Baptist Convention, for his encouragement, assistance, and generosity in so many ways; to the American Baptist Historical Society and the Virginia Baptist Historical Society for the ready use of the rich material in their libraries; and to Mrs. Luther Joe Thompson and Professor David B. Potts for valuable suggestions.

Grateful acknowledgment is due many officers and staff members of George Washington University. President Lloyd H. Elliott, the late President Thomas H. Carroll, Dean O. S. Colclough, and Vice President Harold Bright have given support without which the writing of this history could not have been undertaken. The Director of Libraries, Rupert C. Woodward, has been consistently helpful and generous in many ways. The staffs of the libraries under Mr. Woodward and his predecessor, John Russell Mason, have, like their heads, been uniformly cooperative. Jessie B. Martin, Harvey R. Brasse, H. Earle Newcity, and R. W. Howard have given much valuable technical assistance. Dorothy Thompson and Donald S. Benton have given needed aid graciously and readily.

The loyal assistance of Donald E. McLeod, John M. Sanderson, Jr., and Martin Paul Claussen, Jr., of the staff has facilitated the preparation of the book from the beginning of the project. A very special word of appreciation is due Mary E. Barnes for her assistance in preparing the manuscript and index and the use of her ready knowledge of the materials in the historical collection.

To those named and the many others who should be named, the author expresses his thanks with the humble feeling that without their aid, this history could not have been written.

2023 G Street, N.W.   ELMER LOUIS KAYSER
May 1, 1969

BRICKS WITHOUT STRAW

CHAPTER ONE

Overview:
A Century and a Half
1821-1971

The chapters in *Bricks Without Straw* tell the history of a university rather than the history of its parts. Although there is an occasional flashback to throw light on life in the institution at certain periods, the emphasis is on the University as a whole, a corporate entity. While some of its experiences may have been unique, most of them have been characteristic enough to make this a useful case history in American higher education.

The institution has been known by three names—Columbian College in the District of Columbia, Columbian University, and George Washington University. It has had three major sites—College Hill, Midtown, and the West End. It is significant that all three sites have been located within a relatively limited area in northwest Washington. In a sense, Washington has no hinterland. The city is the District, and the District is the city. The two early became coterminous. A capital city was created by mandate and laid out anew, forming a distinct political unit, virtually sitting astride two political zones. The College really had no choice but to gravitate toward the urban university, and, in fact, to become one of the first truly urban universities. The city itself, then, was a major factor in shaping the institution.

Of equal importance, at least for the first century, was the problem of denominational relationship. In all candor we must say that this problem was more acute in its financial than in its ideological aspects. Pride was strong in the College, as one of the first fruits of the Baptist denomination as a denomination. Denominational contacts were cherished. On the side of the institution, denominational support, since apparently no other was earmarked for its use, was of prime importance. There was no original endowment; in fact, the purchase of College Hill before the Charter was granted was the only one of the College's early financial transactions that was fully funded in advance.

The intent of Congress in chartering Columbian College was quite clear. The petition for a charter which would give the Baptist Convention certain corporate rights, among them the right to engage in education, was summarily rejected. The Charter which was granted imposed upon the College a strictly nonsectarian character, and gave to the Attorney General of the United States the right of inspection and examination. In spite of the Congressional intent, Baptist ingenuity established virtual control by two means. The first was the Charter provision that Trustees should be elected by the contributors in a way to be established in an ordinance by the Board of Trustees. Since the contributors, as defined in the ordinances, were largely individual Baptists and Baptist bodies, the slate drawn up and approved by the Convention was bound to be elected. The second was the fact that the title to College Hill was held by the Convention and the property was leased to the College. Should at any time less than three-fourths of the Trustees be members of the Baptist denomination, the lease was broken.

There was never any subvention or guaranteed underwriting by the denomination. The church relationship authorized and stimulated solicitation of funds from individual Baptists and Baptist bodies. These contributions were supposed to support the academic program, pay for administration and maintenance, and provide funds for plant improvement and expansion. The income from tuition and from boarders was uncertain and indefinite, although the hope was ever alive that some day operating expenses could be fully met from this source. The College was generous to those who wanted to attend. Many a poor boy, looking toward the ministry and armed with a letter from his pastor attesting his Christian character and intention to enter the ministry, would be admitted for reduced fees or no fees at all. Many contributors availed themselves of the right to nominate for scholarships. The number of students registered was unfortunately no index to the amount of tuition that would be collected.

When the indebtedness incurred during the first five years of actual operation reached a dangerous point, alarm became general. When it appeared that someone had to be blamed, Luther Rice, vulnerable because of his poor business habits, was made the scapegoat. The Baptist Convention pointed out that it was not responsible for the support of the College, commended it to the attention of Christian people as deserving of support, and promised continued and prayerful sympathy. The dissolution of the College might easily have taken place. There was a resignation of key Trustees. The unpaid faculty had come to the end of its patience, and offered resignations. The student body, shaken by uncertainties, began to melt away. The exercises of the College were suspended.

One well-timed and intelligent move saved the College. A group of influential Baptists whose names commanded instant respect met in New York on May 9, 1826, and called for the subscription of $50,000 to pay the debt within a period of two years. The subscriptions were to be payable when and if the entire amount was pledged and when the representatives of the group certified that the necessary conditions had been met. Thanks to the generous leniency of its creditors and to energetic fund raising, the College regained its solvency. Although the Convention wished to abandon its role in the nomination of Trustees, the Board itself urged the continuance of the practice. This form of denominational contact it considered desirable and profitable, even though the Convention was, at the time, reasserting its original and primary interest in missions as its sole concern.

The type of church relationship that was developed and maintained during the first quarter-century of the College's history might have gone on indefinitely, but for the slavery issue and the great Baptist schism. When, in spite of efforts to maintain unity, the issue of slaveholding drove a wedge between its northern and southern members, the Baptist General Convention for Foreign Missions, which held title to College Hill, was dissolved. As one of its last acts the Convention transferred the title in fee simple to the College. Thus ended one of the two tangible links in the church connection. The other remained in existence for another quarter-century.

In 1871, because (and the change in temper is interesting) it was thought that a more widely based Board, freed of denominational entanglements, would add to the institution's prestige and open the way for more general solicitation of funds, a change in the Charter made the Board of Trustees a self-perpetuating body. The princely generosity of Mr. W. W. Corcoran, an Episcopalian, who was to serve as president of the Board of Trustees, confirmed the validity of the new arrangement. Also in 1871, a layman was elected president of the College for the first time.

It was toward the close of this lay president's administration that the College, now transformed into a university in educational structure as well as in name, looked again wistfully to the Baptists. In the absence of any other sponsor, it was hoped that denominational pride in an institution which Baptists had started in the national capital would incline them toward undertaking a major part in financing it. The Baptist Educational Society expressed interest but declined support.

The next step was, perhaps, a natural one. Aware that a wealthy Baptist was about to contribute a very large sum to some existing church-related institution, the Trustees in 1898 successfully petitioned Congress to change the nonsectarian character of the Charter, and to provide denominational control by requiring that the president and two-thirds of the Trustees should be members of regular Baptist churches. But Baptist control did not bring the expected millions to Columbian University, and after six years the Trustees asked for the restoration of the original Charter. These six years, 1898-1904, were the only period when the University was sectarian in control by Charter requirement.

In the quarter-century following the restoration of the original Charter, various proposals were made for the resumption of Baptist control, but the character of the University after a century of activity had become fixed. The day for denominational control had passed forever. It is fair to say that almost at any time in the nineteenth century, a proposal for Baptist control joined with insured financial support would have been readily accepted. It took the traumatic experience of 1898-1904, when change to sectarian control failed to entice the expected millions, to end forever a long-cherished idea that financial support might be obtained from denominational sources. The nondenominational character of the University was confirmed when the older idea was subjected to pragmatic test and failed to produce.

In fairness, it must be said that there was never a continuing struggle to free itself of Baptist control. Rice felt that the Trustees put in at the time of the 1826 crisis had such an idea. If they did, it was never carried out. The institution did not throw off Baptist control. It envolved out of it.

Why did the Baptists select the District of Columbia as the site of the mother college of the denomination? They felt that its central position would give permanence, would arouse the interest of those in various parts of the country and, in so doing, strengthen the Union.

The founding of a college in the new capital was an event of considerable importance. Not only had the great Washington urged the establishment there of a national university and many of his contemporaries and his successors voiced the same desire, but it seemed proper that among the institutions of the city should be a college, more broadly based than the Jesuit college in the neighboring city of Georgetown, which would represent in a tangible way the dedication of the new city to culture. The politically eminent of the day were among the contributors to the fund which purchased College Hill. The President of the United States bestowed his blessings on the College, and attendance upon its formal public ceremonies became a fixed social custom. To a young city of less than fifteen thousand inhabitants, a new college was a notable addition. Its student body was drawn from all sections of the Union, with a few foreign students from time to time. Clearly, the early College held a favored position in the life of the city. The modest size of the federal establishment by no means dwarfed the College.

In the absence of public secondary schools, the Academy that was established immediately after the opening of the College was an important addition to the meager educational opportunities available in the city. Offering not only a course for college preparation, but a terminal course for those who planned to enter business and other nonprofessional callings, it gave sound training for three-quarters of a century. With the development of public secondary education in the later nineteenth century it was no longer deemed necessary, or even proper, for the University to maintain Columbian Academy, and the preparatory department was discontinued. In its prime, the Academy contributed greatly to the close ties between city and College.

The loyalty of the city to its College stood the institution in good stead, as the development of colleges in the North tended more and more to lead young men who otherwise would have attended Columbian to go to nearer colleges. This trend was so noticeable that Columbian made special efforts to recruit in the states north of the District, but it was unable to stem the movement that made the College student body largely southern. Luther Rice was quite conscious of what was happening and was apparently not too dissatisfied with the situation. His fund-raising tours in the latter part of his life (he died in 1836) were practically confined to the southern states. The establishment of a Baptist-related college in Richmond was a heavy blow to the College's patronage in the state of Virginia, from which Columbian had drawn students in large numbers. It is easy to understand the concern of a Corresponding Committee seeking a successor to President Binney as it stated the basic problem: "Whether a college standing on Mason and Dixon's line, looking for students chiefly from the Southern Border as one does and having such funds as ours has can sustain itself." In 1860, shortly after he entered upon his duties, the new president, Samson, announced that he was going north to raise funds, it being useless to go south. Soon the Trustees were to authorize the treasurer to accept Virginia currency in payment of students' obligations. Uncertain though it was in value, it was better than nothing at all.

Until the coming of the War of 1861-1865, the local area and its environs had shown no phenomenal growth. In the thirty-year period 1820-1850 the greater Washington area had increased only 28 per cent in population.[1] Washington was still a small city. Although the College was forced to seek its students more and more in the capital area, that area was not furnishing a rapidly increasing reservoir of population from which an increasing number of students could be drawn. All things considered, it was surprising that the College could hold its student body at the level that it tried to maintain. Operating deficits were regular, even though little was spent for maintenance of aging facilities. Instead of building a new and needed structure, the mansard roof on the old college building was raised to provide an additional full story.

The War of 1861-1865 did many things to the city and the College. College Hill was taken over by the government and became the site of important military installations. Shortly after the hospital in Judiciary Square was commandeered, it burned down. The College had few students left, and no facilities for their housing. The student body was reducd to a handful of local youths who were instructed in the homes of the faculty. The government paid the College a rental. Those funds took care of the accumulated indebtedness. They should have been held for the restoration of the property after four years of military occupancy.

The city experienced a great influx of new inhabitants, some temporary, many permanent. A vast staff of civilian employees was required by the War Department, involved as it was in the maintenance of large armies. The Army of the Potomac was organized, and many of its units were quartered in the city and its neighboring defenses. When the War was over, the government still maintained a large personnel in the capital. The Pension Bureau alone was responsible for hundreds of employees. The capital city was magnificent only in its distances. In that war-worn city it was hard to find any traces of L'Enfant's dream. Population growth was henceforth to be of a different order. Out of the chaos was to emerge the orderly city of its designer.

After the War several factors confirmed and hastened the change that had already begun. The College plant was in ill repair; and because the substantial funds needed for its restoration were not available, it was impossible to operate it as a residential college. The expanding city was pushing beyond the old corporate limits. Because the College used only the middle third of its elongated grounds, the authorities saw a possibility of getting a substantial lump sum or a fixed income from the sale of the south plot, nearest the city boundary, or from the subdivision of the area. In line with this possibility, the land along Fourteenth Street, a main artery for north-south traffic, was subdivided for business, and all the remaining land in the south plot was subdivided for residences at a value per square foot a third less than that fixed for the Fourteenth Street frontage. The disposal of the old College property was under way; the sale of the north lot, and then of the College grounds proper, was shortly to follow.

This economic factor was reinforced by another which was both economic and educational. Many of the new civil servants with whom the city now abounded found themselves domiciled in a town that offered very little cultural and educational enrichment. These people worked a short day and were happy to have a chance to attend afternoon classes at Columbian College. The College sensed the demand and, at first experimentally, made administrative adjustments to facilitate the attendance of these employed students. It became quickly obvious that the demand was real and substantial. A very practically-minded president summed up the situation by concluding that there was no reason why instruction should not be given where and when it would be convenient for the people who wanted it and were willing to pay for it.

This decision had deeply significant results. The employed students wanted not only the subjects embraced within the standard undergraduate liberal arts and sciences program. Many were mature people, with degrees, who were seeking advanced courses. Others wanted practical courses such as applied science and engineering. Because the city was the seat of government the need was easily met. Washington had in the government service a vast reservoir of potential teachers of great ability, particularly in the sciences. The employed students wanted courses after working hours, and the government experts, many of them former college teachers, were available to offer instruction at these hours. Part-time students and part-time instructors together increased rapidly and came to occupy a large place in the College's financing and educational organization. The Corcoran Scientific School was organized initially to give this type of educational service to both men and women. Demands for advanced study and the availability of highly qualified graduate instructors made possible the establishment of the School of Graduate Studies in the arts and sciences, which granted both masters' and doctors' degrees and offered graduate courses in jurisprudence and diplomacy.

In the breadth and depth of its educational offerings the College had become a university. This was formally recognized by a change in name in 1873 when, by an amendment of the Charter, Columbian College became Columbian University. Shortly thereafter the University picked H Street between Thirteenth and Fifteenth Streets as the new site. On those two blocks all the University's activities were gathered. Moving out of what had been farm land when it first occupied it—the middle of a rather large acreage, with room to expand—the University now found itself in an expensive but convenient area, the very heart of the financial district. The University occupied high-priced, downtown, city real estate, difficult to acquire. Washington in 1821 was a village. In the 1880's it had already taken on the aspect of a considerable city. At its founding the College had to house and feed the students within its own walls. Sixty years later it could not house its students, nor did it need to. The city was sufficiently large to absorb them without difficulty. Washington was beginning to dress up and the University buildings on H Street were not out of key with their surroundings.

Funds realized from the sale of College Hill, supplemented by any other money that the University could find, even by dipping into restricted funds, did not yield enough to cover the costs of land acquisition and construction on H Street. The University was more deeply in debt than ever before. As it expanded its offerings and tried to make more and more of the universe of knowledge its province, the debt increased. Efforts to raise funds in Washington and to find outside sponsors proved equally ineffective.

A badly conceived economy move, involving among other things the early retirement of two distinguished professors to cut down instructional charges, cost the University the loss of the advantages of the Carnegie pension plan and precipitated a public discussion of the University's ills which brought on the Attorney General's investigation of 1910. A very sick patient underwent major surgery. It was shown that, in order to pay for land and building construction and to meet operating deficits, the institution had used up practically all of its modest endowment. To restore the endowment and lift the debt, the imposing University building and the Law School were sold and a mortgage in the University's favor was put on the Medical School properties. An institution which was not unacquainted with misfortune touched its nadir in 1910. Only the Medical School was housed on University property. Everything else— administration, arts and sciences, law—was in inadequate, temporary, rented quarters.

The coming of Admiral Stockton to the presidency and the purchase of 2023 G Street for a modest sum in 1912 marked the turn in the tide. Strict economy and the patient use of old buildings, slightly modified for college purposes, together with unfailing faculty loyalty and forbearance, made balanced budgets possible and permitted the slow but constant acquisition of small parcels of land for expansion. The Centennial Celebration of 1921 marked the beginning of preparations for the first major fund-raising campaign; and the construction of Corcoran Hall in 1924, the beginning of the building of a new University plant.

The fifteen or twenty years following the crisis of 1910 were rather complicated in their effects on the development of the institution. The Spartan austerity of those years restored public confidence in the University financially and educationally and laid the firm basis for the expansion during the Marvin years. At the same time, to those who look at outward things—and unfortunately many do—the prestige of the University was not greatly enhanced. The city, especially after the First World War, had become more and more monumental with great new structures like the Lincoln Memorial and the buildings of the Federal Triangle. The modest brick structures on College Hill had been looked upon as outstanding when they were built. The University building at Fifteenth and H Streets was massive and impressive and looked quite fitting in the middle of a financial district. But the modified dwellings and built-on classrooms that clustered around 2023 G Street looked too much like the decayed area in which they were located. Public taste was demanding impressive structures, and few of its fellow townsmen knew where George Washington University was.

President Marvin realized this and began, with very meager means, to make the University an architectural fact. Proceeding with great economy, he first made the north side of G Street between Twentieth and Twenty-first Streets with its three major structures a visible representation of the

University. He worked toward the grouping of buildings around this nucleus. People knew then where the University was. The University had started building impressive structures which could hold their own in a monumental city. Generous patrons, and particularly the federal government with outright grants, matching gifts, low interest rates with long periods for payment, made possible the continued policy of building impressive structures, in the best Washington manner, in the University triangle south and east of Washington Circle.

In yet another form, governmental cooperation was exceedingly significant. Even in its early years, the College had looked upon its location in the capital as offering rare opportunity for the close observation of the working of the various branches of the government and for the use of the first-hand knowledge, thus gained, in the total education of the student. As the governmental institutions developed beyond the bare bones of executive, legislative, and judicial business, as such institutions as the Smithsonian and the Library of Congress took form and the burgeoning departments began to develop research activities to strengthen and expand their operations, a new and more intimate contact with the agencies of government was in order. Gradually these agencies, some governmental, some quasi-governmental, began to have importance, through their facilities and research, for practically every department of instruction. The increasingly large group of specialists attached to them offered a rich reservoir from which lecturers and part-time teachers could be drawn. The joint resolution of the Houses of Congress on April 12, 1891, which placed the facilities of the government at the service of educational institutions, formalized for the first time this type of governmental cooperation. By the fortunate fact of its location, the University could make, and has made, continuous and increasing use of these governmental facilities in the city and its environs.

It was, perhaps, by logical progression that this University, as did universities throughout the land, found itself able not only to take from but to give to the government, through sponsored research, types of needed service utilizing academic facilities, personnel, and know-how. This development has had a massive effect on University finances. It has taken a major position in the University budget, increasing commitments but contributing substantial sums to the University's income.

The institution's great handicap through the years had been its lack of money to grow on. Deficits occurred periodically. When they became alarmingly large, a vigorous effort would be instituted to clear them up or reduce them. There had never been, during the first century, any considerable accumulation to finance expansion. With the steady acquisition of land, particularly during the last quarter of a century, building sites were assembled and new methods of finance made construction possible. In the development of a new physical plant, attention was given to student housing and feeding and recreational units. The result was to make the undergraduate student body largely a resident one in an incredibly short time. The part-time student body ceased to have its overwhelming importance and the College again, as in the first period of its history, became basically one with a full-time student body, largely housed on the campus. At the same time the interests of part-time, employed students were in no measure neglected. The University's mission in this area has been so firmly rooted in its history that, regardless of marked expansion in perhaps more traditional fields, it will always be concerned, as well, with those who earn while they learn.

CHAPTER TWO

Missions and Education
1812-1821

America began early in her history to be a land of colleges. At the time of the Declaration of Independence, there were nine colleges, the oldest of them having already arrived at the venerable age of one hundred and forty years. These institutions, stretching from Massachusetts to Virginia, owed their origin to a rugged determination on the part of the Colonists not to allow their youth to grow up as barbarians, as strange as the study of Latin and Greek might seem on the narrow margin of an untamed wilderness. Unawed by difficulties, they were going to provide in the New World the amenities of the Old, as far as they could. Hopefully, they would supply here sound learning in the manner and of the type that they had known in England, consciously or unconsciously conditioned by changing moods of thought, political circumstance, and social experience.

The Revolution brought many changes. Frederick Rudolph has summarized its effects: "The legacy of the American Revolution to the American college was, then, a heavy mixture of French deism, unruly students, state controls, and a widely held belief that the colleges were now serving a new responsibility to a new nation: the preparation of young men for responsible citizenship in a republic that must prove itself, the preparation for lives of usefulness of young men who also intended to prove themselves."[1]

"The preparation of young men for responsible citizenship": This was exactly the motive which led Washington to make his proposals for a university at the new seat of government. Although it never profited from his generosity, the institution which today bears his name has found in his efforts and utterances an urge to strive for his ideal, even though it owes its origin to other men and to other springs of action. Washington's true legacy to American higher education was not his bequest of stock in the Potomac Company, which no institution received, but his faith in education for citizenship which all have accepted.

The idea of a national university was by no means novel with Washington. From the time Richard Rush in 1786 made the first formal proposals for an institution of higher learning, emphasizing graduate study and research, the idea had claimed the attention of many individuals and even of the Constitutional Convention. Washington, as President and as private citizen, was most zealous in its advocacy and even selected a site in the new city, immediately south and west of the area occupied today by George Washington University. Nothing having been accomplished in his lifetime, he left the shares in the Potomac Company, which had been given him by the state of Virginia, "towards the endowment of a University to be established within the limits of the District of Columbia, under the auspices of the General Government, if that government should incline to extend a fostering hand towards it." The fostering hand was never extended, and on May 16, 1825, the stockholders assented to an arrangement whereby all the rights and interests of the Potomac Company were conveyed to the Chesapeake and Ohio Canal Company.[2]

In liquidating the affairs of the Potomac Company, it was arranged that stock in that company could be exchanged for shares of the new Chesapeake and Ohio Canal Company. Stock thus acquired, however, was subject to severe qualification. All holders of stock paid for in cash were to share in the first 10 per cent of net profit per annum. Up to 10 per cent of any profit remaining was to be paid to stockholders who had received shares in return for certificates of debt of the Potomac Company. Finally, if anything remained, up to 6 per cent of it was to be paid to those who had exchanged Potomac Company shares for shares in the new company.

Meanwhile the title of Washington's shares remained vested in the Commonwealth of Virginia until 1832, when, on the petition of Lawrence Lewis to the General Assembly, they and any proceeds were transferred to Lewis, General Washington's surviving executor, his heirs, and his assigns, with the right to appropriate and apply them to the uses set forth in Washington's will. The capital stock of the new company was fixed at $6,000,000, or 60,000 shares of $100 each. Washington's shares of the

Potomac Company were exchangeable for 222 shares at $100 par of the Chesapeake and Ohio Canal Company. That the earnings of the new company would ever produce a sum that would permit payment of dividends to the least preferred class of stockholders was impossible. Lawrence Lewis apparently did not even make the exchange of stock. There is no record of these shares after they were assigned to him by the General Assembly of Virginia.[3]

Although Washington's bequest evaporated in value, his noble words describing his ideas of the function of a university in the nation's capital have remained. They are worth repeating.

That as it has always been a source of serious regret with me to see the youth of these United States sent to foreign countries for the purpose of education, often before their minds were formed, or they had imbibed any adequate ideas of the happiness of their own;—contracting, too frequently, not only habits of dissipation and extravagance, but principles unfriendly to Republican Government and to the true and genuine liberties of mankind; which, thereafter are rarely overcome.—For these reasons, it has been my ardent wish to see a plan devised on a liberal scale which would have a tendency to spread systematic ideas through all parts of this rising Empire, thereby to do away local attachments and State prejudices, as far as the nature of things would, or indeed ought to admit, from our national councils.—Looking anxiously forward to the accomplishment of so desirable an object as this is (in my estimation) my mind has not been able to contemplate any plan more likely to effect the measure than, the establishment of a University in a central part of the United States to which the youths of fortune and talents from all parts thereof might be sent for the completion of their education in all the branches of polite literature;—in arts and sciences—in acquiring knowledge in the principles of Politics and good Government;—and (as a matter of infinite importance in my judgment) by associating with each other, and forming friendships in Juvenile years, be enabled to free themselves in a proper degree from those Local prejudices and which, when carried to excess, are never failing sources of disquietude to the Public mind and pregnant of mischievous consequences to this country.[4]

In the early nineteenth century, a new set of motives was to lead to a remarkable activity in the founding of colleges. While the natural logic of a federal form of government suggested the formation of state institutions of higher learning, denominational loyalty and a sense of mission in the churches inspired the establishment of colleges in vaster numbers. The Great Awakening in its day had made a deep impression on the colleges. The Second Awakening quickened tremendously the missionary spirit in the various denominations. George Washington University owes its origin to this missionary spirit which aimed, by the renewal of the faith of church members generally, to lead them to give generously to the spreading of the Gospel at home and the extension of its teaching *in partibus infidelium*. While the noble utterances of George Washington on the subject of education for citizenship were never forgotten, the appeal was primarily to Christian duty toward the heathen and denominational loyalty. The greater emphasis was on citizenship in the Heavenly Jerusalem rather than in the Earthly Babylon. At a later date the emphasis was to shift, just as radically, to the Washington ideal.

George Washington University is a product of the Second Awakening. Its spiritual origin is to be found in the famous "Haystack Meeting" at Williams College in 1806. For it was in the missionary dynamism aroused by this meeting that Rice, the founder of the University, was later caught up and that determined the whole direction of his life's work.

Luther Rice (1783-1836) began to mature socially, intellectually, and spiritually on his return to his home at Northborough, Massachusetts, from a trip to Georgia to buy timber for shipbuilding at the age of sixteen. He read many pieces of devotional literature, and began to discuss religion eagerly with all who would talk with him. Three years later he joined the Church of Christ, a Congregational church, in Northborough. But he was not satisfied with his church; he was all too well aware of its inadequacies: "corrupt . . . neglectful of its duties."[5]

To improve the local situation, he began to hold frequent "religious conferences" with groups in private homes, where there were prayer, meditation, and exhortation. So marked was his activity that a neighboring Calvinistic minister urged him to undertake formal study in preparation for larger service. Rice was in a state of great concern: "impatience, anxiety, hope, fear, distress, perplexity, confusion, shame, folly, stupidity, etc." He sought "illumination and converting grace."[6] Time seemed to be running out. Death was ever before him. Insignificant incidents became signs and portents of great solemnity. Gradually the skies brightened; he had brief interludes of calm and of "a sweet frame of mind." The moment of unconditional surrender to God came: "I concluded that had I an opportunity, I would actually put a blank in God's hand to be filled as his pleasure should dictate."[7] Clearly Luther Rice was a child of the Second Awakening.

To prepare himself for whatever God should dictate, he entered Leicester Academy, still carrying on his religious work. By sandwiching teaching with study, he was able to make his way. In 1807, at the age of twenty-four, he was admitted to Williams College and, on the basis of his previous studies, was given advanced standing.

In the summer of the preceding year had occurred the famous "Haystack Meeting" at Williams, when five students, driven by a sudden storm to the shelter of a haystack while holding an outdoor prayer meeting, bound themselves to work toward the conversion of the world. Out of their discussions came the formation of a secret society, "The Brethren," of which Luther Rice was a charter member. Looking back over his career late in life, he wrote: "I esteem it the happiest point in my life to have been one of the original members."[8]

From Williams, Rice and some of "The Brethren" went to Andover Seminary in 1810, where, joining with others, including Adoniram Judson, they formed a "Society of Inquiry on the Subject of Missions." Rice became president of the group. Judson seems to have had a marked interest in Asia as an area for missionary effort, which impressed Rice.

As his course at the Seminary approached completion, Rice found himself facing a great decision, for which he had had ten years of active preparation. He had already been licensed to preach, but now he was fully trained for the ministry. What use was he going to make of his life and of his profession? The hand of God was filling in the blank. To Christianize the world was the solemn undertaking and pledge of "The Brethren." Rice was about to begin as he had promised.

The need of one young man, Gordon Hall, to decide immediately whether to remain in the pastorate or undertake a career as a missionary, coupled with the fact that a meeting of the General Association of evangelical ministers in Massachuetts was scheduled to be held in a few days in Bradford, just ten miles from Andover, brought to a head the problem regarding foreign missions which faced the members of the society. The decision was taken, whereupon six of the members signed a memorial, drawn up by Adoniram Judson, to be presented to the General Association. It was a mature document, humble in spirit but characterized by sound practicality. It stated that the members of the group had given the matter careful and prayerful consideration and, on that basis, deemed themselves as devoted until their lives' ends to the work of missionaries. Such was their own conviction; but, with great tact and humility, they inquired of their Reverend Fathers "whether they ought to renounce the object of missions, as either visionary or impracticable." They asked whether they should look to the eastern or the western world, whether they could expect the patronage of an American missionary society or should look to one in Europe for support, and what preparatory steps they should take.

Since the society's deliberations had been carried on in secret, no one outside the group was aware of the depth and intensity of conviction that the memorial expressed. When, at the last minute, a faculty adviser was consulted, he expressed the fear that such apparently precipitate action on the part of so large a group would cause alarm. To reduce the likelihood of such a reaction, it was suggested that only four signatures appear and that the last two—one of them Luther Rice's—be omitted. When the memorial with its four signatures was laid before the association on June 27, 1810, affirmative action was immediately taken. The committee appointed to examine the proposals reported on them sympathetically as "calling for correspondent attention and exertions." It was ordered that there be instituted a Board of Commissioners for Foreign Missions, of nine members, "to devise, adopt, and prosecute ways and means for propagating the Gospel among those who are destitute of the knowledge of Christianity." An immediate investigation was authorized to suggest possible fields of activity. The board approved the readiness of the young men to become missionaries and urged them to continue their studies until the necessary arrangements could be completed. An eloquent appeal for financial support was issued.

The approval of the proposal and the speed with which rapid planning got under way reflect the skill and good judgment with which Judson had drawn up the memorial expressing the desires of the group.

At the second meeting of the commissioners it was reported that four young men had been examined and approved for missionary service. The four were Judson, Newell, and Nott, whose names had been signed to the memorial, and Gordon Hall.[9]

Showing their respect for the proposals, the commissioners sent Adoniram Judson to England to confer with the directors of the London Missionary Society to see if the English group would cooperate financially, and, if so, under what conditions. The London society had had long experience in the field and had considerable financial strength. Prudence suggested that they be approached, even though there was some militant nationalism among the Americans that recoiled at the thought of British control. The London group settled the issue. A formal communication from them was filled with sound advice, born out of their experiences, but the question of support was totally avoided.[10]

On the basis of the fullest information they could assemble, the commissioners decided to establish two mission stations, one in Burmah and the other among the American Indians in the West. Funds were assembled and sailing arrangements were completed for sending the four who had been examined and passed. A day was fixed for their ordination.

At this point Luther Rice, whose name had been omitted from the memorial as presented and who therefore had not been included in the arrangements, came forward and insisted that he be added to the group. Fortified with convincing recommendations, his fervent appeals to the commissioners persuaded them, even though they lacked funds and had some misgivings, to accept Rice and authorize his ordination along with the four previously approved. Rice had to raise the necessary funds within a fortnight. This he did by dint of the most extreme exertions in the dead of winter. The schedule was tight, and there was no time to be wasted. Ordination was fixed for February 6, 1812, allowing him just enough time to get to Philadelphia where three of the missionaries (one acquired a wife on the way) were to embark on the *Harmony* bound for Calcutta.

The service of ordination was held in Salem in the old Tabernacle Meeting House, which was crowded to the doors. The service began at eleven in the forenoon and lasted for four hours. The Reverend Professor Leonard Woods of Andover preached the sermon of ordination, finding his text in Psalm lxvii, and in solemn mood assured his listeners that they were now looking upon these dear young men "for the last time, before you shall meet them at the tribunal of Christ." The Reverend Dr. Samuel Spring of the North Church in Newburyport charged them to let the Lord be their portion, Christ their leader, grace their speech, humility their dress, prayer their breath, the glory of God their object, and heaven their final rest. The Reverend Dr. Samuel Worcester, in giving the Right Hand of Fellowship, formally acknowledged Judson, Nott, Newell, Hall, and Rice as duly authorized ministers of Christ and presented them to God "as a kind of first fruits of his American churches."[11]

Rice wrote in his *Journal* for the day:

6. Thur. Received ordination, together with Brothers Gordon Hall, Adoniram Judson Jnr., Samuel Newell, Samuel Nott, Jnr. in Salem, Massachusetts, as a Missionary to the East Indies. The occasion was solemn and interesting, but worn down with fatigue and agitation of mind, I did not realize it as impressively as was desirable, in an event most sacred in its nature, and under God, probably determining my future lot in life.[12]

On that very evening Nott, Hall, and Rice left in great haste for Philadelphia. On the way Nott was married. There were some delays in sailing which Rice utilized to spread the missionary cause and to collect further contributions. On the evening of February 18, the three missionaries and Mrs. Nott boarded the *Harmony*, which was then riding at Newcastle. They were on their way to Asia.

The voyage, delayed in starting, was wearisome in length and troubled at its conclusion. The time had not been well chosen. France and England were at war; and while the missionaries were at the Isle of France, the United States declared war on Great Britain. When they arrived they found the British East India Company and the officials who carried out its mandates hostile to missionaries and prepared to expel them.

When Rice landed at Calcutta on August 10, he found Judson, who had arrived earlier on the *Caravan*, waiting to greet him. Judson was then seriously engaged in the study of baptism. It was, of course, no new subject for a theologian. In fact both men had given much thought to the problem. When they met in Calcutta, Judson was about convinced that he should make the change to the Baptist faith, and he was baptized. Rice was still inclined to argue. But soon after Judson was baptized, Rice, after some hesitation, applied for baptism and was accordingly baptized on November 1, 1812.

On October 23, two days before he applied for baptism, Rice dutifully wrote the American Board of Commissioners for Foreign Missions of his change in religious sentiments. When the board met on September 15, 1813, it received from its Prudential Committee a very full report on its missionary enterprises up to that time. It also had before it letters from both Adoniram Judson and Luther Rice. In answer, the board formally declared that its relations with the two missionaries were dissolved as of the date of their letters, September 1 and October 23, 1812, respectively. The board's attitude was coldly formal but technically Christian. "They shew us," said the board, "that missionaries are but men."[13]

At the same time that Rice and Judson had been struggling with these problems of the spirit, the authorities had given them new vexations. Harassed by the officials, they had no choice but to leave if they could. By a final stroke of good fortune, Rice and Judson were able to get passage to the Isle of France. Here they parted. Luckily finding accommodations on the *Donna Maria*, Rice sailed for San Salvador and then on to New York.

He had left Judson with great regret and with strong misgivings. Really he had little choice. Rice's health had been bad; a chronic ailment and a proneness to seasickness had made the long outward voyage unpleasant. The concern he had felt over his change in religious convictions had been wearing, and the daily uncertainties that had characterized his stay in India had further undermined his health. The easier voyage back would offer time for recuperation.

Most urgent, however, was the necessity of adjusting his denominational status. Here were two Congregational missionaries—Rice and Judson—appointed and sent out by the American Board of Commissioners for Foreign Missions, who had become Baptists. Both men wanted an amiable transfer of relationship. As we have seen, the board made the transfer easy—it just severed the relationship.

But by becoming Baptists, Judson and Rice had in no way diminished their zeal for missions. Rather, what they saw in Asia had strengthened their determination. Someone would have to undertake the support of Judson and his wife and any others who were sent out. To marshal that support was Rice's task. But here was a difficulty, comparable to one that Rice had faced earlier. When the young men at Andover had decided to offer themselves as missionaries, the memorial that Judson had drawn up had led to the formation of the American Board of Commissioners to organize Congregational support for missions. The Presbyterians later cooperated. But there was no comparable Baptist Board of Missions; in fact, there was no denominational structure with which to work. To create a structure that would throw the organized weight of the Baptist denomination into the work of missions was Rice's problem—and his achievement.

His procedure was wise. When Rice made his formal proposals, he was able to speak in personal terms and point to tangible facts. He began by consulting with Baptist groups and individuals in New England known to be interested in missions. Encouraged by a preliminary survey, he left Boston in the fall of 1813 for a journey to the principal cities from Philadelphia to Savannah, making as many personal contacts as he could preparatory to a meeting in Philadelphia, called for May 18, 1814, of delegates from "the associated bodies of the baptist denomination formed in various parts of the United States for the purpose of diffusing evangelic light, through the benighted regions of the earth."

The form of organization to be adopted had occurred to Rice as he rode on the stage between Richmond and Petersburg. The various local groups should be formed into state foreign missionary societies. These state societies should in turn appoint delegates to form a general society.

The Reverend Dr. Richard Furman was chairman of the Philadelphia meeting. A constitution was adopted establishing The General Missionary Convention of the Baptist Denomination in the United States for Foreign Missions. This body was to hold a triennial meeting to which each regularly constituted missionary society and religious body of the denomination that regularly contributed $100 or more annually to the missionary fund would be permitted to send two delegates. When the convention was not in session, authority was vested in twenty-one elected commissioners who formed the Baptist Board of Foreign Missions for the United States, "with full power to conduct the executive part of the missionary concern."

Individuals who were to play an important part in the early history of the College were assigned leading roles. Rice, a delegate from the District of Columbia, was placed on the two principal committees of the convention. The Reverend Dr. William Staughton, later to be first president of the College, was made corresponding secretary and was elected to the Baptist Board of Foreign Missions, along with the Reverend O. B. Brown, the first president of the Board of Trustees of the College.[14]

The major communications before the board at its first meeting were one prepared by Luther Rice, and a report on recently formed Baptist Foreign Missionary Societies. The latter listed information concerning existing societies as far as possible, estimated an income from them for missionary purposes of not less than $5,850 annually, stated that Rice had been allowed a salary of $8 a week for the thirty-five weeks he had devoted to preparatory work, and reported $1,556.67¾ in the general fund, after expenses.

In his communication, Rice reported on strategic points from which missionary activity could be directed in Asia and South America. In conducting a mission he emphasized the primary importance of a translation of the Scriptures which would involve mastery of the native language and literature, and the location of a printing press at the base of operations. Referring to his own situation, he stated that he had delayed accepting any new responsibility until his relations with the American Board of Commissioners for Foreign Missions had been formally severed. As soon as this was done, he had hastened, with the advice and at the request of his brethren, to make his tour through the middle and southern states. He listed in detail the monies he had received. These were the first fruits of his labor.

The Board of Foreign Missions at their first meeting undertook the patronage of Rice as their missionary to continue his services here "for a reasonable time," and of Adoniram Judson "as a missionary under their care and direction." Rice was to be supplied with credentials stating his appointment and his mission and commending him to the favor of people "wherever, in pursuing the openings of Providence, he may direct his course."[15]

This was the broad grant of authority to the missionary proconsul of the Baptists.

The success of Rice's itineracy militated against his rejoining Judson in Asia. Year after year his commission as the board's agent was renewed. His success in stirring up an interest in missions was phenomenal. The number of new societies formed was amazing. Rice's energy was almost superhuman. He was always on the move, traveling by horse and carriage, gig or wagon, by horseback, by boat, or by stage. On August 30, 1817, he wrote in his *Journal* that in the preceding ten days he had traveled 722 miles, of which about 560 miles were on horseback. There was never a day without preaching or exhortation somewhere—in a state capital, in a courthouse, a meetinghouse, a fine home, or a miserable hovel. Clergy and members of other denominations helped him generously. There was always the contribution—substantial ones of $200 at large meetings down to half a levy from some child or an interested servant. Wherever he happened to be was his only home. He received a few personal gifts of money and considerable clothing, and carried with him some tracts and reports which he sold at a modest price.

Luther Rice by dint of great sacrifice had, rather belatedly it is true, the benefits of a sound literary and theological education in Leicester Academy, Williams College, and Andover Seminary. He no doubt welcomed the position on education expressed by Dr. Furman in his 1814 Address. His own statement to the board at its first meeting had indicated the need for highly literate missionaries, capable of mastering the native languages and literatures. In the Address for the First Triennial Meeting of the General Assembly in 1817, Dr. Furman was able to report action. He stated that the difficulties that some of the pious had raised were "like vapours of the morning vanishing." The original constitution of the convention was amended to include, among other changes, a direction to the board to institute a classical and theological seminary "when competent and distinct" funds had been raised.[16]

From the very beginning of the formal Baptist effort, missions and education were linked together. The Address given in 1814 by the president of the General Assembly of the Baptist delegates for missionary purposes which concluded the printed *Proceedings* was eloquent on this topic. Forming as it did, in effect, a statement of principle, it is most significant.

It is deeply to be regretted that no more attention is paid to the improvement of the minds of pious youth who are called to the gospel ministry. While this is neglected the cause of God must suffer. Within the last fifty years, by the diffusion of knowledge and attention to liberal science the state of society has become considerably elevated. It is certainly desirable the information of the minister of the sanctuary should increase in an equal proportion. Other denominations are directing their attention with signal ardour to the instruction of their youth for this purpose. They are assisting them to peruse the sacred writings in their original languages, and supplying other aids for pulpit services, which, through the grace of the Holy Spirit may become eminently sanctified for the general good. While we avow our belief that a refined or liberal education is not an indispensable qualification for ministerial service, let us never lose sight of its real importance, but labour to help our young men by our contributions, by the origination of education Societies, and if possible, by a general theological seminary, where some at least, may obtain all the advantage, which learning and mature studies can afford, to qualify for acting the part of Men who are set for the defence of the gospel. Improvement of this nature will contribute to roll away from the churches the reproach of neglecting to support the ministry of the word. They will be unwilling to receive for nothing that which has cost their ministers much.[17]

The Board of Foreign Missions in its address to the General Convention called attention to the broad subject of education. A scheme of education laid before the convention received unanimous support and was referred to the board "for maturity and publicity." The report was received at the board's quarterly meeting held in June, 1817. It stated its belief that many wealthy friends were prepared to make substantial contributions and that several thousands of dollars might be easily collected if a start were made. "Numerous youth are waiting to avail themselves of the privilege of a literary and theological Institution, and the widening sphere of missionary work already undertaken, renders an accession of godly and educated youth highly desirable."

At the next annual meeting of the board on April 29, 1818, formal action was taken. Education societies in various parts of the country were urged to cooperate in the effort with the Baptist Education Society in Philadelphia, whose aid had been offered and accepted. The agent was instructed to promote the formation of other societies. The Reverend Dr. Staughton was named Principal; the Reverend Irah Chase, Professor of Languages and Biblical Literature in the contemplated institution; and a comprehensive effort to raise funds was ordered. Under date of May 7, 1818, the corresponding secretary issued a statement regarding the action taken, with supporting arguments, and called upon the board's Christian brethren to direct their immediate attention to the necessity for sending such sums as they could obtain to the treasurer of the board or to the agent.[18]

At the end of his first year of solicitation, Rice, as agent, reported that $1162.06 had been contributed and an additional $75 subscribed for the Theological Institution.[19]

The Second Triennial Meeting of the General Convention, which met in Philadelphia on April 26, 1820, seemed to represent a time of fulfillment. The constitution of the General Assembly was amended to require the treasurer to keep funds for missionary purposes and those for education in separate accounts. The tenth section in the amended constitution put the governance of "an Institution for education purposes," when located, in the hands of the board of managers, as the executive committee of the convention was now designated. This section read:

When the Convention shall have located an Institution for education purposes, it shall be the duty of the Board, under the direction of this body, and exclusively from education funds, to erect or procure suitable buildings for the accommodation of students, and to pursue such measures as may be found most conducive to the progress and prosperity of the Institution. They shall also judge of the qualifications of persons approved by the churches as possessing suitable gifts and called of God to the work of the Gospel ministry, who shall apply for admission as beneficiaries of the Board. They shall have power to appoint suitable instructors in the different departments of education; and determine on the compensation to be allowed them for their services; and superintend, generally, the affairs of the Institution.[20]

The Reverend O. B. Brown, on behalf of a committee, reported on the recommended location of the Institution. The committee desired to eliminate "local politics" and recommended as the place "the seat of the general government." Since it was believed that if literary and theological subjects were both to be pursued under the convention's patronage, they should be kept distinct so that persons could avail themselves of one without the other, the committee believed that "a College, upon general principles for science and literature," would eventually be established. It was, therefore,

Resolved, That the Institution for the education of Gospel ministers, be located at the city of Washington, or in its vicinity, in the District of Columbia; and that the Board be directed to cause its removal thither, whenever suitable preparations shall be made for its reception in that place, and when, in their opinions, such removal shall be expedient.

Resolved, That this Convention accept of the premises tendered to them for the site of an Institution for the education of Gospel ministers, and for a college, adjoining the city of Washington; and that the Board be directed to take measures, as soon as convenient, for obtaining a legal title to the same.— And that the Board be further directed to keep the Institution, already in a state of progress, first in view, and not to incur expenses beyond the amount of funds which may be obtained for the establishment of either of the Institutions.[21]

A committee of five, including O. B. Brown and Rice, was appointed to take immediate measures to procure an act of incorporation for the convention from Congress, "so as to secure the funds of the Convention in the best manner they can."[22]

Out of this action was to develop the chain of incidents that brought about the granting by Congress of a Charter to The Columbian College in the District of Columbia.

It will be noted that all the actions of the convention and the board on educational matters had referred primarily to the Theological Institution, with a College to be eventually established. The form of such an institution was laid down in a "Plan of the Institution" adopted by the Second Triennial Meeting of the Convention.

Certified as possessed of piety, candidates who had had a collegiate or liberal education would be admitted into the junior and, in time, the senior class. These students would receive instruction in the various fields of theology, in the language and interpretation of the Old and New Testaments and in the canons of Biblical criticism; in sacred rhetoric and ecclesiastical history. Students without previous literary training would be divided into the first- and second-year classes where they would study those subjects "which particularly belong to them as students of the Bible and candidates for the ministry." Students in all four classes were "to exercise their gifts in public speaking." "The state and exigencies of the Baptist denomination were to be regarded" in shortening or protracting the period of residence at the Institution. Professors were to be Baptists and ministers of the Gospel, but for those who taught purely academic subjects ordination might be dispensed with. The teachers were to constitute a faculty to govern the Institution under bylaws approved by the board in accordance with the acts and Constitution of the convention.[23]

With the cooperation of the Baptist Education Society in Philadelphia, the board on April 29, 1818, had provided for the inauguration of an Institution in Philadelphia with Dr. Staughton as Principal and the Reverend Irah Chase as Professor. This Institution was in operation and had attracted a fair number of students. Eighteen were pursuing studies there, according to the Address of the Convention at the Second Triennial Meeting in 1820.[24]

The members of the board attended the final exercises of a graduating class of seven members on April 25, 1821. After the awful responsibilities of "the functions of the ministry" had been explained to the graduates "in a most solemn, affectionate and impressive manner," each was awarded a certificate of Christian character and of attendance in the prescribed exercises of the Institution, with honorable dismissal. At the board meeting on the same day there was announced the likely removal of the Institution to Washington in the ensuing autumn.[25]

CHAPTER THREE

College Hill:
The Lot and the Charter
1821-1825

The Institution of the convention was transferred from Philadelphia to Washington twenty-one years after the capital itself had made the same move. Both were modest establishments at the time of the change in location. The office force of the five departments of the government had in 1800 numbered but 137 clerks. By comparison with the size of the Institution a score of years later, even that was a multitude.[1] According to the Census of 1820, the total population of the District of Columbia was 33,039. In the District, then the original ten miles square, were three cities: Alexandria, Georgetown, and Washington, the last the youngest and the largest, with a population of 13,322.

At its Second Triennial Meeting, the General Convention in two significant resolutions had directed the board of managers to move the Institution to Washington as soon as accommodations could be prepared and had directed a committee of five to obtain an act of incorporation for the convention "so as to secure the funds of the Convention in the best manner they can, and in the event of the committee failing, that the Board take measures to procure it."[2]

Progress of a sort had been made along both of these lines to permit the Institution to be moved in the fall of 1821. As to the first, when the board of managers on August 7, 1818, decided "to prepare the way, by the collecting of funds, for the complete organization of the Institution the ensuing spring," a committee of three—Messrs. Cushman, Sommers, and Davis—was appointed to solicit funds, and another committee consisting of Dr. Staughton, Dr. Allison, Elder Jones, and Professor Chase was appointed to solicit books for the library. The success of the first committee was extremely limited. The committee on the library was more fortunate.

There was, however, the vigorous agent of the board at work. Rice wrote to the Reverend Elisha Cushman of Hartford, a member of the board's committee, on August 24, 1819, favoring the location of the Theological Institution in Washington "where there is indeed a most beautiful and eligible site for it. On this subject I wish to have some conversation with you." Rice was preparing for action; indeed, the first subscription he reported "for the lot" was for $20 made by R. W. Latimer of Fayetteville, North Carolina, on August 2, 1819, although real effort begins to show from the middle of September. Subscriptions "for the lot" during the fiscal year 1819-1820 ran far ahead of those "for education purposes," both in amount and in number of donors. In that year 650 donors gave the sum of $3,134.29 for the lot, and 75 gave $133 for the building. Rice and his three colleagues in the effort—the Reverend O. B. Brown, Spencer H. Cone, and Enoch Reynolds—had every right to feel pleased. The first list of subscribers was very catholic in its composition. President James Monroe subscribed $50; John Quincy Adams, Secretary of State, $25; William H. Crawford, Secretary of the Treasury, $25; Return J. Meigs, Postmaster General, $20; Josiah Meigs, Commissioner of the General Land Office, $25; Abraham Bradley, Assistant Postmaster General, $20; Governor John Clark of Georgia, $10. Several Senators and Congressmen were on the list, as were also the famous Captain John Tingey of the Navy and many eminent Baptist ministers. The great bulk of contributions came from Virginia, the District of Columbia, North and South Carolina, and Georgia—areas, interestingly enough, from which the major part of the student body was drawn in the years before the War of 1861-1865.

Reporting to the corresponding secretary of the board on April 26, 1820, that $10,000 had been subscribed and partly paid "for the ground, a lot of 46½ acres—to erect a building and to endow a professorship," Rice said, "This being the result of the incidental attention of an individual, with comparatively little aid from others, and that, too, for but little more than half a year, demonstrates the practicability of accomplishing a most important object in a short time."[3]

"The lot," as it is always referred to by Rice in his subscription lists, became officially known as "College Hill." As far as the earliest land records extend, the lot was in a tract of land known as Mount Pleasant and owned by Robert Peter. By Robert Peter's will of May 10, 1802, his estate was equally divided among his sons, Thomas, Robert, David, George, and James. The part of the tract embraced within the lot was inherited by George Peter and deeded by him on December 11, 1820, to Obadiah B. Brown, who held the property for transfer to the convention.

The property contained "forty eight acres and one hundred and forty four perches, but as it is intended that a road on the east side of said tract of land shall be continued from Fourteenth Street west in the City of Washington to the intersection of the road leading from Georgetown to Rock Creek Church, fifty feet wide, one half of said contemplated road being deducted, also that part of said road running from Georgetown to Rock Creek Church which this survey covers, making together two acres and fifty perches, leave, exclusive of roads, the full quantity hereby sold and conveyed, forty six acres, two roods and fourteen perches." The cost of the property was $6,988, approximately $151.75 per acre.[4]

The road referred to was appropriately named Columbia Road after the College.

The property was immediately north of the boundary (now Florida Avenue) which marked the corporate limits of Washington City. In terms of the present street designations, it ran from Florida Avenue north for almost a half-mile to somewhat beyond Columbia Road and between Fourteenth and Fifteenth Streets. The nature of the terrain, where Cardozo High School now stands, a bit more than a square east of College Hill, suggests the way the elevation of the property increased quite rapidly up to the center part of the holdings. The main college building was located in this central portion, and from it could be seen all parts of the city and of Georgetown. As time went on and streets were cut through the College grounds, appropriate names of academic significance were given them: Columbia, Euclid, University, Staughton, Chapin, Welling, Binney, Bacon (the last five being presidents of the College), and Huntington (said to have been the most popular teacher ever to serve the College). When the modern system of street nomenclature was adopted, the only one of the College worthies whose name fitted into the alphabetical scheme was Chapin. Euclid also held his own.

With property in the hands of a trustee ready to be deeded to the convention and with educational funds collected and being collected, a practical problem arose which made incorporation necessary. The nature of this problem was underscored by an important decision handed down February 3, 1819, on the same afternoon as the more famous Dartmouth

College decision. This decision, in the case of The Philadelphia Baptist Association vs. Hart's Executor (4 Wheaton 1), held "that an unincorporated association could not receive and administer a fund for the training of young men for the Baptist ministry." The question, settled finally by the Supreme Court, had been moot for more than twenty years, ever since a divided decision of the trial court. This specific case must certainly have been in the minds of the members of the convention when, on May 6, 1820, they appointed a committee to procure an act of incorporation "so as to secure the funds of the Convention in the best manner they can." Possibly this action was taken to formalize steps previously taken, since on April 6, 1820, a bill was reported out of the Committee of the District of Columbia to the Senate providing for the incorporation of a General Convention of the Baptist denomination in the District of Columbia. Senator Johnson of Kentucky argued vigorously for the bill, pointing out that it was merely designed to enable a group, about to erect a seminary of learning, to hold real estate, which they already had, and to receive donations. In spite of the Senator's eloquent defense, the basic church-state problem took precedence over the immediate purpose for which incorporation had been desired. The bill was indefinitely postponed, without a decision.[5]

In the next session—the second—of the Sixteenth Congress, Senator Johnson of Kentucky obtained leave on November 30, 1820, to bring in the bill which, after much amendment, finally became the Charter. The bill was read and passed to a second reading. Referred to the Committee on the District of Columbia, it was reported with amendments and read on the next day. When some questions were raised, Senator Johnson replied that the same bill was defeated the previous session "merely because the title, which had been inadvertently and without reflection given to it, had been construed by gentlemen into an indication that the bill was for the incorporation of an exclusive religious society for religious objects alone."

Senator Horsey, who had reported the bill for the committee, stated that he would vote for the bill if certain defects were remedied. He would confine the organization "by express provisions, to objects strictly collegiate and literary." Modes of electing the principal, trustees, and professors should be strictly defined, and no one should be excluded from an office or the benefits of the college on account of his religious opinions. Senator Johnson of Kentucky concurred. The bill was recommitted and other intervening items on the orders of the day were postponed to permit resumption of the debate on the admission of Missouri into the Union.[6]

When the Senate resumed consideration of the bill, as in the Committee of the Whole, it was laid on the table. Discussion was again resumed, and, together with certain amendments and considerations, again postponed. Once again discussion was resumed with further amendments, and on January 9, 1821, the bill was ordered engrossed and read for a third time.

The Senate then informed the House of Representatives that the bill had been passed and asked its concurrence. The House Committee on the District of Columbia, acting without delay, reported the bill without amendment. When it was called for its third reading, a member objected to the procedure and demanded that the ordinary practice be followed in referring the bill to the Committee of the Whole for discussion. So the bill was ordered to lie on the table and be printed for the use of the members.[7]

When the bill was finally called up for consideration by the House, opposition was still very strong. Mr. Storrs raised a great number of objections and was particularly opposed to giving the corporation a right to hold lands in any state in the Union. Though he stated that he was opposed to the passage of the bill in any form, he moved to recommit the bill to the committee with instructions to reduce the number of trustees to twenty-one, to make the members of the Cabinet and the judges of the Circuit Court of the District of Columbia ex officio trustees, with vacancies to be filled by the same body so as to insure a full board of twenty-one at all times, and to establish a visitorial power vested in a joint committee by the Senate and House of Representatives. Mr. Mercer spoke warmly in defense of the bill and protested against its defeat on the ground of hostility to the establishment of any literary institution in the District "which the gentleman from New York [Mr. Storrs] has so broadly avowed." The nature of the session was summarized in the record:

There then arose, on this subject, a debate which occupied the whole of the remainder of the day's sitting, which was desultory in its nature and comprehensive in its objects, embracing the general powers of Congress to confer power by granting acts of incorporation, as well as the merits of this particular bill, and even the Missouri question, somehow or other, wedged its way into the debate.[8]

A final effort was made to restrict any real estate held by the College to the District of Columbia, unless specific consent was given by the legislature of the state within which such real estate was situated. This effort and others to recommit failed, and the bill was read the third time and passed: yeas 79, nays 60. President Monroe approved the Act of Congress on February 9, 1821.

Aside from the general provisions establishing "a college, for the sole and exclusive purpose of educating youth in the English, learned, and foreign languages, the liberal arts, sciences and literature" under the name of "The Columbian College, in the District of Columbia," the Charter contains two very interesting sections, the seventh and the tenth.

The seventh section was added by a vote of 23 to 13, against the strenuous objections of the bill's sponsors. It is good Jeffersonianism:

And be it further enacted: That persons of every religious denomination shall be capable of being elected trustees; nor shall any person either as president, professor, tutor or pupil be refused admission, or denied any privileges, immunities or advantages thereof, for or on account of his sentiments in matters of religion.

In the light of the temper of the Congress as shown in the debates on the bill, it is easy to see that there lurked a suspicion that, although the act to incorporate the convention had been defeated, there would still be a strong denominational influence seeking control. The seventh section was the price that had to be paid for the passage of the bill.

The tenth section is concerned with financial matters and concludes significantly:

That it shall, moreover, be the duty of the said trustees, to cause to be enrolled in the said book or journal the names of all contributors to the institution qualified to vote for trustees, with their respective places of residence, and the said book or journal shall, at all times, be open to the inspection or examination of the Attorney General of the United States; and when required by either House of Congress, it shall be the duty of the said trustees to furnish any information respecting their own conduct, the state of the institution, and of its finances, which shall or may be required.

It was in accordance with this provision that the investigation by the Attorney General was made in 1910. The late Professor Tillema has described this as a feature which was transferred to the Colonies from England where the Attorney General, on behalf of the King as *parens patriae*, exercised the power to inspect and take legal measures for the protection of funds given or granted for educational purposes. The provision in the Charter of February 9, 1821, appears in no other charter granted by Congress. Whether the members of the Congress were conscious of the English usage cannot be said. The final sentence of the tenth section, however, does reflect the sentiment shown in the suggested amendments of Storrs, the implacable opponent of the bill.

Tillema pointed out that the clause in the Charter reserving to Congress the right to revoke or amend, a clause inserted in every later college charter, was clearly the result of the Dartmouth College case. In the Dartmouth College decision the Supreme Court held that the legislature of New Hampshire could not amend the college's charter without the consent of the college trustees, a condition highly objectionable to those who believed that education, as a public function, must be subject to legislative control.[9]

The Board of Managers of the General Convention in a formal resolution thanked all the members of the Senate and of the House of Representatives who had aided in obtaining the Charter, with a special vote of thanks to Senators James Barbour and R. M. Johnson and Congressmen Henry Clay, Charles F. Mercer, John Sargeant, and Henry Meigs.[10]

The Charter provided for the control of the College by a Board of Trustees, not to exceed thirty-one in number, elected triennially by the contributors to the College as provided by the ordinances. They were to be possessed of the usual rights. The College was limited to an income not to exceed $25,000 over student fees. The faculty of the College, no member of which could, while he served as such, be a Trustee, was charged with the enforcement of the rules of the Trustees for the government of students and the recommendation for degrees of such students as had satisfactorily met the requirements. The Trustees were directed to have a proper seal made for the authentication of documents. At the Board's meeting on November 15, 1821, James Peale of Philadelphia was formally thanked "for having gratuitously furnished a drawing of the Seal for the Columbian College, in a stile [sic] highly acceptable to the Board."[11]

Of all the messages of good will which came to the founders following the granting of the Charter, none was more welcome than one from the President of the United States which was quoted again and again in the circulars of the College. On March 24, 1821, President Monroe wrote to the Reverend O. B. Brown, president of the Board of Trustees:

Sir,   Washington March 24, 1821.

I avail myself of this mode of assuring you of my earnest desire that the
College which was incorporated by an act of Congress, at the last session, by
the title of "The Columbian College in the District of Columbia" may accomplish all the useful purposes for which it was instituted; and I add, with
great satisfaction that there is good reason to believe that the hopes of those
who have so patriotically contributed to advance it to its present stage, will
not be disappointed.

The commencement will be under circumstances very favorable to its success. Its position, on the high ground north of the city, is remarkably healthy.
The act of incorporation is well digested; looks to the proper objects; and
grants the powers well adapted to this attainment. The establishment of this
institution within the federal district, in the presence of Congress, and of all
the departments of the government, will secure to the young men who may be
educated in it many important advantages; among which, the opportunity
which it will afford them of hearing the debates in Congress, and in the
Supreme Court, on important subjects, must be obvious to all. With these
peculiar advantages, this institution if it receives hereafter, the proper encouragement, cannot fail to be eminently useful to the nation. Under this impression, I trust that such encouragement will not be withheld from it.

I am Sir, with great respect,
your very obedient servant,
James Monroe[12]

While efforts were being made to obtain a charter, progress was being
made in the preparation of accommodations for the College. Luther Rice
in a letter to the corresponding secretary of the Board of Managers of
the Convention on April 26, 1820, had stated that a building had already
been commenced, 116 feet by 47, which would house 80 to 100 students.
By June 1, 1821, the carpenters' work and the plastering of the main
building were nearly completed. At the first meeting of the Board, it was
announced that buildings would be ready for occupancy September,
1821, and completed by January 1, 1822. The Trustees were therefore
able to state that the Theological Department would open on the first
Wednesday in September, 1821, and the Classical Department on the
second Wednesday in January, 1822.[13]

The buildings were three in number, the College building and two
houses for professors. The main building as completed was 117 feet in
length and 47 feet deep, with a stone basement that had walls 27 inches
thick; the first story of brick, with walls 22 inches thick; the second story
of brick, with walls 18 inches thick; and the third story of brick, with
walls 14 inches thick. The garret was divided into rooms like the main

stories, with dormer windows and fireplaces. On the basement level were a kitchen, a dining room, and a chapel. In the garret there was a room, 30 feet by 16, designed for philosophical apparatus and experiments. On the second and third floors there was a room 11 feet by 17, designed temporarily for a library. In the whole building there were 58 rooms and 60 fireplaces, calculated to accommodate 100 students. The land cost $7,000, and the building with equipment was estimated to cost $60,000. "A well sixty feet deep has been dug adjacent to the building, which proves to be upon a never failing spring of fine water; a blessing which calls for sincere gratitude." All buildings were intended to range with the cardinal points of the compass.[14]

Having been duly chartered, the Board of Trustees of the College were now able to hold real estate. Their immediate interest in obtaining title to College Hill was induced by their urgent need for funds to get the institution in operation. A loan of $10,000 was sought from the Board of Managers of the Convention, the security for which was to be a bond and mortgage on the lot and premises of the College. The Board of Managers at the Trustees' request:

Resolved, unanimously, That it be recommended by the Board, that the land and premises called "College Hill," in the District of Columbia, held by the Rev. O. B. Brown, of Washington, virtually in trust for the purposes of the General Convention, be conveyed by said Brown to the Trustees of "The Columbian College in the District of Columbia"; with an express reservation, in the deed of conveyance, of the right in said premises, of the carrying on of such other operations, or the effecting or locating of such other concerns, besides the establishment for the purposes of education, literature, and science, as may in the mutual judgment of the aforesaid General Convention, or its Board of Managers, and of the Trustees and Faculty of the aforesaid Columbian College, conduce to the promotion of the great objects which the Convention embraces.[15]

At the meeting of the College Trustees on November 24, 1821, O. B. Brown presented the indenture or deed for the conveyance of College Hill "on certain conditions and limitations therein set forth" which were duly accepted, and the property was conveyed by deed, dated November 30, 1821. Such is the simple statement in the Board's *Minutes*, leaving the "certain conditions and limitations" unexplained. Light is thrown on the subject by a report made to the Board of Managers of the General Convention by the College Board of Trustees in 1822 when it was stated that the land and premises had been conveyed:

in such manner as to secure to the Convention the use and occupancy of such part or parts of the same, as may, in the mutual judgment of said Convention, with its Board, and the Trustees and Faculty of said College, conduce to the great objects the Convention embraces.[16]

The actual situation was rather complicated. The indenture is described as being in two parts, but really there are two separate indentures, both of them recorded on December 11, 1821.

The first is an indenture made November 30, 1821, between Obadiah B. Brown and the Trustees of Columbian College. It granted the parcel called College Hill to the Trustees for a period of one thousand years, for which the Trustees were to pay one peppercorn, if demanded, on the first day of each September. If the terms were complied with, the parcel was to be deeded to the College in fee simple at the end of the thousand-year period. There were, however, a reservation and a proviso. Brown reserved for himself, his heirs, agents, and employees, the right to enter at any time and for any purpose and to occupy and enjoy a part of the parcel not to exceed one-fourth of the whole property. Until such time as Brown exercised this right, the College was to have use of the entire parcel. It was further provided that if at any time more than a fourth of the Trustees were not elected from the list nominated by the Baptist Convention the whole of the property should go to the convention.

The second is an indenture made December 10, 1821, between Obadiah B. Brown and the General Convention of the Baptist Denomination. In it Brown referred to the indenture made with the Trustees granting them College Hill and the exception made giving him rights over one-quarter of the parcel. These rights, reserved for himself, Brown now assigned to the convention.[17]

A more effective method of retaining Baptist control, in spite of Congressional intent as expressed in the debates on the Charter and in Section 7 of the Charter as passed, was found through the provision in Section 2 for the election of Trustees "by the contributors of said college, qualified to vote, in such manner, and under such limitations and restrictions, as may be provided by the ordinances of the college."

The Board of Trustees on April 19, 1821, adopted a set of ordinances in the light of facts asserted in the preamble: that the College had been virtually originated by the General Convention; that the establishment and premises on College Hill properly belonged to the convention; and that it was essential that the College be conducted in accordance with the views and wishes of the convention. Contributors qualified to vote were defined as the representatives of associated bodies of the Baptist denomination donating to the College not less than $50 annually or to the objects of the convention not less than $50 annually, of which at least $5 was designated for the College. If such an associated body contributed $100 or more annually, two "contributors" were constituted, and for each additional $200 annually an additional "contributor" was constituted. Contributors were to elect Trustees from a list of nominations of at least fifty persons furnished triennially by the convention before the first Monday in May. A vote of three-quarters of the total number of Trustees was required to amend the ordinance.

Section 7 of the Charter stood in lonely grandeur. Whatever could be done within the Charter to hold the College within Baptist control had been done.[18]

CHAPTER FOUR

Faculty and Students
1821-1825

The first educational unit to get under way on College Hill was already in being as the Theological Institution of the convention in Philadelphia. The "Plan of the Institution" had been formally adopted at the Second Triennial Meeting of the Convention. The Reverend Dr. William Staughton had been appointed Principal, and the Reverend Irah Chase, Professor of Languages and Biblical Literature. In the spring of 1821, the first class was graduated at Philadelphia, with the members of the Board of Managers, meeting at the time in that city, attending in a body.

The Theological Department of Columbian College was scheduled to move to Washington on the first Wednesday in September, 1821. At the meeting of the College Trustees on October 5, 1821, it was duly reported that the Institution had opened September 5 with 11 students and that Professor Chase was on hand and ready "to observe until further directions the rules which had been observed in the Theological Institution in Philadelphia in which he had been a professor." [1]

Most of the students who had been approved and recommended by the churches of which they were members "as having been called of God to the ministry of the Gospel" were indigent and looked to the funds of the Board of Managers for sustenance in whole or in part. One of them was directing the Preparatory School, others were rendering assistance in it or otherwise employing themselves to help meet expenses. Hardly opened, the Institution was already feeling the pinch financially. Students would undoubtedly offer themselves in larger numbers in the future and increase the need for funds for their support. Although the Institution's funds were exhausted, signs were apparent which justified an optimistic outlook. The question was raised, however, whether such students in the Theological Department "shall have the advantages of a complete course of classical education." In the operation of the Theological Institution in Philadelphia the year before the removal, a debt of $1,909.01 had been incurred.[2]

When the College, or, more properly, the Classical Department, began its first term on January 9, 1822, there was a total student body of 30, classified as follows: Theological Department, 3; Sophomore Class, 7; Freshman Class, 10; Preparatory School, 10.

On the opening day, the following faculty was publicly and solemnly inducted into office:

> The Reverend William Staughton, D.D., President of the College
> The Reverend Irah Chase and the Reverend Alva Woods, Professors in the Classical and Theological Departments
> Josiah Meigs, Esq., Professor of Experimental Philosophy
> Thomas Sewall, M.D., Professor of Anatomy and Physiology
> James M. Staughton, M.D., Professor of Chemistry and Geology
> Rufus Babcock, A.B., Tutor

Shortly thereafter, William Ruggles, A.B., was elected as a second tutor, thus beginning the longest consecutive period of teaching in the history of the University.[3]

In his address at the opening of the College, the reverend and learned President Staughton delved deeply into the pages of sacred and secular history to emphasize universal obligation and concern in the education of youth from the beginning of time. This same obligation, he said, had been recognized by "the venerable forefathers by whom our country was colonized. . . . Scarcely had they begun to till the earth for their subsistence, before their views were directed to the culture of the mind. The trees of the forest furnished their academic groves where their youth were educated in whatever could contribute to use, and ornament, and liberty, and honour, and virtue. . . . It was far from being the sentiment of the General Convention of the Baptist Denomination, or of any of the individuals who have been concerned in the erection of the building in which we are this day assembled, that a liberal education is an essential qualification in a Christian minister." He was convinced that many men, not so privileged, had been called of God into His service and had been wonderfully successful. "But these very men are, for the most part, among the first to regret that the treasures of knowledge have, to them, never been unfolded, and many of them are among the most liberal encouragers of theological schools."

The president felt that liberal studies, particularly of languages, should be begun as early as possible. "Pious youth called by the churches to officiate in the ministry of the Gospel, should beware lest the golden period for mental improvement for ever escape them. The observations I am offering are predicated on the fact that our college embraces a Theological as well as a Classical department." While Columbian College at the time was open chiefly to classical and theological students, President Staughton looked forward to the day when "additional edifices will soon be erected, where lectures will be delivered in the Institutes of Law and in Medical Science."

He offered devout gratitude to the Father of Lights, in whose name "the foundation has been laid; and to the charge of his gracious Providence, the destinies of the Columbian College are, with humility and satisfaction, confided." Appreciation was expressed to the President of the United States and others of distinction who had made known their approbation. For Luther Rice there was a special tribute:

The friendship which has long subsisted between the Agent of the Board of Managers of the General Convention and myself, would subject me to the imputation of a mistaken partiality, were I to state half the sentiments I entertain of his toils, his integrity, and his ardour. His works shall praise him, and collect around his character the grateful affections of the friends of Religion, of Literature, and of Man.

In a resounding peroration President Staughton beheld the rising metropolis within sight of Mount Vernon where dwelt Washington, "the hero, who, with the Eagle for his standard, fought the battles of his country, achieved her liberty, illumined her councils, and, leaving her a legacy of paternal advice and patriotic example, in peace expired." It was a habit of the Jews to hold ceremonies of inauguration by the side of running water as if in hope that the services of those who were being set apart, like the stream, might refresh and fertilize and continue. "Alas! it is the lot of mortals to die!—Rivers will pursue their meanders to the sea, when upon us the night of death shall have fallen. Yet, surely, we may be permitted to express our strong desire, and fervent supplication, that as long as the adjacent Potomac shall flow, this seat of learning and virtue may flourish, a blessing to the District—to the Union—to the World."[4]

Academic requirements for the governance of students in Columbian College had been laid down at an early meeting of the Board of Trustees. The first session, which was to begin on the second Wednesday in January, was to end on the second Wednesday in July; and the second session, beginning on the first Wednesday in September, was to end on the third Wednesday in December, "making this the Commencement Day." There has been some speculation as to the reason for beginning sessions on Wednesday, a custom that was followed for over a century. The records throw no light on the subject. The best explanation that has been offered was that the middle of the week was selected so that travel on the Lord's Day would not be necessary in most cases.

In this first statement, maintenance of high academic standards was demanded in no uncertain terms. "The Committee [on opening the College], in common with all the members of the Corporation, feel a strong solicitude that the establishment should possess an elevated character; and even in the outset, they are decidedly of opinion that the requirements for admission, and the course of study should not fall below the standard of institutions holding a distinguished rank among the American colleges." The admission requirements for the Theological Department, unlike the very specific ones governing the Classical Department, were general and indefinite by design. Inasmuch as that department planned to admit "students as may be" without their pursuing the course leading to the A.B. degree, "no particular point of literary attainment needs be specified as required for admission."

For the Classical Department it was quite different. "The applicant for admission should in the judgment of the committee be able to sustain a reputable examination in English Grammar, the general outlines of Geography, Arithmetic, Latin Grammar, Greek Grammar, Virgil, Sallust, Caesar's Commentaries and Cicero's select orations, Latin and Greek Testaments, and Dalzel's *Collectanea Graeca Minora:*—be capable of correctly translating English into Latin:—and produce satisfactory evidence of a good moral character. For advanced standing he should be able to sustain an examination in all the studies previously attended to by the Class he wishes to join: and no student from any other College should ever be admitted without a certificate from the President or Faculty of said College, that he left it without censure."[5]

The course of study prescribed for the College was designed in the freshman year to link the preparatory studies with those that were to follow and to give the students a common base from which their advanced work could proceed. The freshman was required to give continued attention to Latin, Greek, and English, and to geography, mathematics, and algebra. Some attention was given to history and antiquities, with constant exercise in reading, speaking, and composition. For the sophomore there were required: history and geography; elements of chronology; rhetoric and logic; logarithms, geometry, trigonometry, mensuration, surveying, navigation, conic sections, and Euclid's *Elements*. The junior studied natural "phylosophy," astronomy, chemistry, fluxions, natural history, history of civil society, natural religion, and revelation. For the senior were required: natural and political "phylosophy," metaphysics, ethics, analogy of religion to nature, and theology. "Through the whole course, attention to all learned languages, criticism, rhetoric, and oratory [is] to be maintained."[6]

The schedule of fees to be paid, in the light of present costs, seems unbelievably modest. There was a $10 fee for admission, a fee of $30 for the first session, and $20 for the second session. All students were required to board in unless special permission was given by the Superintending Committee. The charges were $10 in advance for board, washing, fuel, and candles, and $5 every third Wednesday, with balance due, if any, at the end of the session. An estimate by the steward, submitted to the Board, fixed the cost of food per student on the basis of the West Point bill of fare, at something less than 25 cents per day. Each student was supplied with bed and bedding at $3 for the first session and $2 for the second; room and furniture, $5 for the first session and $3 for the second. The library fee was $1 per term. For the steward's salary, $2 was charged for the first session and $1 for the second, and a like charge was made for servants' hire. For personal laundry the charge was 37½ cents per dozen pieces.[7]

Detailed regulations governing the conduct of students were laid down.

At the beginning of every term, each student was required publicly, immediately after morning or evening prayers, to sign a declaration that he had read the laws of the College and solemnly promised to obey them under "the penalty of private admonition, public admonition, suspension, or expulsion."

Students were required to attend "punctually and respectfully" morning and evening prayers, all other services directed by the president or faculty, and public worship on the Lord's Day in the College Hall or in an approved congregation. A record of attendance was kept in the Merit Book.

On the Sabbath, students could not leave the College premises or use any musical instrument.

Honorable and gentlemanly deportment was to be maintained in all respects. Association with vicious company or with a person suspended or expelled from the College, playing with dice or at cards, billiards, backgammon ("or any such games"), contention, falsehood, intemperance, injustice, profaneness, immodesty, uncleanness, or any kind of immorality would be punished. Students could not throw stones or anything else within a hundred yards of any building.

Students were not permitted to keep a servant, firearms or any other deadly weapon, gunpowder, or horses or dogs. No student could be absent from his room after nine o'clock from October 1 to March 1, or after ten during the remainder of the year, "at which hours the doors shall be closed." They were admonished to pay strict attention to cleanliness in their persons and in their rooms, not to spit on the floor or drive nails in any part of the building. They were required to wash themselves and clean their shoes in the place appointed for the purpose, and they were not to throw water or anything else from the windows.

Damages done to any part of a building or its furnishings were to be charged to the person responsible and repaired so that "the damaged part is as good and comely as when new." If done by parties unknown, the damage was assessed on the students at the discretion of the Superintending Committee. Any cutting of the woodwork or defacing by making any kind of mark or removing or breaking glass was to cause, for the first offense, public admonition; for the second, suspension; "but for the third offense he shall certainly be expelled."

Students were not permitted, in or near any building, to smoke a pipe or Cigar. (The capital is used in the rules, perhaps to note that this is the more aristocratic of the two forms of smoking. The first cigarettes were yet to come.) Likewise, students were not allowed to keep any ardent spirits or intoxicating liquors of any kind, unless prescribed as medicine.

Students who had been expelled could not enter the premises, and other students were not allowed to associate with them. Sacred respect for the property of persons living adjacent to the College was solemnly enjoined. When required, students had to give evidence in cases of violation of the laws of the College. Failure to do so or any manifestation of ill will toward a student who had done so was deemed punishable as contempt of the faculty.

In term time, no one was permitted, without faculty approval, to go to the city or any neighboring town, or to enter any tavern or public house in the county. Fines for unexcused absence from the College were 25 cents a day; for absence or tardiness from class, 10 cents; and for each day overdue on a library book, 10 cents. No club or society of any kind could be formed except under faculty authorization and subject to faculty rules. These are but a part of the requirements governing the deportment of students as set forth in the Laws of Columbian College adopted by the Trustees.[8]

Shortly after the faculty was inaugurated, titles for its senior members were fixed by the Board, each of three members holding appointments in both the Classical and the Theological Departments. President Staughton was designated Professor of General History, Belles Lettres, Rhetoric, and Moral Philosophy in the Classical Department, and of Divinity and Pulpit Eloquence in the Theological; Professor Chase, Professor of Learned Languages in the Classical, and of Biblical Languages and Literature in the Theological; and Professor Woods, Professor of Mathematics and Natural Philosophy in the Classical, and of Ecclesiastical History and Christian Discipline in the Theological. The versatility of these reverend and learned scholars arouses our deepest respect.

The position of the president for a time was somewhat ambiguous. The Reverend Dr. William Staughton (1770-1829), a native of Coventry, England, was perhaps the greatest pulpit orator of his time in the Baptist denomination. He came to this country at the urging of Dr. Richard Furman shortly after his graduation from Bristol Theological College, when he already had many valuable personal contacts in his native land. He began a highly successful career of preaching and teaching which moved him progressively from Georgetown, South Carolina; to New York City; to Bordentown and Burlington, New Jersey; and to Philadelphia, where he founded the Sansom Street Church. Dr. Staughton played an important part in the organization and work of the convention and of its board, where he held the key position of corresponding secretary. In the development of the board's educational policy he had a decisive role. When the Theological Institution in Philadelphia was started, he was appointed principal; and when the move to Washington was planned, he was asked to continue in that position. The Institution, as set up in Washington under its Charter, took the form of a full-fledged college, instead of remaining a training school for ministers of the Gospel. In what was really the great organizing meeting of the Board of Trustees of the College, held on April 19, 1821, just two months after the Charter had been granted by Congress and approved by President Monroe, Dr. Staughton was nominated President of Columbian College.[9]

The president's salary was fixed at $2,000 per year, with a house furnished. However, while Dr. Staughton still lived in Philadelphia, the salary was set at $40 per week for the periods that he was in Washington. As soon as funds permitted, professors were to be paid $1,500 per year; in the meantime, they received only $800.[10]

Word of the Trustees' tender of the presidency to Dr. Staughton naturally got to Philadelphia, and before he could take the matter up with his people in the Sansom Street Church, a letter was officially approved by the church and sent to him through John Owens, the clerk. The members of the church had hoped that the earlier rumors would prove false, but now that the choice had been made, they wrote him in great concern. So unsettling had been the effect of the news that all their efforts were paralyzed. They could not raise funds to reduce the debt on the church or even to meet their current expenses. The letter called attention to the phenomenal success that had crowned Dr. Staughton's labors there and expressed the fear that if he left, bankruptcy and the disintegration of the church membership would result. Dr. Staughton wrote them that he had not raised the question with them because his own mind had not been made up. He assured them that nothing but a sense of duty would ever cause him to leave Philadelphia. He felt that duty required him to assist in the arrangement of the affairs of the College for the next eighteen months at which time the convention would elect a president. He proposed to fill in at the College during the interim. That course he followed.

On May 15, 1823, Enoch Reynolds, the secretary, on behalf of the College Trustees, wrote to the people of Sansom Street, in a mood of conciliation and consolation, asking them to make the sacrifice and release their pastor to the College. As Dr. Staughton had told the Board on November 15, 1821, it was a sacrifice for him also. He was leaving a church of from five to six hundred members, with a regular congregation of a little less than two thousand, for a young college hardly able to support a president. It was for that reason that he proposed the interim service, when he would be ready two or three times a year, and two or three weeks at a time, to come to the College. When the convention met in Washington in 1823, the College Trustees informed its members that "it is highly important that the President move hither, and the Board are willing to guarantee him a support, till his salary shall be permanently assured."[11]

Obeying the call of duty, President Staughton severed his connection with the Sansom Street Church on May 26, 1823, and preached a farewell sermon to a weeping congregation. The College now had a president in residence.[12]

To provide the College with proper teaching aids, Professor Alva Woods was directed to proceed to England and, if necessary, to the Continent, to procure complete "phylosophical apparatus," specimens in geology and mineralogy and "other articles of curiosity," and books for the library. Addresses to Baptist churches in Great Britain and on the Continent were to be prepared for him. Professor Staughton of the Medical Department was also to proceed to Europe as soon as possible for study and investigation of medical teaching and to supplement the efforts of Professor Woods. They were absent for a year. Professor Chase, who was abroad at this time, having been granted a leave of absence for reasons of health, joined his two colleagues at various points during their sojourn.

In view of the meagerness of the resources of the College, the expenditures of Professor Woods for books and apparatus seem considerable. While the library in 1825 contained 3,034 volumes, it cannot be determined how many of them were packed in the six wooden cases and two trunks that were sent over in the *Electra*, Captain George Robinson, in the summer of 1823. The books purchased were valued on the invoice at 523 pounds 7 shillings. The philosophical instruments were valued at 400 pounds 8 shillings sixpence.[13]

Not the least important of the efforts of Professors Woods and Staughton was the solicitation of contributions. The solid reputation of President Staughton stood them in good stead. The eminent Joseph Butterworth, son of a Baptist minister in Coventry, member of Parliament and co-founder of the British and Foreign Bible Society, wrote that he was highly gratified to note that the president of the College was his highly respected friend. Though he had not seen him for nearly forty years, he knew of "his rising reputation and of his extensive and increasing sphere of usefulness," and as a mark of respect and affection for the president, he sent a contribution of 20 pounds. Other contributors of sums up to 50 pounds included, among his countrymen, Lord Bexley, the Chancellor of the Exchequer; the Bishop of Durham; Lord Ashburton, of Webster-Ashburton Treaty fame; William Wilberforce, the philanthropist; Thomas Babington, uncle of the historian Macaulay; and Hannah Moore. The

Honorable Richard Rush, then American Minister at London and later a Trustee of the College, was also a subscriber to the fund.[14]

So hospitably was young Staughton treated in England that his solicitous father felt called upon to write him that his parents were delighted to find him dining with notables like Rush and Wilberforce, but, he added, "You have too much good sense to become vain by such attentions on the one hand, and to undervalue them on the other."[15]

Before the work of the Classical and Theological Departments had begun on College Hill, plans were under way for expanding the work of the College. On May 16, 1821, consideration was given to the establishment of a preparatory school; on November 24 of that year it was decided to establish a Medical Department, to be opened eighteen months later. The Preparatory School was ready to begin operations when the Classical Department opened, and Samuel Wait, who also served as a tutor in the College, became the first principal. Every student, immediately upon entrance in the Preparatory School, was required to begin the study of Latin.[16]

Although a delay of a year and a half had been planned before the Medical Department was to open, Dr. Thomas Sewall and Dr. James M. Staughton, the president's son, both of them professors in the Medical Department, were inaugurated at the time of the formal opening of the College. In the interim, Dr. Staughton was to go to Europe to perfect himself in the branches he should teach. The Board undertook to pay his expenses up to $1,000 a year during this period.[17]

After a much longer delay than had been planned, bylaws and regulations for the Medical Department were adopted by the Trustees on October 19, 1824. It was ordained that in the central part of the city courses should be given in anatomy and physiology, surgery, theory and practice of physics, materia medica, chemistry, obstetrics, and diseases of women and children. Before a student could apply for the ticket of any professor, he had to be enrolled in the Department at a fee of $5. For each ticket he paid $10, making a total of $40 for the courses given. The cost per ticket was increased to $15 shortly thereafter. Medical students could attend lectures in the Classical Department without charge. To be graduated, if he were not a Bachelor of Arts, a candidate had to satisfy the faculty of his classical attainments, attend each professor during two full courses, and be at least twenty-one years of age. He must enter his name with the dean and deliver an inaugural dissertation on some medical subject at least thirty days before the close of his course. Not only would candidates be examined by the professors, but they must stand a public examination in defense of their dissertations. There was a fee of $20 for the examination and $5 for the diploma.[18]

The first course began on the last Wednesday in March, 1825, and was given in a building rented for the purpose on Tenth Street, N.W., near D Street. Dr. J. M. Toner gives the house number as 477. These rented quarters were so inadequate that a group of faculty members bought a lot at the northeast corner of Tenth and E Streets and built there the structure where the third course of lectures was given in 1826. This first home of the Medical Department was described as "large and commodious, consisting of three elevated stories, with the roof peculiarly constructed for the admission of light into all apartments appropriated to anatomical purposes." On the ground floor were a lecture room, and the laboratory and rooms of the Department of Chemistry; on the second floor were rooms, public and private, of the professors of the theory and practice of medicine, of materia medica, and of the institutes of medicine and medical jurisprudence; and on the third floor were the anatomical theater and the rooms of the professors of anatomy, surgery, and obstetrics. Lectures were held in this building until 1834, when the activities of the Medical Department were suspended for five years. When the faculty was reorganized, lectures were resumed in this building on the first Monday in November, 1839. The Medical Department now occupied, as a tenant, the building which it had formerly owned, because the property had been sold to General John P. Van Ness. He leased it to the faculty for five years beginning November 1, 1839, at an annual rental of $600. As a matter of grace, he remitted $50 of the first year's rental to compensate partially for a bonus of $100 that the faculty had to pay to be released from an agreement to rent much less desirable quarters for the same period in Purdy's Hall at Four and a Half Street and Louisiana Avenue. Annual lectures were given in the building at Tenth and E Streets until 1844, when the Medical Department moved to the Washington Infirmary.[19] While degrees in medicine were granted by Columbian College, the College had no financial responsibility for the Medical Department; the latter's faculty handled all these matters at their own risk.

The inaugural lecture at the opening of the Medical Department of Columbian College was delivered by Dr. Thomas Sewall, Professor of Anatomy and Physiology. It was a rather magisterial discourse and has remained a treatise of considerable interest, tracing as it does in some

Luther Rice (1783-1836),
Founder of Columbian College.

The only known likeness of Rice; cut by Emily Redd
of Caroline County, Virginia, prior to 1830. (The
Virginia Baptist Historical Society.)

Buildings on College Hill, adjoining the City of Washington, in the District of Columbia.—

A building sufficiently spacious for the accommodation of a hundred Students, and two others for the accommodation of Professors, are erecting, and funds, needed for their completion, are respectfully solicited. Subscriptions will be thankfully received and faithfully applied: and it is believed they will contribute to the national welfare.

Luther Rice. Agt.

The above is recommended by.

Wm H Crawford

J. C. Calhoun

Saml H Smallwood

Josiah Meigs

Wm Wirt

R J Meigs Jr

An appeal for the contribution of funds toward the construction of the buildings on College Hill, signed by Luther Rice as agent, with supporting signatures of William H. Crawford, Secretary of the Treasury; John C. Calhoun, Secretary of War; Return J. Meigs, Jr., Postmaster General; William Wirt, Attorney General; and others.

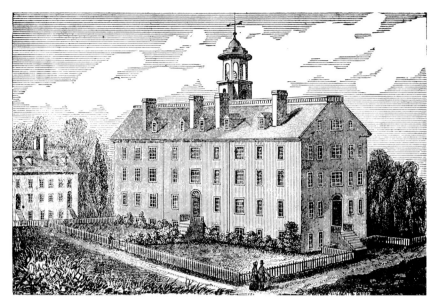

Above: The original College building on College Hill, constructed in 1820-1822. *Below:* The first building of the Medical Department, northeast corner of Tenth and E Streets, erected by the Medical faculty and occupied by the school, 1826-1834 and 1839-1844. The building was sold, and afterward, as shown, was used for commercial purposes.

Left: Enoch Reynolds, first Secretary of the Corporation, 1821-1826. (Courtesy of Mr. Reynolds Marchant.) *Below:* Obadiah B. Brown, first President of the Corporation, 1821-1827. (Reproduced by permission from Dorothy Clark Winchole, *The First Baptists in Washington, D.C.*)

Henry Clay. As a member of Congress, he was a powerful ally in obtaining a charter for the College. He attended the First Commencement. (From the collection of the Library of Congress.)

John C. Calhoun. A strong supporter of the College, he attended the First Commencement. (From the collection of the Library of Congress.)

The Marquis de Lafayette, guest of honor at the First Commencement. (Portrait in the House of Representatives, U.S. Capitol; reproduced from the collection of the Library of Congress.)

President James Monroe signed the charter and attended the First Commencement. (From the collection of the Library of Congress.)

William Staughton, D.D., first President, 1821-1827. (Portrait by Peale in the University Collection.)

Stephen Chapin, D.D., second President, 1828-1841. (University Collection.)

Joel Smith Bacon, D.D., third President, 1843-1854. (University Collection.)

Joseph Getchell Binney, D.D., fourth President, 1855-1858. (University Collection.)

John Withers, Trustee, 1832-1861. Principal benefactor of the early College. (University Collection.)

John Quincy Adams, principal creditor of the early College. (From the collection of the Library of Congress.)

Columbian College,

4th. Year *1st.* Term, ending *13th July* 1825

Mr. *Levering Thomas* Dr,

Tuition, ...	$ 30
Boarding, *10* weeks, at *2* per week	20
Library, ...	2
Steward, ...	4
Room and furniture, ...	9
Bed and bedding, ...	5
Coal, *11* bushels, at *40* per bushel,	4·40
Wood, ...	50
Lamps, ...	2
Blacking shoes and boots, . .	2
Servants' hire, ...	3
Washing, 3½ doz. at 37½cts. per doz.	1·25
Average of damages, ...	1·75
Private damages, .	
	$ 84·90

Received Payment,

Treas.

A student's account covering all expenses for a term (1825).

detail the historical development of medical science and teaching in this country. He looked with guarded optimism to the role which the new Medical School would play. "We do not expect to accomplish in a day what has been found equal to the labour of years, in those schools that have gone before us. If success await the enterprise, it is only through a series of persevering efforts, and self-denying labour, that we shall reap its fruits, or receive its rewards. . . . Who knows but that it may be reserved to this school to make some new discovery in medicine, which shall commence a new era in the science or furnish the world with the remedy for some fatal disease which now eludes the powers of medicine?"[20]

One more new educational venture was attempted in these early years. Just a few days after the plan for a Medical Department was first brought forward, the Board of Trustees decided to establish a Law School "at no distant date." After a delay of more than four years, a Law School was organized, on February 3, 1826; and the Honorable William Cranch, Chief Justice of the Circuit Court of the United States, and William Thomas Carroll, Esq., later clerk of the Supreme Court of the United States, were elected professors.[21]

Judge Cranch, described by President John Adams as "a nephew of mine, and to me very much like one of my sons," served as a judge of the United States Circuit Court of the District of Columbia for fifty-four years. He served as reporter of the United States Supreme Court Reports and, in addition, published five volumes of the Reports of the United States Circuit Court of the District of Columbia and the Patent Decisions which he rendered on appeal from the Commissioner of Patents. Several of his sons were students in the College, as was also his son-in-law, William Greenleaf Eliot, Jr., the grandfather of T. S. Eliot.

Professors Cranch and Carroll drew up a "Digest of By-Laws and Regulations" for the operation and government of the Law Department, which in its first article set forth the contents of the course: "Which course shall embrace so much of the Common and Statute law of England as may be considered applicable to this country, the Constitution and Laws of the United States, the laws in force in the District of Columbia, and the Constitutions and Laws of such of the several States as the Professors may find it convenient to lecture upon."[22]

Judge Cranch delivered the introductory lecture on June 13, 1826, at the courtroom in the City Hall. The *Daily National Intelligencer* in its account of the occasion reported: "The lecture was grave and lucid, and seemed to give great satisfaction to the audience, amongst whom, with other learned and distinguished persons, we noticed the President of the United States."[23]

Thus auspiciously inaugurated, the Law School functioned until about two years later, when the unfortunate state of the College's finances forced its discontinuance. Judge Cranch's resignation was accepted by the Trustees on December 21, 1828. Since its reopening in 1865, the Law School has had an unbroken history.

Still another department had been proposed by Luther Rice to the Board of Trustees as early as December 30, 1822, indicating an interest in the development of research in the field of natural science. He called the projected unit a "Phylosophical Department and General Repository" for research, discussion, and the accumulation of whatever material illustrated natural history. The College's interest was to be brought to the attention of officers of the Army and the Navy who might be in a position to collect materials of educational value. The department was not established, although an approach was made to officers in the armed forces. Commodore Porter was formally thanked by the Board on March 26, 1825, for his gift of Noahevian ornaments, a war conch, and an idol, and for his offer to make collections for the museum, for which a room was set aside.[24]

The Theological Department, in a sense the senior branch of the College, did not flourish. Successive reports of enrollment showed a decreasing number of students, although of the early graduates of the College practically half continued to enter the ministry of the Gospel. No degree in theology, divinity, or sacred studies, in course, was conferred. Professor Irah Chase, who had taught in the Institution at Philadelphia, came to Washington at the time its activities were transferred there in the fall of 1821 and seems to have carried the major load of the courses in theology.

On May 25, 1825, at a well-attended meeting of Baptist ministers and laymen from New England held in the First Baptist Meeting House of Boston, it was decided that the interests of the denomination required the establishment of a theological school near Boston. At the request of the meeting, the Massachusetts Baptist Education Society took the initiative, and its Executive Committee fixed upon Newton Center as the location of the new institution. The Reverend Irah Chase was called from Columbian College and set up a course of study. He began to offer instruction in Newton Theological Institution on November 28, 1825. At first he taught in his own home in Newton, pending the acquisition of property and the remodeling of an existing structure on it. The new institution was chartered by the General Court of Massachusetts on February 22, 1826. In 1931 Newton Theological Institution and Andover Theological Seminary affiliated, and in 1965 they merged as the Andover Newton Theological School in Newton Center, Massachusetts.[25]

When Professor Chase left Columbian, financial difficulties in the College were already becoming critical. On December 14, 1825, the Board appointed President Staughton to have "particular charge of the Theological Department, one other professor to be appointed when funds were available." From that time on, the report by classes of students registered lists none for the Theological Department.[26]

A report of the examination of students of the College at the end of each term regularly appeared in the *Columbian Star*, a periodical published in Washington under Baptist auspices, "devoted to the maintenance of Christian truth, the diffusion of religious intelligence, and the promotion of science," and such other information as is sought in ordinary newspapers.[27]

The writer of the report of the examinations at the end of the first year was particularly eloquent, when, after detailing the subjects covered in each of the classes of the Theological, Classical, and Preparatory Departments, he made a special appeal for the Preparatory School:

It must be gratifying to every lover of sound learning to know, that while the Trustees and the Faculty of this College are exerting themselves to lead the youth committed to their care, through the best and highest course that can be pursued at a University, they duly appreciate the importance of the Preparatory School. For it is there that the foundation of scholarship must be laid. He that is poorly fitted for College will feel the sad effects through the whole range of his studies, and most probably, through life.[28]

The fall of 1824 was a festive period in the life of the young College. In October, the aged Lafayette on his farewell visit to the United States came to Washington as the guest of the city. Escorted by troops and delegations of citizens, he was received by the Mayor, Roger C. Weightman, in the rotunda of the Capitol. The entertainment for the distinguished visitor was lavish, the appropriation for its cost being the largest single appropriation for the year, and $900 more than was spent on the public schools during that period.[29]

In a spirit of great festivity on the evening of Lafayette's arrival, rockets were set off in large numbers, and the houses of many citizens were brilliantly illuminated. The College building, standing in unobstructed view on the heights north of the city, had the lights in the eastern, southern, and western fronts of the building, "amounting to several hundred," ignited almost simultaneously. On the top of the building, on the southern front of the cupola, was placed a transparent star eight feet from point to point. At ten o'clock all the candles were extinguished simultaneously, as suddenly as they had been lighted. The effect must have been magnificent. "On the whole," reported the *Star*, "we do not recollect having ever seen a more splendid illumination of a single building, in any of our cities, than was presented in the lighting up of this elegant edifice."[30]

Lafayette was to return to Washington in the course of his extended tour. The *Daily National Intelligencer*, in its issue of December 11, 1824, announced: "General Lafayette will return to the city in time to be present at the Commencement of the Columbian College, on the 15th instant, and on the 16th will depart for Annapolis, reaching the seat of Governor Sprigg on that day, and Annapolis on the next."[31]

This was the first Commencement. The following official notice appeared in the daily press:

COLUMBIAN COLLEGE

The First Commencement of the Columbian College, in the liberal arts and sciences, will be holden on Wednesday next.

The procession will be formed at the College, and repair to Dr. Laurie's Meeting House, on F Street, between Fourteenth and Fifteenth; where the exercises of the day will begin *precisely* at half past 10 o'clock A.M.

The parents and guardians of the young gentlemen connected with the Institution, the Clergy of the District, and the friends of learning generally, are respectfully invited to attend.

General Lafayette and Suite are expected to honor the exercises with their attendance.

Copies of the Order of Exercises will be distributed at the house.

By order of the Faculty.

Wm. Ruggles, *Sec'ry*

College Hill, Dec. 13, 1824[32]

As the secretary's announcement stated, the place appointed for the Commencement was "Dr. Laurie's Meeting House." This Presbyterian Church was located on the south side of F Street west of Fourteenth on a plot of land now occupied by a part of the New Willard Hotel. It had been built in 1807 through the exertions of the Reverend James Laurie. The seating capacity of this room, 60 by 100 feet, was in excess of six hundred people, if the main floor and the semicircular galleries were used. Because of its size and excellent acoustics, the room was frequently used for conventions, concerts, and scientific lectures.[33]

The Board of Trustees at its meeting on December 2 had issued its *Mandamus* for the conferring of degrees and had appropriated $500 to defray the costs of Commencement Day. All students appearing at the ceremonies were directed to wear black silk gowns, "all of one and the same fashion," which could be purchased or rented from the College at a cost of $3.[34]

The procession formed at the College at nine-thirty o'clock and moved to the meetinghouse. Fortunately the weather was unusually fine and "the house was crowded with an intelligent and fashionable auditory." Present were the President of the United States, General Lafayette and his suite, the members of the Cabinet, and many members of the two Houses of Congress. Music was furnished, as it continued to be for many years, by the United States Marine Band.

After President Staughton's invocation, two sophomores spoke. The first was John Boulware of Virginia, who later became tutor in the College; he died in 1829. His topic was "Responsibilities of American Youth." The second, John W. James of Virginia, later an Episcopal clergyman, spoke on "The Superiority of Grecian over Roman Literature." Two juniors followed. Thomas D. Eliot of the District of Columbia, later a Congressman from Massachusetts, took as his topic "Timoleon and Washington." Baron Stow of New Hampshire, remembered in College history for his later feud with Luther Rice and in the history of his denomination as a highly successful pastor in New England, spoke on "The Influence of Mathematics on the Mind." Each of the three members of the graduating class was heard: Alexander Ewell of Virginia on "The United States," Albert Fairfax of Virginia on "The Spirit of Liberty," and James D. Knowles of Rhode Island on "The Philosophy of the Active Powers of Man." Knowles, who was a professor in Newton Theological Seminary from 1832 until his death in 1838, concluded his oration with a valedictory address. The president conferred the degrees and delivered "an eloquent and truly paternal" Baccalaureate Address, which was followed by the Benediction.[35]

The press was enthusiastic in its reports of the Commencement. "It was one," said the *Daily National Journal*, "which, in the opinion of

competent judges, would have done honor to any of our older universities. Indeed it exceeded all expectations. Every part of the performance
evinced talents and mental cultivation of a high order." "To the President, who has always honoured the institution with his confidence and
kindness," said the *Daily National Intelligencer*, "the scene of the day
must have been peculiarly gratifying, as we are sure his presence was to
the Trustees and Faculty of the College, who justly estimate the liberal
disposition he has shown towards it."[36]

After the exercises, the Trustees and faculty returned to the College
to receive Lafayette and his suite. The General arrived at half-past three
and was received by the Trustees and faculty. Escorted by the Reverend
Obadiah B. Brown, President of the Board of Trustees, and Senator
James Barbour, Lafayette passed through a double line of students to the
College chapel where the President, the Reverend Dr. Staughton, welcomed him "in a brief address in which the elegance of the scholar, the
gratitude of the patriot, and the piety of the divine, were finely blended."
"You have come, Sir," he said, "not like Æneas driven to a foreign shore
by unpropitious winds; not like Ulysses, searching an absent son; but
like the good old patriarch, Jacob, you have formed the resolution, 'I
will go down and see my child, ere I die.' "[37]

Lafayette, in a gracious response, expressed his thanks for the honor
done him, the pleasure with which he had witnessed the Commencement,
and his wishes for the prosperity of the College. Each student was then
introduced. The General shook hands with each one and spoke to all the
students in terms of paternal affection. Following the reception, General
Lafayette and his suite, the Secretary of State, the Secretary of War,
the Honorable Henry Clay, and other distinguished guests dined with
the Trustees and faculty at the President's house. Such was the first
Commencement Day.

Many of the students who greeted the College's guest on that eventful
day wore blue ribbons and gold badges bearing an inscription in Greek.
This was the insignia of the Enosinian Society.

The first and by far the most important student society organized was
the Enosinian. On March 6, 1822, just two months after the College was
opened, a group of students held a meeting for the purpose of establishing
a debating society. In the preamble to its constitution, the members
declared that they were "actuated by a desire of improving ourselves in
knowledge, eloquence and every accomplishment by which we may be
the better prepared for any station in life." They were "convinced that

nothing will better tend to effect this purpose than the united exertions and active operation of a well-organized literary society." There were fifteen charter members. A year later, another society, the Ciceronian, was formed, and the two societies jointly celebrated the Fourth of July for several years. Both societies flourished until financial difficulties in 1827 caused a suspension of the College's activities. As soon as the College resumed its activities in 1829, Enosinian likewise resumed. The Ciceronian Society was not revived. Much later, in 1850, the Philophrenian became the second literary society. General Lafayette and his son were the first honorary members of the Enosinian Society. The society established its own library, which by the middle of the century contained 1800 volumes. *The Enosinian Bee*, which was established in 1838, was a folio page with a printed heading; it contained at least three-fourths original material and was read at each meeting by the editor. When the number of sheets reached a convenient thickness, they were bound in a volume and placed in the society's library. The room in the old College building in the east end of the top floor, where the first meeting was held, remained the permanent meeting place. Handsomely furnished, it was designated as Enosinian Hall. "Enosis," the poem by Christopher Pearse Cranch of the class of 1831, derives its name from the motto of this society of which he was an active member.[38]

The brilliance of the first Commencement Day served to justify high hopes for the future success of Columbian College. At the beginning of the second year the student body had increased to 46, and in September, 1824, the year of the first Commencement, the registration figures showed a total of 103, a very remarkable gain.[39]

The College was feeling the pressure of numbers to such an extent that the Board authorized construction of a second large building "in line with the west of the present building, similar in size and appearance."[40] In May, 1825, the Board of Managers reported to the General Convention that the foundations had been laid and that the work was progressing.[41]

The days of optimism were coming to a close. When the Baptist General Convention met in its Fifth Triennial Meeting in New York a year later, the fact that the College was in trouble and its future uncertain had already become generally recognized.

CHAPTER FIVE

Crisis

1825-1828

Columbian College was but five years old when it was called upon to face its first great crisis. Basically financial in nature, the crisis gradually widened in scope and threatened the very life of the young institution. In the light of the close interlocking of the Board of Managers of the Convention and the Board of Trustees of the College, it is difficult to believe that both these bodies were not equally aware of the true financial condition of the College.

Dr. Staughton was long the corresponding secretary of the Board of Managers, and then its president at the same time that he was president of the College. The Reverend O. B. Brown was a member of the Board of Managers and then its vice president while he was president of the College Trustees. The Reverend Luther Rice was treasurer of the College Board of Trustees and agent of the convention. Enoch Reynolds was secretary of the Trustees and a member of the Board of Managers.

The annual reports of the Trustees to the managers were invariably encouraging in general terms. In April, 1821, the convention's committee was "satisfied that existing circumstances justified the decision of the Trustees on the expediency of opening the establishment at an early day." According to the report in 1822, "Every circumstance indicates the hand of God in all our operations. Daily inquiries show that this College is becoming a subject of general notoriety, and encourages the hope that it will rapidly extend its usefulness, and obtain, at no distant day, much greater patronage than the hopes of its friends had anticipated." In 1823, the Trustees reported that outstanding claims, if collected, would liquidate all of the College's debts. In 1824, the Superintending Committee declared that "the confidence of complete ultimate success in relation to the great objects of the College is unimpaired." "The Columbian College continues to prosper," was the optimistic view expressed in the 1825 report. The Fifth Triennial Meeting of the Baptist Convention in New York in April, 1826, heard an entirely different story.[1]

Regardless of the brave show it had made, the College never had claimed, nor did it do so then, that it had basis for the belief that it was in good financial shape. It did not have sufficient funds to cover the cost of initial construction on College Hill. It had to borrow $10,000 to start operations. There had been fancy calculations from time to time to indicate that eventually the College could pay operating expenses from student fees, but meanwhile annual deficits piled up. Strong dependence had been placed on Luther Rice's fund-raising abilities. But the details of administration kept *Treasurer* Rice at the College for lengthy periods and kept *Agent* Rice away from his collecting trips. There was the usual gap between amounts subscribed and monies collected. Much was paid in scrip and was subject to heavy discounts. Finally there came to general knowledge debts hitherto not realized, arising out of Rice's maladroit efforts at investment.

In spite of the generally favorable conclusions in the reports, it would be grossly unfair to say that the College's financial plight had been willfully concealed. In fact, it was usually referred to at the same time and often in the same document which, elsewhere, would be optimistic about the College's future. The founding fathers of the College were men of great faith, faith in God and faith in the College's mission. Some way or other, God would provide. Luther Rice and his colleagues were never idle but were always actively thinking up ways and means. Efforts confidently embarked upon either failed entirely to produce or else produced funds far below the level of the College's needs.

The $10,000 which had been sought at the outset as a loan from the Board had been negotiated with great difficulty. The Board of Directors of the Boston Mission Society had been particularly hostile to the idea. From the very beginning the type of constant concern under which Rice was to labor was apparent from his letters in the field to the president of the College Trustees. On September 5, 1821, he wrote: "I hoped that the banks would *renew* for once rather than *protest*. . . . Besides what I have written for in New York, I will use my utmost endeavors here [in Providence]—so that if *protested*, I hope we will be able to pay without suit." That, even in the fall of 1821, he was working on a shoestring is made clear in a letter of October 24: "I wish all that we have in the banks in the District was in two or three notes, instead of nearly twenty— then by paying a little on each every discount day no doubt we could get along."[2]

There also was always an abiding hope that government funds might be made available, either as a loan or a gift, to ease the institution's financial embarrassment. Columbian College did not lack warm friends and supporters in the Congress of the United States, and they were active in its behalf. Their arguments were eloquent and persistent and must have seemed completely convincing to those who had a deep interest in the College. But there was a hard core of opposition, holding firmly to their fixed ideas of church-state separation, that was joined in sufficient numbers by those who were not firmly committed, to block aid to Columbian College.

Early in 1824 the Trustees of the College directed that a memorial be prepared for presentation to the Congress soliciting a loan of $50,000 for ten years. The Board emphasized that the College was of national locality, consideration, and benefit, "and although originated by Baptists was founded on the most liberal principles as laid down in the charter." In his report on his committee's consideration of the memorial, the Chairman of the Senate Committee, the Honorable James Barbour, recommended aid in the form of lands belonging to the government in the District of Columbia. The report was not acted upon during that session.[3]

Printed appeals for funds were constantly being issued. In general, they followed a uniform style. A characteristic appeal was the one addressed "to the Friends of Religion and Science" dated March, 1825. The Trustees declared that the founders, "encouraged and sustained by the strong representations of the great Washington and his illustrious successors," although "destitute of pecuniary resources," had "looked for the only means of accomplishing the object in the generosity of an enlightened and liberal public." They referred to the purchase of the lot, the construction of buildings, the granting of the Charter, and the enjoyment of "the confidence, approbation, and patronage of the President of the United States, the Heads of the Departments of the Government, and many distinguished citizens."

They listed the parts of the establishment—the Classical Department, the Preparatory School, the Theological Department, and the Medical

Department—as in operation, with a Law Department shortly to be organized. There was a faculty consisting of the president, seven professors, and five tutors, with nearly 150 students coming from twenty-one of the twenty-four states, one territory, and the District.

Funds were needed for an additional college building and the liquidation of existing debts. A sum of $110,000 had been expended for the lot, buildings, equipment, costs of collection, and the purchase of $20,500 of bank stock. Subscriptions, wills, legacies, etc., amounted to $114,000, of which $54,000 was uncollected. This left unpaid $50,000 of the costs, to which had to be added $12,000 interest, making a total debt of $62,000. This was reduced by the value of bank stocks in hand, and $10,000 which would be realized from the uncollected subscriptions, making a net debt of $30,000.

The Trustees asked if there were not 30,000 among 10,000,000 people who would give a dollar each to clear up the debt and "experience in giving it, the high satisfaction of completing a design obviously conducive to the welfare of our country."

The modest amount requested of each individual in this appeal was not characteristic. Fifty-dollar subscriptions were asked for in the later and even more urgent appeal in 1826. From time to time efforts were made to raise, by subscription, endowments for the president and various professorships. The agent and other collectors in the field received funds and subscriptions in any form they were offered; Rice's accounts show the donation of some pieces of jewelry to the cause. By way of identifying solicitors, large and impressive printed certificates were prepared, to be filled in, signed by the officers of the College, and authenticated by the corporate seal.

The constant pressure on Luther Rice as treasurer and agent became increasingly severe. Facing him constantly were demands for running expenses and for meeting payments on outstanding obligations. So harassed was he that at times he would ask his friends to refrain from telling of his proposed visits to College Hill for fear that he would be besieged by creditors were his presence known. Not only was Rice collecting for the general concerns of the College, but his custom was also to open subscription books for special projects, such as the endowment of professorships and of the presidency. In addition to the collection and disbursement of College funds, he still had the responsibility of collection for the convention's missionary activities. Over and above these concerns, Rice was directly involved in publishing matters.

The *Latter Day Luminary* was published five times a year and cost 25 cents per copy. It reported in great detail the activities of the General Convention, its Board and committees. At the Triennial Meeting of 1820, the committee on the *Luminary* reported that the first volume of the work had been issued, consisting of 91,000 printed copies. It was understood that the *Luminary* should be self-supporting. A balance of $17.25½ remained after the completion of the first volume, with some additional payments on account expected. In 1822, Rice reported for the publishing committee that the *Luminary* would thereafter be published monthly at a cost of $2 per annum, and that the *Columbian Star* would be issued weekly on Saturdays at a cost of $3 per annum and delivered to subscribers in the District on the day of publication. It was hoped that by increasing the number of issues per year and extending the coverage to include matters of general interest, the circulation would be vastly increased and a considerable source of revenue for the convention be opened up. Rice was responsible for the finances, much of the administration, and the promotion of these publications, thus adding to an already impossible burden.[4]

Yet Rice could still write to O. B. Brown when his troubles were mounting, "I no more sicken at the work now than I did five years ago."[5]

To understand the grave crisis of 1826, we must recall that, at least to the Baptist Convention, education came second to missions. The logic of this position cannot be challenged. In the preamble to the first constitution the delegates stated that they had convened "for the purpose of organizing a place for eliciting, combining, and directing the Energies of the whole Denomination in one sacred effort for sending the glad tidings of Salvation to the Heathen."[6]

True it is that Dr. Furman, the president, did make a reference to education in the Convention Address, but he underscored the efforts of the body as "directed chiefly to the establishment of a foreign mission," with home missions to "enter into the deliberations of future meetings."[7]

When the constitution was amended and passed on May 2, 1820, the new article inserted to provide for an institution for educational purposes stated specifically that it should be financed "exclusively from education funds."[8] It seems to have been generally accepted that education funds and mission funds would each be used specifically for the purpose for which they were given and for no other purpose.

This separation of funds was never made by Rice in his curious bookkeeping. His receipts and expenditures for all purposes, including his own personal expenses, were entered day by day in his *Journal*. Moving rather rapidly from place to place as he did much of the time, collecting for missions, education, periodicals, and special funds, perhaps it was too much to expect him to keep an orderly set for books. When the time came for a report to the convention or to the board, he would undertake to separate debits from credits and one account from another, and produce an itemized report down to the smallest items, even to gifts of 6¼ cents at times. He frequently protected himself by saying that any inaccuracies noted would be corrected in a later report. Some men have a genius for keeping orderly accounts. Luther Rice certainly did not. When criticism came, it was difficult to meet.

At the meeting of the Board of Managers in May, 1825, Rice was referred to in terms that amounted to a vote of complete confidence: "The Agent of the Convention, the Reverend Luther Rice, continues his unwearied course, alike in relation to missionary and collegiate concerns. His health remains vigorous, and his labors, above measure, are active and unbroken. Self-devoted to the service of the Saviour, he feels the vows of God are upon him, and these sacred vows he is endeavoring incessantly to discharge. It is the sincere wish of the Board that all his self-denying and generous purposes may be realized."[9]

Evidently in preparation for the Fifth Triennial Meeting of the Convention, scheduled to be held in New York a week later, the president laid before the Board of Trustees on April 19, 1826, what the *Minutes* describe as "sundry statements comprising the accounts of the College." These were referred back to him with instructions to prepare them in a proper manner. While these papers are not so identified, it is more than likely that they were Rice's unorganized records which were so baffling and time-consuming to those who made an effort to digest them and produce a balance sheet. Certainly there had developed a deep concern for the College's financial standing, deep enough to become a matter of general knowledge. Whether sudden crisis had developed or whether patience, long tried, had finally grown weary enough to break through the haze of optimism and engage realities is hard to say.

Dr. Staughton, the president of the College, from the account given in the *Memoir* by Lynd, his son-in-law, seems to have had the same views with reference to the institution's finances that were held by so many others. "He had," wrote Lynd, "unbounded confidence in those who managed the pecuniary concerns of the college, and while the note of complaint was swelling louder and louder, in different sections of the country, he seemed to view it merely as the result of hostility to the institution. He entered into their defense, on every suitable occasion, with ardor." Lynd tells us that Staughton never let pecuniary details occupy his mind. He had decided that the College's difficulties were trivial. He had to change his mind, however. Writing to his son from the convention in New York he expressed real concern: "I look for a great struggle in New York, but I have the good hope that righteousness and truth will prevail. Perhaps brighter days are before us."[10]

Certainly no better proof that crisis was at hand could be sought than the action of Luther Rice himself in taking the floor on the first day of the convention on April 26, 1826, and moving the appointment of a committee of eleven "to investigate the conduct of Luther Rice in what may be considered as belonging thereto on his own individual and personal responsibility, in what may be considered as belonging to his official relation to this body, and in what may be considered as belonging to his official relations to the Columbian College, and report to this body." Rice followed this resolution with another. Noting that his name did not appear on the list of nominees for election to the College Board, approved by the convention, he moved that his name be included on the list, but the session was adjourned. On the following morning the motion was called up, but by formal resolution it was postponed, and a resolution was adopted calling for immediate action to determine the financial condition of the College. Rice's motion was referred to a committee for its suggestion of some viable arrangement at that afternoon's meeting. The committee made the following report to which Rice gave his formal agreement:

> Mr. Rice having declared his determination to devote his time to the collection of funds for the College, and never again to perform any part of the service of disbursing monies on account of the College, unless specially directed so to do by a resolution of the Board of Trustees; and having also expressed his determination to retire from a seat in the Board of Trustees, provided he shall be found in the opinion of the Convention on the investigation which he has invited, unworthy of that office, it is the opinion of the Committee that his name ought to be placed on the list for Trustees.

The report was accepted and Rice's name was added.[11]

The groundwork had now been laid for a complete exposé of Rice's entire financial operations. As was usual, when Rice's report as agent for the past three years was presented, it was referred to the appropriate committee for examination and audit. In utter frustration, the Committee on Agents' Accounts reported that they had been referred to earlier numbers of the *Luminary* and *Annual Reports* and a recent Manuscript Account, and that they were not able "to accomplish an investigation from such resources." Rice was ordered to furnish a Manuscript Account current to the committee by the following morning.

Dealing with another facet of Rice's operations, the committee on the *Star* and the *Luminary* was directed to inquire into the state of the property occupied by the publishing concern, which Rice had estimated to be worth $10,000 and had agreed to deed over to the convention. The committee prepared and presented a very detailed and circumstantial report. Although they lacked full documentation, they had interviewed many persons who had had some connection with the matter and had thus been able to fill in the narrative. The mood of the committee was eminently judicial and fair. There could be no defense for sloppy bookkeeping, especially if it resulted in applying funds received for one purpose to another. Yet Rice did have a plea. If he had been unbusinesslike, so had the convention. Rice and his colleagues were profoundly impressed with the need for the *Luminary*, and later for the *Columbian Star* with its greater frequency, as instruments of communication to keep the members of the denomination at large informed of the activities of the convention and its representatives and thus increase the sense of involvement of Baptists generally in the vital work that had been undertaken. Conscious of a generally felt need, Rice with characteristic impetuosity had gone ahead when the convention was based at Philadelphia and acquired and equipped a printing establishment there. He had done the same thing when the board shifted its base to the District of Columbia. Other than a requirement that the publications should be self-supporting, there was no formal arrangement as to the financial relations of the printing concern with the convention. In addition to the two periodicals, general printing was also done. Rice was the proprietor of the establishment.

The property and equipment that Rice bought for the printing office in Washington cost $11,150. The real property, consisting of two brick houses valued at $10,000 by Rice, he turned over to the convention, with the understanding that the proceeds should be applied to his benefit until an amount equal to what he owed on the property was realized. When the property was deeded over, a committee of the convention was supposed to run the printing concern; but Rice had continued to operate the business and had applied sums paid in for the periodicals to meet the debts of the College.

At the time the report was made, Baron Stow had recently leased the offices and premises, had discontinued the *Luminary*, and was running the *Star* on his own responsibility. The committee faced two problems: the debts of the business before, and after, the transfer of the property. Rice claimed that what had happened before the transfer of the property was his own business and that the convention should be concerned only with what happened afterward. The committee acknowledged that it lacked the necessary data to make a positive determination of the amount involved. "No leger [sic] or daybook had ever been kept in the office. The whole pecuniary accounts were noted in a subscription book. Mr. Rice informed us that he has always made minutes in his journal of whatever monies he has received, but that these minutes are scattered through his journals ever since the work began." An accountant was at work on these papers, but it would be a month before he could finish his task. The committee was at sea. The accounts were now cold, some of them nine or ten years old. There was no way of knowing which subscribers had paid and which were in arrears. The committee had also found a flaw in the deed. Part of the land used was not included in the parcel transferred to the convention. Since the Triennial Meeting would have adjourned long before anything definite could be known, the whole matter was referred to the Board of Managers, with power to act. Rice was absolved of any intentional wrong or design to injure the convention.[12]

On May 5, the convention heard the report of the committee on the conduct of Luther Rice that had been called for by Rice's own resolution on the first day of the meeting. It stated that they had heard several witnesses, examined their charges against Rice, and given him a chance to refute them. Nothing was found affecting his moral character, but many imprudences and indiscretions, some of which he acknowledged, were found. By way of illustration a short history of Rice's transactions was given. The report would seem, in a way, to absolve him from censure through the period of the convention of 1823, by saying that he presented an account of his operations up to that time. "But whether they were fairly understood by the Convention is very doubtful." Of the various transactions entered into "in conjunction with the Board of Trustees of said College" after that time, two were considered as very imprudent.

On his own private responsibility, certain houses were purchased of Col. R. M. Johnson to a large amount, and which were afterwards received by the Board of Trustees as College property, which have heretofore yielded very little profit to the College, while it has burdened it with a debt of fourteen thousand dollars. Through him a claim of Mr. McKenny against the United States government was taken up, amounting to eleven thousand dollars. This also failed in affording funds to any considerable amount, while it loaded the College with the whole debt of eleven thousand dollars.[13]

Upon hearing the report, the convention resolved that no charge as to immoral conduct had been substantiated, that the urgent embarrassments of the College partially mitigated his imprudences, and that it appeared that Mr. Rice was a "very loose accountant . . . with very imperfect talents for the disbursement of money."[14]

The committee on the concerns of the College reported to the convention on May 6, 1826. The report was discussed in the morning and throughout the afternoon sessions, and a resolution of the greatest significance was adopted. The preamble declared that experience showed that the connection between the missionary and educational concerns of the convention had helped neither one, and that the convention could exercise no control over the affairs of the College which would be beneficial to the institution or would maintain public confidence, as evidenced by a recent decision of the Attorney General. The decision thus alluded to but not described was one given to O. B. Brown, president of the Board of Trustees, in reply to a personal inquiry, made of Attorney General Wirt, if the election of trustees could be held in New York City. The Attorney General ruled that elections must be held in the District of Columbia, the seat of the College. For these reasons the Trustees were asked to amend the ordinances by placing the nomination of Trustees in the hands of some body other than the convention, "taking care to preserve to the Baptist Denomination the effective control of the institution." Recalling the general but erroneous impression that the convention was responsible for the debts of the College, the convention declared that if the Trustees followed the course recommended in the list of nominations recently furnished by the convention and if the Trustees' policy was such as to inspire public confidence, they would use their influence and exert their powers to free Columbian College from its embarrassments.[15]

In the closing moments of the Triennial Meeting, it was announced that certain members of the convention had held a consultation to consider ways and means of relieving Columbian College. Their request that their minutes be added to those of the convention was approved. This conference, in the Oliver Street Baptist Meeting House in New York, was a major factor in securing the continuance of Columbian College.[16]

With great boldness these friends of the College cut the Gordian knot by making specific recommendations, which, under the circumstances, could not be rejected. A committee of five men of considerable distinction was set up to insure public confidence: the Reverend Messrs. R. B. Semple, L. Bolles, William T. Brantley, and Jesse Mercer, and the Honorable James Thompson. They recommended that measures be taken to reform the "One Hundred dollars system," a scheme by which donors were permitted to send students to the College. The system as a fund-raiser was self-defeating, and was made all the more so by inaccurate records, so the College never knew exactly what its obligations were. The next recommendation called for prudent retrenchments and economies in the operation of the institution. Measures were to be taken at once for raising a sum of $50,000 in subscriptions of at least $50 each from responsible persons on condition that the whole sum be subscribed within two years, subscriptions to be payable in sixty days after the entire amount had been subscribed and on the certification of the committee that the financial condition of the College warranted their payment. The group recommended that the Board of Trustees of the College fill the present vacancies on it, the first ones with citizens of the District of Columbia named on the list of nominations. By way of change in personnel, the Reverend Elon Galusha was urged as treasurer to succeed Rice. The employment of Rice and such other agents as were necessary was recommended to collect outstanding subscriptions, to obtain subscriptions for paying the interest on the College debt and defraying its current expenses, and to solicit for the $50,000 fund.[17]

Following the suggestions of the New York group, an appeal was drawn up over the signatures of O. B. Brown and Enoch Reynolds, president and secretary, respectively, of the Board of Trustees. The appeal, which was distributed on May 18, 1826, listed, in general categories, liabilities amounting to $83,028.60 and assets of $85,557.65, a balance of $2,529.05 over debts. However, because of the heavy interest on so large a debt, the carrying charges were excessive; and because so many subscriptions, notes, and outstanding accounts would probably fail of collection, at least for a time, it was judged that the actual debt of the College was on the order of $30,000. The Board therefore sought to raise $50,000 immediately.

At the Board meeting where this statement was authorized, Rice resigned as treasurer but agreed to act in that capacity until other arrangements could be made. He was, however, to continue as agent, together with the Reverend Messrs. David Benedict, Jonathan Going, and Elon Galusha, and the Honorable John B. Yates. The Reverend Elon Galusha was asked to move to Washington as soon as possible and assume the duties of treasurer. Committees were to be appointed to see what retrenchment could be made in the expenses of the College and to ask the government to take back the obligation of McKenny and give up its claim against the College.

Accepting election as treasurer to succeed Rice, the Reverend Elon Galusha was released by his own church to permit him to move his home to Washington and devote his whole time to the College's concerns. He embarked upon his task with great energy and dedication. No better evidence of his zeal could be sought than the statement he had printed on September 1, 1826, bearing the bold heading:

READ—RESOLVE—ACT

THE CRISIS IS AT HAND

It is a lengthy document of approximately five thousand words, eloquent, and in places melodramatic, calling on denominational pride coupled with patriotic sentiment, human sympathy, and common business sense. The purpose of the document was to stimulate the drive for $50 subscriptions to complete the $50,000 fund. In a note to Professor Ruggles, written on a copy of the statement, Galusha said, "I find that by sending this statement to an individual more effect is produced upon his mind, than by an hour's talk without it." His dominant appeal was to save the College with its glorious prospects for the Baptists. His arguments ran the whole gamut: to add to Baptist prestige, to protect the Baptist name from disgrace, to prevent discouragement to potential donors who had made previous gifts, to prevent "Episcopalians, Unitarians, or Infidels" from building on their ruins or profiting by their misfortune; to save embarrassment from seeing "a powerful establishment rising up under the auspices of Government." To those who would respond to the need were offered the affectionate thanks of the writer, the eternal gratitude of the denomination, the approbation of a good conscience, the smile of benevolence, and a fond recollection in heaven![18]

President Brown of the Board of Trustees reported that an election had been held on the first Monday in May and that 27 persons had received the required majority of votes cast and had been declared elected. Among these was Baron Stow, who became secretary of the Board two months later, succeeding Enoch Reynolds, who resigned. To fill vacancies in the Board caused by the failure to elect a full slate and by resignations, the recommendations of the New York group were followed. James Barbour, Secretary of War; Richard Rush, Secretary of the Treasury; John Mc-Lean, Postmaster General; Samuel Harrison Smith, president of Washington Bank; and Roger C. Weightman, mayor of Washington, were elected. Since they were public men with wide administrative experience, it was expected that they could add great strength to the Board and increase public confidence in the College.[19]

The new members of the Board became active at once. Baron Stow, the new secretary, was also editor of the *Columbian Star* and was thus in a strategic position to wield great influence. A graduate of the College in the class of 1825, he had a wide acquaintance among Board members, faculty, graduates, and students. He became, in a very special way, Luther Rice's *bête noire*.

At a Trustees' meeting late in May, 1826, a letter was read from the Reverend John Kerr of Richmond, severely censuring Stow's report of the General Convention in the *Star*'s issues of May 6 and May 13. The Board referred this letter as an additional item for investigation to a committee appointed the previous day and now instructed to inquire into the correctness of statements made in the *Star* implicating the conduct of Luther Rice. It was also to investigate and report on the pecuniary condition of the College. The Board ordered its action and the names of the committee members, Messrs. McLean and Smith, published in the *Star*.[20]

As the days went on and as tensions increased, this linkage of the new Trustees, Stow, and the *Star* came to suggest to the beleaguered and badgered Rice the formation of a conspiratorial apparatus against him and against the College and its originators. Certainly many of the Board's actions in the ensuing weeks and months were highly businesslike. They prohibited any new notes being given, and they ended the $100 system. Banks and other creditors were asked for a moratorium until January 1, 1827. Sound systems of procedure were set up for the treasurer and the steward, the only two officers authorized to make expenditures. A new schedule of student charges not to exceed $180 per annum was set up. Rice's books were turned over to Samuel Smoot for a detailed audit. These were wise measures whose only fault was that many of them were about five years too late.

The effort to get a full picture of Rice's financial relations with the College did not produce rapid results. Samuel Smoot, to whom the treasurer's accounts had been turned over for examination, arrangement, and summary, was a graduate of the College and, for a time, principal of the Preparatory School. Smoot understandably had his difficulties with the fragmentary memoranda and haphazard journals he had to handle. Once he gave up the task, encouraged to do so by Rice, but was ordered by the Board to resume. The new men, basically anti-Rice in view, controlled the Board for a period of six months. Although the majority of the full Board was probably never militantly anti-Rice, the quorum requirement was low, meetings were called on short notice, and the new men living in the District were able to attend meetings which, for one reason or another, out-of-town men frequently had to forgo.

Many of the resolutions show the hostility of this group to Rice. On September 18, 1826, Rice was asked to state his view of his agency and produce records of what he had received in subscriptions and cash toward the $50,000 fund. Rice asked for a month's time to prepare his reply. A month later to the day, the Board opened up on Rice with a broadside in a series of resolutions that lacked nothing by way of directness. The preamble stated that, as a result of the recommendation of the New York group on May 15, 1826, Rice was appointed agent to collect subscriptions, that Rice had returned to the College for a considerable time and had not informed the Board of his intentions in the discharge of his agency. Since the Trustees had obligations in this respect, they directed Rice to state his intentions so they could discharge their duties. Inasmuch as it might actually be shown by the facts that Rice was indebted to the College in a large amount—a fact probably not known to the New York meeting, to the convention, or to the Trustees at the time of his appointment—an unusual situation was created. Considering "the delicate and important circumstances," the Board left to Rice the course to be pursued. If he saw fit to continue the agency, he must state, before his departure, the compensation expected and the services to be rendered, maintain strict accounting, and make regular payments to the treasurer. Personal donations to any agent were prohibited. The action was ordered printed in the *Columbian Star* over the signature of the secretary. Rice protested, and O. B. Brown tried to have the order to publish rescinded; but with Rice present and voting, the motion to rescind was lost 5 to 7. Rice presented a written protest against the publication of the resolution as, in his opinion, "uncalled for and of injurious tendency."[21] On November 8, he told the Board that he would not leave until he had finished a statement of his accounts.

On February 23, 1827, in a letter to the Board of Trustees Rice presented his claim for compensation for services for five and a quarter years,

amounting to $5,250, and entered into an examination of "a report pur-
porting to 'embrace a general account current between Luther Rice, as
Treasurer, and the College,'" made on August 5, 1826, and showing a
deficit of $26,008.69. As a result of alleged "omission, under-credit, and
over-charge," Rice claimed an overpayment on his part of $40.27, rather
than a deficit. This, he said, he could ultimately show. He had already
spent four months on his accounts, and to do the job completely would
require at least six or eight months more. Meanwhile, the situation would
permit no delay. The subscriptions toward the $50,000 fund were, by
agreement, to be canceled if the full sum were not subscribed within two
years. Rice therefore suggested suspending the examination of his accounts
so that he could go forth to raise funds. A set of resolutions was adopted,
stating the facts in Rice's letter, accepting, for the time being, his allega-
tions as to "omission, under-credit, and over-charge," and directing him
to give his attention to securing subscriptions and collecting funds.

Printed in the same four-page leaflet with this letter was a second
letter from Rice to the Board, dated March 14, 1827, referring to the
final report of the Committee on the Financial Concerns of Columbian
College, which had acted under instructions from the convention at its
Triennial Meeting in 1826. He protested again that the deficit of
$26,008.69 was determined without any reference to him. In this second
letter he referred bitterly to the new men who had been brought into the
Board and who had resigned several months later. These men, he said,
"were brought into the Board by the honorable and conciliatory spirit
of compromise indulged by myself and my friends." If they meant by
this method of leaving to embarrass the College, it was consistent with
their whole line of action as an effort to take the College out of the
control of those who had brought it into being. If, as alleged by Rice,
they had not indulged in such tactics as tying Galusha up at the College
for two months and him for six months when they should have been in
the field, the $50,000 would have been entirely subscribed and partially
collected. With the College now free from "party collisions" he was
optimistic over the chances of completing the fund within the two years
allowed.[22]

In the period between the writing of each of these two letters, published
together in the leaflet, a series of events had occurred which account for
the optimistic conclusion of the second letter. The resolutions of October 18, 1826, mark the high tide of success of the anti-Rice group. Rice
counseled the president of the Board, O. B. Brown, to see always that he

had enough Baptists around so that the hostile members of the Board could not muster "the active majority on the spot." "Smith," he wrote to Brown, "will not be satisfied until he gets the college out of the hands of the Baptists."[23]

When the Board resolved that, in the light of his explanations and his claim for compensation, Rice suspend his work on his accounts and go into the field to raise funds, Rice had triumphed. The Board had taken his word and continued his agency. There was a wholesale exodus from the Board. Stow resigned as secretary and as Trustee. Five other Trustees resigned.[24]

Rice had been exceedingly hostile to Baron Stow, and his hostility was reciprocated. Stow had come into a position of great power for so young a man. As secretary and member of the Board, he had immediate access to full information, at the same time that his control of the *Star* gave him an excellent medium of communication both locally in the District and throughout the denomination. Rice looked upon him as a fellow conniver with Smith of the Board and with Ruggles of the faculty, ready to deliver the College over to non-Baptists. Rice's claim that Stow had garbled accounts of official action in the *Star* to put him in an unfavorable light was investigated and declared groundless. Rice was sufficiently goaded by Stow to take to the public prints in a counterattack. To put an end to what was assuming the proportions of a scandal, the First Baptist Church, of which both men were members, held a meeting, reported in its records of November 10, 1826, as a result of which a reconcilation of a sort was effected, and the parties agreed to cease their recriminations against each other.[25]

Rice was evidently satisfied by the outcome. On November 23, he wrote to a friend that all was settled and that he and Stow were on good terms again.[26]

Baron Stow was shortly to move on to fields of greater usefulness. He was ordained October 24, 1827, and entered upon a pastorate in Portsmouth, New Hampshire. After five years, he moved on to the Baldwin Place Church in Boston, which he served with great effectiveness for forty years.

The Rice–Stow controversy indicated the general tension that dominated the College administration. In the year 1827 President Staughton resigned; Secretary Stow resigned; the steward, Robert P. Anderson, resigned; and a number of Trustees resigned. The faculty individually and as a body offered resignations.

Internally, the College was at a low ebb in morale. The members of the faculty had many grievances, not the least of which was unpaid salaries. The financial stringency which had so long afflicted the College had led to shabby treatment of a loyal teaching staff. Payments on salary, rather than salary, had been doled out tardily and were now greatly in arrears. The faculty, and particularly Professor Ruggles, had protested consistently and vehemently. It was generally known that their resignations were ready for presentation at any time.

On March 19, 1827, Luther Rice brought to the Board word of a disturbing situation. "It had been intimated," he stated cautiously, "that a spirit of restlessness prevails amongst the students and a disposition on the part of some to leave the Institution." The Trustees immediately requested their Financial Committee "to enter into a free conversation with the Faculty" and to take whatever steps they deemed necessary. Consultation with Professor Caswell (later president of Brown University) and Professor Ruggles made it quite plain that the disquietude was due to the very generally known condition of the Institution's finances and the fear that the faculty was about to resign. To dissuade the faculty from leaving, the professors were offered a lien on the library if they would agree both to stay until the end of the year and not to leave later with less than three months' notice. Tutors who needed money to move would be paid in cash, and claims of the College against individuals were assigned to furnish the necessary funds.[27]

The student enrollment for the year 1826-1827 had been reported as: Theological Department, 1; Classical Department: Seniors 13, Juniors 5, Sophomores 14, Freshman 20; Preparatory School: First year 10, Second year 6, Third year 4; Unclassified 4; Total, 77.[28]

On March 26, the Financial Committee asked the Board's opinion as to the desirability of continuing the operation of the College. Demands for payment were coming from every side—tradesmen, artisans, banks, individual creditors, and faculty members. O. B. Brown stated his belief that first attention should be given to the payment of the faculty.[29]

A month later the Trustees asked the College's creditors for a breathing spell, to permit the use of funds for current expenses and to give a pledge not to bring suit or execution against the College for a period of two years. The resignations of Messrs. Caswell, Ruggles, and Conant, which had been presented to be effective as soon as other instructors could be appointed, were laid on the table. Six days later, the resignations, to which that of Tutor Heath had been added, were again presented. The Board was told that the faculty had dismissed all students. Again the faculty's resignations were laid on the table. Feeling in the Board against the faculty was very strong, and attention was given to the propriety of bringing suit against Caswell and Ruggles, the two senior members, for damages caused the College by resigning without due notice and informing the students before notifying the Board. A committee was appointed to visit the students and take whatever measures they deemed necessary.[30]

The committee convened with the students in chapel. It would help any students who wanted to stay in the city to find cheap board. If they stayed at the College they would have the usual commons; and if they could not afford other quarters, the committee would give them places in their own homes. Ten students signed a statement declaring their intention to stay at the College. A vacation was declared from May 1 (the next day) until the first Wednesday in September and it was promised that efforts would be made to get sufficient faculty.[31]

The Trustees' offer to give the faculty a lien on the library to secure their salaries and thus dissuade them from leaving was formalized by a resolution of the Board adopted on March 26, 1827, and formally recorded as an assignment of property on April 12, 1827. Certain claims of the College against private individuals were assigned to Professor Ruggles, Professor Caswell, and Thomas Conant, a tutor. Ruggles and Caswell were each given a lien claim on all the books and pamphlets in the library to the extent of $550 on the express agreement that each was to continue his duties until January 1, 1828, provided that "the College shall continue so long in operation" and that each should give at least three months' notice thereafter of intention to leave.[32]

At a meeting of the Board on May 9 it was reported that the professors had rejected this arrangement and again presented their resignations.[33]

The blows that had fallen upon the College had been particularly distressing to President Staughton, a highly sensitive man whose great distinction had been publicly recognized for many years. He was hardly prepared for crisis and threatened failure. Staughton had been consistently the optimist until the hard facts had cut the ground from beneath him. He felt personally aggrieved and used to say in his family, "I am familiar with humiliation." With what he hoped was the strengthening of the Board by the addition of several distinguished Trustees in 1826, he felt the tide had turned in the College's favor. He was in Charleston, South Carolina, on a fund-raising tour in the South when news came to him of the resignations of some of these men from the Board. He was shocked and, as he wrote his son, did not know what to do or what to say to people. "The constant cry among the friends of the College is, 'Doctor, any news from Washington today?'" On March 22 he wrote that he would probably send in his resignation immediately. "God only knows what I have suffered since I have been in Charleston."[34]

His resignation, dated in Charleston March 23, 1827, was laid before the Board of Trustees on April 11, 1827. For a man who wrote eloquent prose and graceful poetry, the laconic nature of his letter tells much:

> Rev. O. B. Brown, President of the Board of Trustees
> Sir:
> I request you to communicate to the Board of Trustees, my resignation of the office of President of that Institution.
> > Yours, with due respect,
> > Wm. Staughton[35]

Dr. Staughton was elected president of Georgetown College, Kentucky, in 1829, but did not live to enter upon the office. He died in Washington on December 13, 1829, in the sixtieth year of his age. His funeral was an occasion of public sorrow. "All the clergy were present, even the Roman Catholic apostolic Vicar. The trustees, faculty and students of all the departments of the college, made arrangements and walked in procession. The house was surrounded by hundreds, who could not procure entrance. The Rev. Mr. Brown spoke, Dr. Chapin and Dr. Laurie prayed."[36] Thus the College honored in death its first president, who by his personal eminence had added so greatly to the prestige of the young institution.

With the resignation of President Staughton, an era in the College's history was rapidly drawing to a close. By action of the Trustees, all the property of the College was conveyed in trust to three distinguished citizens—John P. Van Ness, James Corcoran, and George Bomford—to be held by them for the benefit of the creditors. The deed setting up this trust is a formidable document of fifty folio pages. The indenture, made December 15, 1827, was recorded ten days later. The document set forth the metes and bounds of the property. It provided that at any time or times after September 15, 1828, the Trustees might sell the lot or parcels of ground and premises with their appurtenances, after due advertisement, and pay off the debts of the College. It was further provided that in the same way "the philosophical apparatus, implements, instruments, maps, charts, household stuff and furniture, goods, chattels, and effects of every whatsoever mentioned in the schedule marked A" should be held and sold in the same fashion, any surplus money to be paid over to the Trustees of the College.

Schedule A contains a catalogue of the books belonging to the library in 1825, numbering in all 3,034 volumes; a copy of an invoice of six cases of philosophical instruments ordered by the Reverend Alva Woods, listing each of the items; a general statement showing the value of each of the cases of instruments and each of the six cases and two trunks of books; and a complete inventory of the furniture, goods, and "affects" [sic] of the College, made by the steward on May 14, 1827.

Despite its cold legal formality, there is high tragedy in this document. All that was material that Luther Rice and his co-laborers had been able to accumulate was apparently about to fall away. A noble effort seemed to be on the point of failure.

Luther Rice, founder, defender, and chief fund-raiser of the College, resigned from the Board, followed shortly by O. B. Brown, the president of the Board. As the time drew near for the scheduled resumption of the College's operation, a resolution of the Board extended the vacation hopefully until arrangements could be made for paying the debts.[37]

The resignation of the Reverend Obadiah Bruen Brown from the presidency and from membership on the Board of Trustees was particularly significant. When Luther Rice began to identify himself with Baptist concerns in the District of Columbia, Brown was already pastor of the First Baptist Church, which he was to serve in that capacity for half a century. Not only was Brown the pastor of an important church; he was also a man of affairs, a leading citizen with broad personal contacts locally and nationally, and recognized as a leader in his denomination. It is not too much to say that his services to the College were second in value only to those of Rice. He was one of the small group that raised the funds and purchased College Hill. He was active in supporting missions, particularly those in Africa, and in espousing the cause of education in his denomination. He was the first president of the Board of Trustees. Because Dr. Staughton's acceptance of the office of president of the College was long delayed and when accepted made possible his presence in Washington only for limited periods at infrequent intervals, Brown virtually had to serve also as President of the College. With Rice in the field, he had also to take over many of the treasurer's functions. Rice never hesitated to ask anything of Brown—to write letters, to confer with individuals, to placate creditors, and very often to guarantee funds by his own endorsement. Without him, Rice would have been ineffective in large degree, for Brown was what Rice was not—orderly, methodical, and practical. In the days of bitter controversy, Brown stuck faithfully by Rice, and Rice gave Brown his fullest confidence.

As embarrassing as were the indefinite suspension of its academic activities, the withdrawal of so many important figures from places of leadership, and the existence of wholesale ill will in the College community, the massive weight of heavy indebtedness was perhaps even more distressing. Each effort to draw up an accounting of Rice's financial relation to the institution produced a different amount of the alleged shortage. Each was countered by Rice with his familiar formula of "omission, under-credit, and over-charge," producing a result favorable to him as treasurer and agent.

Without attempting to draw up a balance sheet—because that was virtually impossible even a hundred and forty years ago—it is at least illustrative to point out some of the major areas and sources of indebtedness. One of the more succinct statements on the question of the debt was made by Rice in his letter of February 23, 1827, to the Board of Trustees, when he pointed out that some of the deficit antedated the College Hill operation. The operation of the Theological Institution in Philadelphia, before its removal to the District, had resulted in a deficit of $6,665, which, with interest charges, had risen to $9,237.18. There had been greater costs than had been provided for in the construction of the main College building and in the expenses of the agency. There had been unusually high charges in the form of premiums on drafts, protests, and discounts on noncurrent bills, in addition to heavy interest charges on sums borrowed from banks and from individuals. Then there was the debt incurred through Rice's curious attempt at investment which had resulted in obligating the College to the government for a substantial sum.

The *Christian Secretary* of Hartford, Connecticut, in its issue of May 10, 1828, reported that the inquiry had been frequently made, "How did the College become indebted to the government in the sum of $30,000, without having received a consideration of equal value?" A letter from Rice answered the inquiry. So involved was the answer that it is best given in Rice's words:

The facts are: A friend of mine held two large houses and lots at Greenleaf's Point in the City of Washington, which had come into his hands to secure a debt for a relative of his, who was, at the same time, a debtor to a bank in Cincinnati, Ohio, in which bank the government had made deposits of money arising from the sale of public lands in the western country; but the said bank was failing, and the government likely to suffer loss. He proposed to convey to me the said two dwelling houses and lots—that my obligation should be given to the government, with a lien upon the property—and the government give his relative credit in the aforesaid failing bank in Cincinnati. The arrangements were agreed to; the conveyance of obligation executed; and thus I became a debtor to the government in the sum of $14,000. This was in 1820.

A few years only had passed by when application was made to Congress for a loan of $50,000. The house rejected the application; but a bill was got up in the senate to make over to the College certain debts, including mine, due the government, and other property, in all to the amount of $30,000; and the bill came within two or three votes of passing.—This fact, and the remarks and suggestions of several members of Congress, produced the belief that if the College were the direct debtor to the government it would not be difficult to obtain a relinquishment of the obligation. Under this impression —considering that the arrangements concerning the two houses at the Point had been entered into by me solely for the purpose of enabling me to prosecute more successfully the objects of the College—and fully expecting that Congress would give up the claim in a short time, the Board of Trustees consented to make an obligation to the government in lieu of mine, which was, therefore, cancelled; and hence, the College became indebted to the government $14,000!

To this was added the sum of nearly $12,000, in the following manner: Col. McKenney was indebted to the government to that amount; but held a claim against the government for say $8,000. He proposed that the College obligation should be given to the government, and the amount of his claim, when obtained, paid over to the College, and the balance that would be due the College from him, be paid by installments quarterly out of his salary. It was expected his claim would be allowed soon; would become the same in effect as a loan from the government, which might remain an indefinite period without being repaid, and perhaps ultimately become a donation. This was finally agreed to, and the College was then a debtor to the government to nearly $26,000.[38]

Apparent losses incurred through Rice's bad management by no means explained the total deficit. The College had never been properly financed. An initial loan of $10,000 was required to get it under way, and deficits in running expenses had resulted in a mass of loans from individuals and from banks.

In the early computations, the liabilities were about balanced by the assets, consisting mainly of the grounds and improvements on College Hill. On later reckonings the liabilities tended to soar above the assets. The problem was approached by almost equal expenditure of effort in two directions: whittling down the claims by appeals to the creditors and soliciting subscriptions to the $50,000 fund.

A Bill for relief of Columbian College, in the District of Columbia, passed by the Congress in the spring of 1828, freed the institution from its liability to pay the United States the sum of $30,000, inasmuch as the College had received no benefits from its indebtedness to the government. The Trustees, in accordance with the provisions of the Act, deeded the houses on Greenleaf's Point to the United States. Thus was removed the largest single item of indebtedness.[39]

In order to tie in with the method of solicitation then being employed, the ordinances fixing eligibility to vote for Trustees were changed. Any Baptist group giving not less than $50 had one vote, two votes for $100, and an additional vote for each added $50. Any Baptist pastor giving $50 became a voter for life.[40]

Student charges for the future were fixed at $200 per year: $30 for tuition and $100 for board for the first session, and $20 for tuition and $50 for board for the second session.[41]

The Bank of the United States, Philadelphia branch, agreed to relinquish $5,698.22 of the sum due that bank.[42]

On April 19, 1828, the committee that was established at the New York meeting on May 9, 1826, to certify when, within the two-year period allowed, the financial returns would warrant the payment of sums subscribed to the $50,000 fund, certified that the subscription was completed and that the conditions of payment were fulfilled. Commenting on this, the *Columbian Star* took a very conservative position. It expressed the hope that subscribers would pay promptly and, if possible, increase their contributions. The *Star* observed that the debts of the College were stated at $102,000, that the various banks had relinquished a part of their claims, that the other creditors would be paid 65 per cent of their claims, and that the net amount would then be $71,027, for which the College had in view only $67,440. To meet this deficit of $3,587 the College could only fall back on old claims which had gone long unpaid. The *Star* commented that none of these debts had ever been authorized by the convention. The *Star* might have added that the certifying committee had acted just in time.[43] The two-year period allowed would have expired in less than three weeks' time, and all the subscriptions would then have been canceled automatically. While, all things being considered, it is fortunate that the certifying committee acted when and as it did, the picture was actually less favorable than they knew. New claims came in amounting to $4,000, and but $33,000 of the $50,000 subscribed was paid in. There was still a large debt!

The Board was not aware of this, any more than were the members of the Committee. Ever since President Staughton's resignation, they had been casting about for a new president. On August 28, 1827, the Reverend Daniel H. Barnes of New York was elected. He demanded, as conditions of his acceptance, the right to remodel the statutes and ordinances, a veto on the appointment of all teachers and agents, the same perquisites as the presidents of Brown University and Union College, and a salary of $2,000 per year, payable quarterly in advance and to be raised to $3,000 as soon as possible, the same to be secured by bonds of responsible individuals for ten years at least. The Board could only regret that these conditions could not be met and on October 20, 1827, informed Barnes that the position had been offered to another. The new choice was the Reverend Dr. Stephen Chapin of Waterville, Maine, who was offered the post with a salary of $1,500 and free rent in a good house. He accepted and was formally elected on June 20, 1828.[44]

CHAPTER SIX

Financial Recovery
1828-1859

The College's major problem from the very beginning was financial. The College was assailed by demands from all quarters; hence it was not surprising that the vacation declared first from May 1, 1827, to the first Monday in the following September should be finally extended until arrangements could be made for paying the debts of the institution. All seemed to depend on the completion of subscriptions to the $50,000 fund within the two-year period allowed as a condition of the payment of the pledges made. The schedule was barely met, and within two months, on June 20, 1828, the Reverend Stephen Chapin was formally elected second president of Columbian College.

Stephen Chapin (1778-1845) was a native of Milford, Massachusetts, a graduate of Harvard, and, like Luther Rice, a Congregational minister turned Baptist. At the time of his election, he was Professor of Theology in Waterville (now Colby) College.

President Chapin's administration (1828-1841) was devoted to the arduous task of releasing the College from all indebtedness. On May 9, 1842, the Board announced that this great objective had been achieved; and on the twenty-fourth of that month at a service of special commemoration in the College Chapel, solemn thanksgivings were offered to Almighty God for His saving mercy.

So central had the problem of finance been that it is revealing to survey the steps taken in the Chapin, Bacon, and Binney administrations to meet the continued difficulties which, though harassing, did not again force a suspension of the institution's activities.[1]

Luther Rice, looking back at the distressing situation into which the College had fallen in the late 1820's and from which it was slowly extricating itself, summarized rather adequately the causes of the trouble:

First. Four unfortunate errors produced in the first instance, the embarrassment of the institution, viz.: going in debt, too much cost and parade of faculty, incautiously crediting students and supporting beneficiaries without means, and my remaining so much of my time at the college to assist in managing its affairs, instead of being constantly out collecting funds.

Second. This erroneous course was fallen into more readily, because at the time, funds were circulating freely through the community, and subscriptions and collections were easily obtained. But when debts had been contracted, an over proportion of faculty employed, students largely indulged on credit, with beneficiaries on hand, a great change took place in the financial condition of the whole country; still hoping this state of things would prove only temporary, the corrective was not immediately applied, as it ought to have been, and serious embarrassment, at length, began to be felt.[2]

Each of these errors was to some degree guarded against, but never completely enough, as the College resumed its functions. In some cases, the Trustees by overcaution increased the institution's trouble. To eliminate "too much cost and parade of faculty," the teaching staff was cut so far back that it could no longer provide adequate instruction. Teachers' salaries were pared down so far and payment was so partial and irregular that a rapid turnover in staff resulted, much to the discouragement of an *esprit de corps* at a critical period. As has been mentioned, in 1842 the Board was able to announce the College's release from indebtedness. There was slow growth during the Bacon and Binney administrations. It was not apparent in the size of the student body, which tended to fluctuate erratically and was at best an unpredictable source of revenue from tuition. It was to be seen, instead, in improvement in administration. There was a new caution in matters financial. Efforts were made to reduce the amount of outstanding rights to nominate students with credit for tuition, an unfortunate lien placed on the College's receipts as a device to attract subscribers to special funds.

Comprehensive financial reports were regularly made to the Board and scrupulously audited by select committees. Individual members of the staff were not allowed to incur obligations in the name of the College without formal appropriation. Even the Executive Committee's power to authorize expenditures was called in question at times. This closer scrutiny given for the first time to business matters provided a real basis for developing financial policy. The Board now knew what the proceeds from fees would probably be and what the invested funds would yield, and also the difference between these amounts and the standing expenses of the College. While their sights were never set high enough, they tried to figure out the necessary increases in endowments to take care of the deficit.

All of these moves indicated progress. Had the Trustees been able consistently to improve their procedures along this line, the way to financial solvency might have been found. But a new set of circumstances was to create new difficulties and plunge the College again into a period of grave uncertainty. The problem of slavery, with its attendant features of sectionalism and states' rights, added a new source of trouble to the difficulties that Luther Rice had so candidly stated.

Despite all the improvement in financial administration, there was one area within the College that cried for reform, and there was no reform. In fact, the pressure for funds exaggerated and compounded a serious practice that was to be spelled out, word for word, in the Attorney General's Report of 1910. The Trustees did not protect the endowment. Time after time, appropriations for running expenses were made from uninvested endowment funds. In a growing enlightenment in matters financial this was a tragic blind spot.

Relations with the Baptist Convention remained ambiguous. In 1826 the convention had asked to be relieved of the task of nominating members of the Board of Trustees. The Trustees were, however, anxious to maintain the connection. In a resolution of September 10, 1828, they stated very frankly that the College could not prosper without extensive patronage and that the best way to obtain the patronage of any religious denomination was "through some representative body." They asked, therefore, that at the coming session of the convention a slate of at least fifty persons be nominated to be submitted to the contributors for election as Trustees. They earnestly requested the convention "either themselves to retain the powers of said nomination in future, or to take steps to have an Education Convention organized for this purpose, or any other [steps] tending to the prosperity of the College and the general interests of edu-tion."[3]

The convention, acting upon the Board's resolution, stated that since the Trustees did not consider the action with reference to the College taken at the last convention as imperative, and that since the patronage of no other Baptist group had been obtained, those who had been valiantly working to sustain the College deserved the encouragement of an acceptance of their request. A list was accordingly drawn up and submitted to the contributors for election.[4]

Following this precedent, a list of nominations was prepared and approved at the Seventh Triennial Meeting in 1832,[5] at the Eighth Triennial Meeting in 1835,[6] at the Ninth Triennial Meeting in 1838,[7] at the Tenth Triennial Meeting in 1841,[8] and at the Eleventh Triennial Meeting in 1844.[9]

At the special meeting of the convention held in New York on November 20, 1845, a committee of three was appointed to inform the College Trustees of the contemplated change in the organization of the convention so that they might make plans for the future elections of Trustees.[10]

At the adjourned session of the convention, meeting under the new name of the American Baptist Missionary Union, on May 21, 1846, the convention relinquished "all right, title, and interest which they may have to the real estate, or any other property, belonging to or in the possession of Columbian College, in the District of Columbia."[11] The transfer in title was duly made, and now, after a quarter of a century, the Trustees of the College held their real property in fee simple.[12]

In its evolution, the convention had now gone full cycle. Started in 1814 as an organization to further and support missionary enterprise, it had adopted education in 1820 as a major concern by an amendment to the constitution, putting the governance of "an Institution for education purposes," when located, in the hands of its Board of Managers. In 1826, pointing out that the connection between the missionary and educational concerns had helped neither, the convention had asked the Trustees to amend their ordinances so that the nomination of Trustees would be placed in other hands, "taking care to preserve to the Baptist Denomination the effective control of the Institution."

The Trustees realistically enough equated Baptist control with Baptist support. Overtures were not made to other Baptist bodies, and the Board clearly demonstrated by its requests to the Convention for nominations at its Sixth, Seventh, Eighth, Ninth, Tenth, and Eleventh Triennial Meetings that it still desired this denominational tie. At times, the request was a simple and formal one, but at other times it was accompanied by a lengthy communication.

In 1835, in asking for the Convention's nominations, the Trustees called attention to the grant of city lots from the Congress; to the success that was crowning their efforts to gain new pledges; to a student body of 50, of whom 21 were professedly pious, with 17 of their number looking toward the ministry; to the activities of a student Society for Missionary Inquiry; and to the number of young men who had gone forth to serve the church and public institutions.

In 1841, the Trustees made an eloquent plea for support. They pointed out that 60 students were necessary to meet the salaries of the faculty, that there were only 28 enrolled, and that, of these, only 20 were full-pay students. In 1844, the Trustees' letter joyously announced that the College's debts had been paid.

At its adjourned meeting in 1846, the convention accepted an Act of Incorporation granted by the Legislature of Pennsylvania on March 13, 1846, entitled "An Act changing the name of the association known as 'The General Convention of The Baptist Denomination in the United States for Foreign Missions and other important objects relating to the Redeemer's Kingdom' to that of 'The American Baptist Missionary Union' and for altering and amending the charter of the same," and also an act of the Legislature of Massachusetts passed March 25, 1846, for the same purpose. It was resolved that when the convention adjourned it meet on the third Thursday of May, 1846, for purposes of organization as the American Baptist Missionary Union.

The Acts of Incorporation and the new constitution were specific: "The single purpose of the said Baptist Missionary Union" was *missions*. They were back again to the constitution of 1814 in their sole dedication to missions. The relinquishment of the title to the College property[13] was a matter of cold logic.

Just how profitable in a financial way was the patronage that was symbolized by the convention's nomination of Trustees cannot be estimated. With a desperate need to get support wherever it could be found, it was perhaps wise at the time to hold on to the Baptist connection. True it was, there was no subsidy from denominational sources; but, in the appeal to individuals, Trustee nomination could suggest sponsorship and open Baptist purses more easily. The main drive for funds was directed toward Baptists, the agents were Baptist ministers, and appeals to denominational loyalty were not lacking. It was unfortunate that the yield was so meager.

The possibility that the government might be a source of financial assistance was ever present in the minds of the Trustees. General Washington's frequently reiterated interest in a national university and the bequest in his will, the sponsorship of his idea by many of his successors, the frequently expressed interest of Presidents, especially Monroe, in Columbian College, and the very regular attendance of Presidents and Cabinet members at the Commencements—all of these suggested that the College might legitimately claim assistance from the federal government. The Congress did in the spring of 1828 pass an act to relieve the College by freeing it from liability for the payment of $30,000, a debt incurred by Rice in some of his more naïve ventures in finance.[14] This Congressional relief, along with the relinquishment of $5,698.22 of a sum due The Bank of The United States, Philadelphia Branch, helped tremendously in the 1826-1828 period when the $50,000 fund was being raised. It did not, however, end recourse to Congress for later assistance. The Memorials continued to be sent. They next bore fruit when, by an act of Congress approved July 14, 1832, there were granted to Columbian College city lots to the value of $25,000 to be selected and valued by the Commissioner of the Public Buildings. The proceeds of the sale of these lots were "not to be otherwise used by the said trustees than as a capital, to be by them forever hereafter kept vested as aforesaid."

In accordance with the act, Joseph Elgar, commissioner, selected and conveyed to the College 180 city lots.[15] Because of the pressure of immediate obligations, the Trustees requested and received a supplemental act approved February 28, 1839, authorizing them to sell as many lots as were necessary to raise the sum of $7,000 to be applied toward the corporation's debts. By April 23, 1841, sufficient lots had been sold to realize the $7,000; notes amounting to $4,187.39 which had been taken for the sale of lots were still in the treasurer's possession. It was stated that the amount of these unpaid notes plus unsold lots valued at $5,858 would make up about $10,000, which remained to be invested in the endowment fund. An examination of the records in the office of the Recorder of Deeds made in 1910 showed that from 1839 to that time 170 out of the 180 lots originally granted had been sold for a total consideration of $70,822.93.[16]

In the early financial history of the College, the agent played an important role. Luther Rice had been treasurer and agent. Because of the serious difficulties brought about by this dual role, the two offices were generally held by different individuals after Rice's time. There was a period following the difficulties in 1826 when several agents were commissioned to raise funds; but this changed gradually, and there was a single agent. In the 1840's and 1850's this office became a very powerful one, for not only did the agent raise funds but he also supervised their expenditure. Two of the most important agents during the period were the Reverend A. M. Poindexter of Virginia and the Reverend W. F. Broaddus of Kentucky.

Appointed on August 29, 1845, Poindexter was given the task of raising $50,000 as a permanent endowment, an amount considered adequate to produce an income which would close the gap between expenses and income. When he resigned two and a half years later he reported that he had raised $25,413.30 in cash and pledges. Something more than half of this amount was in the form of unpaid subscriptions, $3,003.24 of which was collected by his successor. In attempting to collect these unpaid notes the new agent often heard the excuse that the subscriptions were not to be due until the whole $50,000 had been pledged. In a letter on October 13, 1852, Poindexter denied that he had ever made such an arrangement.[17]

Poindexter's successor, after a four-year interval, was the Reverend W. F. Broaddus, whose activities were devoted to raising a $40,000 endowment fund. This amount was determined by the offer, in 1852, of John Withers of Alexandria to give $20,000 to the endowment if matched by an equal sum from other sources by the end of the year. Broaddus reported to the Board on May 12, 1853, that he had secured $20,000.06, thus matching Withers' offer.[18]

John Withers (1776-1861), a native of Alexandria, was the most generous of the early benefactors of the College. A Trustee from 1832 until his death, it would appear from the records that he never failed to respond to an appeal for funds. His conditional offer of $20,000 came at a critical time for the College. President Bacon, overwhelmed by the College's difficulties, had offered his resignation. Withers' action was a prime factor in causing the president, at the Board's request, to withdraw his resignation. When Broaddus reported to the Board on May 12, 1853, that Withers' offer had been matched, the time allowed had been exceeded, but Withers paid as he had undertaken. This was but one of his major gifts. At one time, when because of financial embarrassment he could not pay a subscription when called upon, he paid the interest to the College until he was able to pay the principal. While it is impossible to state the exact total of the gifts he made to cancel debts, repair buildings, and increase the endowment, the amount would seem to aggregate almost $70,000.

(Withers was one of the few persons buried at College Hill. His remains were reinterred in the University lot at Oak Hill Cemetery, Georgetown, in 1884. The grave is marked by a large granite obelisk.[19])

The College during these trying years had no more constant friend than John Quincy Adams. Withers was its principal giver, but Adams was its principal creditor. From the time he contributed $25 to the fund for the purchase of the lot until his death almost thirty years later, he gave generously of his means, his advice, and his presence. Judge William Cranch, the first Professor of Law, the father of three graduates of the College and the father-in-law of another, was his first cousin. During Adams' long residence in Washington he attended Commencements and public exercises of the College with great regularity. He was a friend and adviser of President Chapin, although they did not see eye to eye on the Smithson bequest.

In 1824 and 1825 Adams loaned the College about $13,000 which with later loans and interest brought the total of its indebtedness to him up to $20,000. This was secured by a mortgage on the College property.

A deed recorded June 6, 1829, stated that Adams was the holder of four certificates of stock representing $3,500 in the aggregate and equal therefore to 35 shares in the loans to the College. In addition, it stated that Adams held a bond for $7,500 with interest and another for $2,050, making a total indebtedness on the part of the College of $16,912.50. To this was added a debt of $642.50 to Mrs. Adams which her husband had assumed, making a grand total of $17,555. Adams consented to discount this loan at 32 per cent if given "security for the eventual payment of the residue with lawful interest thereon." In the light of these facts, the College conveyed to Adams all of its land, its buildings and their contents, with the agreement that if the College paid $11,410.75 on or before June 1, 1830, together with interest, the deed would become void, and the evidences of the College's indebtedness would be surrendered. Until default, the College was given the right to occupy and use the premises.[20]

While the College was thus indebted to Adams, the Smithson bequest netting $508,318.49 came into the possession of the United States Treasury. The question to be determined then was how should this money be used to increase and diffuse knowledge among men? Should a university be established? Adams was deeply interested, and President Chapin went to him in some alarm. If the money were used to set up a college or university, Chapin felt that Columbian College would be destroyed. Adams set his fears at rest by telling him that he did not believe the Smithsonian Institution would be a college or a university, "but altogether of a different character." He had in mind a research institution. When the increasing needs of the College for immediate relief became more pressing, President Chapin changed his position and inquired of Adams hopefully if the College could get any aid from the Smithson Fund. Adams had not changed his position. "And as the principal debt of the Columbian College is to me, I can be instrumental to no arrangement which would result in the payment of the College debt from the Smithson Fund." Adams could not be moved. The new Institution took on the form that he had in mind.[21]

The inability to pay Adams or even at times to pay interest when due was a source of particular embarrassment to the College. At each interest period herculean efforts, often without success, were made to pay Adams the sum due. On some occasions, a well-timed gift from Nicholas Brown of Providence saved the College embarrassment on this score. On October 20, 1837, Adams wrote George Wood, the Treasurer, regretting the necessity which compelled him to require payment of the interest due the preceding June 1, amounting to $684.64. The request did not procure results at the time, because a year later Adams wrote again. On June 13, 1838, the treasurer was ordered to give him a note for $1,369.38 for two years' interest on the debt up to the first of that month. On January 23, 1839, it was reported that the debts of the College amounted to $30,086.47, of which $13,227.27 was owed Adams. By October 12, 1840, the debt had been reduced to $11,581.74, but six months later it was up to $12,-038.29. The treasurer was then directed to pay Adams $684.65, the interest due for the year, and $300 on account of the principal. Adams' request to be paid in specie led to the adoption of a resolution that read:

Resolved, that the Board appreciate the kindness and liberality which Mr. Adams has constantly exhibited toward the College, as well as the lenient course he has pursued, as its principal creditor, in the long indulgence which he has granted, and that the Board fully admit the justice of his demands to receive the money to be paid him in the lawful currency: but in consideration of the fact that the funds which have been received for payment of the debt are not of that character and that the other creditors whose course in most cases has been equally kind and lenient, have been paid in paper, the Board hope that Mr. Adams when informed of the great difficulty which has been experienced in obtaining such funds as we have, will waive his request to be paid in specie and receive such funds as we have paid the other creditors.

On March 5, 1842, Adams signed the following receipt:

Received of Andrew Rothwell Treasurer of the Columbian College eight thousand seven hundred and ninety-six 23/100 dollars in full of the amount due me on the mortgage of the College property including interest. $8,796.23.

J. Q. Adams[22]

Adams along with many of his fellow creditors had accepted a settlement at approximately 60 cents on the dollar.

No formal deed of release was recorded until June 4, 1859. Then Charles Francis Adams and other heirs of John Quincy Adams, after stating the original size of the debt, "from time to time enlarged and extended," declared that the $8,796.23 was accepted by Adams on March 5, 1842, "in full of the aforesaid debt including interest due him" and that they therefore reconveyed the property to the College.[23]

At the state funeral of John Quincy Adams on February 25, 1848, in the civic procession from the Capitol to the Congressional Cemetery marched the faculty and student body of Columbian College.

In trying to develop a solid financial basis during these critical years, the Trustees had used every device that ingenuity could suggest. They persuaded the Triennial Convention to ignore its mandate of 1826 and resume the nomination of Trustees. What tangible results this produced is problematical, although the convention, as it was about to pass out of existence, did give the College the College Hill property in fee simple. The Trustees memorialized the Congress incessantly and received $25,000 in city lots and the relinquishment of a claim for $30,000. As major financial achievements, they were able to complete the $50,000 fund in 1828 and to match John Withers' gift of $20,000 in 1853. They sought, but rarely ever with complete success, funds for professorships, the presidency, repairs, and new construction. There was a sad lack of donors on the scale of John Withers and John Quincy Adams. At significant points the Trustees achieved freedom from debt, but never security for the future. In 1859, the year of President Samson's election, the assets of the College were rated at $151,095.

CHAPTER SEVEN

Growth and Operation
of the College
1828-1859

The *Columbian Register* for May 3, 1828, carried an official notice under the heading "Columbian College" which began: "The Trustees of this institution have the pleasure of announcing to the public that the course of instruction will be recommenced on the 14th day of the present month. Through the liberality of its creditors and the determined and generous efforts of its friends, the College will now go forward in its career of usefulness." The first session was to be a short one, three months in length, with instruction given by Professor Ruggles and Tutor Boulware of the class of 1826. Then after a month's vacation, on September 10, a standard session of two terms was to begin, with President Chapin joining Professor Ruggles and Mr. Boulware in giving instruction.

The Reverend Stephen Chapin (1778-1845), a graduate of Harvard, assumed his office as President of the College and Professor of Moral and Intellectual Philosophy, and Belles-Lettres, shortly after the resumption of instruction. He had been a Congregational clergyman and, like Luther Rice, entered the Baptist ministry. After serving as a pastor for a brief period, he became Professor of Theology in Waterville (now Colby) College, remaining there until he came to Columbian in 1828. The Trustees of Waterville College in accepting his resignation were pained by the thought that they "must give up to distant strangers, a man who has done the highest honor to the station that he has filled, been a common and sincere friend to the pupils under his charge, and who has sustained the rank of one no less distinguished as a philanthropist, than beloved and admired as a divine." It was "a pleasing thought" that "the rising generation of the South may profit by the instruction of the ripest of scholars, and the example of the best of men."[1]

The *Washington Chronicle* on July 12, 1828, called him "one of the first men of our nation in point of piety and literary attainments."

The second session after the resumption of instruction included a first term from the second Wednesday of September, 1828, to the third Wednesday of December, with the longer second term running from the second Wednesday of January to the second Wednesday of July, 1829. The charges for the three-month term were:

Admission fee, payable once	$10.00
Tuition in the College Classes	20.00
Tuition in the Preparatory School	12.00
Library, room, furniture, and bed	8.00
Table, washing, fuel, lights, and servants, per week	3.00

Nonboarders paid a total fee of $29.50 in the College and $21.50 in the Preparatory School.

The charges for the six-month term were:

Tuition in the College classes	$30.00
Library, room, furniture, and bed	18.00
Table, washing, fuel, lights, and servants, per week	3.00

Nonboarders paid total fees of $47.50 in the College and $27.50 in the Preparatory School.

It was pointed out that the total charge for tuition, board, etc., not including books and stationery, would not exceed $200 for the year.[2]

When the students returned after their "vacation," they found the physical appearance of the College substantially unchanged. The new building which had been authorized four years before, to be located west of the College building and to be similar to it in size and appearance, was still far from completion. In fact, the gaunt walls of the West Wing apparently stood as sad evidence of too ambitious planning until 1842, when the material in them was sold for $300 and the proceeds used for improving the appearance of the College building.[3]

The curriculum was virtually unchanged when instruction was resumed, although in 1827 a system of gymnastic exercises was introduced, the expense not to exceed $200 per annum. Just what the system included and what equipment was used are not disclosed. In fact, we have to wait for light on this subject, and shall perhaps wait in vain. It is not until

1860 that we hear about a gymnasium. In that year President Samson announced the erection of a gymnasium, "the College erecting the shed and the students fitting up the interior."[4]

The growth of the faculty in size was slow, and of salaries even slower. In 1841, thirteen years after the resumption of instruction in the College, the situation seemed unchanged. The Committee on the State of the College, reporting to the Board, stated that expenditures for the year were $3,550, as against $1,375 received from students. These expenditures were salaries for President Chapin, $1,300; Professor Ruggles, $1,375; Tutor Chaplin, $675; and other expenses, $200. To make these very modest sums more realistic, it should be borne in mind that the receipts mentioned were those for tuition only. The steward collected charges for rooms, food, and personal services from the students; and the net over and above his expenses was his salary. The president and the faculty were provided with living quarters according to their rank, in addition to their salaries. The president was also assigned a few acres for raising vegetables for his own use, and the steward was permitted to cultivate for his own profit areas in the College property not otherwise reserved. Viewing this small faculty as the irreducible minimum, the College had struggled on until its whole accumulated debt was discharged in 1842.[5]

In light of the small income received from tuition, it was astounding that so much free instruction was given to young men preparing for the ministry. It was poor financial policy for an impoverished institution, but a magnificent display of Christian charity. A report presented to the Trustees in 1847 showed the value of the instruction given candidates for the ministry during the six preceding years as $4,013. In addition to this, $907 worth of tuition was given under the system of $100 rights, and $192.70 of tuition to two others, basis not stated. In other words, $5,112.70 was given away in tuition for which current fees were not paid.[6]

That in spite of its ups and downs the College was held in high esteem was shown by a request from the faculty of the Hamilton Literary and Theological Institution (now Colgate University) in July, 1844, that the Trustees and faculty of Columbian College confer upon regular graduates of the Hamilton Institution the degrees of Bachelor of Arts and Master of Arts on satisfactory certificate from the faculty of the Institution on the completion of the required course and worthiness "in other respects, the Institution to pay the graduation fee and other expenses." The request was granted, and in two years the College conferred forty-five Bachelor's degrees and one or maybe two Master's degrees for the Institution. When, on March 26, 1846, the New York Legislature granted a college charter to the Collegiate Department of the Institution, it was no longer necessary to use Columbian's degree-granting power.[7]

The years of President Chapin's administration (1828-1841) had been years of retrenchment marked by a sturdy resolve to free the College from its accumulated debt. This one aim was pushed with strict singleness of purpose. As has been suggested, long-range objectives were for the time ignored. Educationally the College, at best, stood still. When in the year following Chapin's resignation the Board was able to discharge its debts, attention began to be given to the improvement of teaching and to the improvement of the College and its grounds.

A building for the use of the Preparatory School was erected on a lot belonging to the College at Fourteenth and N Streets. The structure was of brick, 25 by 30 feet, and two stories in height. The School had had a checkered career, as shown by the fact that in the first twenty-six years of its existence (1822-1848) it had no less than seventeen principals, eleven of them serving for a single year or less. Steps were taken in 1848 toward a permanent engagement with Zalmon Richards, who unfortunately served for only two years (1849-1851). He was to achieve distinction in the world of education as Superintendent of Schools of the District of Columbia and first president of the National Education Association. In the year of Richards' resignation, the Preparatory School property was sold for $2,500. After an interval of two years, George S. Bacon was appointed to take charge of the school. At a cost of $730 the roof of the building housing the philosophical equipment was raised to form a second floor, and provision for the Preparatory School was made in the remodeled building. So as not to involve the Board in any liability, the teacher was paid from the fees of the pupils. In 1859 the Board ordered that the studies of the Preparatory School be arranged in a three-year course and that this curriculum be published in the College catalogue. Preparatory School students taking subjects in the College paid an additional $5 per course, but not over $10 in any case. The obvious need for such a school in the District had prompted the Board to recommend to the Trustees of the Public Schools of the City of Washington that they send a few of the advanced pupils to pursue their studies at College Hill, the expenses to be paid out of the School Fund.[8]

In the final years of President Joel Smith Bacon's administration there was renewed evidence of a determination toward improvement in the

College's program and equipment. There was constant demand for an increase in the number of faculty as essential to further success and growth. On October 13, 1852, a communication from the faculty insisting upon the need for two new professors "present and teaching" was laid before the Board. Because of the 31 students enrolled, 20 of them new, an additional tutor was necessary. Anxious to raise standards, more thorough and extended examinations were called for at the end of each term, with a special committee being brought in to attend the examinations. The faculty took favorable notice of improvements in the outside appearance of the buildings and grounds but was very critical of the badly used and unattractive furniture, which they asked be replaced at once by new, "tastier" furnishings. They recommended a complete revision of the College bylaws. The Board authorized the sale of two Eleventh Street lots for not less than $3,200 to provide funds to be disbursed under the Trustees' direction. The lots actually brought $4,075.

Over a six-month period the faculty sent up additional recommendations of considerable importance. The scientific course was to be separated more distinctly from the classical course and put in a regular department with English and mathematical studies. The course was to embrace three years and offer its own specific degree. In this course mathematics was to be extended to include engineering, and work in the natural sciences was to be increased. The degree of Master of Arts "in course" was no longer to be given on the basis of an accumulation of courses beyond the requirement of the Bachelor's degree, but was to be awarded on the basis of a well-sustained examination on a definite course of study.

In its report to the Board on June 2, 1853, the Committee on Library and Apparatus was critically constructive. The library contained 6,000 volumes, most of them on theological subjects and for the most part the result of chance donations. It was not adequate for the use of the professors in preparing their lectures, and their modest salaries would not permit the purchase of these scholarly materials at their own expense. The students procured books for their own use. Particularly lacking in the library were books of reference and classical authors in critical editions. Treatises on branches of science were totally wanting. Also needed were histories of literature, English classics, and the best works in history, ancient and modern. In other words, it appeared that the library lacked everything. It was recommended that a beginning be made with small appropriations. A fortunately timed gift of $75 from

Isaac Davis, distinguished Massachusetts statesman, founder of the Davis Prizes in Public Speaking and friend of Luther Rice, was immediately assigned for the purchase of books. The library, the Committee reported, was housed in two small, pleasant rooms, the ones that had been assigned to it when the College building was erected. More room was now needed; the library should be reorganized, and a catalogue prepared.

The apparatus on hand was mostly for mathematical and natural philosophy. The equipment was of superior quality and in good condition, but more attention was required to the needs of chemistry, geology, and botany.

Considering the various suggestions made, a committee on rearranging the studies made four specific recommendations: that the faculty prepare a schedule for a three-year scientific course of study leading to the degree of Bachelor of Philosophy, that a new professor be appointed in the Department of Natural Sciences, that a definite grade of attainment be set for the degree of Master of Arts, and that examining committees in the several branches be appointed to attend the College examinations. The first Ph.B.'s, five in number, were conferred in 1854. A change was made in the College calendar so that, instead of splitting the session in two unequal parts, a single session was fixed to run from the last Wednesday in September to the last Wednesday in June.

Never before in the institution's history had such interest and concern been manifested in educational organization.[9]

In their efforts to bring about these improvements, the Trustees and faculty had, for the first time, the organized support and encouragement of the alumni. The Alumni Association of Columbian College was formed at a meeting of twenty-seven graduates on July 14, 1847. Six years before, on April 18, 1841, a meeting of alumni had been held in Baltimore. At that critical time they expressed full confidence in the institution, then in the final throes of its successful effort to remove its indebtedness. They emphasized the need to raise a fund to support a professorship in the College. Each of those present took the responsibility for raising his share of the fund, and the Board was asked to provide an agent to collect the pledges. Robert Ryland of the class of 1826, later president of Richmond College, was the chairman of the group. It was at their request, in October, 1852, that Thomas S. Brackenridge of the class of 1825, who had already won distinction as a landscape architect, prepared a comprehensive plan for the improvement of the grounds of the College and proceeded with the work.[10]

One important change was made in the governance of the College. As stated in the preceding chapter, the Trustees had prevailed upon the Triennial Convention to continue the practice of presenting to the subscribers to the College a list of nominees to be voted on for election to the College Board of Trustees. But as Andrew Rothwell, on behalf of a Trustees' committee, reported to the Board on April 22, 1847: "After the last and final meeting of that body [the Triennial Convention] in the city of New York in May last, it was by formal resolution seperated [sic] and dissolved, its constituents now forming too [sic] seperate [sic] bodies." The Trustees had therefore to review the machinery of election to the Board. After examining the Charter and Ordinances, the committee recommended that no change be made in the Ordinances inasmuch as none was necessary, since the existing requirements would be met in full if the Board would set up a list of subscribers entitled to vote. Individual contributors could not vote except as representatives of associated (i.e., Baptist) bodies contributing to the funds of the College, one vote being allowed for each $50 contributed. By adopting these recommendations, the denominational relation was retained, but the convention was no longer in existence to serve as the nominating body.[11]

In the effort to improve the appearance of the grounds and to increase the facilities, the entire property was enclosed by a wooden fence almost a mile in length; a gravel walk was laid from the College building to the boundary (now Florida Avenue); a steward's house was built; and the roof on the College Building was raised to gain an additional full floor.

The steward's house was erected in 1855, north of the professors' houses and west of the College. The main building was three stories in height, with a back building of two stories. The main house was 40 feet deep with a frontage of 28 feet, the back building 30 feet deep and 16 feet wide. The lower floor, supported by pillars, was used as a dining hall; the second floor, as quarters for the steward's family. Five rooms on the third floor were used for boarders. The cost of $3,850 was paid in installments on the builder's demand as various stages in the construction were reached. The money, characteristically enough, was taken from uninvested endowment funds, to be repaid with interest as soon as possible.

Five years later, in 1860, when the College had a record enrollment of 71 students and the Preparatory School 65, further expansion was undertaken at a cost of about $10,000, raised by subscription. A new roof was built on the College building and raised so as to make the attic, formerly only a half-floor lighted by dormer windows, a full story. A new addition of three stories, 40 by 18 feet, was made to the steward's house, and provision was made for heating the public buildings of the College by steam. At the same time the gymnasium was being erected.[12]

These changes and additions were made against a background of growing concern as to the desirability of selling some or maybe all of the institution's holdings on College Hill. When money was needed for the building of the steward's house in 1855, a committee of the Board was directed "to look into the expediency of marking off a portion of the College grounds, to be arranged into lots and sold by the square foot for residences under restricted conditions of improvement to aid the College finances." For the time no action was taken.[13]

Four years later, in 1859, a Trustees' committee was appointed to consider the removal of the College to the city and the discontinuance of the dormitory system and of the Steward's Department—in other words, to cease being a residential college. Inasmuch as each year the College seemed to be falling short by $1,800, it was figured that an additional endowment of $30,000 was needed to close the gap. Therefore, the Board looked with favor on selling the southern portion of the College land, the part immediately adjacent to the city, for an asking sum of $30,000 but with a minimum of $25,000 in mind. This was an area of 21 acres, south of the College Lawn. They did not favor general subdivision because of the cost of grading and culverting. They authorized the sale of city lots, including some of the Congressional grant of 1832. After full consideration, however, the Board decided that it was inexpedient to move the College to the city and that for the time the dormitory system and the Steward's Department would be continued.[14]

While the question of moving to the city and selling ground on College Hill was motivated largely by financial considerations, there was also a desire to avoid the grief as well as the expenses incurred by boarding students. Student protest against the Steward's Department, its service, and its food was frequent and insistent. Life would be happy freed of this nuisance, with generous funds in hand from the sale of land and attention limited to the business of instruction. Investigation showed, however, that Washington of the 1850's could not absorb in its limited housing such a student body or insure the likelihood of proper feeding.

Stewards took their position at their own risk and expense, and their income was derived from the profits made on the operation. Initial agreements, incident to a steward's appointment, were designed to keep

him from cutting too many corners and to insure the students a sound
basic diet at a fixed rate.

Stephen Prentiss, who was appointed steward in 1859, was required
to maintain a neat and orderly table at which he himself should preside,
unless in the president's judgment he was needed elsewhere. A suitable
number of civil and capable servants were to be available. Meals had
to be ready punctually at the hour fixed by the faculty. The steward
was required to report students guilty of waste or any impropriety for
discipline, "but in no case shall such charge depend merely upon servant's
testimony." Two grades were provided, a "best table" to cost no more
than $3 per week and a "cheap table" to cost no more than $2 per week.
Students at the cheap table were to wait on themselves after provisions
had been placed on the table.

The bill of fare for the best table provided for:

Breakfast: Fish or cold meat, warm rolls and cold loaf of bread, warm corn
bread, tea and coffee, white sugar for tea, brown sugar for coffee, butter,
molasses;
Dinner: Soup, roast fresh meat of two kinds or one kind of roast with ham
or boiled meat cold, Irish potatoes and rice, sweet potatoes and other vegetables
in their season, provided that there could always be at least two kinds on
the table, corn bread, a sufficient supply of all seasonings, a dessert twice a
week of pies, puddings, or some equivalent;
Supper: The same as breakfast except meats and molasses and occasionally
warm bread.

The bill of fare for the cheap table included:

Breakfast: Warm corn bread and cold wheat bread, butter;
Dinner: One kind of meat, fresh meat twice a week, vegetables, one kind
of potatoes and rice, molasses, bread;
Supper: Cold bread, crackers twice a week, molasses or butter.

The steward was allowed to charge for laundry, such as a towel, a sheet,
a pillow case, 50 cents per dozen.[15]

In its circulars, the College had always emphasized the healthfulness
of its location and its unfailing supply of good water. There is little
record of serious illness. During an epidemic of cholera in the city in
1832, *The Globe* reported: "Not a single case has occurred at this
College. Indeed, no spot in the Union surpasses it in healthfulness."[16]

There is a record of a single threat to the salubrity of the College before the War of 1861-1865. At the Trustees' meeting of October 10, 1855, the president spoke of a noisome stench which contaminated the atmosphere and apparently had resulted in some cases of illness at College Hill. A letter from William J. Stone, a neighbor, which was read to the Board went into particulars. The noxious effects which had been felt had their origin in two large buildings, one of them 450 yards east of College Hill, where the city's detritus was gathered, preliminary to final disposal. Mr. Stone (whose property happened to be located between College Hill and the nearer of the two buildings) asked the College to urge the Board of Public Health to take measures to insure professors and students (and Mr. Stone?) "the universal right of pure air to breathe." The authorities apparently took effective measures to abate or eliminate the nuisance, since there is no further mention of this threat to the College's claim of a salubrious location.[17]

Student conduct was generally satisfactory. Discipline was strict, and the rules laid down in the original bylaws were strenuously enforced. Then, as now, expulsion required action by the Trustees on the recommendation of the faculty. The concurrence of the Board appears to have been automatic. The number expelled does not seem excessive. Mention of student behavior in the press is generally laudatory in the formal expression of the times. The *Washington News* of October 14, 1848, went beyond the usual bounds of enthusiasm in its praise when it stated:

The students of Columbian College, we are satisfied (and we have excellent opportunities of judging), will compare advantageously with those of any other college both in mental culture and moral deportment. We have heard of no outbreaks among them nor sprees, nor skylarking, which are ever and anon occurring in other similar institutions. The young gentlemen seem deeply impressed with a proper sense of self-respect, and whenever they visit the city, they conduct themselves with the utmost propriety, in all respects as become gentlemen. We venture to assert that none of the last year's class was ever seen in any improper place, or indulging in any unbecoming deportment; and we trust and believe, that the class of the scholastic year that has just commenced, will sustain the high and exemplary character of its predecessor.[18]

Whether, in making his evaluation, the writer in the *News* was aware of the Arnold case which had occurred the year before is not known, nor is it known what moral judgment he would have placed on Arnold's activity. From the tenor of a letter to the Reverend Baron Stow, a graduate of the College, a one-time Trustee and then an influential minister in Boston, it would seem that there had been considerable discussion of the matter in New England. President Bacon in his letter to Stow stated emphatically:

We have published nothing from the faculty. I have been extremely reluctant to do so. I disapprove wholly of the policy of bringing private matters such as is usually the discipline of colleges, schools and families or other domestic relations, unnecessarily before the public. They can rarely judge of them fairly or impartially. Bad feelings and party spirit are awakened, or perpetuated and much oftener I think injury, than good is done, to all concerned.

To S. S. Arnold of Boston, the brother of the student concerned, President Bacon had written that the faculty, because of the nature of the case, had required Arnold's separation from College, not by an open expulsion but by immediate removal. On March 1, 1847, the Board of Trustees sanctioned the action of the faculty in requiring Henry J. Arnold, because of misdemeanors, to leave the College. No details are given in the Board's *Minutes*.[19]

The facts as set forth in letters by President Bacon were these. Captain Haynes, "a gentleman of wealth and standing came from Va. to take charge of the stewardship of the coll. with the laudable purpose of aiding it by his means, his influence, and his labors, bringing a number of his servants [slaves] with him." Two of Haynes' best servants, "either of their own accord or instigated by others, planned to gain their freedom" by taking advantage of some supposed informality in the mode of their introduction into the District. After they had begun to plan, these two slaves made known their intention to the student, Henry J. Arnold, who "seems to have entered, with a great deal of zeal and earnestness into their plan, and to have offered them aid and encouragement, and to have solicited others, northern young men, to join him in it, clandestinely of course." Only one other student consented to join him, and he later withdrew, leaving Arnold to act alone, against the urgent advice of his friends. Arnold furnished one of the servants with money and a note, said to be directed to a lawyer but lacking name and address. Suddenly the plot was discovered, and the servants were sent to Virginia. The slave Abram who had been aided by Arnold gave the student's name as "his aider and abetter, exhibiting the note he had written and the money he had given him."

This caused strong and indignant feelings against Arnold and created great excitement, requiring all the skill and authority of the faculty to control lest there be an outbreak of violence. Under these circumstances the faculty sent Arnold away, and the Board confirmed their action.

Arnold, excluded from Columbian, applied for admission to Waterville College. In a letter to President Bacon, President D. N. Sheldon of Waterville wrote that Arnold had explained some of the circumstances of his exclusion, but was told that he would not be admitted without a certificate of honorable dismissal unless President Bacon would give him a letter saying that, in his judgment, there was "no valid reason founded on his conduct while a member of Columbian College, why he should not be received into a college in New England." Arnold had repeated his request for admission to Waterville without the required letter. On behalf of the faculty, President Sheldon asked to be informed whether Bacon could give the statement and whether Arnold had violated any college law.

President Bacon's letter of May 8, 1847, lacked nothing by way of directness. He refused to give the letter.

> . . . on the contrary, it is our decided opinion that the course of conduct which he pursued and the principles of action he assumed would have justified and procured his removal from any college, or other institution, or from any well regulated family in the land. . . . In reference to the infraction of college laws, his conduct was a flagrant violation of all the laws (and we have several such), which require in a student integrity of character, correctness of deportment, a due regard to the rights and interests of others, and fidelity to his duties and obligations as a student; and it was for this he was removed from the College.[20]

New problems were arising.

President Bacon's administration (1843-1854) was an eventful one. He had tried with considerable success to achieve greater financial stability, to increase the faculty, to raise standards of instruction, and to improve and increase the College's facilities.

His successor was the Reverend Joseph Getchell Binney (1807-1877), a native of Boston, educated at Yale and Newton Seminary. His great dedication was to missionary work among the Karens. He held a brief pastorate at Elmira, New York, and his three years as president of Columbian College were an interlude. He accepted the presidency on the basis of a three-year tenure (1855-1858) and then resumed his activity in the foreign missions field. The records during his administration indicate great activity on the part of the Reverend George Whitefield Samson, a Trustee who seemed to serve as the intermediary between the Trustees and the faculty. "The College," said President Binney in his letter of resignation, "has nothing to fear in the future with an efficient administration. I should be perfectly willing to trust my reputation on its prosperity."[21]

His confidence seemed to be justified when President Samson, in his annual report for 1860, two years after Binney's resignation, reported a College enrollment of 71 students, a Preparatory School enrollment of 65, and, *anno mirabilis*, an excess of about $1,000 of income over outlay for the year.[22]

Things, apparently, had never looked brighter.

CHAPTER EIGHT

Retrospect:
The College and the
Medical College
1821-1861

T he mortality rate of colleges founded before the War of 1861-1865 was generally very high. While the average rate in New England was low, a study of colleges in sixteen states outside that area showed the amazing mortality rate of 81 per cent.[1]

That Columbian College had survived seemed little less than providential. Aside from serious problems within its own constituency, it was living in a vexatious and uncertain time, when an immature economy was indulging in quixotic behavior. Without any backlog of endowment, the College had constantly to struggle to fill the gap between income and expenditure. It could only look to its friends for donations and hope for increasing registrations that would bolster income from tuition. Unfortunately the same factors which made funds hard to obtain limited the enrollment of full-pay students and increased the demands by beneficiaries who could not pay.

When funds to get the College under way were being solicited, the country was still suffering acutely from the effects of the Panic of 1819. The high level of prices, inflated progressively by the Napoleonic Wars and the War of 1812, had sustained tremendous speculation in land. When the European demand for foodstuffs and cotton dropped off and contraction among the banks started, the price level of domestic commodities slipped. A panic began, causing widespread unemployment, suspension of banks, reduction of rents, and a cataclysmic fall in price levels. Recovery was hardly achieved when again overexpansion, excessive spec-

ulation, and a series of crop failures brought about the suspension of the
New York banks followed by the suspension of those throughout the
country, and the Panic of 1837 was on. Recovery from that panic had
barely begun when the banks, heavily involved in advances to railroads
and other enterprises which could not at once meet their charges, found
their assets tied up and began either to close or to take severely restrictive
measures. In the usual series of chain reactions, the economy came to a
standstill, causing the Panic of 1857. This chapter of economic woe was
the background of the College's effort to find substantial donors.

Of these national problems, first panics, then slavery, became more
and more insistent. The slavery issue had grown right along with the
College. The debates over the Charter were interlarded with discussions
of the Missouri Compromise. The familiar landmarks of the great controversy as it moved out of the hands of the abolitionists and into the
hands of the politicians during the first forty years of the College's
life show the rising tempo of the issue's move toward "the irrepressible
conflict": the founding of the abolitionist movement, the organization
of the Underground Railroad, the gag resolutions against antislavery
petitions, the debate over the Wilmot Proviso, the Compromise of 1850,
the Kansas-Nebraska Act, the Dred Scott Decision, the Lincoln–Douglas
Debates, John Brown's Raid, and the election of Lincoln.

Situated in the Federal District, a location which its sponsors, both
political and religious, thought would forever guarantee it a national
character, the College seemed nevertheless to be drawn irresistibly toward
a southern orientation. As his career developed, Luther Rice, born and
educated in New England, turned more and more toward the South as
the theater of his activities and the center of his affection. True it is that
the reasons for this were not all personal with Rice.

Aside from any ideological interest, the increasing number and attrac-
tion of colleges in the northern states led more and more of their youth
to attend colleges in that area. The authorities of Columbian were conscious of what was happening and tried to keep the student body from
becoming predominantly southern. Notice of an interest in this regard
found its way into the press, but the trend continued up to the outbreak
of the War of 1861-1865.

It would be difficult to comment more emphatically on the desire for
students from the northern states than was done in the *Washington
News* on October 27, 1849:

The class is already much larger than at any period during the last year, and with the usual increase during the progress of the session, we presume long before the next commencement rolls around, every room in the College will be occupied. It is therefore time that the friends of the College should begin to devise the means for the enlargement of its accommodations, as it is now manifest, that it is destined in a very few years, to be one of the most popular institutions in the country. The southern portion of the country duly appreciates the superior advantages of the College owing to its location at the seat of the Government, for most of the students come from that section; and we should like to see more young gentlemen from the northern states coming among us for the same purpose, as this is common ground, belonging to the whole country, and as friendships formed at college are generally of the strongest and most enduring character. We regard this College as one of the strong links in the chain that will bind the Union together, and we cannot therefore, too earnestly call upon our fellow citizens of all parts of the country to give the Columbian College a liberal support.[2]

Seeking support for the College, Rice in his day naturally turned more and more to the area which was sending students to Columbian. During the trying days of 1826-1827, when he was under fire from many quarters, Rice developed a very real suspicion of the North's good faith. He felt that his enemies in the new group of Trustees, with northern support, were trying either to capture the College or to kill it. Rice felt that his backing in the South was solid enough to support him to the limit. He could hardly be more emphatic than he was in writing to O. B. Brown from Petersburg, Virginia, on September 1, 1826: "I have only to add—the *Star* must be taken out of the hands of Baron Stow and the Board must cease covering me with some fresh expressions of disgrace, unanimously every few days, or I am done, and as soon as I strike, depend upon it, you'll find it difficult to raise funds at the South for the College."

Writing to Brown a year later, Rice referred to "the faithlessness of New England" and the possibility that New York might follow the example. He felt that "the reputed perfidy of the North ought to inspire caution." "I am now," he declared, "disposed to believe it practicable to save the College without New England, even without New York, even after all the injuries the North has inflicted upon the concern."[3]

Apparently dependence upon the South was becoming a basis of the Board's policy. In appointing the Reverend Stephen Davis of Georgia as its agent in 1841, the Trustees stated: "That entertaining a deep sense of the generous liberality of the South, in contributing funds for the payment of the debts and support of the College in years that are past, we do now look to them with high hopes that they will give their wealth for its much needed endowment." The Great Baptist Schism, then but a few years off, threw the College into an even greater dependence on the South.[4]

The minutes of the various meetings of the Triennial Convention and of the Board seem to indicate a desire to eliminate as far as possible divisive discussion of the slavery question and its related problems. On May 4, 1841, the final day of the meeting of the Tenth Triennial Convention in Baltimore, it was

Resolved, that the fervent thanks of this Convention are due to our Heavenly Father, that throughout the interesting discussions and transactions of this session, He has caused to prevail so large a measure of Christian affection and harmony.[5]

At the Twenty-ninth Annual Meeting of the Board of Managers in Albany, the Board stated the official attitude. Declaring that it had been extensively understood that at the last session of the convention in Baltimore "the neutral attitude of the Board in relation to slavery was changed," it ordered reprinted, as being still in force, the circular of the Acting Board in the year 1840. The full text therefore appears twice in the records of the Board of Managers.

This "Address of the Board, adopted November 2, 1840," is a document of great significance. Mentioning its concern at the "indications on the part of some of their beloved brethren and coadjutors, to withdraw from the missionary connection in which they have been happily associated for many years," it pointed to the fact "that for the prosecution of this one object the Board of Managers was created; and to this alone (with the exception of a temporary, authorized divergence, to Home Missions and Education) have the operations of the Board down to the present moment been restricted." From this single object they have refused to turn aside or even to indulge in what might have been justifiable expression on controverted subjects lest they endanger their sole mission. Particularly did they refer to "the continuance of Christian fellowship between northern and southern churches." The subject of slavery was clearly irrelevant to the work of Foreign Missions and entirely outside the scope of the General Convention. The members of the Board might act as individuals, they might act within their churches, "but as a Board of the Convention, they can say and do nothing."[6]

A note of alarm that the days of neutrality might be coming to an end was sounded at the very beginning of the Thirty-first Annual Meeting of the Board in Providence on April 30, 1845. The host church, the First Baptist Church in Providence, stated rather ominously in its formal letter of greeting:

We are not unaware of the embarrassments which attend the present meeting of the Board, and the important questions which may be brought before them. We sympathize in these embarrassments, and we regret the occasion which has produced them; and we need not say, it will be especially painful to us, should they give rise to any discussions, not marked by Christian forbearance and Christian love.[7]

The fears of the First Baptist Church of Providence were to be realized. In spite of the strenuous efforts of the Board to suppress controversy, numerous Baptist churches had already put themselves on record. The American Baptist Anti-Slavery Convention, meeting in New York City in 1840, was especially alarming to the South. The Alabama Baptist Convention threatened to withhold funds from the Board and from the American and Foreign Bible Society unless those agencies repudiated all connection with the cause of abolition. If such assurance were not forthcoming, a Southern Baptist Board would be formed. The reverse position was being taken by northern groups. An emphatic declaration of neutrality temporarily restrained the Alabama group from taking action, but the last had not been heard from that quarter. The Alabama convention next inquired what would be the policy of the Board and the convention in making appointments where slaveholding was involved. The Board laid down a statement of policy. All members of the denomination in good standing, whether in the North or South, were eligible for appointment. Contingencies might arise where it would be necessary to make an appointment by which the northern brethren of the Christian community would become responsible for institutions which they could not conscientiously sanction. In such cases, "we could not desire our brethren to violate their conviction of duty by making such appointments" but would consider it necessary that they refer the case to the convention.

The breaking point had been reached. The American Home Missionary Society decided in April, 1845, that hereafter its work could be more expediently carried on in separate northern and southern groups. In May of that year over three hundred delegates from southern churches organized the Southern Baptist Convention in Atlanta. Unlike the Triennial

Convention, it was not a group of autonomous units freely associated for foreign missionary activity. It was a strong, well-organized denominational group carrying out through its own instrumentalities the policies and the general work of a large religious body. Luther Rice would have approved the type of organization but deplored the schism, which brought to an end the Baptist Triennial Convention for Foreign Missions.

A. C. Cole in *The Irrepressible Conflict* observes: "The sectionalism of the fifties, however, bred a demand for greater educational self-sufficiency."[9] In the case of Columbian College, circumstances had made it a sectional institution. The trend was to go beyond that and to make the College almost a local institution. The location of the College, however, prevented it from becoming provincial in outlook. Then, as now, many Washingtonians came from somewhere else.

The situation was explained by President Bacon in a paper that he read to the Board on June 15, 1852. Six weeks before, he had told the Board of his intention to resign. He now offered a formal resignation, which, at the Board's earnest insistence, he withdrew a month later. He served for two more years.

In his statement, the president referred to the period 1843–1850 as an encouraging one. The agent, the Reverend A. M. Poindexter, had been largely instrumental in raising between $20,000 and $25,000 in cash. At the close of 1850, there were 66 students; counting the Preparatory School, there were 100. The graduating class of 24 was the largest in the history of the College. Then a decline took place, due in part to the fact that the faculty was too small to carry on the work but due principally to the great changes which were affecting the whole country. As President Bacon said:

It was about at that time [1850] that the fearful political agitation sprang up which shook all of our institutions, political, social, and moral, to the very foundations. Strong sectional feelings and jealousies were excited—and it was perfectly natural under such circumstances, that there should be manifested in the several states a strong disposition to foster their own institutions, and to concentrate all of their interest and patronage upon them. Pennsylvania was then almost completing an endowment of $120,000 for her University. North Carolina, South Carolina, Alabama, Mississippi, and other states immediately entered upon vigorous efforts to sustain and strengthen their own colleges, and to attract toward them all the patronage in their power. The effect of these proceedings was immediately felt upon the interests of our

College. Several students were withdrawn, and many others were prevented from coming who would otherwise have sought their education here. But the movement which most seriously affected our present condition was that of Virginia in behalf of Richmond College. The friends of that institution after several ineffectual efforts to endow it entered upon a course of measures which thoroughly aroused the local feeling and interest of the state. Having secured the service of our former very efficient Agent, Mr. Poindexter, they entered upon the work of endowment and in less than one year have received something over $60,000 toward that object. From the state of feeling as exhibited at their religious anniversaries in Richmond, one year ago, it was manifest they would be able to control, for the present at least, the interest and patronage of their state, and as most of our students were, as they always have been, from that state, it became evident that the interests of Columbian College must suffer greatly, if indeed it would not be wholly prostrated, unless some powerful means were adopted for counteracting the influence which those movements would naturally and necessarily produce.[10]

He had tried, but found it hard to awaken interest anywhere. "Doubt and discouragement seemed to have settled down on all minds."

These were very direct words from one of the ablest of Columbian's presidents. They did stimulate marked activity within the College, but a great historic force was at work, beyond the control of any group.[11]

Seven years later when President Binney resigned after a brief administration, a Committee on Correspondence for a new President was appointed. In reporting to the Trustees on the nature of the problem before it on February 3, 1859, the committee very plainly accepted the fact that although Columbian had become definitely a southern college it had special problems when it stated: "Now whether a college standing on Mason and Dixon's line looking for students chiefly from the Southern Border as one does and having such funds as ours has, can sustain itself will depend very much on the energy and character, physical, moral, intellectual, that we place at its head."[12]

An individual possessing the necessary qualifications was found close at hand in the person of George Whitefield Samson, who entered upon the duties of his office July 1, 1859. President Samson was a native of Harvard, Massachusetts, and a graduate of Brown and of Newton Theological Institution. He was ordained in 1843 in the E Street Baptist Church, where he served for a few months as pastor, before undertaking a period of study and archeological investigation in the Holy Land. Returning to Washington, he again became pastor of the E Street church, serving until his election as president of Columbian College. Included in his congregation were many distinguished statesmen, among them Amos Kendall, Sam Houston, and Stephen A. Douglas.

President Samson's influence on the great is illustrated by an account of his relations with Sam Houston. Dr. Rufus C. Burleson, later the president of Baylor University, had converted General Houston in a meeting in Independence and baptized him in 1854. The General left shortly thereafter to enter upon his duties as Senator in Washington. "I could but feel," wrote Dr. Burleson, "a profound solicitude for a man converted so late in life and full of stormy passions, about to engage in exciting political discussions so soon after his conversion and baptism." He urged Houston to make Dr. Samson's acquaintance and to hear him preach every Sunday. He also wrote to Dr. Samson "to watch over my young and illustrious convert." Dr. Burleson's advice was sound. The General wrote to his wife: "Tell Bro. Burleson I am safe. God put it into the heart of the great Dr. Samson to call on me and invite me to attend his church regularly and oh, what a treat it is to hear such a preacher every Lord's day, his sermons fortify my soul against the greatest trials I am now called upon to indure."

Samson was a preacher of great evangelical warmth and eloquence and a scholarly man of many-sided interests. He needed but little briefing for his post as president. He had been a Trustee for fourteen years at the time of his election and, particularly during the administration of President Binney, had taken an active and, at times, a dominant role in the affairs of the College. In the crucial years that he served as president (1859–1871), he was in every way adequate to the grueling demands made upon him.[13]

The character of President Samson is shown in an incident which occurred in Washington during the War. A Southern Methodist congregation had erected a new house of worship and had invited Dr. Samson to deliver the sermon of dedication. A newspaper claimed that the church had been erected by disloyal citizens and called on the War Department to place a flag over the house. When President Samson went to the church to preach the sermon, he found that quite an excited crowd of church members, military officers, the district attorney, and others had assembled. Turning toward the district attorney, he said: "Gentlemen, I greatly regret that under existing circumstances, I cannot conscientiously take part in the services proposed." The members of the congregation, fearing that otherwise they would be liable to arrest, urged Dr. Samson to proceed. After some consultation, he said to the crowd: "Brethren and friends, I wish every one present to understand that I alone am responsible for deferring the service of dedication, and I will give my reasons at once to the Secretary of War. On next Sunday, if circumstances justify, the dedication will take place." He immediately wrote a note and sent it to Secretary Stanton. In it he informed the Secretary that he had declined to conduct the service of dedication at the Southern Methodist Church "because the flag was draped over the door." He conducted services in military establishments, he said, almost every Sunday afternoon, where the flag was appropriate, but it was not appropriate at the church. He stood on the principle of separation of church and state and the church was no place where loyalty to an existing government should be tested. An excited crowd, furthermore, was in no condition to give "quiet attention to gospel truth. . . . The placing of that flag over the door was an intimation, from some quarter, that the loyalty of the congregation was in doubt." He had known the devoted leaders of that congregation for years as men "of Christian sincerity and quiet fidelity." He hoped that these people, "permitted, because trusted, to spend months in the erection of their house for separate worship, will be allowed its quiet occupation on the coming Sabbath." Stanton declared Samson "truly brave and right" and the flag was down before two o'clock that afternoon. The next Sunday, the Baptist president of Columbian College in quiet solemnity dedicated a Southern Methodist Church in the northern capital to the worship and the glory of an Almighty God who wore neither blue nor gray.[14]

So thoroughly recognized was Dr. Samson's influence and integrity that during the War, with the permission and encouragement of the Secretaries of State and of War, he visited the President of the Confederate States "to insure the transmission of letters and moneys for humane and Christian purposes and in every way keep alive a Christian interchange" between the temporarily severed parts of the nation.[15]

The outreach of the College during the first forty years of its existence had been remarkable. Although the official attitude of the Baptists toward the College varied from time to time, the institution had served the church well. Of the 300 graduates of the College before the War, 104 became ministers of the Gospel. Among them many are recalled as men of exceptional influence and ability. In the first few classes we find such distinguished names among the clergy as James D. Knowles, A.B. 1824; Robert W. Cushman, A.B. 1825; Baron Stow, A.B. 1825; Stephen G.

Bulfinch, A.B. 1826; Rollin Heber Neale, A.B. 1829. Many became heads of institutions of higher learning: William Greenleaf Eliot, A.B. 1829, chancellor of Washington University, St. Louis; Robert Ryland, A.B. 1826, president of Richmond College; William Carey Crane, A.B. 1836, president of Baylor University; Henry Holcombe Tucker, A.B. 1838, president of Mercer University and later chancellor of the University of Georgia; Charles L. Cocke, A.B. 1839, president of Hollins College; Luther R. Gwaltney, A.B. 1853, president of Judson College and later president of Mercer University; William Lyne Wilson, A.B. 1860, president of West Virginia University and later president of Washington and Lee University; Richard Herndon Rawlings, A.B. 1854, president of Judson College. Many who had taught on the faculty of Columbian later served as presidents of other institutions. Irah Chase founded the Newton Theological Seminary. Alva Woods became president of the University of Alabama; Josiah Meigs, of the University of Georgia; Alexis Caswell, of Brown University; Adiel Sherwood, of Shurtleff College; Rufus Babcock, of Waterville (later Colby) College; Robert Everett Pattison, of Waterville College; and Kendall Brooks, of Kalamazoo. Samuel Wait was the founder of Wake Forest College.

In other fields of activity, several served in the Congress of the United States. Among them, in the House of Representatives: Thomas Dawes Eliot, A.B. 1825, of Massachusetts; William Lyne Wilson, A.B. 1860, of West Virginia, who was also Postmaster General under Cleveland; Frederick Perry Stanton, A.B. 1833, of Tennessee, who was also governor of Kansas; William Alexander Harris, Ph.B. 1859, of Kansas, later a senator. And in the Senate: Daniel T. Jewett, A.B. 1829, of Missouri; Matthew Walker Brooke, A.B. 1831, of Mississippi. Robert Ould, A.B. 1838, was Judge Advocate General C.S.A.; William Benning Webb, A.B. 1844, became a Commissioner of the District of Columbia, and Harvey Lindsley, M.D. 1828, was an early president of the American Medical Association.

Of the alumni who were members of the faculty the best known was Adoniram Judson Huntington, A.B. 1843, Professor of Latin and Greek for half a century. No graduate of the University has ever served as president of the institution in permanent tenure.[16]

Fifteen of the prewar graduates of the College received also the degree of Doctor of Medicine from Columbian. Some families contribute several names to the list of early graduates. There are for example the three sons of Judge Cranch: John, A.B. 1826, the artist; Edward Pope,

The seal of Columbian College, drawn by James Peale
and adopted by the Board of Trustees in 1821. When
the College became a University, the same seal was
retained, with the inscription changed from College to
University first in Latin, then in English.

The College building on College Hill after 1860 when the mansard roof on the
original structure was raised to produce a full fourth story.

Washington Infirmary, in Judiciary Square. An early teaching hospital, it contained both lecture halls and the clinical department. It was the quarters of the Medical Department, 1844-1861.

The Law School, 1865-1884. This building, originally Trinity Church, was located on Fifth Street on the site of the present Columbian Building. Lectures in medicine were also given here while the Medical Department was without a home of its own.

A view down Tenth Street, about the turn of the century, showing Ford's Theatre and, at the northeast corner of Tenth and E Streets, the first Medical School. The peculiar shape of the roof was due to an effort to secure as much daylight as possible for the anatomical department on the top floor. (Washingtoniana Collection, D.C. Public Library.)

Tent wards in Columbian College General Hospital, with the College building in the background. (From a photograph, probably by Mathew Brady, originally in the Ordway Collection. Library of Congress.)

Columbian College and Carver Barracks, Meridian Hill, Washington, D.C., 1864. (From a print lithographed and printed by Charles Magnus, 1864. University Collection.)

A convalescent ward in Columbian College General Hospital. (From a photograph by Mathew Brady in the National Archives.)

George Whitefield Samson, D.D.,
fifth President, 1859-1871. (Brady
Collection, Library of Congress.)

The Medical School, on the north
side of H Street, midway between
Thirteenth and Fourteenth Streets.
In 1865, while being used as the
United States Army Medical Museum, this building was offered to
the College by Mr. W. W. Corcoran.
The Trustees accepted, and turned it
over to the Medical faculty to be
adapted to their purposes. The building was used as a medical school for
two years, 1866-1868.

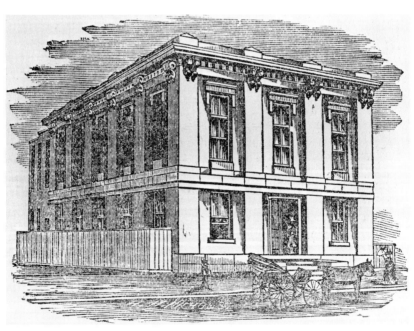

Law School, H Street, east of the University Building, 1899–1910.

In 1868, the Board authorized the enlargement of the building used from 1866 to 1868 as the Medical School. This involved the addition of a floor and other new construction. In this modified form the building was used until 1902.

James Clarke Welling, sixth President, 1871-1894. (University Collection.)

Samuel Harrison Greene, D.D., acting President, 1894-1895, 1900-1902. (University Collection.)

Benaiah Longley Whitman, D.D., seventh President, 1895-1900. (University Collection.)

Charles Willis Needham, eighth President, 1902-1910. (University Collection.)

William Wilson Corcoran, President of the Corporation, 1869-1888; principal benefactor of the University in the late nineteenth century. (Portrait by Mathew Brady [Brady No. 3130], National Archives.)

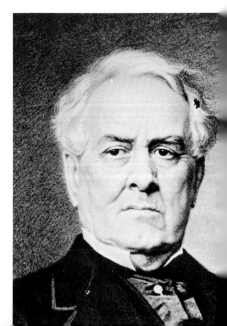

A.B. 1826, the lawyer; and Christopher Pearse, A.B. 1831, Unitarian minister, minor poet, and painter. Five of the Bagby family were graduates of the College in the prewar years. The list of distinguished graduates given above is bound to be incomplete. It does, however, suggest the remarkable output of an infant college.

In looking retrospectively over the first forty years of the life of Columbian College, emphasis has naturally been placed on *the College*, with some attention to its Preparatory School. In an earlier chapter there was some reference to its ephemeral Theological Department, to the brief career of the first Law School, and to the establisment of the Medical Department. Only the last was to have a continuous existence, except for a short break in its regular lectures from 1834–1839, although the professors still continued instruction to private classes, and another break during the latter part of the War of 1861-1865.[17]

Although the Medical School was organized as the Medical Department of Columbian College by authorization of the College's Board of Trustees and its ordinances approved by the Board, it was not subject to the same vicissitudes that afflicted the College proper. Its faculty handled the department's finances generally as a matter of personal risk and received and disbursed funds. Its financial operations were never covered in the Treasurer's Report during these years. On the recommendation of the Medical faculty, the Board made appointments and granted its mandamus for the conferring of the degree of Doctor of Medicine by the president of the College at its own Commencements. As has been previously noted the Board did, at the College's expense, underwrite the cost of young Dr. Staughton's period of study and travel in Europe, preparatory to his serving on the first Medical faculty. There was some interchange between the members of the College and Medical faculties. Some of the Medical professors held appointments in the College faculty and offered college courses in basic sciences, and the various literary courses in the College were open to Medical students to assist them in gaining the acquaintance with the arts that was expected of medical graduates.

Early in its history, the legal status of the Medical Department was challenged. The enabling clause of the Charter established a "College for the sole and exclusive purpose of educating youth in the English, learned and foreign languages; the liberal arts and sciences, and literature." Section 6 of the 1821 Charter gave the faculty the power "of granting and confirming, by and with the consent of the board of trustees, signified by their mandamus, such degrees in the liberal arts and sciences, to such pupils of the institution, or others, who, by their proficiency in learning or other meritorious distinction, they shall think entitled to them, as are usually granted and conferred in colleges." Strictly, in other words, the Charter authorized degrees in the liberal arts and sciences in course, and honorary degrees.

There was presented to the 19th Congress, 1st Session, a "Memorial of Sundry Citizens of the District of Columbia, Praying that a Charter may be granted by Congress to Enable Them to Institute a Medical College, etc." The memorialists did not mention Columbian College but stated that the time had arrived when a medical college should be established in the city of Washington. The names of thirty-six well-known citizens, seven of them physicians, were signed to the memorial. On the same day, February 13, 1826, the professors in the Medical Department of Columbian College presented their memorial in which they traced the history of Columbian's Medical Department, questioned the need and expediency of two medical schools in the District, and disclaimed any desire for a monopoly. Seven days later, on February 20, 1826, the original memorialists presented a counter memorial to the Congress. They pointed out the limitations in the Charter and compared its statement with that in the act of March 1, 1815, giving Georgetown College the right to confer such degrees as are usually conferred by colleges and universities of the United States. They emphasized the significance of the word "universities" and suggested that the Columbian Medical faculty had usurped a power not legally theirs. They repeated their request for a charter for a medical college. On February 22 a memorial signed by an even more imposing group of citizens as to both number and distinction was presented to Congress, asking that "inasmuch as there is already, in successful operation in this District, one respectable institution of that character," another *not* be incorporated. This point of view prevailed.[18]

After this unsuccessful challenge to its right to exist, the Medical Department continued to grow. An announcement in the press in July, 1840, stated that lectures would commence on the first Monday in November annually and continue until the first of March in the Medical College at the corner of Tenth and E Streets. Five professors held chairs, respectively, in pathology and the practice of medicine, chemistry and pharmacy, obstetrics and the diseases of women and children, materia medica and therapeutics, and surgery. Students in surgery observed operations and were allowed to perform the more important ones with their own hands. The entire expense for the course of lectures by all the professors was $70, a dissecting ticket $10 at the student's option. Good board could be procured at from $3 to $4 per week.[19]

In 1847, on recommendation of the Medical faculty, the Board of Trustees added "the National Medical College" to the already cumbersome name of "the Medical Department of the Columbian College in the District of Columbia."[20]

In 1843 the only facilities for hospitalization in the District were those of the Naval Hospital, the poorhouse infirmary, and the jail where the indigent insane were confined. As a result of a campaign launched by the District Board of Health to correct the situation, Congress granted the old jail, vacant since the removal of its inmates to a new building, to the Medical faculty for the purpose of medical instruction and for an infirmary.

The Infirmary was opened when the necessary alterations were completed. The two-story building, with a frontage of about 150 feet, provided lecture rooms, an anatomical museum, laboratory, professors' rooms, and facilities for a large number of patients. Patients paid the steward "a very small sum" for board. Medical attention was given gratuitously by the faculty, who also supplied medicine and advice without charge to the poor, daily between 9 and 10 A.M. in the clinic.[21] President Tyler, who had taken a personal interest in the project, appointed three members of the Medical faculty as physicians in charge. In 1844, at its request, the Medical faculty was given charge of the building, and its professors visited the hospital daily.

During the period from June, 1845, to November, 1848, responsibility for nursing service was assumed by the Daughters of Charity of St. Vincent de Paul. The Sisters of Charity returned to the Washington Infirmary at the outbreak of the War of 1861-1865 and remained there nursing the wounded soldiers until November 4, 1861, when the Infirmary was destroyed by fire. Congress later appropriated $537 to reimburse the Sisters for personal property lost in the fire.[22]

Public opinion did not appear to favor Congressional largess to the Medical School. Some of the local physicians were vocal in their protest at the closing of the hospital to physicians not connected with Columbian. There was even a demand that the building be turned over to the school board for use as a high school. However, the control remained unchanged until, at the outbreak of the War, the hospital was taken over by the government.

To finance the hospital during its first years was a matter of difficulty since Congress restricted its assistance to appropriating funds for the care of paupers. In 1853, an appropriation to enlarge the building and so provide more rooms for indigent patients did permit the addition of a lecture room for the school.

An account of the enlarged Infirmary on Judiciary Square which appeared in the press in 1853 pointed out that the Medical Department's Infirmary was the Marine Hospital of the District of Columbia, to which the Collectors of Customs at the ports of Alexandria and Georgetown could send all seamen requiring medical assistance. The Infirmary and College were situated on a plot of several acres, well removed from any dwellings. No one suffering from contagious diseases was admitted. Its central location made it ideal for receiving emergency cases.

To the enlarged building were added wings three stories high, and a neat cupola. The third floor had a spacious hall in front for the patients' exercise and recreation. The building contained more than one hundred well-finished rooms, accommodating in all at least 300 persons. Ventilation was well provided for, and adequate heat was furnished to all parts of the building.

The development of the Infirmary as a teaching adjunct was a matter of great educational significance. Here was one of the earliest teaching hospitals in the country. As Dean Parks has written: "This early hospital provided students with opportunities for clinical experience not offered at most schools until the turn of this century."[23]

It seems almost tragic that this magnificent teaching adjunct should have been the College's first major casualty in the great war that was about to begin.

CHAPTER NINE

War

1861-1865

On April 24, 1861, President Samson called a special meeting of the Board of Trustees to report that twenty students had left the College owing to the disturbed condition of the country and that more were planning to leave. The Board was asked to consider the possibility of continuing the exercises of the institution. The president had addressed notes to patrons of the College in the city asking for their opinion as to a recess. Two-fifths of the students had given indications of remaining and the professors were willing to carry on, with the exception of John Pollard, a tutor, who wanted to resign, and Professor Ruggles, who was anxious to travel for a time. Inasmuch as the students who had withdrawn had done so on their own initiative, it was felt they were not entitled to refunds. The treasurer was directed to receive Virginia money when tendered rather than permit bills to go unpaid; the Virginia currency would be used to pay the bills of the College when the creditors would accept it. The seniors had already left, and the question of their degrees was postponed for later consideration. It was the sense of the Board that as long as students sought instruction, the College would remain in operation. The students were going to the War, and war would soon come to the College. The city was in a state of turmoil and unrest.

In the forty years that had passed since the granting of the Charter of Columbian College in the District of Columbia, the city of Washington had changed greatly. The District had decreased in area due to the retrocession of Virginia's portion of the territory originally ceded to form the ten-miles square. The total population of the District in 1820 was 33,039; in

1860 it was 75,080; that of the city of Washington was 13,117 in 1820 and 61,122 in 1860. The gain for the District in 1860 over 1820 was even greater than it appears since the later figure did not include the population of Alexandria, which had been retroceded in 1846. This growth in population was reflected in the increase of the number of dwellings in the city. On January 1, 1823, there were 2,346; in 1859 there were 9,769.[1] Gas for illumination and cooking was coming quickly into general use. In 1856 the Washington Gas Light Company already had 1,700 customers, more than 30 miles of gas mains, and some 500 street lights.[2]

Water mains had been laid through the length of the city to the Navy Yard. Great improvement had been made in the grading and graveling of streets. Washington was no longer a city of magnificent distances. The distances were still there. In fact, the majestic width of the main streets imposed a great strain on municipal finance when it came to paving. The magnificence of nature had been reduced by efforts toward a magnificence of man. But man's job was still notably incomplete. The government buildings were in course of construction. Progress had been made toward completing the Capitol, Treasury, Post Office, and Patent Office buildings. The Washington Monument had risen to 170 feet and awaited funds for the resumption of the work. The blocks received from the states, towns, and organizations to be used in embellishing the interior were on display in sheds. There was little evidence of effort toward landscaping. For the time being, stables and shacks often stood back to back with monumental public buildings.

It was this city, trying to become a true national metropolis, that experienced in an especially poignant way the fears and alarms that caused the students in Columbian College, just across the city boundary, to abandon their studies. Less than two years before, grossly exaggerated rumors at the time of John Brown's Raid had thrown the city into panic for fear of an attack on it and an uprising of the slaves. When the real proportions of the raid were known, fears died down. A reorganization of the militia was about the only step taken to improve the defense of the city. The election of Lincoln, followed so shortly by the secession of South Carolina in December, 1860, brought out again all the old fears and many new ones. Would the inauguration of Lincoln involve the city in a wave of violence? If the Union fell to pieces, would Washington, on the border, cease to be the capital?

When the President-elect arrived secretly in Washington on February 23, the need for extraordinary measures was apparent. Breaking with precedent, the inaugural procession was not a civilian demonstration but was like a military expedition, as one historian has written. The militia was federalized and immediately after the firing on Fort Sumter the President, on April 15, called on the governors of the states to provide quotas of the militia.

As the Sixth Massachusetts Regiment, the first of these contingents, passed through Baltimore on its way to the capital on April 19, it was savagely attacked by a mob. To prevent a repetition of this, the city authorities cut the railroads leading to the North, so that for the time no troops could be sent directly from the North to Washington.[3]

The wounded troops of the Sixth Massachusetts were brought on to Washington and placed in the Washington Infirmary, the quarters of the Medical School and its hospital. From that time on, the Infirmary was used as a military hospital, until it was totally destroyed by fire on November 4, 1861. The Medical Department had lost its classrooms and its hospital. After the first battle of Bull Run, when it was necessary to expand rapidly the hospital facilities within the District, the government began to take over buildings and grounds on College Hill.[4] In many cases contingents of troops would occupy areas without formal permission. In June, 1861, the Third Maine Regiment of Volunteers destroyed a large section of the College fence which was used for flooring in the tents, leaving a field of clover unprotected. The Quartermaster agreed to pay $150 for the repair of the fence and $75 for five acres of clover when appropriations were available.[5]

On June 15, 1861, the Board of Trustees empowered its Executive Committee with the president and treasurer to contract with the government for rental of the College building at the rate of $350 per month. The arrangement was made, although it appears that from July, 1862, the government arbitrarily reduced the rent to $250 per month. It was reported to the Board on October 28, 1862, that the steward's house had been taken for $50 per month and that sixteen acres of College ground had been occupied for the erection of barracks for which remuneration was to be sought.[6]

The military were not exactly comfortable neighbors. In the summer of 1861 we find President Samson telling a mournful tale of woe about the encroachments of the several regiments encamped "back of our grounds." The First Maine made a commons of his meadow, from which he cut $50 worth of hay a year, and his garden, which supplied his table with vegetables. His stable was used for their horses and its loft as a guardhouse, his hay to make beds for the men. His carriages were used day and night by loungers and were badly broken and defaced. The College pump was used daily by 3,000 men; it required repairs every week. Life must have been rugged indeed for the Reverend President.[7]

Two major military hospitals were organized on the College grounds, Columbian College Hospital and Carver Hospital. Across Fourteenth Street just outside the College grounds were Mount Pleasant Hospital and Stone Hospital. The capacity of Carver was 1,300 beds; of Columbian, 844; of Mount Pleasant, 1,618; and of Stone, 170.[8]

No one in Washington could fail to see the havoc of war. Listen to Walt Whitman:

As I sit writing this paragraph (Sundown, Thursday June 25 [1863]) I see a train of about thirty large four-horse wagons, passing up Fourteenth Street, on their way probably to Columbian, Carver and Mount Pleasant hospitals. This is the way the men come in now, seldom in small numbers, but almost always in these long sad processions.

His letters show that he devoted much time to the patients at Carver Hospital, which he describes as "a little city in itself" with more "inmates than an ordinary country town." His visits were no doubt a welcome antidote to the drabness of the hospital. "O, I must tell you," he wrote his mother on June 3, 1864, "I [gave] in Carver hospital a great treat of Ice Cream, a couple of days ago, went around myself through about fifteen large wards—I bought some ten gallons, very nice. You would have cried and been amused too. Many of the men had to be fed; several of them I saw cannot probably live, yet they quite enjoyed it. I gave everybody some—quite a number [of] Western country boys had never tasted ice cream before."[9]

The Columbian College Hospital had one distinguished civilian as an emergency patient. President Samson wrote that one day as Mrs. Lincoln was riding down Fourteenth Street from Soldier's Home, where the Summer White House was located, the horses of her carriage bolted and started to dash down the hill, just as they passed the College entrance. The President's wife, in jumping from the carriage, fell and was taken into Columbian College Hospital where she was cared for by Mrs. Rebecca R. Pomroy, who had lost both husband and son in the War and was working as a nurse. Whenever thereafter there was illness in the Lincoln family the services of Mrs. Pomroy were always sought.[10]

On one occasion at least, President Lincoln visited Columbian College

Hospital. Senator Orville Hickman Browning of Illinois records in his diary that on Sunday afternoon, May 18, 1862, the President sent for him and he and Mr. Lincoln rode out to the hospital at the College, "went all through it, and shook hands and talked with all the sick and wounded."[11]

Columbian College U.S. General Hospital was used for the whole four years of the War, from July 14, 1861, to July 10, 1865. The only graduate of the Medical Department known to have served on the staff of this hospital was Marcellus King Moxley (1839-1889), M.D. 1863. Dr. Moxley served as a Medical Cadet from September, 1861, to July 4, 1862, then as an Assistant Surgeon.

A proposal for the purchase of College Hill was made by the Surgeon General of the Army on behalf of the government in the early part of the War. President Samson pointed out:

The College grounds consist of nearly 47 acres, including a strip of land extending from Boundary Street [now Florida Avenue] along 14th Street road and between 14th and 15th Streets prolonged a distance of about one half mile; having a grove of native forest trees in front and another in the rear; including also a triangular shaped piece of ground projecting South of Boundary St. and having a dwelling house upon it, and a triangular strip used as a Cemetery north of the road [now Columbia Road] passing along the northern boundary of the main property.
The Buildings of the College consist of the main edifice, now occupied as a Hospital, a Steward's house with large back building, a Professor's house, a double house for the President, a school building, a new and large brick stable, with other out buildings. All these have been enlarged or improved within two years; and all are or may be heated from the common engine room which heats the College edifice, Steward's house and school building. The entire expense of these buildings, including $5,000 for heating apparatus and $1,000 for drainage has been about $67,000. The land cost originally $7,000; and since that period, 42 years ago, the land in the vicinity has increased about ten fold in value.

President Samson felt that the Board might entertain an offer for the purchase of the property at the low price of $100,000, since the government's occupation made it impossible for the College officers to protect the property or to carry on their duties properly and since there had been some desire on the part of the patrons to move the College into the city. The president hoped that the government, before proceeding with its offers to purchase, would consider the fact that thousands had given of their means to aid the College to be located at this spot for the purpose of promoting the interests of education at the national metropolis. The government did not take the College, but the incident has provided for us, in President Samson's letter, the best description we have of the College property in 1861.[12]

To the College buildings used for the hospital, the government had added several other buildings: a two-story barracks, a baggage house, a kitchen, a drying house, two guardhouses, and five outbuildings.[13]

On December 5, 1861, Colonel W. W. H. Davis of the 104th Regiment, Pennsylvania Volunteers, First Brigade of Casey's Division, appointed First Lieutenant James M. Carver of Company C, 104th Regiment, Pennsylvania Volunters, "General Superintendent for the erection of Winter Quarters for the Brigade."[14]

It was this Lieutenant Carver apparently who designed and supervised the building of the wooden structures in the College grounds south of the College buildings which became known in compliment to him as Carver Barracks. It was in these buildings that a general hospital was opened on April 17, 1862, under the name of Carver U.S. General Hospital. An administration building and six new wards 200 feet in length were added. The capacity of the hospital was further expanded by the use of a large number of tents, thus becoming one of the larger hospitals in the area. Carver Hospital was closed on August 17, 1865.

A century later, it is difficult to see how it was possible to carry on instruction on College Hill, with two major general hospitals with 2,144 beds on the grounds and with added military contingents from time to time camped on the grounds in tents. Each year the faculty reported its firm resolution to continue instruction as long as there were any students.

The effect of the War on College enrollment can be seen from the accompanying figures, reported as of June 30 by the president in his annual reports showing the maximum number of students registered during each of the War years.

Year	College	Preparatory School
1861	82	73
1862	22	31
1863	23	53
1864	31	94
1865	36	106

In addition to carrying on the duties of the president, of a minister of the Gospel, and of a public man, Dr. Samson had to assume personally a large share of the instruction and also, after the resignation of the Reverend Joseph Hammitt in the summer of 1862, the duties of agent. His burden was eased by the high degree of cooperation and good deportment on the part of the student body, upon which he invariably commented in his annual reports. There were graduates each year during the War. Since the College building which contained the dormitory accommodations was occupied in July, 1861, there was no attempt to register boarders, although a few were taken care of in the steward's house. No catalogue was issued in 1862.[15]

The Medical Department's experience was still more difficult, for the Washington Infirmary was taken over by the government for a military hospital and shortly thereafter totally destroyed by fire. Its teaching hospital and lecture rooms were lost to the Medical Department forever.

On June 24, 1862, it was reported to the Trustees that, "two years since," Old Trinity Church on Judiciary Square had been purchased by a member of the Medical faculty with the assistance of the president for $10,000. The last installment had been paid and nearly $4,000 was being spent to fit up lecture rooms, library, and public hall with twelve law offices for rent. The building was to be completed by September first "unless arrested by occupancy as a government hospital." Significantly, reference was made to the desirability of reviving the Law School. The Medical School had been in a bad way, with constant changes in the faculty and the falling off of student enrollment. Prospects had been greatly improved, however, by the knowledge that "a gentleman of this city" was considering giving the College a building for the Medical School. It was recommended that thought be given to a more direct control of the affairs of the Medical Department and especially of any building that might be given the College for the department's use.[16]

To provide for a continuation of instruction after the loss of Washington Infirmary, Dean J. C. Riley reported to his faculty on October 18, 1861, that a building on E Street between Eleventh and Twelfth Streets had been leased. This building was known as the *Union* Printing Office, or as the *Constitution* Office, from the names of the newspapers published there. Dr. Toner in his *Anniversary Oration* in 1866 states that lectures continued in that building "for sometime." Lectures were suspended in 1863-1864 and 1864-1865. In his annual report for 1863, the president stated that the faculty of the Medical School was then occupying rooms in Old Trinity Church and that when that building was "fitted" title would be transferred to the College. Lectures in medicine were resumed in this building, then known as the law building of Columbian College, in 1865.[17]

Matters of great significance were taking form that were to change the whole organization of the College and create the framework for the University. Discussion with reference to the revival of the Law School had been continued by a committee headed by Joseph Henry, the famous scientist and a prominent Trustee. The committee was convinced of the desirability of the project for three reasons: the strategic location of the College in the national capital; the presence here of many young men with college degrees or literary backgrounds, working in the government, but with much time on their hands and looking forward to law; and the authority of the Charter and the prestige of the Law School, begun forty years before, but suspended for financial reasons. The school should have two professors, one for the work of each year, and invite lecturers on special branches such as military jurisprudence, patent law, laws of diplomacy, and consular procedure. Satisfactory completion of two years of study of eight months each from October first to June first would earn the LL.B. degree. A graduation fee of $100 would be charged, the money to be used for contingent expenses, heating, lighting, etc., payment of professors, and the procuring of a library. Decision was delayed for a year, but the project was far from being abandoned.[18]

While the resumption of legal education was being considered, new difficulties beset the Medical School. An impression that had spread around to the effect that the government was going to open a school with free instruction in medicine and surgery, together with other factors, had so affected enrollment that continuance of the Medical School was not justified in 1863-1864. The President's Report for 1864 expressed the hope that the school could be resumed under more favorable auspices and that the Law School could be revived. Modest surpluses in operation were stimulating hopes. Nevertheless in 1864 the Board voted to delay the opening of the Law School and in 1864-1865 lectures in the Medical School were suspended for a second year, but the Law School's reopening was authorized for the fall of 1865.[19]

On July 12, 1865, the Board received Mr. W. W. Corcoran's offer to present to the College the building on H Street, then used as the United States Army Medical Museum. Six months later the Trustees turned over to the Medical faculty all the arrangements necessary to adapt the building to its purposes. The housing problem for medicine and law was now settled in buildings under the College's control.[20]

In the War, which was just ending, the graduates in medicine had played a large role. It would appear that at least 46 served in the Union Army and 24 in the forces of the Confederacy. William James Hamilton White (1827-1862), M.D. 1848, Surgeon U.S.A., who fell at the Battle of Antietam September 17, 1862, was the first medical officer killed in the War.[21] Dr. Alexander Yelverton Peyton Garnett (1820-1888), Professor of Anatomy, a surgeon in the Confederate Army, served as physician to President Jefferson Davis.[22] Another graduate of the College, John Wesley Clampitt, Ph.B. 1861, played a professional role in a sequel to the tragedy of Lincoln's assassination. He was counsel for Mary E. Surratt in the trial of the conspirators for the killing of the President.

Dr. John Frederick May (1812-1891), A.B. 1831, M.D. 1834, Professor of Surgery, figured in the great national tragedy—the assassination of the war-time President—at two points. Renowned as a surgeon, he was called to the bedside of Lincoln, probed the wound, and confirmed the opinion that nothing could be done to save the President. He was to figure also in the confused aftermath of the assassination: Dr. May identified the corpse of John Wilkes Booth.

In a paper written by Dr. May in 1887 and not published during his lifetime, he tells that some time before the assassination "a fashionably dressed and remarkably handsome young man" had come to his office and introduced himself as Mr. Booth. He was playing an engagement then with Miss Charlotte Cushman and was much annoyed by a large and constantly growing lump on the back of his neck which he wanted the surgeon to remove. The surgeon told him that he would operate only on condition that Booth would suspend his engagement and take a complete rest, explaining that the wound would close without a scar if he remained quiet, but if it broke open it would leave a large and conspicuous scar. Booth said he would not break his engagement and that the doctor must operate. Upon Booth's insistence the doctor removed the tumor and the wound healed with the likelihood of but a slight scar. About a week after the wound started to heal, Booth came to the doctor with the wound wide open, saying that following the action of the play Miss Cushman had embraced him with such force and so roughly that the wound was opened. An ugly scar resulted. Time passed and Dr. May was summoned to the Navy Yard to go on board a ship anchored there to see if he could identify a body as Booth's. When he saw the body he declared that it bore no resemblance to Booth. He described the scar, and when the corpse was turned, there it was. When the body was placed in various positions, Dr. May began to make out the lineaments of Booth. Never, he wrote, had a greater change taken place. The Adonis he had known was now a haggard corpse, with skin discolored and facial expression sunken, a harrowing picture of starvation and exposure. But it was Booth. The lower right leg was greatly contused and completely black from a fracture of one of the long bones. Dr. May wrote his account after Giteau's assassination of President Garfield, and he concluded with the observation that "none but *madmen* has assailed with murderous intent the Chief Magistrate of the nation since the foundation of the Republic."[23]

CHAPTER TEN

Reconstruction
1865-1871

In the early months of the War, Washington decreased in population. Civil servants with southern sympathies left, many of the residents sent their families away to what they thought were places of greater safety, and those who had homes elsewhere made their way to them. Work on public buildings was stopped and many mechanics and laborers were thrown out of employment. The supply of food and other necessities moving into the District had been interrupted, and prices skyrocketed. Temporarily the city was in bad shape; but within a few months, with the building of defenses under way, the organization of militia forces from the District, and the moving in of troops from the states, calm returned, and rapid improvement began.

The assembling of tens of thousands of troops to form the Army of the Potomac transformed the capital city into a vast military camp. West of Twenty-first Street and south of G Street down to the wharves on the river there was a vast series of depots for all types of military supplies and equipment and huge corrals for tens of thousands of horses and mules. Large unoccupied areas throughout the District were used for military encampments, and schools and churches were commandeered for hospital use. Demand for labor, skilled and unskilled, grew. Civil employees of the government increased in number tremendously. All forms of business were stimulated. The population jumped from the sixty-odd thousand shown in the 1860 census to 140,000 reported by the police board in 1863, plus the constantly varying military population. This radical increase in size and the change in the nature of the population brought special problems of their own. Washington had become a large city, and a large city with large-city problems was the outlook for the future.[1]

Circumstances were rapidly developing which were to transform Columbian College into an urban university. When Joseph Henry, the chairman of the Trustees' Committee, had recommended the reopening of the Law School, he had mentioned the number of young men who were working for the government and who were considering law as a profession. The number of civil servants had vastly increased, and many of them (though Henry's observation had been restricted to the law) would no doubt be interested in study in the liberal arts and sciences, not only at an undergraduate but at a graduate level. Government clerks at the time enjoyed bankers' hours. Offices were closed at three in the afternoon and adherence to the closing hour seems to have been loosely enforced. Frequently a block of work was assigned for the day, and when that was completed many employees felt free to leave.

The lectures of the Medical faculty had traditionally begun in the late afternoon, as did those in law when that department was reopened. Practicing physicians and surgeons came to lecture in medicine; likewise, among Henry's recommendations for the Law School was one that visiting lecturers in special branches of the law be utilized. In the College, work in the regular classes, held in the forenoon and early afternoon, was supplemented by lectures offered later in the day. The employed student, or "the late-afternoon student" as he was called for decades, was constituting a more and more pronounced area of interest. Likewise the utilization of the part-time teacher, often a government expert who gave lectures in his specialty, was becoming more general.

Not without bearing was the growing renewed discussion of the advisability of moving the College from College Hill to the center of the city. As we have seen, this discussion had begun even before the outbreak of the War; but the decision had been not to move the College to the city.

No sooner was the War over than President Samson laid before the Trustees a plat of the College's south grounds "that might be disposed of to advantage." This was the preliminary to positive action.[2]

The grounds south of the College lawn were divided by streets and alleys according to the plat. A strip of land on the west of the area was to be laid out as an alley with a width that varied from 10 to 18 feet, and surrendered to the Levy Court for a public road, provided the party on the other side of the strip dedicated enough of his holding to make a street

50 feet wide. The two streets running east and west, that had just been opened, were to be named Staughton and Chapin. On the basis of an expert appraisal, lots fronting on Fourteenth Street were to bring an annual rental of 6 per cent of their valuation, the latter based on 25 cents per square foot, during a ten-year lease, the lessee to pay all taxes. These lots could not be occupied by stores for the sale of spirituous liquors or "any other traffic not previously approved by the Board." Lots fronting on Boundary, Staughton, and Chapin Streets could be used only for dwellings and outbuildings for family and residential purposes. They were offered on a ten-year lease at an annual rental equal to 6 per cent on an appraised value of 15 cents per square foot, the lessee to pay all taxes. The College was responsible for grading streets and alleys; the lessee, for grading the lots on a scale conforming to the streets, and for laying foot pavements in front of the lots. Leases could be perpetually renewed, but the valuations were to be fixed every ten years by a committee of three: a Trustee, the lessee, and a member nominated by them. In his Report for 1867, the president estimated that the rentals would add $4,200 to the annual income.[3]

These measures suggested the shape of things to come: the gradual disposal of all the property on College Hill and a relocation of the College. In the same Annual Report for 1867, another item of great significance appeared. The president reported the success of the effort, favored at the annual meeting in the preceding year, "to gather an evening class of advanced pupils." He recommended increased consideration of this project. During the second term 30 to 40 young men "had asked for this privilege." The fees they paid had been sufficient to pay four professors $140 each and the instructor in French $90 for this added service, a most welcome addition to embarrassingly inadequate salaries.

In spite of the appearance of what we recognize today as clear evidence of trends toward future change, strenuous efforts were made to improve the existing plant. Just before the War large sums had been spent on buildings and grounds. By the summer of 1865, the government had repaired the damage done to the main College building resulting from its use as a hospital. What was left of John Withers' legacy of 1853 was used to restore other buildings and grounds. A new Preparatory School building was erected on the College grounds at a cost of $8,450 and was named Withers Hall. The Law building was vacated after years of occupancy by the Medical faculty, and the building on H Street given by W. W. Corcoran was surrendered by the War Department as a Medical

Museum and turned over to the Medical School on November 1, 1866. Two years later, the building was greatly enlarged to afford adequate facilities for instruction.

In the refurbished main College building, a cause of much complaint was removed by providing new furniture for the students. For each boarder there were an iron bedstead, mattress, two pillows, chair, study table, and washstand for which he paid $10 annually. For each nonboarder, there were a study table and chair for which the fee was $5 annually. Rooms were inspected once a week.[4]

A resolution of July 27, 1865, authorized the faculty to remit one-half of the tuition fees of orphans and the fatherless.[5] In his Annual Report for 1867, the president made an earnest appeal for the endowment of scholarships to support pupils from the public schools. Twelve years before, the Trustees of the Public Schools of Washington had been urged, in the absence of a public high school, to send a few of the advanced pupils to the College at the expense of the school fund. It was now hoped that this number could be increased through the creation of scholarship endowments of $8,000 each, which would underwrite the expenses of a student during his preparatory and college years. Such a scholarship was established by the Honorable Amos Kendall in 1869 through a gift of $6,000 in the name of Calvary Baptist Church.[6]

Aside from endowed scholarships, various individuals were each assuming the obligation to pay the tuition fees of a student.

Student enrollment from the final year of the War to the last year of the Samson administration is shown in the accompanying table. The figures are taken from the president's Annual Report submitted each June; the number of graduates each year are shown in parentheses.

It will be noticed that there was a general build-up in enrollment until 1868, and then a gradual decline. The fact that the close of the War released many young men who returned to their studies explains in part

	Academic (College and Preparatory)	Medicine	Law	Theology
1865	142 (7)	—	—	—
1866	167 (5)	17 (4)	108 (36)	—
1867	213 (4)	29 (4)	198 (59)	—
1868	189 (11)	35 (8)	210 (105)	—
1869	184 (12)	60 (10)	173 (71)	20 (—)
1870	183 (7)	70 (12)	168 (68)	18 (—)
1871	140 (11)	54 (10)	167 (82)	18 (—)

the growth during the earlier years. The falling off in the later years caused President Samson great concern.

Just as the hostilities were ending, the Trustees took a significant step in the Board's gradual evolution from being highly denominational in character to being more truly public. The right to vote for Trustees in the triennial elections, which had been restricted to contributing denominational organizations, was extended to permit eligible individual contributors to vote.[7]

Many of the projects which had been planned during the war years came into fruition. A general reconditioning of all the buildings and grounds was got under way. The Law Department was revived and began instruction in 1865, with John C. Kennedy instructing the junior class, and William M. Merrick the senior class.

After the Law Department had been in highly successful operation for two years, a plan for its permanent organization was adopted. No other department was to be liable for the expenses of the Law Department and all of the latter's income was to be devoted exclusively to its own support and advancement. Student fees, office rents, donations, and all other receipts were to be appropriated in the following order:

1. Payment of necessary expenses for maintenance;
2. Salaries of professors and fees of lecturers;
3. Increase of the library under direction of the Law faculty;
4. Liquidation of the debt on the Law building;
5. Creation of a fund for endowment.

The president of the College was to be ex officio lecturer on ethics, and special lecturers were to be appointed at the discretion of the faculty. The department was to be under the supervision of the Trustees' Committee on the Law School with the consent of the faculty. Salaries of professors were set at a minimum of $2,000 and a maximum of $3,000. Until the minimum was reached, all the surplus after maintenance costs were paid was to be prorated among the professors. After the minimum was reached, half of the surplus was to be prorated until the maximum was reached. Student fees were $80 for the first year, $70 for the second. The policy of annual election of professors was rescinded.[8]

In the spring of 1868, a theological department was again established. It was not to have any special denominational complexion in its requirements. Its general instruction was to be that common to all theological seminaries of evangelical Christians. Its students were to look to clergy of their own denominations for instruction in areas specifically relevant to their own communions. The department embraced four "schools": Biblical interpretation, Christian theology, church history, and ministerial duties. Although the College was anxious to increase its income from student fees and shortly thereafter raised the tuition fee of academic students to $60 per annum, a nominal fee of $5 per term was charged theological students, with the expressed intention of seeking outside aid from friends. Resident members of the College faculty were appointed to the chairs: President Samson, theology; Professor Huntington, Biblical literature; and Professor Shute, church history. The student body of 20 during the first year included six Presbyterians, eight Baptists, two Episcopalians, two Methodists, and two Congregationalists.[9]

In the death of Amos Kendall on November 12, 1869, the College lost one of its most distinguished supporters. Although he held office for only four years, two as a Trustee and two as president of the Board of Trustees, his influence on the history of the institution was exceedingly great. A native of Massachusetts and a graduate of Dartmouth, he moved to Kentucky where he was called to the bar. He became editor of several papers, the *Argus of Western America,* published in Frankfort, being the best known. With powerful political connections, he came to Washington and achieved great influence as a member of the "Kitchen Cabinet." As Jackson's Postmaster General he freed that department from debt. The memorial resolution adopted by the Trustees declared that "to his sagacity and skill we owe the early development of the telegraph." "His mature years," the Trustees declared, "which in God's providence have been crowned with great prosperity have been devoted to the interests of humanity"; they were given to the building of an Asylum for the Deaf and Dumb, since adopted and enlarged by the government (Gallaudet College at Kendall Green, D.C.), the creation and endowment of Sunday schools, and the erection of a stately temple for the worship of God (Calvary Baptist Church). His benevolences to the College were many, including the endowment of the scholarship which still bears his name. President Samson had in him a warm supporter and influential friend.[10]

One Trustee who, during the period, gave almost daily attention to the affairs of the College was Andrew Rothwell, a member of the Board from 1835 until his death in 1883 and, for brief periods, its secretary and treasurer. Deacon Rothwell was an outstanding leader in the Baptist community and a most useful member of the Board. No other Trustee was as regular in attendance at meetings, as assiduous in auditing financial statements, heading committees, and preparing reports.

The College was able to assemble a faculty of high quality, though of inadequate size, in the first years following the War. William Ruggles was still there. He was a member of the original faculty and his connection with the institution extended over a period of fifty-five years until his death in 1877. Ruggles served as spokesman of the faculty in all the delicate negotiations with the Board when the staff was being either tardily or partially paid. A man of great determination, he was unyielding in his convictions and emphatic in their expression. His was the great continuing influence during the first half-century of the College's existence. A versatile scholar, he taught both the natural sciences and mathematics, and the social sciences.[11]

The Reverend Adoniram Judson Huntington, A.B. 1843, has been described as the best-loved member of the faculty. A gifted teacher and an able classical scholar, he had served in the early 'forties as principal of the Preparatory School and joined the faculty on graduation from college; here he served for fifty-one years, a period broken at times by active work in the ministry.

Edward T. Fristoe began his long period of service as teacher of mathematics and science in 1855, his special interest being in the field of chemistry, which he taught for a generation. The Reverend Samuel Moore Shute came to the College in 1859 to teach the classics, but was best known as a teacher of English and the author of an Anglo-Saxon manual. The service of these men extended over decades and fixed the academic tone of the institution.[12]

There was another member of the faculty who could not claim the long term of service of these men, but who is of great interest in his own right. He served as professor of Latin from 1865 to 1871. William Lyne Wilson (1843-1900), born in what is now West Virginia, was a graduate of the College in the class of 1860. Although physically frail, he joined a Confederate quartermaster outfit stationed in the middle Shenandoah Valley, taking with him a trunk full of books for his intellectual pleasure. But the rather sedentary life of a quartermaster did not suit him, and on April 1, 1862, he joined the Twelfth Virginia Cavalry in which he served as a private until the surrender at Appomattox. He rode in the Shenandoah Campaigns, was captured and exchanged, and fought at Brandy Station, the Wilderness, Spotsylvania Court House, Cold Harbor, and on the Petersburg-Appomattox front. His letters to his mother and his diary describe in graphic and often classical language the waning of the "Southern constellation." His epitaph for the Confederacy was *Ilium fuit* (Troy was). On his return to civilian life, his plans for the immediate future were settled when his Alma Mater called the gifted young alumnus to her faculty as professor of Latin. Tradition has it that his first lectures were given in the uniform of a Confederate cavalryman. He married the daughter of Professor Huntington. He made good use of his time, for in the evenings and on Saturdays he studied law in the Law Department, which had just been reestablished. Wilson determined to enter into the practice of law, but as an ex-Confederate this was not allowed him until 1871, when he formed a partnership and hung up his shingle at Charles Town. Becoming involved in politics, he worked up from city attorney of Charles Town to delegate to the Democratic National Convention. But education beckoned again. Elected president of West Virginia University, he had hardly entered upon his duties when he was nominated and elected to the House of Representatives, where he served until his defeat in 1895. President Cleveland appointed him Postmaster General. He is credited with the establishment of rural free delivery and the introduction of the private penny postcard. With the conclusion of Cleveland's second term, Wilson was not to be relegated to the Democratic shadows that accompanied a long Republican regime. Accordingly, he accepted the presidency of Washington and Lee University. He died October 17, 1900, a victim of tuberculosis. He was one of the truly great alumni of the College.[13]

In discussing the College, it is easy to overlook the role played by the Preparatory School during the post-War period. The school enjoyed generous patronage and its enrollment always exceeded that of the College. Its burgeoning income from tuition was a major addition to the institution's finances. A normal channel for admission to Columbian College and preparation for other colleges, the preparatory course was also a terminal course for many youths who intended not to enter one of the professions but to pursue banking, mercantile, or other careers. No public secondary education was available in the District, and Columbian Preparatory School met the need, at least for a limited group. There was a constant concern on the part of the Trustees and faculty to add to the school as many worthy and gifted youths from the public schools as possible, by means of scholarships paid through the school fund, special endowments of the College, or the liberality of individuals. The courses in the Preparatory School and the College were integrated so that qualified prep students could anticipate degree requirements by taking single courses in the College. The work was carefully supervised and the standard of instruction was high. From 1861 to 1884, the principal of the Preparatory School was Otis T. Mason, A.B. 1861, who served the College later as professor of anthropology and Trustee after he had become curator of ethnology in the U.S. National Museum. He achieved great distinction through his researches on the American Indian and his epoch-making ideas about the classification of primitive implements.[14]

When Dr. Samson assumed the duties of president, the College was about to arrive at its peak enrollment, only to have the student body melt away almost completely with the coming of war. As we have seen, the War, for the period of its duration, virtually transformed College Hill into a military installation. In that confused setting President Samson attempted, with the assistance of a skeleton faculty, to carry on the business of instruction. Circumstances forced him to be president, professor, and business manager all at once in these abnormal conditions. He solicited, received, and disbursed funds. During the greater part of the War period he was conducting fifteen class periods a week. Problems arose with frequency, decisions had to be made, and action taken without delay. A strong, positive man was needed and Samson was just that.

The conditions that prevailed at the end of his administration should not have been unexpected. They can best be understood by noting first a series of communications between the Board of Trustees and President Samson. On April 13, 1870, the president presented his resignation to the Board. He gave four reasons for his action. His term of office had already reached the limit "beyond which his most efficient predecessors had declined to go." His own small property had been exhausted; and his salary, drawn from the academic fund, was out of proportion to the services rendered by others. With the Law and Medical Departments in their own buildings, and with the oversight of the former now separated from the duties of the president, the functions of his office could be performed by someone less dependent on the income he would receive as president. There was a great need for a suitable building for the library, and apparatus and funds had to be sought. The principal donors had been the former and present presidents of the Board. Some wills with favorable bequests had been written, but he had no distinct donors in view.

Unwilling to accept this resignation, the Board tried to make proposals which would, in part, remove the president's reasons for relinquishing his office. His salary was increased to $2,500, a building would be erected as soon as there were any chances for its successful funding, and the president was asked to give his time as agent for six months, with salary and expenses. These offers were made May 24, 1870.

In his reply to the Board just a week later, on May 31, Samson wrote at length because he feared that the Board did not fully understand the background of his action. In a way that none of his predecessors had ever done, he cited the history of the College to put his position in the proper setting:

Your first President compelled to assume an agency, saw the College decline, and his administration lasted about five years. The second and third gave practical attention to the finances, were each favored with able agents and both held their positions during terms of about eleven years. The fourth secured efficient aid from members of the Board, but was aided by no agent and his office terminated in three years with a debt accumulated solely for salaries of instruction amounting to about $9,000. Instructed by this example, the efforts of the fifth President were devoted to secure a scale of improvement graduated by the income of the College: his strength being given to the immediate work of instruction and his leisure to finances. Before the War, improvements were steadily made, the salaries were promptly paid and a small surplus in the Treasury was every year secured. During the War, the improvements ceased, but the debt was all paid off, while the Faculty were also promptly paid. Since the War so large attention has been given to improvements that too large a proportion of the income has been devoted to these, and thus withdrawn from the first necessity, the small salaries of the Faculty which is their only dependence. In this the President has made it a point of honor and duty to share the inconveniences to which all the Faculty have been subjected. If the President serves as agent it would be detrimental to all departments. The Agent should be directly responsible to the Board.

The president's mind was unchanged. He ended his letter: "I am unable to reach at present the decision they have asked."

Still the Board did not act on the resignation, but appointed as agent the Reverend A. D. Gillette, D.D., Professor of Pastoral Duties in the Theological Department, when a sum sufficient for its endowment had been raised. Gillette was meanwhile to act with President Samson, giving his entire time as agent and receiving as compensation a commission of 5 per cent. In assigning the agent's duties, the Board evidently still had in mind the complaints the president had set forth in his letters of resignation and explanation. Funds were to be collected to liquidate the liabilities of the academic department, to erect an academic building, and to complete a fund for the endowment of the president's office and for a chair in the Theological Department.

Anxious not "to shrink," Samson withdrew his resignation in his Annual Report on June 27, 1870.

By the time the annual meeting of the Board in 1871 rolled around, attitudes had stiffened. Samson looked back "on a year of labor too severe to be continued." Up to this time the *Minutes* of the Board had been kept without showing any indication of disagreement. In fact, the *Minutes* of the meetings of April 13, May 24, and May 31, 1870, were not entered in the *Journal* until after Samson's resignation was withdrawn. The *Minutes* for the Annual Meeting in 1871 show a marked air of determination. It was recommended that all agents' commissions be canceled and immediate reports called for; that no contracts be made unless authorized by the Board just elected; that a committee of four Trustees be appointed to investigate and report on a schedule of property, debts and liability, the condition of the College buildings and their contents, and also of the Law building; that a statement be made regarding College laws and ordinances, the character of the catalogue—whether accurate or not—and necessary changes in the Charter, laws, and ordinances. Every one of those elected to the Board who had not signified his acceptance in writing before the next meeting of the Board was to be considered as having declined. All attorneys having in hand papers, property, and business of the College were to report to the Board through the secretary. All tenants were to pay rents in full at once. No copies of the 1870-1871 catalogue were to be circulated until further action. The recommended committee of four Trustees was appointed to take over the functions assigned to it and was given both access to all records and the power to call for any information. No action was taken on the president's Annual Report at this time; but on July 12, more than two weeks later, the president was instructed to strike from it all matters not relating to his duties and acts as president. He and Dr. Gillette were notified that their agencies were terminated, and final reports were called for. No catalogue was to be printed, no printing or advertising was to be done, and the recently prepared catalogue was not to be published.

Ten days later, on July 22, 1871, President Samson's revised report was presented and his resignation was accepted, his salary to continue to the end of the vacation. The Board assured him of its "sincere respect, warm affection, and hearty desire for his welfare and happiness." Neither the final Annual Report nor the revised report appears in the *Minutes* of the Board.[15]

President Samson's own draft of the original Annual Report for 1871 was in his personal papers. This report was comprehensive in its scope. It discussed current trends with reference to the elective system and to scientific instruction in American colleges. Reasons for Columbian's decline in reputation were discussed, particularly with reference to the condition of the buildings and an inadequate faculty. Difficulties in financial management and division of responsibilities were very pointedly indicated. Under the headings of "Improvement of Real Estate," "Debts Incurred and Methods of Meeting," and "Legacies," he gave an account of his stewardship. The section on the "President as Agent" pointed out the difficulty of his dual position. "Future Demands of the College" listed major needs, and "Matters Personal to the President" ended with his final resignation.

It is difficult to understand why the administration of President Samson closed so ambiguously. The answer is to be found in his conception of the presidency, in his own ideas as to priority, in the enormity of the tasks he had to perform, and in the special problems facing a college that was developing into a university.

The Charter of 1821 provided "that the head or the chief master for the said college shall be called and styled 'the president,' and the masters thereof should be called 'professors and tutors,' " and that neither, while they remained such, should be eligible for the office of Trustee. The president, professors, and tutors were styled "the faculty of the college," which was empowered to enforce rules and regulations governing students, to grant degrees on the mandamus of the Board, and to issue proper diplomas or certificates in evidence thereof.[16]

The president was thus the head of the faculty, and his Charter powers were simply those that devolved upon him in this connection. President Samson was always careful, in his communications to the Board dealing with academic matters, to observe this particular relationship. He was a teaching president and the functions of his office in this regard were particularly congenial to him. He insisted upon sharing with his faculty colleagues when funds were not available for full and prompt payment of salaries. Educational recommendations to the Board were made in the name of the faculty. Acting as a schoolmaster involved no pose on Samson's part. He was well trained and well traveled. He knew intimately the history of Columbian College and wrote and thought with that background in view. Though an accomplished pulpit orator, fired with great evangelical fervor, his educational writings and communications are written as a lay educator would write them. They are not crowded with pious platitudes or laden with Scriptural allusions. Samson was prepared to serve as president within the Charter definition.

The times, however, were to deny him the luxury of serving as such. Other duties were forced upon him in administrative, financial, and promotional areas. Still he insisted on the priority of matters academic, both in his own activities and in the allocation of the College's interest and meager funds. The prompt and full payment of the faculty, in his judgment, took priority over all other expenditures. Providing adequate facilities for instruction followed as a close second.

These matters academic, basically so agreeable to him, represented a full-time assignment. But circumstances added other assignments, less congenial and more arduous. His college plant had become a military installation, even though instruction was still being given to the students who remained. When it seemed desirable to dispense with the services of the Reverend Joseph Hammitt as agent, the full responsibilities of that post fell upon the president, who became in effect business manager, solicitor of funds and students, and collector of pledges. This was in addition to his presidential duties and his fifteen class sessions a week. It settled down to a killing schedule, one in which Samson was at the College from Monday to Friday and in the field on his work as agent from late Friday to early Monday each week. In spite of his desires and to the detriment of his health, he had had to assume practically the entire burden of academic and financial administration.

Samson had protested, but the War prevented any easing of the load. When it ended, a business agent was appointed to take over the duties of registrar and steward, and was ordered to report directly to the chairmen of the appropriate committees of the Board. This appointment was made ostensibly to relieve Samson of some of his burden on College Hill so as to permit him to push his agency more actively. The president saw that a division of responsibilities had been created and he pointed out that the registrar and steward should be subject to his supervision, but the Board ignored his recommendation. Thus he saw appropriations being made for physical improvement and faculty salaries going unpaid.

Added to this erosion of the president's powers on College Hill, there was the question of the Law School. When the rules were drawn up for the conduct of the school, the president was made lecturer on ethics. He was given no other specific function, the Law Department actually being operated by the Trustees' Committee on the Law Department through its Law faculty. The Medical Department had always been autonomous to a large degree.

The real situation was that a true university was beginning to take form. The time was running out when a president of the College, whose function was close to that of a dean today, could handle a group of schools in a more or less detailed fashion. It was unfortunate that the War period had so vastly increased the duties and the reach of the president. It made what followed seem very drastic and an affront to a man who had performed herculean labors for the institution.

The Board's insistence that Samson continue the agency was perhaps his prime reason for his resignation. If the Trustees had lightened his burden by appointing an agent rather than by administrative circumvention, he might have decided differently. Of one thing he was certain. The whole history of the College demonstrated that no president could serve without an efficient agent, and hope for success.

President Samson's administration was a difficult one. The nation experienced a civil war, and the College was in the midst of it. But the College was also in the beginning of an age of transition, during which the institution underwent momentous change. Two years before the close of the Samson administration, Mr. W. W. Corcoran, Washington's most distinguished citizen and one of the institution's most liberal patrons, became president of the Board. It called as Samson's successor the eminent scholar and public man, Dr. James C. Welling.

Without the dedication, intelligence, and industry of George Whitefield Samson, Columbian College might have been a casualty of the War of 1861-1865.

CHAPTER ELEVEN

The Age of Welling
1871-1894

The great achievements of President Samson had been to pay off the debt incurred during the administration of his predecessor, to keep the College alive and maintain its dignity during the War, to provide housing for its various departments, and to lay the basis for a full resumption of its activities. Like Moses, he had led it over a troubled journey, but another man was to lead it into the Promised Land. The imminence of change was evident in much of Samson's policy: the College was bound to become a university. The transition was made by a peculiarly happy partnership of the president and the head of the University Corporation who, working closely together, provided the educational leadership, the vision and practical sense, and the financial support that were required.

W. W. Corcoran, the District's most distinguished citizen, already a major benefactor of the College, was elected president of the Board of Trustees on November 30, 1869, to succeed the late Amos Kendall. On August 11, 1871, James Clarke Welling, Professor of Belles Lettres in Princeton University, formally accepted the office of president of Columbian College. In a sense, President Samson's resignation—offered, then withdrawn, and again submitted—had been pending since April 13 of the preceding year.

Just a short time before President Welling's election, the Legislative Assembly of the District of Columbia, at the request of the Trustees, passed on July 25, 1871, "An Act for the relief of Columbian College, in the District of Columbia." Since an act approved January 21, 1871, had vested executive power in the District in an appointed governor, and legislative power in an elected legislative assembly, it was the territorial legislature that passed the act of July 25, 1871. By it the original Charter was amended to permit the College to apply the proceeds from any sale of its property to pay off existing indebtedness and to put its property and equipment in good condition. To replace the existing Board of Trustees, the act created a corporation of the College. Its members were to be elected by the Trustees chosen in May, 1871, and were to consist of thirteen Trustees, residents of the District of Columbia, and thirteen Overseers. The president of the Corporation and its secretary-treasurer were to be selected from the Trustees. The Corporation was to meet annually; the Trustees semi-annually, quarterly, monthly, and occasionally as required. The creation of a Board of Overseers, whose members would be relieved from the obligation to attend any except the annual meetings, provided a means for relating to the College influential men living outside the District.[1]

While no real estate or other property could be sold by the Trustees without the vote of the Corporation, other routine matters could be handled by the Trustees; since by the provisions of the act they were residents of the District they would be available for meetings at any time. Administrative efficiency was thus achieved by this modification of the Charter.

The President of the United States, the Chief Justice of the United States, the Attorney General, the Governor of the District of Columbia, and the Delegate of the District of Columbia were made honorary members of the Corporation, without vote.[2]

President Welling had been in touch with his predecessor, and the thoroughness of his briefing is shown by the fact that his force was immediately felt. Accompanying his letter of acceptance was another communication demonstrating this fact very clearly. He stated flatly that he did not desire to be charged with the financial administration of the institution, that he would give his first attention to the internal administration of the College. As a move toward economy, the Board had failed to reappoint two professors. This, said Welling, would work injuriously to the standards of instruction. He asked and got an additional tutor in mathematics and an instructor in French, and salary increases for Professor Huntington and Professor Shute. The new president lacked nothing by way of directness in dealing with his Board. When requests that repairs be made to make the president's house more livable had not been complied with, he wrote: "The many inconveniences to which I have been subjected at the threshold of my administration induce me to request that the ceremonies connected with my inauguration be postponed to as late a period as practical during the coming month."[3] The repairs were made.

Because of Mr. Corcoran's uncertain health, Judge John A. Bolles was elected vice president of the Board so that a presiding officer would always be available. A committee of five was appointed to inform Mr. Corcoran of this arrangement and to say that they would be glad to confer with him regarding such a plan as might be deemed wise and expedient for converting Columbian College into a national university bearing his name. After consideration, Mr. Corcoran very graciously declined the honor and suggested the name "The Columbian University."[4]

The inauguration of the sixth president was held on Monday, November 6, 1871, in the Congregational Church at Tenth and G Streets; a large and distinguished company was present. Prayer was offered by the Reverend James A. Cuthbert; Dr. Samson delivered his farewell address; the choir sang an ode written for the occasion by the Reverend Stephen P. Hill; the vice president handed the keys to President Welling, who then delivered his address. The Reverend Cleland K. Nelson pronounced the benediction. Mr. Corcoran was present but was unable to participate physically.[5]

At the first annual meeting of the newly constituted Corporation, W. W. Corcoran was elected president, William Stickney secretary and treasurer, and John A. Bolles vice president. By ordinance the names of the various branches of the College were fixed as follows: the Preparatory School of Columbian College, Columbian College, the Law School of Columbian College, and the Medical School of Columbian College.

In 1872, on the recommendation of the Medical faculty the degree of Graduate in Pharmacy was for the first time conferred upon six young men who had completed a regular apprenticeship in the drug and apothecary business and also attended two full courses in pharmacy. The degree of Bachelor of Philosophy was replaced by the degrees of Bachelor of Letters and Bachelor of Science. A bequest from the estate of the Reverend Romeo Elton, amounting to $8,742.88, was gratefully accepted as a basis for the endowment of the Elton Professorship of Mental and Moral Philosophy. At the same time another proffered gift was gracefully declined.[6]

Mrs. Maria M. Carter, who had previously subscribed $1,000 to found a scholarship for some deserving young man, had offered, through President Samson, a gift of $5,000, the income from which was to provide for the tuition of female students. In her letter of July 31, 1871, Mrs. Carter had proclaimed her conviction: "I am unable to see why the influence of women may not be profitably transferred through the austere forms of the Collegiate recitation room." Dr. Samson thought that Mrs. Carter's wishes could be "indirectly met in Columbian College." Just how was not specified, but the intending donor was thanked for her kindness in making the offer. For eight months the matter waited for a decision from the Trustees. Finally the Board decided that it was "not deemed expedient to accept the proposition of Mrs. M. M. Carter until some plan can be fixed upon for the kindly proffered donation to the education of women." Coeducation must wait.[7]

While President Welling had been careful to stipulate that he was not to be burdened with financial administration but was to be concerned with the internal affairs of the institution, his plans for development obviously required funds of a size hitherto unknown to the College. Here is where his partnership with W. W. Corcoran, the president of the Corporation, was valuable.

William Wilson Corcoran was born in Georgetown in 1798, the son of Thomas Corcoran, a Charter Trustee of Columbian College. Engaged in mercantile affairs in his native town during his early life, after 1828 he became more and more involved in banking activities, and in 1844, in partnership with George W. Riggs, he bought the old Bank of United States. His firm carried the burden of handling the heavy loans made by the government in the Mexican War. In August, 1848, with $12,000,000 worth of a 6 per cent loan of 1848 on hand, with the demand steadily falling below what Corcoran and Riggs had paid, Corcoran went to London, in spite of efforts to dissuade him, and sold a substantial amount of the stock, raising the market price to 119½ and making a handsome profit. In 1854, he withdrew from the firm and retired from active affairs. He was already over seventy when he became a Trustee and president of the Board. His health was uncertain and he was frequently unable to attend meetings or, if present, to preside. But his interest in the institution and his close knowledge of its affairs continued to the end of his life. This was not the only educational institution that profited by his generosity. William and Mary College, the University of Virginia, and Virginia Military Institute also knew him as a benefactor. In the city of Washington, Mr. Corcoran established and endowed the Corcoran Gallery of Art and its school, the Oak Hill Cemetery, and the Louise Home for gentle-women.

At a special meeting on October 7, 1872, the Corporation, at Welling's suggestion, resolved that an effort be made to increase the permanent endowment to $250,000. Two months later it was reported to the Board that Mr. Corcoran had proposed the donation "of a very valuable tract of land, called 'Trinidad,'" adjoining the city limits. In a letter to the Trustees, the donor spelled out his conditions. The gift of Trinidad was in no way to cause any relaxation in the efforts to raise the $250,000 endowment; the principal of the donation when realized was to be funded and kept forever intact, and Dr. Welling was to remain at the head of the College. To further Mr. Corcoran's intent, if $100,000 of the $250,000 were not raised in cash by January 1, 1875, or if for any reason, other than death, Dr. Welling should cease to be president, the donation of Trinidad would be revoked. The Trustees immediately took steps toward a change of name, resolved on the introduction of courses in agriculture and mechanical arts as a basis for a request for a land grant, and decided to maintain a "Corcoran School of Science and Art" with the income from the Trinidad gift. The aid of the Smithsonian Institution and other scientific organizations was to be sought in setting up the Corcoran School. Authorization was given to move the Preparatory School and any of the collegiate departments to within the City. Certain changes in the Charter were to be sought from Congress.[8]

The legal change of name from Columbian College in the District of Columbia to Columbian University was effected by an act of Congress approved March 3, 1873. By this legislation, which supplemented the original Charter of 1821, the name of the institution was changed, the limit on an annual value of $25,000 of the Corporation's property was removed, and the number of Trustees was increased to twenty-one and the number of Overseers to twenty-one, exclusive of the president of the faculty, who was made an ex officio Trustee of the Corporation. The act of the territorial assembly, approved July 25, 1871, was affirmed, but with a stated restriction prohibiting the sale of any land granted by Congress or of real estate given by any person or persons for use other than that provided for in the Charter, legislative act, will, devise, or grant governing the gift.[9]

This piece of legislation was of great importance. For the first time, it made the president of the institution a member of the governing board. It looked forward to the creation of a true university endowment without legal limit as to size but protected by law from use for any purpose other than that specifically stated by the donor. These changes were made by the Congress as a result of recommendations made to the Board by Dr. Welling.

The supplemental act of Congress was formally accepted by the Corporation on March 31, 1873, and on May 24 of that year the beginning of a new era in the life of the institution under its new name, the Columbian University, was formally celebrated by a gala banquet at Wormley's Hotel at Fifteenth and H Streets. This hotel, owned and operated by a Negro, William Wormley, was one of the most exclusive in the city and was famous throughout the nation for its extraordinary cuisine.

The assembled company was one of great distinction, including President Grant and his Cabinet, members of the diplomatic corps, senior officers of the armed services, and eminent scholars. The response to the first toast, "The Columbian University," gave President Welling an opportunity to explain the university movement and its relation to Washington as a great educational center. The Attorney General, George H. Williams, spoke for legal education; the Secretary of the Smithsonian Institution, Professor Joseph Henry, for science; Charles Astor Bristed, for the classics; William Beach Lawrence, for jurisprudence; and the French Minister, the Marquis de Noailles, for "the Communion of Scholars in the Republic of Letters."[10]

President Welling had now established a legal basis for the presidency which gave him the setup he desired and which clearly reflected a resolve to protect against the situation that had harassed his predecessor at the end of his administration.

The University at once made an effort, through the appointment of an agent, to collect the $100,000 toward the $250,000 endowment fund by January 1, 1875, to secure the Corcoran gift of Trinidad. Although its efforts yielded $103,381 in cash and pledges, less than the required $100,000 was in cash. Welling acknowledged that technically the gift had been forfeited, but was correct in expressing the view that so interested was Mr. Corcoran that he would accept what had been done "as an earnest of our ultimate triumph." Mr. Corcoran made a further subscription of $4,000, payable when the $100,000 cash was in hand, and paid $2,000 on account. The full sum not being realized, the remaining $2,000 was not paid. Mr. Corcoran, however, deeded Trinidad over to the University as part of the endowment. It was sold for $85,000, plus $20,000 to quiet some outstanding claims. With the donor's acquiescence, $10,000 of this sum was "borrowed temporarily" to pay for the equipment of the new Corcoran Scientific School. In 1886, Mr. Corcoran made a further gift of $25,000 to the Corcoran Fund, as the new endowment was designated.[11]

The time selected by President Welling and the Corporation for making a determined effort to raise a real endowment was a propitious one. On June 24, 1873, the treasurer had reported that the institution was free from debt, $33,000 on that account having been paid during the two preceding years. This was the time to go ahead.[12]

Just as the old College was expanding into the new University, the greatest of its teachers passed from the active scene. At the end of 1873, Professor William Ruggles asked to be relieved of the duties of his chair and they were temporarily assumed by President Welling. Appointed a tutor in 1822, Ruggles had been a member of the faculty for more than a half-century and had served three times as acting president.[13] Four years after his retirement he died on September 10, 1877, at Schooley's Mountain, New Jersey.[14]

On April 25, 1873, by the authority of the Executive Committee of the Board of Trustees, a statement called "Plan of the Columbian University" was issued, with the request that all persons interested in the enterprise communicate with President Welling or any member of the Executive Committee. This was probably the first draft of Welling's "University Idea."

The first project mentioned in the document was the foundation of a School of Science bearing Corcoran's name, and a "Polytechnic School." Great emphasis was placed on the availability for use in scientific education of the personnel and the apparatus of the many government establishments here. "In so far as these national establishments may be utilized for educational purposes, they constitute *a vast permanent endowment*, worth many millions of dollars, but costing nothing in the use that is thus made of them." The School of Science was to furnish instruction in these branches:

1. A course in mathematics, mechanics, and astronomy;
2. A course in physics;
3. A course in chemistry and metallurgy;
4. A course in natural history (zoology and botany);
5. A course in physical geography, meteorology, geology and paleontology;
6. A course in ethnology, archeology, and anthropology.

It was hoped that this School of Science would have available, through Mr. Corcoran's benevolence, an endowment of $200,000 yielding "at the lowest" $12,000 annually. This sum plus the revenue from tuition fees would not be adequate for the establishment of such a school in any city other than Washington. The equipment available from government laboratories and the wealth of scientific learning represented by government personnel from which teachers could be drawn would make such a school possible there.

The Polytechnic School would furnish special practical instruction in at least the following:

1. A course in surveying;
2. A course in civil engineering proper, or the science of construction;
3. A course in dynamical engineering or the science of machinery;
4. A course in agricultural chemistry.

To these would be added, as the crowning adornment of the University, a School of the Fine Arts, embracing architecture, sculpture, and painting. The resources of the Corcoran Gallery of the Fine Arts would be available for use in the same way that government establishments would be utilized in scientific instruction. The work of each of these schools would not be tightly compartmentalized, but in every way possible each was to be auxiliary to the other. The same would apply to the relations between the recommended new schools and the College. If the recommendations were carried out, the University would consist of the following "distinct but confederated departments: the Preparatory School, the College proper, the Scientific School, the Polytechnic School, the Medical School, the Law School, and the School of Fine Arts."[15]

When the administration came to implementing these recommendations, consideration was given first to the projected Scientific School. Attention to scientific instruction was by no means a new concern of the institution. Among the first faculty inducted into office on January 9, 1822, had been Josiah Meigs, Professor of Experimental Philosophy; and two members of the Medical faculty who were given appointments in the College before medical instruction began, Dr. Thomas Sewall, Professor of Anatomy and Physiology, and Dr. James M. Staughton, Professor of Chemistry and Geology. At the same time that he was purchasing a library in Europe, Professor Staughton was acquiring "philosophical apparatus," and in 1823 he sent back on the *Electra* instruments valued in excess of 400 pounds.

The original requirements for the first degree in arts had included considerable study of mathematics in the first two years: algebra, logarithms, geometry, trigonometry, conic sections, and the *Elements* of Euclid, with such practical courses as mensuration, surveying, and navigation. The junior year called for "natural philosophy," astronomy, chemistry, and fluxions, and in the senior year there was more natural philosophy.

In 1853, the faculty had formally recommended to the Board, through President Bacon, that a scientific course distinct from the classical one be set up. The sciences were to be put in a regular department, instruction in which, with English and mathematical studies, would form the backbone of a three-year course leading to a special degree. Instruction in the natural sciences was to be extended, and some attention was to be given to engineering. With this expansion in mind, a committee undertook a survey of the College's existing facilities. They found the library almost completely wanting in treatises in all branches of science, and in need of additional space. A newly received gift was appropriated for the improvement of the library. The committee reported the scientific apparatus as of superior quality and in good shape, but they felt that further provision must be made for chemistry, geology, and botany. At Commencement in 1853, the honorary degree of Doctor of Laws was conferred upon Matthew Fontaine Maury, the great oceanographer. In July, 1853, the faculty was authorized to set up the schedule of instruction for a three-year scientific course leading to the degree of Bachelor of Philosophy. Five members of the class of 1854 were graduated and received the new degree. The degree of Bachelor of Philosophy was abolished in 1872 and the degrees of Bachelor of Science and Bachelor of Letters (B.L.) were substituted for it.[16] At the time of this change in degree designation, discussion of a new scientific school was already under way.

A committee of five was appointed "to consider the best practical course of instruction [in the proposed Scientific School], to correspond with eminent teachers and lecturers, and to report to the Corporation, as soon as possible, the details of such a course, and the probable expenses of each department. That said committee also report upon the expediency of making the compensation of each professor depend, in part at least, upon the number of his pupils; and also if some of the advantages of such a course cannot be made available to women." President Welling was chairman of the committee; among its members was the eminent scientist, John Wesley Powell.

The committee brought in an elaborate report. In order that such a school may fulfill its theory and mission in all directions, it was recommended that instruction be offered in the following departments: English, modern languages, mathematics, physics, chemistry, metallurgy, civil, mining, mechanical, and topographical engineering, geology, biology, drawing and architecture, and philosophy, including pedagogy. Not all of these departments would be started at once, but as demand indicated and the straitened resources of the University permitted. Certificates of proficiency would be given if only a partial course of study was taken. For completion of the studies in any department, a corresponding degree, such as Civil Engineer or Mining Engineer, would be granted; for completion of studies in a number of confederated departments, proper degrees such as Bachelor of Science and Doctor of Philosophy would be granted. Although outside of the areas referred to the committee, "as a fitting complement to the foregoing scheme of studies" the future establishment of a School of Political Science was recommended, with a course of studies running at least through two years and leading to the degree of Doctor of Philosophy.

It was proposed that the question of the admission of women should "not be decided by a hard and fast line, but that the faculty of each school should make the determination with the approval of the Corporation." This was felt desirable because the faculties of the Scientific School, the Medical School, and the Law School depended on the income of those schools for their salaries. The College was excluded from this general procedure; the decision as to the admission of women remained in the hands of the Corporation, to be made "in its own wisdom."

As to the salaries in the Scientific, Law, and Medical Schools, the committee made no further suggestions. These schools were "administrated by night," and in the main the teaching was done by instructors gainfully employed during the day. With the president and the College faculty, the situation was different. All their working hours had to be given to the College. If any one of the other units did not produce revenue adequate for its maintenance or if no general fund could be raised to make up the deficit necessary to pay professors or officers who gave their whole time to their duties, "it would only remain for the Corporation to suspend such department, School, or College."

To provide furniture, fixtures, apparatus, and supplies for the conduct of a scientific school, an aggregate expenditure of $25,000 was roughly estimated. Since the Scientific School would use at night the same quarters the College used during the day, no additional quarters would be required. In drawing plans for a new University building, it was earnestly recommended that provision be made for an assembly hall, holding five or six hundred, that could serve as a meeting place for scientific societies and as a hall for popular lectures. The committee asked for authorization to enter into discussion with eminent men of science to see how many would be willing to join in the enterprise for a contingent share in the fees of the school.[17]

When the new University building on the southeast corner of Fifteenth and H Streets was completed, there was issued a *Prospectus of the Corcoran School of Science and the Arts of the Columbian University, Washington, D.C.* (Washington, 1884), following closely the lines of the recommendations of 1881 and announcing that the exercises of the school would open on the first Wednesday in October, 1884. The dean was Edward T. Fristoe, Professor of Chemistry, and the faculty included such famous scientists as Simon Newcomb (astronomy), Lester Frank Ward (botany), Theodore N. Gill (zoology), Otis T. Mason (anthropology), and Cleveland Abbe (meteorology). The *Prospectus* announced that for the accommodation of employed students, the exercises of the school would be held in the evening, between six and ten o'clock. The inaugural address was given by John W. Powell on October 1, 1884. It was an eloquent speech, surveying the whole field of human culture as evidence of the humanistic significance of science.[18]

Late in 1886, the Medical faculty made an earnest appeal to the Trustees for an addition to the Medical School building, offering to pay a substantial amount of the carrying charge on the loan that would have to be made. Agreeing to pay 5 per cent interest and 2½ per cent into a sinking fund, the faculty was authorized to proceed with the planning of an addition on a lot to the rear, given by Mr. Corcoran, at a cost not to exceed $10,000. At the next annual meeting of the Corporation, a Department of Dental Surgery, in connection with the Medical School, was authorized. In their communication to the Corporation, the Medical faculty expressed a desire for a closer connection with the governing body of the University than in the past. The old surplus-sharing arrangement for salary was no longer working advantageously. During the past sixteen years the faculty had averaged less than $300 per year for each professor, although in 1885-1886 the share of each had been $600.[19]

In spite of negligible salaries, the Medical faculty, in addition to the $10,000 borrowed for the enlargement of the building, paid out of their own funds in excess of $2,000 for fitting the interior, providing gas fixtures, paying the architect's fee, and obtaining apparatus for the new Dental School.[20]

President Welling had always been greatly interested in the establishment of a School of Politics and Jurisprudence. Committees appointed to consider the project had been discouraged by the low state of the University's finances. But President Welling did not give up. The appointment to the Law faculty of Justice John M. Harlan, Associate Justice of the Supreme Court of the United States, as lecturer on constitutional law in 1889, and of his colleague Justice David J. Brewer as lecturer on the law of corporations in 1890, encouraged the president, no doubt, in believing that distinguished and learned public men could be enlisted to teach in a School of Comparative Jurisprudence.

At its annual meeting in 1890, the Corporation decided upon the establishment of a school of jurisprudence and political and social science. In the fall of 1892, at a special meeting of the Board called at the president's request, plans were discussed for "a still higher graduate school for the comprehensive and scientific study of the Comparative Jurisprudence of the world" to be established as an integral part of the University and to be begun in 1893-1894. In accordance with the Board's instruction, the president had gone to Europe the preceding summer to consult with leading authorities. He had conferred with various British scholars, including Sir Frederick Pollock, and had arranged conferences with some of the outstanding scholars of the Continent, among them Professor Paul Vinogradoff, when the news of the untimely death of Professor Edward T. Fristoe, Dean of the Scientific Faculty, called him back to the University. Dr. Welling had, however, engaged in a voluminous correspondence with scholars all over the world and had well-thought-out plans which the Board considered.

Lectures in the School of Comparative Jurisprudence were to be held each day in the morning and afternoon and would be open to college students and to all others who could profit by them. The doctor's degree in philosophy or laws was reserved for those with basic academic training, a reading knowledge of French and German, and at least two years of attendance at the lectures of the school. The studies of the first year could be taken in connection with the School of Practice, whose one-year course led to the master's degree in law. In this way, the requirements for the bachelor's and master's degrees in law and the doctorate could be met in a minimum of four years.

The president, Professor H. E. Davis, and the Trustees' Committee on the Law School were designated as a group to raise funds or take such other steps as were necessary. If a surplus for the year 1893 permitted, $3,000 of this amount was to be appropriated for an extension of the work of the Law School in the direction of a School of Comparative Jurisprudence.[21]

Meanwhile, modest progress was being made by the Scientific School. Due largely to the ingenuity of the instructor, a new physics laboratory was equipped and made available. A mechanical engineering laboratory was authorized, to be paid for by contributions from the students, matched by personal contributions from members of the Board. The school was granted permission to set up a one-year graduate course for the Master of Science degree, and a three-year graduate course for the doctorate, a reading knowledge of French and German being required. The Graduate School was authorized to give the professional degrees in engineering and the Ph.D. degree in 1892. Under an earlier Board action, two Ph.D. degrees in course had been awarded in 1888 to members of the faculty, Andrew P. Montague and James Howard Gore, who had "pursued graduate studies far in excess of the requirements prescribed for the degree."[22]

The appointment of Charles Edward Munroe, the eminent chief chemist of the Navy, as Professor of Chemistry in the College and the Scientific School to succeed Professor Fristoe brought to the University an outstanding scholar whose influence was felt immediately. The chemical laboratories were completely renovated and the work of the department fully reorganized.[23] Professor Munroe's influence was equally apparent in the establishment and development of the School of Graduate Studies.

Proceeding with the expansion of the University, President Welling, on March 14, 1893, reported to the Trustees in accordance with a resolution adopted at the previous annual meeting of the Corporation concerning graduate study. That resolution had directed the faculties of the College, the Medical School, and the Corcoran Scientific School "to devise schemes of graduate studies in their respective departments, and to report the same to the Board of Trustees during the coming scholastic year." The statement of the president, embodying the conclusions of the various faculties, was concerned primarily with the College and the Corcoran Scientific School. The status of the Law School had been previously determined by the Corporation; the Medical School lacked the proper laboratories for advanced scientific investigation.

As to the problem of a staff, Welling noted the difficulty in asking distinguished scholars to take posts on a graduate staff without the offer of adequate compensation. There had, however, been ready response to the University's request and the president was able to recommend for addition to the faculty a slate of more than twenty, including several outstanding names: General A. W. Greely, the explorer (geography); Asaph Hall (higher mathematics); Harvey W. Wiley of Pure Food fame (chemistry); Cyrus Adler (Oriental history); and Frank W. Clarke (chemistry). A group consisting of President Welling, Dean Charles E. Munroe, and eleven senior professors was set up as "The Board of Directors of Graduate Studies" to exercise the general functions of a faculty.

The candidate for a master's degree had to hold a bachelor's degree from a reputable institution, spend at least a year in advanced study, pass a satisfactory examination, and present an acceptable thesis. A student holding a B.S. in Engineering could become a candidate for the degree of C.E. or E.E.; and upon the completion of a year in the advanced study of engineering, the passing of an examination, and the presentation of a satisfactory thesis, he could receive the degree.

The candidate for the degree of Ph.D. had to hold a master's degree in science or arts or the equivalent, and qualify in French and German. Three topics for advanced study were to be selected: one major subject and two collateral subjects in which the student had to pass a satisfactory examination. Two years of study were required. A thesis embodying the results of research in the major field must be presented, printed, and successfully defended before a board of experts.

Tuition fees were to be distributed and apportioned as in the Scientific School. Matriculation fees for graduate students were to constitute a fund for the payment of clerks.[24]

President Welling looked upon the School of Graduate Studies with special pride. To him it was the capstone of the educational structure he had sketched when he came to the presidency and had worked toward unceasingly. In speaking to the Corporation at its annual meeting in 1893, he recalled that this last important act of his administration brought to fruition an idea that was almost as old as the College itself. It was, he said, "only just to say that the seminal idea of such a school for the propagation of advanced learning dates almost from the origin of the institution. As early as the year 1822, Luther Rice, who deserves to be held in lasting memory as the 'Founder of Columbian College,' had projected an 'annex' to the College to be called the 'Philosophical Department' in which special provision should be made for the cultivation of 'advanced studies' beyond the limits of the ordinary college curriculum." He pointed out that the idea had been formally approved in 1823 when a circular letter was sent to all officers in the armed forces asking assistance in collecting illustrative materials and specimens for instruction. Unfortunately the financial embarrassment of 1827 postponed the project. It had now been realized. A public reception of the Graduate Faculty on May 25, 1893, was attended by fifteen hundred guests. In the following fall, President Welling, although then in uncertain health, formally inaugurated the school.[25]

These many changes in educational organization and in the expansion of the institution's offerings represented the first of the major achievements of President Welling. It is perhaps necessary to point out that along with them went a definite change in the character of the student body. The Preparatory School and Columbian College remained as they had been, giving their full time to education. Every one of the other departments was designed by the arrangement of its schedule of instruction to make its offerings available, and in some cases primarily available, to those who had regular employment and pursued courses in the late afternoon and evening.

The second of the major accomplishments of the Welling administration was to move from College Hill and to group all the departments of the University in the heart of the city. As has been said, there had been many serious discussions, extending over decades, before College Hill was abandoned. Financial need invariably precipitated these discussions. As early as 1855, a committee of the Board had been appointed to consider the expediency of subdividing and selling a portion of the College grounds. No action was taken. Four years later even more serious consideration was given to selling off the southern portion of the grounds without subdivision. Again, no action was taken. During the War the Quartermaster General raised the question of the purchase of College Hill by the government. President Samson saw some virtue in the proposal but did not encourage it. In 1865, however, he had prepared a plat of the south grounds, looking toward the sale of this major parcel. A plan for leasing individual plots was presented.

The War had given the College a brief period of relative freedom from financial worry. The College's expenses had been cut to the bone and the rental paid by the government yielded a steady income. As soon as the War was over and the College began to resume its full activities, deficits again began to accumulate. By herculean effort the institution was able to free itself from debt in 1873. Unfortunately, this was merely a repetition of past history in which deficits had been the rule. By extreme effort they would be paid off and there would be a breathing spell. The effort, however, was never successful in building up a reserve or creating an effective endowment. Deficits would begin to pile up again, and so it went. Time after time proposals were made to sell off unproductive land held by the College. Money was tight in the 1870's and sales at advantageous prices were hard to make.

The Law School during the first decade after its revival had been self-sustaining and generally revenue-producing. However, at a special meeting of the Board in 1875, the president had to report that the first rush of students from the various government offices had ceased and that the competition of two newer law schools was being seriously felt. The Law School was no longer self-sustaining.[26]

In spite of financial difficulty, Welling had lost none of his enthusiasm for his university idea. Washington was no place for a small college. None was needed, and such an institution could be maintained much more cheaply elsewhere. The nation's capital demanded a great university. Welling suggested the advisability of selling College Hill and urged action without delay.[27] In 1878 the Board offered to sell the north grounds to the government for the Naval Observatory at a price of 10 cents per square foot, and expressed a willingness to receive offers for other ground which it had available. The offer was not accepted.[28]

The high confidence which had characterized the announcement in 1873 of the University's intention to establish a School of Science seemed misplaced as, year after year, the plan failed of realization. The problem was not a simple one. Added income was needed. New quarters, conveniently located in the heart of the city, were essential. A committee reporting on the situation toward the close of 1880 spelled out the reason for the delay: failure to realize anticipated funds. The assessed values of Trinidad, unproductive property in the city, and the college grounds plus an estimated value of $50,000 for the buildings on College Hill only totaled about $223,000. A sum much less than this would be realized at a forced sale. Even if a productive piece of property on Third Street, with an estimated value of $17,380, were sold, the total proceeds would fall short of the $200,000 that had been stated as necessary to yield adequate income for the support of the new school. To add to these woes, the current rate of interest had fallen to between 4 and 5 per cent. Postponement was recommended.

President Welling was loath to make this decision. Something, he said, must be done. Taxes were eating up the institution. The University was $10,000 in arrears already, and each year taxes were adding $1,000 more to the expenses—about the amount of the College's yearly deficit. The president's dictum was direct and explicit: "Since we cannot execute what we projected, we must project what we can execute to the extent and compass of our means." Two days later, in a special meeting, the Corporation authorized a loan of $12,000 secured by a mortgage to pay taxes.[29]

An ingenious maneuver, probably not without deeper significance, was executed to relieve the University of part of its tax burden. The Medical School had been financially autonomous, with the faculty members deriving their salaries directly from the student fees. At a special meeting the Board resolved: "That the National Medical School, the Medical Department of the University, is hereby declared to be an integral part of the University system and that until further notice the salary of each of the professors of the school be fixed at one dollar per annum." Citing this resolution, the University requested the Commissioners of the District of Columbia to include the medical property in the general exemption of the University's property used for its educational purposes. Through their secretary, William Tindall, the Commissioners granted tax exemption from the date of the resolution but refused to waive the University's obligation for taxes on the medical property prior to that time.[30]

When the Corporation held its annual meeting in 1881, it heard a dismal report on registration. The College had only 39 students in attendance during the year. The president felt that the requirements for graduation were too severe as compared with those in the older universities; and henceforth, instead of having to get diplomas in all seven schools (i.e., departments), students would be required to get diplomas in only five, with certificates of proficiency in the others, to qualify for the bachelor's degree. To ease the financial situation in the Law School, professors' salaries were fixed at $2,400 for eight months, with an additional $600 or as much as practicable to be paid at the end of the academic year. A basic report by a select committee of five had been prepared and the Corporation adjourned to meet in ten days' time when full attention would be given to this report.[31]

The later meeting was significant. The report was specific. The investigations by the committee disclosed that the income from rents, interest, and dividends alone amounted to $7,084, or about $1,000 above teachers' salaries. Other expenses ran to $6,630 per year. The taxes for six years had amounted to $14,129, or $2,354 per year. Unless reductions were made, the College deficit for the next year would be on the order of $5,000. Law, Medicine, and Preparatory could make their way; the burden was the College. Therefore, a reduction in the number of professors and the elimination of one janitor were immediately called for.

The committee made no attempt to gloss over the situation. Its language was baldly realistic. The cause of the shrinkage in enrollment, it declared, "is doubtless the forlorn condition of rooms and appliances." The walls were not as white as might be. The tables and chairs were very common-looking, many of them fearfully hacked with knives, making the whole appearance "cheerless and repulsive." The chemical apparatus was "old and insignificant" and the geological specimens were in "rough-looking, dirty cases." "Valuable works of art were nearly ruined by their surroundings." The library books, many of them old and worthless, were in the topmost story of the building. "In short, the whole establishment is behind the times and well adapted to disgust students and parents." The advantages of a beautiful location were negated by the distance from the heart of the city, now that the dormitories were no longer used.

Washington, the committee declared, wanted no ordinary college. With theological education as one of its aims when originally established, that function was given up years ago and was well carried on elsewhere. The city was entering a new era. Many young men and women wanted courses in the University at a convenient place and time. It seemed folly to ignore them and go on losing property in the dull and almost useless routine of former years. "We must remodel our course of instruction, adapt it to the wants and surroundings of the city and bring it into the midst of those we would instruct." The principal of the Preparatory School went so far as to say that with a favorable location in the city he could double the student body.

The appointment of a special committee was ordered to consider and report upon "a plan for the entire reconstruction of the Schools of the University so that we may offer to the people of every class the privilege of high education and establish here an Institution that will teach what people will pay for learning."

The economies called for at an earlier meeting were put into effect: salaries were reduced, one professor was not reappointed, and a janitor was discharged. Once again the sale of the College's city property as soon as possible was authorized. As matters for the committee's consideration it was proposed that the property of the Law building on Fifth Street be sold, provided a site for the College and rented quarters for the Law School could be found, or that arrangements be made for a building to house all the schools but the Medical School. Special consideration was to be given to the needs of the College and the Preparatory School.

The die had been cast. The days of College Hill were rapidly coming to a close.[32]

When the Corporation met to hear the committee's report in November, President Welling explained the various alternatives that were available and had been considered. The clear preference of the committee for a site was the southeast corner of Fifteenth and H Streets, a parcel containing 20,200 square feet. Unfortunately the price of $75,000 seemed far beyond the University's means and put this location out of the question. There was a possibility on the north side of H Street, one square east. Using the site of the Medical Building as a nucleus, certain adjacent parcels could be acquired that would form a holding of 10,700 square feet, large enough for a structure to accommodate all departments. The University could sell its unimproved property in the city, assessed at $13,890; the Third Street house, valued at $17,380; the Law building, worth $18,070; and eleven acres in the northern tract of the College land at $4,000 per acre. These sales would have an anticipated yield of something in excess of $93,000, with any deficit being met by the sale of more of the College land. As an alternative the University could put up a building on the Law School site to provide revenue and make up the difference by selling more acreage on College Hill.

The decision was made to select the Medical School site, to acquire the adjacent lots available, and to sell more land. With full confidence, plans and specifications were ordered and on December 3, 1881, the erection of a building to house all departments was authorized.[33]

However, on January 11, 1882, the president of the Corporation added to his already many benefactions the offer of a vacant lot 95 feet by 153 feet 5 inches at Vermont Avenue and Eye Street. The Board immediately stopped the further acquisition of property around the Medical building and voted not to carry through the erection of the proposed structure. A major part of the north grounds of the College property amounting to 16,442 acres was sold to Mrs. Mary D. Biddle of Philadelphia for $49,326, thus putting some cash in the treasury to work with. Unfortunately, on investigation the lot offered by Mr. Corcoran, usually called the Arlington lot, was found too small for the type of building proposed. Clearly the location at Fifteenth and H Streets was the favored one. The ever-generous Mr. Corcoran agreed to bear a burden of $30,000, equal to the value of the Arlington lot, should the institution build on the southeast corner of Fifteenth and H Streets. The Corporation made another decision: A building to house all the departments except the Medical School was to be constructed at the favored site, with the cost limited at the time to $75,000. The erection of a building for the Preparatory School in the area was authorized at a cost not to exceed $18,000. The remaining property on College Hill, amounting to 18 acres, was ordered to be sold as quickly as practicable. This decision held, and for a quarter of a century the activities of the University were centered in midtown on H Street, between Thirteenth and Fifteenth Streets.[34]

The institution was at a great turning point in its history. College Hill was gone. For forty years the College had rested in a truly bucolic setting. Then for the frenzied four years of civil war, it had been a vast military installation. For the next twenty years College Hill had seemed to live on borrowed time. No real doubt existed that the College must be moved into the city. Too pressed by debts to move and too burdened with taxes to stay, the College spent years in discussing what to do. In its entire history the institution had really had only one operation completely financed in advance. Luther Rice and his colleagues had raised the necessary funds when the land north of the boundary was bought, before there was a charter or a college. But from then on, whatever was done was done by borrowing and individual solicitation. Congress did donate $25,000 worth of city lots, and in the early days there were a few generous donors like John Withers, and to a lesser degree John Quincy Adams and others. Generous as they were, their benefactions could hardly be described as princely. What they contributed did not go in full measure to a supporting endowment but was usually eaten up by annual deficits and modest expenditures on the physical plant. When what had been farmland became suburban property and then was subdivided into city lots, "the lot" that Rice and his confreres had bought yielded the funds which helped make the midtown location possible.

The change in site was no more radical than the change in student body. The early College had drawn boarders from all parts of the eastern seaboard. The steady growth of colleges in the northern states and, with the approach of the War, the slavery question had drawn off students from the North and made the student body predominantly southern. The rapid development of Richmond College, particularly, cost the College much of its patronage by Virginia Baptists, long a mainstay. The War nearly limited the student body to the District of Columbia. After the War, the South was impoverished and hardly prepared to send students to Columbian. An effort was made by electing Trustees, and later Overseers, from Maryland to develop in that state the type of patronage that Virginia had furnished before the War. This effort was less than fully successful and the College found its dormitories unused and its faltering enrollment made up largely of students from the District.

The outreach of the institution was then extended in an unexpected fashion. The great expansion of the civil service during and following the War brought to Washington many young men who were interested in taking courses for professional training or personal enrichment that were available after their working hours. The tremendous response from this group in the early years of the Law School gave added emphasis to the opportunity for extending the services of the institution. When President Welling formulated plans for a scientific school, he had clearly in mind the demand which existed for instruction after working hours. As the discussion for the removal from College Hill to the city went on, more and more thought was given to this potential source of a vast body of students, drawn from all over the country, resident here temporarily and anxious to learn while they earned. The best way to cultivate this patronage was to offer the courses at a convenient place at convenient hours. The poverty of the College made it eager for students. Circumstances were most favorable for educational services and financial profit to go hand in hand. Idealism and solvency would be equally served by shaping the University's offerings so that, as the committee in charge of the site frankly asserted, the institution would teach what people would pay for learning. With this policy in force, what had started as a traditional college took on the full mission of an urban university.

Immediate steps were taken to implement the Corporation's decision to relocate. There had been only 37 students in the College and 64 in the Preparatory School during 1881-1882. It was ordered that operations be conducted in the city the following year when the College would utilize a building on the lot at the corner of Fifteenth and H Streets until spring. By that time it was hoped that the Medical School would be able to accommodate the College. It was planned to break ground for the new University building early in the spring. The treasurer's report for the year shows that the property at Fifteenth and H Streets had been bought for the very reasonable price of $60,000, and that the ground for the Preparatory School west of the Medical property had been acquired for $2,565.87 cash, subject to a deed of trust for $4,434.13 held by the Louise Home.[35] When the academic year 1882-1883 opened, the College was in the old building at Fifteenth and H Streets. It was ready to move to the Medical School as soon as building plans required the clearing of the new site. There had been some delays in the construction of the new Preparatory School whose 55 students were still at College Hill, but by December the new building would be ready for occupancy. The total cost of building and equipping the Preparatory School was $27,039.[36]

In December, 1882, Welling reported that the University was enjoying "a good measure of prosperity." Registration was up: Preparatory 65, College 40, Medicine 69, Law 165; a total of 339. The very gratifying increase in registration in the Medical School, the president explained, was "mainly due to the large number of government employees drawn to the city by the clerical work of the Pension Bureau and other departments of government." The same factor was eventually to help all the branches of the University.[37]

Great care was taken in planning the new University building. Advice was sought and obtained from Princeton and Johns Hopkins University and their suggestions were embodied in the plans. Of all those submitted, the plans of William M. Poindexter were looked upon with most favor, although those submitted by Joseph C. Hornblower had many desirable features which the Board wished embodied in the final drawings. Poindexter estimated the cost at $71,300, or $75,300 if extra room were added. The Poindexter plan was accepted, but, on the recommendation of the Johns Hopkins authorities, provision was made for putting all the laboratories in a separate building or annex.[38]

For easy identification, the property at College Hill had been divided into three major parts: the south plot; the College grounds, the center part where the buildings were located; and the north plot. A small area north of Columbia Road was devoted to the cemetery. Before the cemetery area was sold, the bodies interred there were removed. President Welling reported that precise locations and names were unknown because the headstones, never having been replaced, were all mislaid. Included among those buried in the cemetery was John Withers, the most generous of the College's early benefactors. President Welling was authorized to have all of the bodies removed to Oak Hill Cemetery and to have a suitable monument erected to John Withers.[39]

The south plot had been subdivided by B. O. Carpenter into building lots which were leased and sold. The north plot was sold to Mrs. Mary D. Biddle for $49,326, and the middle plot of 596,938 square feet to General William M. Dunn in behalf of his wife, Elizabeth Lanier Dunn, for $87,500, with the building materials and contents reserved and the right of occupancy of the professors' houses permitted until June 30, 1883.[40] The old furniture of the College, described in such drab terms by the Trustees' Committee, was auctioned off by Duncanson Brothers for the colossal sum of $83.98. The total yield from the sale of the entire property in the middle plot with its improvements amounted to $89,275.[41]

The last piece of property belonging to the University on College Hill, the west half of lot 42 in the South Grounds (on Chapin Street, west of Fourteenth Street), was sold to Mrs. Mary D. Biddle for 30 cents a square foot in 1883.[42]

The requiem for the old College home was sung by the Board of Trustees in its annual report to the Corporation on June 18, 1883:

It would be eminently seemly for us to unite with you in dropping some natural tears over the demolition and disappearance of the old College building on College Hill, if amid the urgent calls of the living present and the quickening inspirations of the nascent future, we were not rather called to forget the things that are behind and to reach forth to the things that are before us. But while we are in the midst of putting up a new building, to be erected in largest part from the proceeds of the lot of ground purchased in the year 1819 by the Founders of the Columbian College, we may most properly confess our obligations to the good men who in their day and generation were enabled to "build better than they knew," because they labored in faith and hope. Other men labored, and we are entering into their labors. For the actual brick and mortar which composed the old College building there is no need to make lamentations, now that it has disappeared from the face of the earth. As a *College* building it represented a style of architecture which has become obsolete, while its appearance of dilapidation and decay, on the leading thoroughfare of our city, was a standing advertisement to the discredit of the Corporation. Even the members of the Corporation itself refused to subject their sons to the hardships and mortifications of such a residence and regretfully sent their children, of late years, to other and more prosperous institutions.[43]

There was not as much nostalgia as might have been expected in the Board's statement. It seemed to reflect the anguish of hopes frustrated in the past along with a defensive attitude to silence any criticism. It is not inconceivable that its tone was affected by startling information that the Corporation had recently received. The College grounds which had been sold to Mrs. William M. Dunn for $87,500 had been sold by her three weeks later to William C. Hill for $142,026—a profit of more than $54,000.[44]

After hearing the Board's report, the meeting of the Corporation was adjourned and the members proceeded to the site of the new University building to lay the cornerstone. The demolition of the old structure on the site which had served as the temporary home of the College was begun on September 19, 1882. The contract for construction was awarded to William C. Morrison, whose bid was $67,839, well within the limit set by the Corporation.[45]

The new University building was occupied by the College, the Law School, and the newly established Scientific School in September, 1884. The structure was four stories high with a frontage of 121 feet on Fifteenth Street and 64½ feet on H Street, with an annex extending back on the south line 156 feet. The façades were of pressed and molded bricks with terra cotta ornamentations, all especially designed. Ascent to the main floor was by steps 12 feet wide and to the floor above by an ornate staircase 7 feet wide. The main floor contained the Law Lecture Hall 45 by 60 feet with a seating capacity of five hundred persons, the Museum, the University Library, the Law Library, the president's office, the Reception Room, and one lecture room. The upper stories contained lecture rooms, professors' studies, the Chemistry Lecture Hall, the Enosinian Society Hall, and other rooms. In the basement, only a foot below the pavement level, were several lecture rooms, the Assay Department, and service and storage rooms. The pavilion surmounting the building was reserved for astronomy or graphics. The chemical laboratories were in the annex on the south line of the lot, insulated from the main building by a heavy brick wall. Brick partitions and iron beams made the building fire-proof. The building was steam heated and had an elaborate system of ventilation reaching every room.[46] The total expense for building and equipping the new University building was $94,416.84.[47] Because of delays in construction, the College shared the Preparatory School's building during the year 1883-1884, and the opening of the 1884-1885 academic year was postponed until September 15 to allow time for the completion of the structure.[48]

The coming of a new age is graphically illustrated by the fact that on October 21, 1891, the Board authorized the installation of electric lights on the whole first floor of the University building, which had then been in use for seven years, and the treasurer was authorized to have a telephone put in on July 27, 1892. But the most significant evidence of a new age was the invasion of the University's academic halls by women. Toward the end of Dr. Samson's administration Mrs. Maria M. Carter had offered a gift of $5,000 to endow a scholarship for a woman student. In the early days of the Welling administration this gift was courteously refused until some plan for the education of women could be fixed upon.

That the question had been a matter of some public attention is evident from a report of the opening exercises of the Law School on October 13, 1869, in the columns of the Washington *Morning News* on the following day:

The noticeable feature of the evening however, to the community at least, was the presence in the school of the irrepressible Mrs. Lockwood, of Union League Hall–women's rights discussion notoriety. It is understood that she is anxious to study for the bar, and will endeavor to be admitted to the school. It was noticed that the idea of female students met with approbation from many of the sterner sex, who are doubtless contemplating what pleasures they will have in going through the mazes of legal disquisitions in the company of the fair and lovely characters whose presence in the schoolroom will be so comforting. . . . By all means let the ladies initiate themselves as students of law. When they get admitted to the bar, and come to be members of legislatures and members of Congress, etc., we will have less spouting in the halls of legislation, and a greater regard to honesty in public matters. The "rings" will then, perhaps, have to give way to a better condition of things, and the millennium be nearer than most people suppose.

The Law faculty, however, had a different view.

The report of the committee of five, authorized by the Corporation on June 18, 1881, suggested that the question of admitting women be referred to each of the faculties of the several schools for recommendations to the Corporation, the College alone excepted, admission there being reserved for the decision of the Corporation "on its own wisdom." This report was accepted in 1883, and at the annual meeting of the Corporation the following year the president presented the results of his consultation with each of the faculties. The Law faculty declared that "the admission of women into the Law School was not required by any public want. In the whole history of the institution only one woman has applied for admission and her wants were amply supplied by the Law School of the Howard University in this city." The Medical faculty said that because of inadequate space it would be a physical impossibility. With added accommodations, the admission of women would probably be favored on certain conditions, not yet particularized, "for that woman has a mission in the medical service of the future, can hardly admit of question." The faculty of the College believed that the real proportions of demand should "be ascertained by offering opportunity of a monthly examination in college studies to all such as shall be found capable and willing to pursue them, and if as a result of such tentative proceeding, it shall be found that the want is greater than can be supplied in this way, that the Corporation should throw open the doors of the College without restriction on the ground of sex." In addition it was generally felt that the Corcoran Scientific School being open to women, it was not necessary to arrange for female education under the auspices of the College.

The question, however, was not to be allowed to rest. In a letter of December 10, 1884, four women—Ellen W. Cathcart, Sarah S. Scull, Alice J. White, and Clara Bliss Hinds—asked to "be allowed to enter their names as applicants for tickets to the course of Lectures delivered before the Medical students of Columbian University." On the following day this letter, with one signed by the dean and all the full professors, was sent to the Board, requesting authority to admit the four women on the same footing as men were admitted. The faculty went on to explain:

Since it may appear somewhat wayward on the part of the Faculty to have changed its decision since the last meeting of the Board of Trustees, it may be stated: That the signers of the foregoing petition having, by permission of the Faculty attended the lectures this winter (but without matriculation or other official recognition) and having found that the inconvenience from want of proper retiring rooms (which the Faculty had thought would be an obstacle to their attendance) is not in reality an insuperable difficulty, but one with which they (the ladies) are quite willing to put up, the objection on the part of the Faculty to the admission of female students is withdrawn. So far the conduct of the male students toward the female ones has been uniformly polite as stated by the ladies themselves, and no objection on the part of the male pupils has been made to the admission of females.

The Board granted the authority.[49] Clara Bliss Hinds, class of 1887, was the first woman who received the degree of Doctor of Medicine from the University. A year later the Board issued its mandamus for the conferring of the degree of Baccalaurea (sic) of Science on the first two women graduates of the Scientific School, Elizabeth Preston Brown and Louise Connolly.[50]

In the College, coeducation began, albeit hesitantly, with an action taken by the faculty on September 24, 1888: "Voted that Miss Mabel Nelson Thurston might enter the College course by paying the matriculation fee and standing examinations once a month with each of the members of the faculty." In the following January the College faculty voted to permit Miss Thurston to have her examinations at her home. In September, 1890, the Board of Trustees noted that the preceding year it had accepted four women as nonpaying students and extended the same privilege for 1890-1891. Miss Thurston having blazed the trail, the Board accepted coeducation in the College as a *fait accompli*, as seen in the rules and regulations adopted by the Corporation on June 16, 1890:

2. That no student under twenty-one years of age shall be admitted to Columbian College unless he or she shall pursue studies in at least three schools of the College, and shall embrace in his or her selections at least twelve hours of attendance or recitations or lectures per week.

The same set of rules and regulations betrayed a continuing concern about coeducation. The faculties of the College and the Scientific School were to be visited by the appropriate committees of Trustees to receive their advice and consultation in matters of discipline "and in particular to consider what additional rules, if any, may need to be established in view of the coeducation of young men and young women in the same classes and in the precincts of the same building."[51]

In 1892, the Medical faculty asked that coeducation be ended after seven years of trial. All proposals to solve the problem on the basis of a separation of the sexes in all instruction and operations involving "what the faculty deem a strain on modesty" seemed impracticable. They would involve either dual instruction or the establishment of a women's medical school, neither of them feasible from a financial point of view.

The first of Welling's achievements was his reorganization and expansion of the institution's educational program. The second was his regrouping of all of the University's activities in the heart of the city. The third was the establishment of an endowment fund. Each of these was, of course, closely related to the others and much has already been said with reference to the third of Welling's major objectives.

The institution had never had any substantial endowment. In the main, its fund-raising energy had apparently been exhausted in making up annual deficits and providing modest expenditures for property maintenance. In 1832 by act of Congress approved July 14 of that year, city lots worth $25,000 were given to Columbian College for the endowment of professorships, but at the institution's request permission was given in 1839 to sell $7,000 worth of the lots to meet outstanding debts. In 1845, the Reverend A. M. Poindexter was appointed agent to raise what was referred to as the $50,000 permanent endowment. Mr. Poindexter's efforts produced $25,413.30 in cash and pledges. The collections on account of this fund amounted to $11,396.60. In 1851, the Reverend W. F. Broaddus was appointed agent to raise a $40,000 endowment fund. John Withers offered to give $20,000 as soon as others had given a like sum. The net proceeds of this effort amounted to $14,111.97, railroad bonds valued at $2,000, and a house and lot on Third Street, eventually sold for $14,300. While there were other professorship, scholarship, and prize funds, none of them exceeded $6,000 in value. In the administration of these funds, the Trustees had been quite casual, frequently applying uninvested endowment funds to the payment of current operating deficits.[52]

When President Welling entered upon his duties in 1871, he notified the Board by letter that he did not desire to be charged with the financial administration of the institution. Fortunately, he had by his side an able and generous financier. William Wilson Corcoran had been elected President of the Board of Trustees two years previously, succeeding Amos Kendall. No sooner had Dr. Welling been settled in office than he persuaded the Board to declare its intention to raise a $250,000 endowment. Mr. Corcoran offered a powerful incentive to encourage the prompt raising of the fund. If $100,000 of the total amount sought were raised by January 1, 1875, and if President Welling would pledge himself to remain, he would give the institution the Trinidad tract adjoining the city of Washington. The details of these matters have been discussed earlier in the present chapter. They are mentioned here to show how President Welling was immediately involved in matters financial. Although failing to meet in full the financial objectives set from time to time, the president continued unabatedly to labor for a real endowment fund during all of his lengthy administration. His association with Mr. Corcoran brought him help in two ways. The University received gifts of a size far exceeding anything it had known before, and the president had a strong ally in his insistence upon better financial administration. Mr. Corcoran's death on February 24, 1888, was a serious personal loss to Dr. Welling, to the University, and to the District.

The statement announcing his death to the Corporation suggests the extent of the University's indebtedness to William Wilson Corcoran:

It is not too much to say that the Columbian University in its present reconstitution, in its new habitation, and in the enlarged scope of its operations is essentially his creation. He gave to us our Medical Building and the ground on which its extension has just been erected; he laid the foundation of the only permanent endowment which the University has ever had, for in 1873 the University not only had no endowment but was $30,000 in debt and had spent in current operation every dollar of its invested funds; he gave to us $30,000 for the erection of the beautiful building in which we are today assembled, and only two years ago at the annual meeting of that date, he added the munificent gift of $25,000 to our permanent endowment and presented a costly work of art for the adornment of the general hall of the Preparatory School.[53]

The president of the University, Dr. Welling, was elected to succeed Mr. Corcoran as president of the Corporation. President Welling must have felt singularly alone as he stepped into the place of the University's elder statesman and greatest benefactor. He had formulated at the beginning of his term of office a University plan for the expansion and development of the institution's educational organization. Before he laid down the burdens of his office he had seen the capstone placed on his organizational structure. True, there was much yet to be done in its development, but his idea had taken institutional form. It is doubtful if he would have pushed ahead as ambitiously as he did without Mr. Corcoran's counsel and financial support. All that Mr. Corcoran had hoped for had not been realized. The funding he provided did not prove as adequate as he had hoped; but, instead of practically nothing at all, the treasurer's report the year of his death showed: invested funds for scholarships, $24,875; the Corcoran Endowment Fund, $170,429.60; miscellaneous, $4,700—a total just over $200,000.[54]

The educational plan as laid out would have required continued benefactions on the order of Mr. Corcoran's for its conservative development and financial support. There was no W. W. Corcoran in sight. Without delay the president brought to the attention of the Corporation the formation in Washington on May 17, 1888, of the American Baptist Education Society. As a representative of the interests of the University, Dr. Welling was instructed to attend the next meeting of the society in May, 1889, in Boston, to present the claims of the University. He wrote a 32-page pamphlet entitled *The Columbian University: Notes on Its Relations to the City of Washington Considered as the Seat of a National Baptist University* (Washington, 1889).

In this pamphlet, President Welling, in appealing for "one or two or three millions of dollars . . . which would suffice to confirm the Columbian University in the undisputed possession of the educational opportunities which it is now powerless to utilize," dwelt with great emphasis and detail on his standard argument: that the modest sum he mentioned could, with what the government offered here, command more than could fifteen or twenty millions invested elsewhere. "If," he wrote, "there be any who are tempted to say that the Baptist denomination of the United States has no need for such a seat of highest learning, either for its own sake or for the sake of Christian civilization and culture in our land, I cannot here attempt a formal argument against that thesis. No such argument should be necessary in the face of facts full of admonition to the Christian scholar."

The president was encouraged by what he heard and in June, 1889, he told the Board of greatly widened interest in the University on the part of "men of the clearest light and foremost understanding in the whole Baptist denomination." Interest had even extended beyond the Baptists, since it was recognized that the University must be "unsectarian." A committee was expected to bring in recommendations to the Baptist Society's Board of Managers. When this committee's report was acted upon, Dr. Welling thought that the Corporation should meet in special session to consider "our University outlook." At this session the president referred to the fact that the society had raised nearly a million for the founding of a new college in Chicago and that a committee had "minutely inquired into the surroundings of the University problem in Washington and submitted a detailed report." The committee recommended a "junction" between Crozer Theological Seminary at Chester and Columbian University and referred the proposal to the authorities of the two institutions for their opinions. Dr. Welling pointed out that theological education had been a prime consideration of the founders. The Board sent to Crozer a resolution of salutation and willingness to discuss, but the "junction" was never effected. The Board next proceeded to discuss the "enlargement and development of the institution as a National University," with the thought of raising a million dollars. Toward this end, it was recommended that the Board of Managers of the Education Society be petitioned to furnish a modest sum to defray the salary of a financial agent or itself undertake active steps to raise an adequate endowment. A formal commendation to the Baptist denomination of the University's efforts to enlarge the endowment was the extent of the society's contribution. The hope for a Baptist connection which would solve the University's financial problems had not been abandoned. It was merely waiting to rise again.[55]

The last years of President Welling's administration saw the University, in his glowing terms, "lifted on a flood tide of prosperity." This happy appraisal of the situation was based largely on a favorable turn in the size of the student body. An increase in the number of civil servants, particularly through the expansion of the staff of the Pension Office, brought in many who sought professional training, particularly in law, and advanced work in the arts and sciences. When President Welling entered upon his duties in 1871, the total number of registered students was 326. At the end of his service twenty-two years later, the number had grown to 902, and the faculty had more than doubled in size. The president's constant insistence on the availability of government libraries and equipment for the purposes of instruction was given legislative sanction by the Joint Resolution of the Houses of Congress on April 12, 1892, putting the government's libraries and collections in Washington at the disposal of institutions of higher education.

One matter above all others seemed to give Dr. Welling great concern as his tenure neared its end. He recalled that $10,000 had been borrowed from the Corcoran Endowment, never paid back, and "may be forgotten"; that $38,434 of the same fund was used for standing debts incurred for the University and the Preparatory buildings; that $16,000 from the sale of Trinidad applied to the debt violated the spirit and intent of Mr. Corcoran; and that later debts of $18,000 and $4,434 had never been refunded. This practice he heartily and justifiably condemned not only as a matter of bad faith but as a loss of much-needed endowment income.[56]

Dr. Welling's long years in office had not been interrupted by any substantial period of leave for rest and recreation. He requested the grant of a vacation on account of the uncertain state of his health on October

24, 1893. On January 25, 1894, he asked to be relieved of the presidency at the end of the year. Feeling a marked improvement in his physical condition, Dr. Welling found it unnecessary to take the lengthy period of rest that he had requested. But in June, 1894, a lack of strength forced him to ask permission to go at once to his home in New England. In a simple and unaffected style, he thanked his associates for their support and friendship and reiterated his faith in the University.[57] Three months later, on September 4, 1894, he died suddenly at his home in Hartford, Connecticut.

James Clarke Welling (1825–1894) was for forty years intimately connected with the capital city as journalist, educator, Trustee of the Corcoran Gallery of Art, Trustee of the Philosophical Society, member of the Board of Visitors of St. Elizabeth's Hospital, a founder of the National Geographic Society, and Regent of the Smithsonian Institution. As literary editor and associate editor of the *Daily National Intelligencer* his voice was an important factor in shaping opinion during fifteen critical years in our national history. Returning to this country after a sojourn in Europe, he served briefly as clerk of the Court of Claims, president of St. John's College in Annapolis, and professor of rhetoric and English literature at Princeton, leaving his professorship there to become president of Columbian. While an act of Congress changed Columbian from College to University legally, Welling, supported by W. W. Corcoran's generosity, changed it in fact. The University today is substantially as Welling set it up. Whatever it has achieved and whatever measure of greatness it may achieve in the future can be looked upon in large degree as the lengthening shadow of this man.[58]

CHAPTER TWELVE

Reverses
1895-1910

U pon President Welling's resignation, a committee from the Board of Trustees was immediately appointed to select a successor. In the interim, the Reverend Samuel Harrison Greene, D.D., pastor of Calvary Baptist Church, was asked to serve as the executive head of the University. On the recommendation of the committee, the Board of Trustees elected as the new president the Reverend Benaiah L. Whitman to take office September 1, 1895. Dr. Whitman was a graduate of Brown and of Newton Theological Seminary. After serving for two years as pastor of the First Baptist Church of Portland, Maine, he was elected president of Colby College in 1892. Three years later he became the seventh president of Columbian University.[1] His brief administration was but an interlude between the high promise of the Welling era and the frustrations of the Needham administration.

Dr. Whitman was, in a sense, pledged to carry out the Welling plan which involved rounding out the academic organization, as had already been discussed and authorized, and providing new and adequate housing for the University units in the H Street area. Each of these objectives involved major sums of money for its realization, and Whitman had no Corcoran by his side. Efforts to find substantial donors were fruitless. The new president could only turn in the direction in which Welling had turned following Corcoran's death: to the Baptists and their education society. This source yielded nothing. The only alternative, now that the University occupied substantial parcels of downtown real estate, was to mortgage these holdings to the limit. The unfortunate consequences of this policy were soon to be evident.

While the financial picture had darkened, basis for hope in another area was already apparent. The College's real endowment had always been its faculty. In the later days of the Welling period and in the Whitman years, there came to the University the group of men whose personal dedication and teaching ability really made possible the continuance of the College and the maintenance of scholarly standards in spite of financial crisis.

Howard Lincoln Hodgkins, a graduate of the College with high honors, had begun to serve the University in an official connection before he received his degree. While still in college, his great ability led to his appointment as a teacher in the Preparatory School, thus beginning an official relation which lasted for the remainder of his life. Transferred to the College faculty as a professor of mathematics, he was almost immediately placed in offices of administrative responsibility, serving at various times within the first two decades of his career as director of the Summer Session, dean of the Scientific School, and dean of the University. As secretary, he was the one who kept the alumni organization alive and vigorous. The records disclose a wide range of activities that he carried on as the trusted adviser of presidents and Trustees. The frequent resolutions of appreciation that appear in the Trustees' *Minutes* show the high regard in which the young scholar was held.

Charles Edward Munroe, who had succeeded Fristoe, was another of this group of outstanding faculty. He added great prestige to the Department of Chemistry and was particularly responsible for the development of the Corcoran Scientific School and the School of Graduate Studies, both of which he headed as dean.

William Allen Wilbur came to the University as principal of the Preparatory School. When the Preparatory Department was discontinued, he became professor of English; later his title was changed to dean of Columbian College.

Hermann Schoenfeld in Germanic languages and literature, George Neely Henning in French, Charles Sidney Smith in the classics, and Charles Clinton Swisher in history and political science also joined the faculty in this period and spent the remainder of their academic careers at the University. In the sciences, several government specialists became part-time members of the faculty and rendered distinguished service for many years.

These men furnished the continuum as the University emerged, not entirely happily, from the midtown location, fixed its new center in the West End, and began its period of new growth.

In the early part of the Whitman period, many administrative changes were made, largely carrying out earlier recommendations of President Welling. A summer session was authorized, first as a part of the Scientific School and later as an independent unit.[2] Tuition in the College was fixed at $120 per year; in the Academy at $100 per year.[3] It was determined to increase the length of the course for the bachelor's degree in law to three years and for the master's degree to four years beginning October 1, 1896, but this date was postponed.[4] The change in requirements for the bachelor's degree in law was finally made effective beginning October 1, 1897.[5]

The master's degree in law was provided for in the ordinances adopted for the School of Comparative Jurisprudence and Diplomacy. This school was to offer instruction in interstate commerce law; political history and science; Roman law; comparative constitutional law; public international law; conflict of laws; history of diplomacy and treaties; and political geography and its relation to political history, boards of arbitration and proceedings thereon. Instruction was given in a two-year course. The successful completion of the first year entitled students who already held the bachelor's degree in law to receive the degree of Master of Laws. Those who completed the two years might receive a degree in diplomacy. The expenses of the school—with the exception of heat, light, and fuel —were to be paid from fees. Any amount left over from fees was to be divided among the four professors. A percentage of the amount received through gifts and other sources was to take care of heat, light, and fuel.[6]

These ordinances were prepared and presented by Charles Willis Needham, a member of the Board of Trustees at the time, who seemed to be the president's educational mentor. When the new School of Comparative Jurisprudence and Diplomacy was set up, he became its dean. In accordance with the provisions of the Charter, he then had to resign from the Board of Trustees. He was, however, almost immediately elected its secretary and his influence continued unabated. These ordinances were adopted October 12, 1898.[7]

In order to give the Law School, which had been located in the main University building, additional needed room, Mr. Needham proposed and the Board approved the erection of a building on H Street, immediately east of the main University building, to contain three lecture rooms, two moot court rooms, and offices. The cost was not to exceed $40,000.

The new building was ready for occupancy on January 4, 1899; its cost was approximately $35,000. The building, fronting on H Street, was 61½ feet on each side, three stories high; the top of the cornice was 49 feet above the pavement level. It was heated by steam. The exterior was faced on all four sides with gray Ridgway bricks. The entrance portico had granite columns from Mitford, Massachusetts, with terra cotta capitals. On the ground floor were Jurisprudence Hall, 30 by 50 feet, and the offices for the dean of the School of Comparative Jurisprudence, the dean of the Law School, and the secretary of the Law School. On the second floor were the office of the president, faculty rooms, and two lecture halls each 28.34 by 30 feet in area. On the third floor were two moot court rooms, a reception and smoking room, and a library 30½ by 58 feet.[8]

The formal inauguration of the School of Comparative Jurisprudence and Diplomacy was held on November 15, 1898, in the presence of the President of the United States and his Cabinet, with addresses delivered by Justices Harlan and Brewer of the Supreme Court of the United States; Secretary of the Treasury Gage; Sir Wilfred Laurier, Prime Minister of Canada; and John W. Foster, former Secretary of State.[9]

In addition to this newly organized school, the University acquired another academic unit by accepting the faculty and curriculum of the National Veterinary College, with the understanding that this new unit would not be a charge on the University, but would have a relation similar to that of the Medical and Dental Schools at the time. Two years later, the Veterinary School decided to limit itself to graduate work.[10]

On the site of the old Law building on Fifth Street there was erected the Columbian Building, a modern office structure designed to be rented for law offices. It was considered a part of the Corcoran Endowment because it was built with endowment funds and the rentals produced a sizable increase in the income of the fund. The building was opened December 1, 1898.[11]

After three-quarters of a century it was felt that the Preparatory School had fulfilled its mission, and the discontinuance of Columbian Academy was recommended. At the same time it was proposed that the Preparatory School building be utilized as a hospital, which gave the Medical School a teaching hospital again.[12]

"The Original Thirteen," Columbian College, 1899-1900. Miss Thurston is second from the left in the back row.

The University building, southeast corner of Fifteenth and H Streets, 1884-1910. It originally housed all the departments of the University except the Medical and Preparatory Schools.

The Medical School, north side of H Street between Thirteenth and Fourteenth Streets. *Left to right:* The first building was originally built (1883) as the home of the Preparatory School; the second was built as the University Hospital (1902); and the third, the Medical School, was built on the site of its predecessor (1902). During the period 1887-1921, the Dental School shared the quarters of the Medical School.

The football squad of 1908. The most successful team in the athletic history of the University, they were the South Atlantic Champions, with a season's score of 255, opponents 28.

Fifteenth Street, looking north from Pennsylvania Avenue, shortly after the turn of the century. The University building at the southeast corner of Fifteenth and H Streets is in the right center.

The College of Veterinary Medicine, 2113-2115 Fourteenth Street, 1908-1918.

William Miller Collier, tenth President, 1918-1921. (Library of Congress Collection.)

Charles Herbert Stockton, ninth President, 1910-1918. (Library of Congress Collection.)

Left: Howard Lincoln Hodgkins, President pro tempore, 1921-1923. (University Collection.) *Above:* William Mather Lewis, eleventh President, 1923-1927. (University Collection.)

2023 G Street, 1912-1938. The first building occupied when the University was relocated in the West End. Originally built for St. Rose's Industrial School, renamed Lisner Hall by the University. In the residence to the right of 2023, Henry Adams had rooms in 1869-1870. The residence to the left was the home of the Easby family.

Woodhull House, northeast corner of Twenty-first and G Streets, 1912. Later the office of President Hodgkins.

Porter House, northwest corner of Twenty-first and G Streets, 1912. Later the office of President Collier.

Quigley's Pharmacy, southeast corner of Twenty-first and G Streets, 1912.

Patterson House, southwest corner of Twenty-first and G Streets, 1912. Later the office of President Lewis.

New Masonic Temple, Thirteenth and H Streets, and New York Avenue. Upper two floors were used by the Law School, 1910-1921.

School of Pharmacy, 808 Eye Street, 1906-1919.

In the development of the Medical School and University Hospital during this period, a dominant role was played by Dean Emil Alexander de Schweinitz, the eminent bacteriologist.

Ordinances establishing the University Hospital were adopted "for the purpose of providing clinical instruction for students." The hospital was to be maintained by donations, fees from patients, and $1,000 annually from the receipts of the Medical School.[13] The hospital was opened November 1, 1898.[14]

Dissatisfaction had long been felt with the relation of the Medical and Dental Schools to the University. These schools were now brought within the financial structure of the University. The Medical building, its equipment, furniture, and apparatus were turned over to the University, which became responsible for the unpaid portion of obligations assumed by the faculty from time to time for the improvement of the building and its equipment. The same building and the same faculty would be used, but the University undertook to pay a salary of $1,000 annually to each of the seven members of the Executive Committee of the Medical School, and an additional $500 to the dean for a period of five years. A division of the surplus was provided for. The two major professors in the Dental School were each to be paid one-sixth of the receipts; the remaining four-sixths was to be paid into the general funds of the Medical School.[15]

The inadequacy of the Medical building became speedily apparent. The Medical School faculty proposed that Dr. A. F. A. King, who had been dean from 1879 to 1894, be authorized to undertake the solicitation of funds for a new medical building and hospital. Dr. King's efforts yielded no funds; and after consideration for many months the Board authorized borrowing $360,000 at an interest rate not to exceed 4 per cent, in part to pay off the mortgage on the Widdicombe property which had been previously purchased. This lot, 100 feet on H Street with a depth of 145 feet, was located between the Medical School and the old Preparatory School building and was formerly occupied by a stable. The remainder of the loan was to be used to construct a new building for the Medical School and to build on the Widdicombe lot a new hospital with private rooms and wards for clinical instruction.[16]

The construction of the new Medical Building and the Law School brought together, for the only time in the University's history, all of its schools in a single group of buildings constructed by the University. Tragically, this situation continued for only a decade. It was at this time, symbolically it would seem, that the University began holding one Commencement in which all the schools and colleges participated.[17] It might also be noted that from this same period, due largely to the insistence of graduates, all diplomas were for the first time written in English instead of Latin.[18]

President Whitman sought and obtained a change in the constitution of the governing board of the University. As we have seen, an act of the Legislative Assembly of the District of Columbia, approved July 25, 1871, provided for a college Corporation of thirteen Trustees and thirteen Overseers. An act of Congress, approved March 3, 1873, removed the $25,000 restriction on the yearly value of the College's property, changed the name of the institution to Columbian University, made the president a Trustee, and increased the number of Trustees and Overseers to twenty-one each.

The amendment sought by President Whitman and approved by the act of Congress on March 18, 1898, returned to the old system of a Board of Trustees of twenty-two members, one of whom was the president, but with this further and significant change: that the president and two-thirds of the members of the Board must belong to the Baptist denomination. For the first time in its history, the institution was, by law, actually under Baptist control.[19]

The Corporation accepted the changes in the Charter and prepared to put its provisions into force on June 1, 1898.[20]

It was evident that the University, hard pressed financially, was to follow the opening made by President Welling and appeal to the Baptists for aid. In 1899 the Board formally thanked the richest Baptist of the day for a donation of $2,500 for the current expenses of the School of Comparative Jurisprudence. Many had entertained hopes that Mr. Rockefeller's benevolence would be of a somewhat greater degree.[21]

A few months later the Trustees resolved to lay "the affairs and interests of the University before the Baptist Education Society for counsel and to secure its aid." The Board's representative who conferred with the officers of the Baptist Education Society was told that the society could not possibly make any contribution. He talked also with President William R. Harper of the University of Chicago, who expressed interest but made no suggestions. The effect of this was most depressing.[22]

President Whitman, expressing his own conviction that he was no money-raiser, presented his resignation and asked its immediate acceptance. His resignation was accepted, to take effect April 30, 1900.[23]

During the Whitman administration, the University sustained, for the only time in its history, a major financial loss through the dishonesty of one of its senior officers. Robert H. Martin, in the words of President Whitman, had in a brief time come "to the practical headship of the University." Already in the employment of the University following the death of Mr. Robert C. Fox, the secretary and treasurer, he had gradually taken over the functions of the offices held by Mr. Fox. He had even been placed on the Board to make him eligible to hold the offices, until a change in the rules made membership on the Board no longer a requirement for holding these offices. He had also been elected registrar and, as such, received all fees from students. With this combination of offices, he was free of any checks on his actions.

One day while Martin was away, a woman appeared at the office to make a payment on an obligation. When the bookkeeper looked in his ledger for a statement of her account he could find none, even though she declared she had been making her payments regularly to Martin. The bookkeeper was Charles W. Holmes, who later became treasurer and served the University with great fidelity and distinction for more than forty years. Under Mr. Holmes' careful scrutiny, other irregularities began to come to light. It first appeared that Martin had embezzled $840 of collections from the Trustees' fund. Martin made good this amount and was removed from office. Shortly afterwards, he acknowledged the embezzlement of $4,000 more. The Trustees settled with his bondsmen for this sum, only to find later that the total amount of his defalcation was $25,850.81, according to the audit of the accountant, William E. DeCaindry, and Martin's own acknowledgment.[24]

In present-day terms, the amount seems almost trivial. For an institution trying to make ends meet with but little success, it was a disaster. It could have paid the interest on the University's debt for more than a year. In forcing the adoption of better business methods, it was a blessing in disguise.

The Spanish American War occurred midway in the Whitman administration. Unlike the War of 1861-1865 and the great twentieth-century wars, its impact on the University was relatively slight. In his Annual Report for 1898, the president summarized the situation in a single paragraph:

It is a matter of pride that when the call for volunteers was issued, our students were not slow in offering their services. Not many have been able to take the field, but their failure was due to the inability of the government to use them and not any unwillingness on the part of the students. To meet the needs of those [whose] services were called for, provision was made that no student need lose his standing because of absence. The College faculty voted to recommend that a senior in good standing should be allowed his degree, although not present at the final examination because of the call of the government. The faculties of the professional schools arranged to give prospective graduates their examinations out of the regular order, as would best meet their needs, whether before going or after their return.[25]

Among the students called into active service was a member of the junior class. He elected to stay in the military service after the War, expecting naturally that a tour of duty in or near Washington within a reasonable time would give him a chance to complete his requirements for a degree. Twenty years and another war passed before the opportunity came. He did complete his requirements for the degree, and in 1919 the degree of Bachelor of Arts was conferred upon him "as of the class of 1899." That man was William Lendrum Mitchell (1879-1936), General "Billy" Mitchell, pioneer advocate of air power in national defense.

While at the turn of the century many young and vigorous men who in their day were to become legends were being added to the College faculty, ties with the institution in its earlier days were passing. In 1899, the Reverend Robert Ryland of the class of 1826, the oldest alumnus of the College at the time, died. He was the founder of the University of Richmond and served as its president from 1844 to 1866.[26]

In 1896, the Reverend George Whitefield Samson, the fifth president of the College (1859-1871), who had guided its destinies during the troubled days of the War of 1861-1865, passed on. He had gone from the presidency of Columbian to New York as the president of Rutgers Female College, hoping to achieve there the success he had known in Washington. Laboring much of the time without salary, he had hoped that one of the religious bodies that had organized the institution would undertake its support or that the College could be associated with some university in a Barnard-Columbia or Radcliffe-Harvard type of relationship. His efforts, heroic as they were, failed.[27]

In 1900, Adoniram Judson Huntington (1818-1903) became Professor Emeritus of Greek. A graduate of the College in the class of 1843, he had taught in the Preparatory School in his senior year; served as tutor in Latin and Greek, 1843-1846; as professor, 1846-1849, 1852-1859, 1862-1882, 1882-1900; and as dean of Columbian College, 1897-1900. He was described by those who knew him as "the best-loved man who has ever been connected with the University." His term of service in the College was exceeded in length only by that of William Ruggles.[28]

While these honorable names suggest the antiquity of the College, the other branches of the University did not lack figures of great distinction. President Welling had declared at the end of his long and fruitful administration that men would find "the future glory of the University in professional education and higher learning."[29]

To look at the eminent names on the faculties of these various schools would seem to indicate that Welling's prophecy had early fulfillment. To mention but a few, there were Walter Reed (medicine), Theobald Smith (bacteriology), Frederick Russell (medicine), Harvey W. Wiley (chemistry), Otis T. Mason (anthropology), Lester F. Ward (botany), Cleveland Abbe (meteorology), Justice John M. Harlan (law), Justice David J. Brewer (law), John W. Foster (international law). Two of the men just named were graduates of the College: Otis T. Mason of the class of 1861 and Lester F. Ward of the class of 1869.

Otis T. Mason (1837-1908) was principal of the Preparatory School from 1861 to 1884 and probably contributed more to the development of that school than any other individual. He became interested in ethnology and in 1872 became a collaborator in ethnology at the Smithsonian Institution to assist in the arrangement and classification of its collections. In 1884 he gave up his post at the Preparatory School, was made Professor of Anthropology, and became curator of the Department of Ethnology of the National Museum. His ideas about classification proved to be epoch-making in the field of ethnology. He was recognized as an outstanding authority on the American Indian, and his *Handbook of American Indians* has been described as a "monumental work."[30]

Lester F. Ward (1841-1913), "Father of American Sociology," was a soldier in the Union Army. Discharged because of wounds received at Chancellorsville, he secured a position in the Treasury Department and began to attend classes at the College. He received his B.A. in 1869, his LL.B. in 1871, and his M.A. in 1872. In 1881, Ward became assistant geologist in the United States Geological Survey; later he became the Survey's geologist and paleontologist. Here his scholarly ability and deep scientific interest rapidly developed him into a scientist of great repute in the field of paleontology. His wide-ranging intellectual interests and his broad scientific background gradually led him more and more into the field of sociology. His eminence here was fully established by his great two-volume work, the title of which, *Dynamic Sociology* (1881), was to give a name to a school of sociological thought. Called to a professorship at Brown University, Ward spent the last few years of his life there in the leisurely pursuit of his studies and in writing.

Ward is perhaps the supreme example of the employed student who attained great eminence in the world of learning. He was a man of tremendous erudition and amazing industry. His knowledge of foreign languages included the classics, all the languages of western Europe, and a reading knowledge of Sanskrit, Russian, Chinese, and Japanese. A recent biographer credits him with nearly 600 publications.[31]

Dr. Samuel Harrison Greene served as president *ad interim* for two years. Then Dean Charles Willis Needham was elected and took office without delay.[32] As his first formal report to the Board of Trustees shows, he knew the University in all its detail and was in a position to evaluate the situation he would have to face during a trying administration. President Whitman had carried out, but not funded, the "University Plan" of his predecessor.

As a prelude to a discussion of the problems of the Needham administration, a few observations should be made. Columbian was now, in a true sense, an urban university. Its educational plant was located midcity in the heart of the financial area. It was completely nonresident; it had no dormitories and no facilities for feeding students. The Corcoran Scientific School, offering all of its courses after working hours, was gaining in enrollment more rapidly than the College or any of the other schools. The work of the graduate and professional schools was also, in large part, designed for the part-time or the late-afternoon student.

Although the buildings were grouped, the schools and the College had not yet been completely integrated into the University system. Pockets of autonomy still remained in some areas. Many professors were still paid as salaries a percentage of the fees collected for their courses. The expenses of administration were neither clearly delineated nor fairly apportioned. Certain necessary adjuncts to instruction, particularly the libraries, had been woefully neglected. Student enrollment continued to grow, however, and the total—1,383—was impressive.

This continued growth in enrollment was important, for student fees were almost the sole source of income. The Corcoran Endowment had not increased as its founder had hoped. Just what the effective endowment was is almost impossible to say; certainly it was not highly productive. Shifts in funds were frequent. The Board had been cavalier in handling funds whose use was supposed to be restricted, and robbing Peter to pay Paul was, at times, almost an accepted policy. Struggling to meet instructional costs with student fees rarely left a surplus. Extraordinary expenditures were met by the best device that could be thought of. There was no money to grow on.

Finally, an attempt to assume a posture that would encourage donors resulted in a reduction of the pool of potential givers. The supplemental act approved March 18, 1898, which provided that the president and at least two-thirds of the Trustees be Baptists, made Columbian a denominational institution. The famous Section 13 of the original Charter which provided that there should be no religious test for president, trustees, professors, tutors, and students had been in effect for seventy-one years and, although circumvented at times, had not been violated. This surrender of the institution's birthright as an independent university did not impress the American Baptist Education Society or any wealthy Baptist to the point of supporting a worthy and ancient, but impecunious, Columbian University. Rough days were ahead before the University could find its bearings and sail into less troubled seas.

In the two-year interval between the resignation of President Whitman and the election of his successor, the functions of acting president were exercised by the Reverend Dr. S. H. Greene, pastor of Calvary Baptist Church, who had served in the same capacity in the interim between President Welling's resignation and President Whitman's election. To assist him, Dr. Howard Lincoln Hodgkins, who was himself to serve as president during a later interregnum, was made dean of the University.[33]

On June 18, 1902, Charles Willis Needham (1848-1935) was elected the eighth president of the University. He was a lawyer by profession and had practiced in Chicago and Washington. A member of the Board of Trustees and for a time its secretary, he had resigned as a Trustee when he became the organizer and first dean of the School of Jurisprudence and Diplomacy. He had been a most active member of the Board of Trustees and had a detailed knowledge of the University, its corporate structure, and its financial problems. In the energy and imagination with which he planned the work of the School of Jurisprudence and Diplomacy he was not only following the line of his own intellectual predilections and professional interest but completing the educational structure that Welling's "University Plan" had envisioned. As president of the University, he brought forth a new conception of university organization which was never to take final form because of economic difficulties and, perhaps, better educational thinking. His administration of eight years was a significant one, but not because it was one of the happiest periods of the University's history.

His contemporaries laid heavy blame on the president; but after the several decades that have passed, the question of responsibility no longer seems so simple. He acted with his Trustees. He failed to raise the large sums needed, and so did they. There is, however, much evidence to show that the effort was made. The greatest names in business and finance appear on the list of contributors, so these men were undoubtedly approached and their gifts were certainly gratefully received. The modesty of their donations in proportion to the size of the fortunes they represented makes their gifts seem to be tokens of encouragement rather than indications of any desire or intent to be substantial patrons of the institution.

President Needham was a strange mixture of idealism and practicality. His judgment at times could have been better, his actions more discreet. Other presidents had suffered from similar limitations. It was President Needham's lot to serve as the head of the University in critical years, during which he had to face the cumulative results of bad policy on the part of earlier presidents and Boards as well as to bear the burden of his own mistakes. When, after he had tried every device he knew, he heard cries of criticism from many quarters and saw his support shattered and gradually disintegrating, he took the only course and withdrew.

From the start President Needham saw to it that his Board of Trustees was aware of the financial situation. At the beginning of his first academic year, when his administration was but a few months old, the president in his first Report to the Board stated the situation about as plainly as it could be stated. The income from all sources for the year, it was estimated, would amount to $83,000, the expenditures to $98,000. This anticipated deficit of $15,000 for the year, added to the existing deficit, made a total of $25,767.76 in new income that would have to be provided during the current year.

The work of Columbian College, he reported, was being conducted without a dean and there was little association between the men carrying on the work of the institution. There were a lamentable lack of unity and an alarming absence of college atmosphere and spirit.

The Corcoran Scientific School was "a night school." Night schools, he emphasized, did not appeal to men of large means in the endowment of college work. Students in the Scientific School did not feel that they were members of the University. The president urged that class hours be changed from the evening to the late afternoon, from four o'clock to six-thirty, and that libraries and laboratories be open until ten o'clock. He made the same recommendations regarding the School of Graduate Studies. In every department, except the Medical and Dental Schools, classes would be given from 9 A.M. to 6 P.M.[34]

A year and a half later, it was decided to provide classroom work in medicine in the forenoon, in addition to the afternoon hours, for those giving their full time to study.[35]

No longer were students who were employed during the day called "night students." They were now "late-afternoon students," even though circumstances were at times to force an unorthodox extension of the "late afternoon." The great demand for college work after business hours in the years following the War of 1861 to 1865, the circumstances surrounding the creation of the Corcoran Scientific School and the considerable student support that it drew, and the bringing of the University to the heart of the city to provide easier access for the employed student—all these factors had led to a great experiment in part-time education and the creation of a true urban university. This had been hailed as a great leap forward, a widening of educational services and of support for educational offerings. Now President Needham, faced with a great financial problem and thinking about attracting outside support rather than about tuition from an enlarged student body, sought to define and restrict part-time work to bring the University picture more within the accepted academic pattern. In furtherance of this effort, his administration undertook a consistent policy for the encouragement and development of student activities.

To achieve a sense of unity and to cut down administrative overhead, the president offered a "New Plan," the successor of Welling's "University Plan," the blueprint which had been followed for a score of years. In a sense the capstone of the Welling structure had been the School of Jurisprudence and Diplomacy, of which Needham himself had been dean. The consolidation that the "New Plan" recommended was facilitated by the fact that Columbian College had had no dean since the death of the venerable Adoniram Judson Huntington in 1900, and the arts and sciences branches were under the general control of Howard Lincoln Hodgkins, as dean of the University.

The president proposed that Columbian College, the Corcoran Scientific School, and the School of Graduate Studies be discontinued as separate entities and that all of the work in the arts and sciences be organized on the basis of subjects. Instead of deans and colleges there would be departments, each with a head professor, an assistant professor, and instructors. In place of the faculty there would be two councils. A President's Council would include all the heads of departments and the deans of the professional schools. A University Council would include the president, all professors in the arts and sciences, and the deans and designated professors of the professional schools.

The head professor was to divide each subject into a two-year cultural course, a third-year specialized course, and a course for original research. All graduates of approved secondary schools were eligible for admission to the college course, the degree of bachelor of arts being granted upon the successful completion of three years of work. Ten or twelve of the twenty class-hours of the third year could be taken in one of the professional schools. This plan was put in operation October 1, 1903. One dollar from each matriculation fee was set aside for the support of athletics.[36]

The continued deficit in operating costs, comprising what was called "the floating debt," continued to give the president great concern. This debt, made up of bank loans, increased from year to year, and was but a part of the picture. There was also the staggering debt of $360,000 secured by a mortgage on the University's property and largely incurred in construction of the building on H Street. "Borrowing money to put up new buildings," said Needham, "was bad business." The president had no magic formula for getting the institution out of debt. "It is improbable," he told his Trustees in January, 1903, "that our friends will help us until we help ourselves by putting the University on a sound basis. For a long time, the experiment has been tried of enlarging the work, thereby increasing the expenses beyond the income in the hope that the additional work done and the increased reputation of the University would attract friends to the University and secure financial aid. This experiment has failed and it simply remains for us to return to the old-fashioned formula of reducing expenses to meet the income."[37]

The president was in dead earnest. A drive for $500,000 was started, to pay off the floating debt and to buy a new and more desirable site. The University Hospital was opened for patients on February 28, 1903, and it was hoped that its operation would yield a sizable surplus. The report made to the Board at its fall meeting in 1903, however, blasted those hopes. The cost of the new hospital had exceeded the estimate by $9,920.96 and on its operation for a half-year it had lost over $600.

The total capacity of the hospital was 125 patients, with forty rooms for the reception and treatment of private cases. There were two wards of twelve beds each for the general medical and surgical diseases of women, a like number for men, a ward of eight beds for maternity cases, a nursery of twelve cribs, and a children's ward of eight beds.[38]

It had been necessary to increase the floating debt to $40,000 at 5 per cent. The interest on this loan and on the loan of $360,000 amounted to $17,840, a figure slightly more than the normal operating deficit.

To add to his discouragement, the president found it impossible to raise funds as he had hoped. He was facing constant objections to the denominational character of the institution's control. He was incessantly being asked why Washingtonians did not do something for their University.

The University did not lack students. The opening registration in 1903 showed: Arts and Sciences, 287; Medicine, 215; Dentistry, 71; Law, 314; Jurisprudence and Diplomacy, 40; total, 927.

The president was embarrassed that literature sent out over the country had promised new buildings, dormitories, and a setup for real student life. Much had been promised, nothing done. There were, he said, enough students living in boarding houses to fill five or six dormitories. "With these burdens upon us and before us, we approach the problem of the development of the University as almost one of life and death. The University cannot go on in its present condition very long." Needham was disheartened but not defeated. He recommended, and the Board agreed to, a request to Congress to restore to the Charter the original prohibition of religious tests and to repeal the provision in the recent amendment requiring that two-thirds of the Board and the president be Baptist in their religious affiliation. The president recommended that the Columbian Law Building on Fifth Street, valued at $225,000, be sold; that the proceeds be used to buy Van Ness Park at Seventeenth Street and Potomac Park for $161,343; and that a dormitory, to be called Corcoran Hall, be erected on the north side of this five-acre plot. When some Trustees objected that the Columbian Building represented the Corcoran Endowment and should not be used, Needham responded that this was a proper use since the dormitory would yield an income.[39] Two loans of $100,000 and $62,000 from Riggs National Bank and the Washington Loan and Trust Company, respectively, produced the cash which purchased the Van Ness property, the site where the Pan American Union's building was later constructed.[40]

The property itself was of considerable interest. It was part of the vast real estate holdings of "Davy" Burnes, one of the original proprietors in the District, which had been inherited by his daughter Marcia, reputed at the time to be the richest heiress in the United States. Marcia Burnes married John Peter Van Ness, a wealthy member of Congress from New York and later Major General in the militia. Mrs. Van Ness built a great mansion house on the lot near the modest old Burnes cottage. It was a most elegant structure, 70 by 40 feet, with six bedrooms and necessary dressing rooms and a small dining room on the second floor; a large dining room, library, salon, butler's pantry, and den were on the first floor; and a huge kitchen below was equipped with a dumb-waiter to carry food to the butler's pantry. A glass-enclosed conservatory was included in the plan. Hot and cold running water in all parts of the building was a novel feature in this elaborate creation of the great architect, Benjamin Henry Latrobe, hardly to be expected in a house completed in 1816.[41]

Sketches and plans for the improvement of Van Ness Park were quickly drawn by the architectural firm of Hornblower and Marshall, laid before the Trustees, and adopted with the understanding that modifications could be made.

The changes in the Charter and bylaws were formally approved by the Board on February 20, 1904.[42]

With the proposed changes undoubtedly used as an occasion to renew, hopefully, earlier contacts with Mr. John D. Rockefeller, a contributor to Columbian University years previously, it had been ascertained that he would interpose no objection to the projected changes in the Charter. It later appeared that his contribution had been the only one obtained during the period of Baptist control of the Board, and that his waiver would be useful in meeting any objections that might be raised.[43]

As the University resumed its nonsectarian character under the provisions of the original Charter, showing that hope from the Baptist denomination (if not from individual Baptists) was about extinguished, what looked like a promising opportunity opened up in a new quarter.

In August, 1897, a group of representative women had met in conference in Washington, D.C. As a result of their deliberations, there had been incorporated in September, 1898, a George Washington Memorial Association to advance and secure the establishment in the city of Washington of a university "for the purpose and with the objects substantially set forth in and by the last will of George Washington" and "to increase the opportunities for the higher education of the youth of the United States."[44]

These patriotic ladies were not the only ones whose minds and efforts had turned in this direction. Since 1869, the energetic and resourceful John Wesley Hoyt had been crystallizing his ideas along the lines of a national university. Hoyt was a versatile man, a student of law and medicine, teacher at Antioch in the days of Horace Mann, president of the University of Wyoming, government official, author, propagandist, and natural-born organizer. In his advocacy of a national university he became involved in a long and, at times, acrimonious controversy with President Eliot of Harvard. He labored endlessly, by his own personal effort and through various organizations, to get the support of Congress or of a major philanthropist. For a time the George Washington Memorial Association, through the Washington Memorial Association, which with the Academy of Sciences it had helped form, put its support behind a Washington Memorial Institution and helped encourage Hoyt in his desire to see a national university. In the winter of 1903, Hoyt wrote to the University relative to a movement for a national university, suggesting a conference with a view to turning the influence of the organization he represented to the building up of Columbian University. The letter was tabled to await consultations with the president. As chairman of the National University Committee, Hoyt wrote again to the University in May, 1904, but his letter was merely read, considered, and placed in the files.[45]

When Hoyt's second communication was received, the University was already deeply involved in negotiations with the George Washington Memorial Association. In a letter of February 18, 1904, Mrs. Archibald Hopkins, the president of the association, wrote that her Executive Committee had urged favorable action on proposals made by the University's president the previous December. "If," Mrs. Hopkins wrote, "they decide to erect a Washington Memorial Building on the site which you propose to give for the purpose, the George Washington Memorial Association would ask you and your Board of Trustees to consider taking the name of George Washington University for the postgraduate department of your greater University." It is easy to suspect Hoyt's influence in the form of the proposal: a memorial which was to be a great center for advanced study.

The Board of Trustees asked President Needham to continue negotiations, inviting the association to construct in Van Ness Park a memorial building to be used as the administration building of the University; it would offer facilities for lectures, research, and discussions in University courses and by scientific societies.[46]

The Memorial Association had been busily seeking subscriptions and gifts. About $50,000 had been subscribed; $16,000 of it had been paid in cash and part of it was made dependent upon raising $50,000 more. When $100,000 had been reached in cash and subscriptions, work on the memorial building was to be commenced. On May 2, 1904, President Needham was able to report that an agreement had been reached whereby the association agreed to raise funds estimated at $500,000 to build the central building in a proposed group in Van Ness Park, to be known as the George Washington Memorial. Plans were to be approved by both boards. The building was to be used as an administrative building and was to contain an auditorium for lectures and for international and scientific gatherings. The structure was to belong to the University, which undertook the complete cost of maintenance. The University promised, as permitted by an act of Congress, approved January 23 of that year, to change its name to George Washington University upon completion of the building, which name was to be held in perpetuity. The association agreed to raise the necessary funds, the agreement to become binding upon formal acceptance by both boards.

The arrangement was made with the understanding that the University would be nondenominational and would give primary emphasis to postgraduate work.

Because Columbian had been the name of the institution for eighty-three years, and because around that name were centered much history and much sentiment, it was recommended that there should be created, under the general laws of the District of Columbia, an auxiliary corporation known as Columbian College to have control of all academic undergraduate institutions. The name Columbian College, it will be remembered, had ceased to be used when, under the Needham plan of reorganization, all work in the arts and sciences had been grouped together under the designation Department of Arts and Sciences. The relations between the College and the University were not to be disturbed except that the control of the College was to be vested in its own Board of Trustees, at least a majority of whom would be nominated by the Trustees (and, as it happened, from the Trustees) of the University. For the present, financial management would remain with the University, which would also grant the College's degrees. The head of the College would be an officer of no higher rank than dean.

All of the president's recommendations with reference to the agreement with the association, including the change of name, the use of the Van Ness property, and the reorganization of Columbian College, were adopted. A committee set about drawing up a charter for Columbian College, which was duly signed and certified and filed with the Recorder of Deeds June 22, 1904.[47]

The use of the old name, Columbian University, ceased with the close of the fiscal year, August 31, 1904. Plans went steadily forward for the realization of the George Washington Memorial. The association felt sufficiently encouraged to express the hope that the cornerstone of the memorial building could be laid February 22, 1905. An architectural competition was set up with great care. The program was prepared by the professor of architecture, Percy Ash. Five leading architectural firms were invited to compete in presenting a general scheme of buildings for Van Ness Park, and definite plans for the memorial building, each to receive an honorarium of $200. The General Park Commission was asked to determine the winner among the architects. Costs of the competition were to be shared equally by the University and the association, but costs of the plans for the building were to be defrayed by the association alone.

Reporting to the Board in November, 1904, President Needham noted a great growth in college spirit. Total candor would have required that he also note the great bitterness on the part of many alumni at the loss of the old name, Columbian University.[48]

The president spoke with pride of the success of the changes that had transformed the Department of Arts and Sciences into a day school, with all classes ending by 6:30 P.M. He pointed out with great satisfaction that in 1901 only 17.6 per cent of the students in arts and sciences attended day-time classes before 6:30. In 1904, 100 per cent were day-time students, with 37.4 per cent completing work before 4:30 P.M.

William Allen Wilbur, head of Columbian Academy until its discontinuance and then Professor of English in the College, was made acting dean of the newly incorporated Columbian College. For the time being, the College would be supported by the University, but the president looked forward to an early date when the College would have its own administration and classroom buildings and dormitories. Then the College's own Board of Trustees could take over. Dormitories, Needham thought, were necessary, for while there had been a great growth in college spirit, it could develop to the fullest extent only if there were dormitory life.

The president was encouraged by an increase in the number of full-time students in the Graduate School and by the fact that the first beginning class in law in the morning had drawn from 35 to 40 students. As far as the School of Jurisprudence and Diplomacy went, the picture was not so pleasant. Lack of funds to increase the faculty was holding down the enrollment. Because of its evening schedule, the Dental School had been taken off the list of its national association, much to the chagrin of its students.

There had been a general increase in the number of students. At the time of the president's Report on November 16, 1904, the registration was: College, 387; Graduate, 55; Medicine, 290; Dentistry, 63; Law, 408; Jurisprudence and Diplomacy, 40; total, 1,243.

The financial picture for the year 1903-1904 had been encouraging. The treasurer's Report showed income of $342,761.21 from all sources and expenses of $342,502.93. While this indicated a surplus, it was felt that actually there would be a deficit on the order of $6,000, a very small one in the light of past history.

New educational bylaws were adopted, fixing the organization of the University as follows:

> Department of Arts and Sciences: Columbian College (B.A. and B.S.), and School of Graduate Studies (M.A., M.S., degrees in Engineering, and Ph.D.)
>
> School of Medicine (4 years leading to M.D.), School of Dentistry (3 years leading to D.D.S.)
>
> School of Law and Jurisprudence (3 years leading to LL.B., plus 1 year to LL.M., plus 3 years to Doctor of Jurisprudence)
>
> Department of Politics and Diplomacy (2 years leading to M.Dip., 3 years to Ph.D.)

To this was added a Department of Architecture.[49]

The adoption of a new name necessitated an appropriate change in the University insignia. Apparently there had never been any formal adoption of colors for Columbian. The seals on the early diplomas were attached to ribbons of varying light colors, but blue and gold had come to be generally used. On the recommendation of the University Council, the Board ordered that beginning February 22, 1905, the colors of the University should be the buff and blue of General Washington's uniform as preserved in the National Museum. Modern colorimetric examination of the original has made possible in recent years an accurate reproduction of the Continental buff and blue. Columbian University had used the old seal of Columbian College, replacing the word "College" with "University." This was the seal drawn for the College in 1821 by James Peale, showing the lion and the lamb together and above them the opened book. A seal drawn by Frederick D. Owen, B.S., 1905, M.S. 1906, was adopted, using the University colors. The outer circle showed the words "The George Washington University, 1821"; inside the circle there was a shield with an open book in the upper portion and in the lower portion "the face of George Washington taken from the Stuart picture," with the motto *Deus nobis fiducia* between the outer circle and the shield. This motto did not appear on the Peale seal, although for many years it was occasionally printed on the cover of the catalogue just below the seal.[50]

From every indication it would seem that the convocation of February 22, 1905, inaugurating the use of the new name, occasioned great enthusiasm. President Needham in his address reported on the reorganization of the work of the University, begun two years previously. He was particularly pleased that the Medical School was about to discontinue night classes, so that the closing hour of 6:30 would be uniform practically throughout the entire University. With characteristic eloquence, Mr. Justice Brewer, the convocation orator, delivered the keynote speech for the new era that all expected to dawn.[51]

A fortnight after the convocation, an act supplemental to the original Charter was approved, giving the University power to organize colleges for "special lines of educational work"; educationally they would be a part of the University system but would have independent financial foundations.[52]

Under this act, Columbian College was incorporated as an independent organization in all financial and legal responsibility, although the president had earlier stated that "at present" financial management would be directed by the University. In the same way, the Washington College of Engineering was incorporated.[53]

These arrangements were ephemeral. Because they were found embarrassing in later negotiations when an effort was being made to get an extension of the Morrill Act, they were suspended; and unified control, which in actuality had never ceased, was formally reestablished. In a somewhat different category, the National College of Pharmacy was taken over as an affiliated college.[54]

The enthusiasm engendered by the adoption of a new name, the possibility of a new site in a strategic location, and the reorganization of the University could not blind the Trustees to the existence of a critical financial situation. The floating debt was becoming unmanageable and temporary relief was sought in the usual fashion—the debt had to be refinanced. The president recommended and the Board approved an increase in the debt secured by the University's property. A loan of $360,000 was increased to $450,000. It is disheartening even today, to see what that loan, representing practically the full borrowing capacity of the institution, produced net. After the $360,000 outstanding was paid, the floating debt and the balance on the Van Ness loan taken care of, and the expenses of the deal and overdue interest met, a balance of $24,601, less in amount than the operating debt for a single year, was all that remained. It was, in fact, little more than one year's carrying charges on the loan of $450,000 accepted from the Fidelity Trust Company of Philadelphia for five years at 4.4 per cent.[55]

If President Needham's faith faltered, his utterances did not betray it. At Commencement in the very same month that the Fidelity Trust Company's loan was negotiated, he declared in his address:

We are entering upon a new era of our institutional life. The past, covering a period of over three-quarters of a century, has been honorable and is worthy of the respect and veneration of men; we have agreed to enter upon a new and a larger life; to make the institution a University in the broadest and best sense, and have reorganized upon a foundation, broad enough for all to stand upon who are interested in higher education at the National Capital. With a supreme purpose to make the University worthy of support,—the equal of the best institutions in our country, we turn our faces today, with courage and hope, toward the future.[56]

A new possibility of help appeared, indirect in a way but very significant. When Andrew Carnegie became a trustee of Cornell University in 1890, he began to become more and more aware of the low economic status of college professors and of the hardship many of them faced in retirement. To meet this problem, he set up an endowment of $10 million, later increased to $15 million, to provide free pensions to faculty members. It was estimated that there were only 92 private nonsectarian institutions of higher learning, with a total faculty of 3,100 receiving about $6 million in salaries annually, which were of sufficient academic excellence to qualify for participation. Since the average annual salary was about $2,000 it was felt that the foundation's income of $500,000 would be sufficient to set up free pensions for retired college teachers 65 years and over, with at least thirty years of service, amounting to one-half of the average of the individual's salary over his final five years of employment.[57]

The University applied for participation in the Carnegie program. The foundation was concerned over the denominational contacts which the institution had had. To meet this question, the Board resolved: "That the President and Secretary of the University certify to the Carnegie Foundation the following statement of the Board of Trustees: namely no denominational test is imposed in the choice of trustees, officers, or teachers, nor in the admission of students, nor are any denominational tenets or doctrine taught to students in the George Washington University."[58] Having satisfied the foundation of its eligibility, the University was admitted to participation in the pension plan.

Adding to his duties, President Needham, who had been Dean of the Law School, was now, as Professor of Law, assigned courses in that school at a substantial increase in salary. This adjustment in the Law School was made necessary by the resignation of Professor W. A. Maury, who had taught in it since 1878. An individual of the greatest distinction, learned in the law, highly gifted as a teacher, Maury ranks among the most eminent men in the history of the University.

In spite of the limited resources of the institution, President Needham felt that a proper president's house should be provided. The University purchased 1710 N Street with the provision that the president should pay the interest on the encumbrance, taxes, and 5 per cent on the monies paid out. It was not an entirely satisfactory arrangement.[59]

Amidst all his problems, Needham was able to claim achievement of one long-sought-for aim, very dear to his heart. Reporting to the Board in the fall of 1906, he could declare that George Washington was "no longer a night school or a University whose prime purpose is to educate government clerks," and he offered the figures to prove it.[60]

The great need that faced the University forced consideration of great efforts. The futility of random solicitation for funds by individuals had been long demonstrated. All efforts to raise money by Trustees, faculty, graduates, the Memorial Association, and other groups were now combined, under the general control of the Board of Trustees, in a committee headed by Professor Mitchell Carroll. This committee was given a long-range as well as an immediate objective. It was to proceed at once to the raising of $2,500,000, of which $600,000 was to go toward the erection of the Memorial Building and $900,000 for additional grounds (only five acres had been acquired in the Van Ness purchase), with $1,000,000 for endowment. As soon as this initial $2,500,000 was subscribed (payment could be made in cash or in five annual installments), a drive for $7,500,000 was to be launched. Of this, $1,500,000 would be spent for buildings and $6,000,000 reserved for a permanent endowment.[61]

In view of the stated building program for which funds were to be solicited, much depended on the possession of an adequate and appropriate site. The five-acre Van Ness plot, although strategic in location, was woefully inadequate for the group of monumental structures planned. More land in the area would have to be acquired, and prices were high. There was yet another and very grave embarrassment. The Potomac frequently overflowed its banks and, at this time, a marsh extended in places up to B Street, now Constitution Avenue. A hue and cry was raised that this would be a very unhealthy place to locate a university with hundreds of students. Soundings made by members of the Engineering faculty indicated that water was found in some places very near the surface. One of the major critics of the use of the site fortified his complaints with an offer of land and building in Chevy Chase, Maryland, if the Van Ness site were relinquished. His criticisms were met by formal assurance from the Superintendent of Sewers that the use of a canal as an open sewer in Potomac Park adjacent to the property would be discontinued and filling would be begun within a year, and a statement from the Health Officer that health in that locality compared favorably with that in other parts of the city. The Chevy Chase offer was declined.[62]

Professor Carroll's committee got under way with great vigor to publicize what was designated "The George Washington University Movement." The first meeting of citizens and alumni held at the New Willard Hotel on February 25, 1907, seemed to indicate certain success. In its columns on the following day the *Evening Star* described a scene of amazing enthusiasm in which the chairman, the Honorable H. B. F. Macfarland, one of the Commissioners of the District of Columbia, "over and over again found it impossible to put a motion to adjourn, so eager were those present to announce their own subscriptions or those of someone else to increase amounts already given." In one hour, the very respectable sum of $82,000 was subscribed.

The Building and Endowment Fund Committee, as a matter of strategic approach, suggested that the first step in connection with raising the initial $2,500,000 be directed toward a material object, the building of a Columbian College building as an appeal to local sentiment. This building would be erected on a *new* site.

On February 16, 1907, the Trustees accepted an offer from Elihu Root, Secretary of State, submitted through Mr. C. C. Glover, for the purchase of the Van Ness property for the sum of $200,000, Mr. Glover generously donating his fee as a very substantial contribution to the fund. The property was to be used for a structure housing the Bureau of American Republics.[63]

To facilitate the addition to the Board of men of wealth who might be disposed to aid the University in a major way, the number of Trustees was increased to twenty-seven. What was to be an interminable discussion of new sites immediately got under way. The Columbia Heights Citizens' Association brought out a twelve-page booklet presenting the advantages of their area. "From a sentimental, historic, and practical standpoint," the association declared, "the site on Columbia Heights embodies features which cannot be duplicated." Interestingly enough, they first dwelt upon the "sanitary effect of location" of the site they recommended, 200 feet above the Potomac. The association was proposing a site immediately east of the south half of old College Hill. Containing 23⅓ acres and extending north from Florida Avenue between Fourteenth and Eleventh Streets, it was just about half the size of Columbian College's original holding.[64]

The first and continuing preference was for Oak Lawn, or the Dean Estate, at the northeast corner of Florida and Connecticut Avenues, available initially at a cost of $550,000, plus an agreement to build on the site within five years, at a cost not less than $150,000, Dean Hall, in memory of the former owners. Later statements in the campaign literature of the committee said that the University had an option to buy for $800,000. The site was an impressive one and considerable enthusiasm was raised by the prospect of acquiring it. Generous subscriptions were received. Unfortunately, however, they were conditioned on the purchase of a specific site. When the purchase failed to go through, the subscriptions became null and void and their payment wholly voluntary.[65]

Professor Mitchel Carroll resigned as chairman of the Committee on Site, Buildings, and Endowments in January, 1908. His functions were eventually taken over by Dr. Richard D. Harlan as representative of the University.

While these matters of finance were taking up so much of the administration's energy, some educational changes were being made. On the recommendation of the dean, the Medical School resumed the admission of women in 1906 by accepting the registration of Mrs. Alice W. Downey. Although the faculty declared that this action created no precedent, two more women were admitted the following fall.[66]

The title of Harriet Stratton Ellis, head of the Women's Department, was changed to Dean of Women, and the Department of Law and Jurisprudence became the Department of Law. Continuing its policy of cooperation with the schools, under certain conditions teachers in service were given scholarships equivalent in value to one-third of the regular tuition charge. William Carl Ruediger, later dean of Teachers College and provost, was appointed to the faculty as Assistant Professor of Educational Psychology in 1907.[67]

The Department of Politics and Diplomacy was made a separate and independent college under the name of the College of Political Sciences; it gave graduate and undergraduate instruction in history, politics, economics, international law and diplomacy, and related subjects. To the faculty of the new college were appointed William Ray Manning (diplomatic history), W. W. Willoughby (political science), Howard Lee McBain (political science), and Henry Parker Willis (finance).[68]

In 1908, Latin was removed from the requirements for the degree of Bachelor of Arts, and the degree of Bachelor of Science was discontinued. Beginning with the year 1909-1910, work in medicine became full-time.[69]

While President Needham felt that scholarship was better served by full-time than by part-time study, he was also anxious that the institution over which he presided should conform to the traditional college picture, because, as he so often stated, donors were not interested in supporting a night school. He was interested in donors. It was part of this same concern which led him to foster student activities, manifestations of "college spirit," more energetically than had any of his predecessors. During his administration, the Trustees regularly granted full scholarships to the editors and business managers of student publications. Not infrequently the president referred to student activities in his Reports to the Board.

The Association of Class Presidents as an overall steering committee undertook a systematic reorganization of undergraduate activities. An editorial board of the University annual, *The Mall*, later known as *The Cherry Tree*, was established. The weekly student publication, *The Hatchet*, was put on a firm basis. The work of the four debating societies was coordinated by an Intercollegiate Debating Council, made up of a student member from each society, two members of the faculty, and two alumni. In competition, the teams, usually debating in series Georgetown, Virginia, and Washington and Lee, maintained a fine record. After a bad season in 1903, when only two games out of seven were won, football was showing great progress, competing with teams such as the Carlisle Indians (Jim Thorpe's great team), Bucknell, Washington and Lee, V.P.I., Maryland Agricultural College (now the University of Maryland), and Georgetown. The lack of a practice field under the University's control was a serious handicap and during 1907-1908 the football team was allowed by the American League to use their ball park for a rental of $300. Nevertheless the team of 1908, coached by Fred Nielsen, compiled an impressive 8-1-1 record, even though the 6-0 game with V.P.I., which clinched the South Atlantic championship for George Washington, was delayed in starting until 4:45 P.M. by a heavy snowstorm that blanketed the field in Blacksburg. Baseball was slowly building up substantial student support. Other successful organizations were the Classical Club, which arranged public meetings addressed by visiting scholars, the Glee Club, the Dramatic Club, and the Tennis and Chess Club.[70]

The Alumni Association again became an active force in the life of the University. Organized first in 1847, it had met regularly until 1861 and, again after the War, from 1865 to 1874. After a break of twelve years, the association resumed its activities in 1887. During the Needham administration, local alumni groups were organized in many large cities throughout the country. In the fund-raising activities of the period, efforts were directed toward raising $150,000 for an Alumni Hall on the new site, to be conducted as a club for local and visiting alumni. Significant recognition of the importance of alumni support was given when, in increasing the number of the Trustees, the Board on May 6, 1909, authorized the alumni to nominate each year two from their number to serve three-year terms as Trustees.

At the same time that closer relations were being developed with the graduates, a plan was put in operation to promote improved communications between the faculty and the student body through regular conferences of the deans and class officers. A student employment center was also set up.

Rooms were set apart in the University building to provide comfortable meeting places for the students' Y.M.C.A. and Y.W.C.A. The two associations had charge of one chapel service each week and held a joint

meeting on the first Wednesday of each month. In their work with the
chapel, they aided in maintaining the University's oldest institution, one
which was not ended until 1967.[71] When the Baccalaureate Sermon was
discontinued in 1968, it might be said that the secularization of the
University was completed.

All of this very normal activity would seem to indicate that business
was going on as usual. An affiliated college, the College of Veterinary
Medicine, was organized according to the new plan,[72] with Dr. David
Eastburn Buckingham as dean.

Active discussion of a site still went on as though the University were
financially able to move at will. Definitely, it was not. As the year 1907-
1908 drew to a close, the estimated deficit for the year was $54,008.
When the Financial Committee offered its tentative budget for 1908-1909,
it showed a deficiency of $69,296.35, leaving a sum of $16,540.67 to be
found, "after all liquid cash and unencumbered property has been disposed of." The committee declared "the condition most grave."

Some money was being collected. J. P. Morgan made the first subscription, one of $5,000 for the College of the Political Sciences; and
Andrew Carnegie gave $1,000 for books for its special collection, the
Mount Vernon Alcove. But of the meager amount that had been paid
in cash for the Buildings, Site, and Endowment Fund, $13,501.32 had
already been used for general expenses. To save money, President Needham recommended the elimination of deans, the discontinuance of all
technical work, and the reorganization of the College's offerings to
emphasize the sciences. But he recommended that the College of the
Political Sciences, considered a gem in the academic crown, be continued,
with an enlarged faculty. At the next meeting of the Board, the president
was asked to submit a detailed plan for the reorganization of the
undergraduate program so as to decrease the amount and extent of work
offered.[73]

The Financial Committee, now thoroughly alarmed, continued its very
pointed warnings. Time was running short. If large endowments or
subscriptions were not made within a few months, all nonself-supporting
courses would have to be withdrawn. The situation was so serious that
all senior members of the faculty must be taken into the Board's confidence at once.

The president presented and the Board adopted the requested report
on retrenchment. He recommended that the work in the Arts and
Sciences be grouped under two deans—one for undergraduate, the other

for graduate courses—and the total of salaries held to $45,000; that medicine, dentistry, and the hospital be put on a self-supporting basis; that salaries in law be reduced by $4,400; and that the appropriation for the College of the Political Sciences and the general expense account be reduced by $8,500. It sounded dismal, but Needham was not dismayed; his confidence was quite unshaken: a windfall was in sight. He was ready to count chickens before they were hatched.[74]

President Needham's hope rested on a piece of pending Congressional legislation. This bill, supplementary to the Morrill Act of 1862 and its various additions, and known as the Gallinger-Boutell Amendments, would extend to the University the benefit of the funds annually appropriated under the act and would make the Secretary of Agriculture, the Secretary of the Interior, the Secretary of Commerce and Labor, and the Commissioner of Education members of the Board of Trustees ex officiis. As the president told the Trustees on March 8, 1909, this act had passed the Senate without dissent on the last day of the session just ended, had been reported favorably by the House Committee on Agriculture, but reached the House too late to be acted upon. It was reintroduced in the Senate at the Special Session of the Sixty-first Congress.

If the University were recognized as *the* University in the District to receive Morrill Act funds, it would get from that source $40,000, which later would go to $50,000 annually. Strong opposition came from various quarters, but particularly from President Edmund J. James of the University of Illinois, chairman of a committee on a National University of the Association of Presidents of State Universities. Oddly enough in a strong statement two years earlier, President James, with the School of Politics and Diplomacy particularly in mind, had declared that the University was "well adapted to develop into a University that will do work of national importance, provided, only that it now receives adequate financial support from the people of the Republic."

The bill was again before the Congress for passage. So as not to complicate matters the corporate organization of Columbian College and the College of Engineering was temporarily suspended. The president was optimistic; but should no money be received from other sources to meet the $70,000 needed one year hence, he recommended, and the Board agreed, increasing the mortgage on the H Street property when the loan was renewed. The president was advised to make known the plight of the University to the faculty and to those who were being asked to contribute, but not to the press. Because it was feared that a reduced registration would result, advanced requirements for law and medicine were postponed until a later time to be fixed by the respective faculties. The president was asked to find a purchaser for the H Street property, reserving to the University the right to rent the premises for from three to five years.[75]

While waiting in vain for favorable Congressional action, President Needham received a letter from Mrs. Susan Whitney Dimock, President of the George Washington Memorial Association, dated April 14, 1909, enclosing two resolutions which had been offered by Dr. Charles D. Walcott, Secretary of the Smithsonian Institution, a member of the Association's Board and also a Trustee of the University until his resignation in 1910. Mrs. Dimock's letter was written in a spirit of pacification. She insisted that she and Needham were not working against each other, that each had his loyalty but that the end result they sought was basically the same. The enclosed resolutions were direct and to the point. The first declared that, the Van Ness property having been sold, the association had withdrawn from its agreement with the University; the second, that Mrs. Dimock was given discretion whether to present the resolution to President Needham or not. Characteristically she did the difficult but courteous thing.

At the same Board meeting as the one at which Mrs. Dimock's letter was read, a committee of the President's Council, consisting of Deans Munroe, Wilbur, and Hough, submitted a schedule which showed the minimum number of teachers and assistants required by each department to carry on necessary work. With this as its chart, the Budget Committee, with Mr. John B. Larner as chairman, went to work on paring down the 1909-1910 budget.[76]

The committee recommended that the office of dean of women be eliminated; that Professor Mitchell Carroll be granted leave for a year and that his work be carried by Professor Charles Sidney Smith and an assistant; that Professors James Howard Gore and J. McBride Sterrett be retired as eligible for Carnegie pensions; and that the work in mathematics be distributed and no new appointment be made in philosophy, thus saving $2,200. On the assumption that the Medical and Dental Schools and the hospital could care for themselves, these and other changes would, it was reported, bring instructional costs down to a figure close to the estimated receipts. Although Dr. Gallaudet solemnly warned his fellow Trustees that these changes could cause great injury to the University, the recommendations were adopted, and the chairman of the committee expressed the hope that there could be a reduction in the expenses of the

College of the Political Sciences, which had had a charmed life and had escaped serious retrenchment. Efforts to meet the financial crisis by merely cutting instructional costs to balance expected income were not enough. There was still administrative overhead and the burden of carrying heavy loans. The deficit for 1909 to 1910 was bound to approach $50,000.

To meet this deficit, loans were granted by the National City Bank of New York and Riggs Bank of Washington; these, with a mortgage to be placed on the president's house if it was not sold, would carry the cost of conducting the University, not to the end of the next fiscal year, but only to April 1, 1910. In this dark hour when the Medical and Dental Schools and the hospital were expected to earn their way, Dr. William Cline Borden, a graduate of the University, was appointed dean of the Medical Department, a position he held with great distinction for a generation.[77]

The days of the administration, maybe even of the University itself, seemed numbered. The sad state of the institution's financial structure was now generally known and publicly discussed. Particularly aggrieved were the members of the teaching staff. While the principles of academic freedom and tenure were not then fully codified as they have since become, they were not unknown. Faculty meetings became a forum for bitter and acrimonious exchanges. For many years, a story was repeated that at one faculty meeting a senior professor challenged the figures presented by the president. Needham curtly rejoined, "Professor, you know, figures do not lie." The answer came right back, "No, Mr. President, but liars figure." An aroused Alumni Association appointed a committee, with A. S. Worthington its president and a leader of the bar as chairman, to make an investigation to ascertain the facts in the case as a background for alumni assistance. When the committee asked leave to go over the records and to interview employees in the financial office, the president declined to do anything more than give them copies of published material; he denied them access to the original records.

The Board of Trustees itself began to crumble. Dr. H. C. Yarrow, a most active and useful Trustee, resigned because he disapproved of the policies being followed. Senator Newlands withdrew, pleading the pressure of official duties. Because of the Board's failure to heed the warnings he had so consistently given and because he had no faith in the estimates laid before the Board, Mr. Hennen Jennings resigned; in closing, he expressed the belief that before the University became bankrupt, it should be turned over to the District of Columbia government to operate. Mr. Eugene

Levering refused to approve the budget unless the faculty were told that probably salaries could not be paid in full the next year. The veteran educator of the deaf, Dr. E. M. Gallaudet, thought that a full and detailed public statement should be made at once to answer with the truth what had been appearing in the press.[78]

In the midst of this confusion, a well-directed bomb exploded in the form of a letter to President Needham from the Carnegie Foundation for the Advancement of Teaching, dated June 4, 1909, and read to the Trustees the next day. It was written by Dr. Henry S. Pritchett at the direction of the Executive Committee of the Foundation. He addressed himself first to the question of endowment. As of August 21, 1907, the University had reported a productive endowment of $219,832.96, but in a financial statement as of October 3, 1908, a productive endowment of only $123,500 was shown. The rules of the foundation required that any institution in its retiring allowance system have a productive endowment of at least $200,000, the minimum requirement for maintaining fair educational standards.

Moving on to academic matters, he reported that an investigation he had just had made showed that announced standards of admission were not enforced. While the College showed reasonable care in enforcing admissions requirements, more than a third of the enrollment was made up of special students. The College of the Political Sciences and the Division of Education gave little regard to requirements. The Law School was lax in requiring four years of high school for entrance. The Medical School frequently evaded its requirements; if it had enforced them, it would have been so reduced in enrollment that it could not continue.

Then Dr. Pritchett went on to the question of the arbitrary retirement of two professors "in the prime of their active teaching," in order to save money. This he declared was "a blow at academic dignity and academic freedom." He had made his case: the Executive Committee "informs you with great regret that the relation of the George Washington University as an accepted institution is terminated with this date."[79]

Professors Gore and Sterrett were made professors emeriti. Members of the faculty petitioned the Board to confer upon them the honorary degree of Doctor of Laws at the 1909 Commencement. The recommendation was tabled. Both of the men almost immediately resigned from the emeritus status. Nine years later each received the honorary degree of Doctor of Letters and resumed his place on the faculty's roll of honor. Although they did not receive the official accolade at the 1909 Commencement, they did not go without honor on this occasion. Amid a great ovation, the student body presented each one with a silver loving cup as a token of esteem and respect.

The Board decided to move slowly until the president could confer with Dr. Pritchett. Meanwhile, they determined not to call a meeting of the alumni, reconsidered one appointment in the College of the Political Sciences to save the amount of a substantial salary, and authorized the Dental School to give evening courses.[80]

When the Board met at the beginning of the 1909-1910 session President Needham reported on his conversations with Dr. Pritchett during a two-day visit at the latter's summer home at Plymouth, Massachusetts. The difference of almost a hundred thousand dollars in the two statements of productive endowment, a fundamental question from the standpoint of the foundation's regulations, was not given the expected important place in the president's recapitulation of his talks with the Carnegie executive. His report showed clearly the influence of the tension between president and faculty. Dr. Pritchett, the president assured the Board, did not know of the faculty's opposition to his policy of improving the standards of the work being done and of his struggle to introduce modern scientific methods of instruction. He pointed out the caliber and output of the professors who had been brought in since 1905. Needham contended that his objectives and those of the foundation were based on the same principles, particularly his efforts to broaden the curriculum in science, with more attention to laboratory work. He defended the admissions policy. If, he told the Board, Pritchett had been properly informed of the true state of things earlier, the action of the foundation the preceding spring would have been different. Because he felt that the Carnegie official seemed cooperative, the president asked him to send down a special fact-finding committee. Dr. Pritchett refused, not wanting to set a precedent; but the optimistic president expected that he might come down in person.

The general tone of the president's Report was one of hope. He was able to report increased registration for 1909-1910, though there had been "some unfortunate press stories." Reporting to his fellow graduates on November 30, 1909, the president of the Alumni Association, E. C. Brandenburg, stated that he was "compelled to record the fact that during the heat of an internal controversy which occurred some months since in our University, the Board controlling and managing this [Carnegie] foundation saw fit to remove us from the list of those entitled to this recognition. Coming at the time it did, we regret to be forced to believe that this action was largely the outgrowth of this disagreement and without the mature consideration which doubtless does and should control this body of intelligent men in reaching their conclusions."[81]

If no progress had been made in matters of finance, the president could point with satisfaction to increasing evidence of student activities and school spirit. It was with real pride that he pointed out that sixteen fraternities and three sororities had chapters in the College. The four debating societies were active. While in 1900 there had been no athletic organization, there was now football, baseball, track, rifle, and some boating, and a weekly and an annual publication. Notwithstanding the serious disadvantages under which the students had to practice, they had resorted "to the remarkable spectacle of football practice by electric light." Both the student Y.M.C.A. and Y.W.C.A. continued active, and at the opening of the college year prepared an excellent *Student's Handbook* with information as to rules and customs, locations of libraries and classrooms, office hours and student organizations.[82]

There remained one ray of hope which somewhat illumined the dark financial picture during these days when the buoyancy and ingenuity of college youth were giving a new social life to the University. Final action had not been taken by Congress on the Gallinger-Boutell Amendment to the Morrill Act, designating The George Washington University as the institution in the District to receive annual appropriations provided under the act for a college in each state offering work in agriculture, the mechanical arts, and certain other subjects. Particularly crucial was the testimony offered at a hearing on February 25, 1910, by President James of Illinois. President Needham asked his Board for approval of a formal reply to this testimony. The approval was given. In his rebuttal, Needham stated that he felt it had been developed so fully in the hearing that there could now be no question that the District was entitled, like each of the states, to an equal amount of financial aid. The question was, which university should be designated. He called attention to the nature of the University in the light of its Congressional Charter and later supplementary legislation, in form private, but in some sense public. Its nonsectarian Charter was in no way endangered by the recent Columbian College incorporation. In answer to the objection that these funds, if granted, might be used for all subjects, the president pointed out that courses in agriculture and mechanical arts required instruction in both general subjects and basic science. Needham gave figures which are of interest in the light of the Carnegie Foundation's findings. He reported a total of $312,000 of assets, $335,800 of endowments, and $21,000 of trust funds to show total assets of $669,000. As a matter of fact, progressive borrowing had reduced the Corcoran Endowment to $16,000 productively invested; and of the Congressional Professorship Endowment Fund, lots estimated as worth $32,000 remained unsold, so that this fund could be restored, it was hoped, to almost $50,000.

The president challenged the right of anyone arbitrarily to rule on the condition of funds or to say when professors should be retired. Should there be created a federal university, Needham was certain that the District of Columbia could not support both it and George Washington, and that the federal university would kill George Washington. President Needham's reply did not produce the passage of the desired legislation. There was a new wave of resignations from the Board.[83]

On April 27, 1910, Charles Willis Needham presented his resignation as president of George Washington University. Five days later, it was accepted.

The presentation of the president's letter of resignation was followed immediately by the reading of a letter from the Attorney General of the United States, stating that pursuant to a resolution adopted by the House of Representatives on April 25, 1910, he was about to proceed to an investigation of the financial condition of the University. The action of the Attorney General was based on provisions of Section 10 of the original Charter of 1821. This section required in considerable detail that the Board of Trustees keep certain records of all their proceedings, of their bylaws and ordinances, and of all property—real, personal, or mixed—which should at all times be open to inspection by the Attorney General; "and when required by either House of Congress it shall be the duty of said trustees to furnish information respecting their own conduct, the state of the institution, and of its finances which shall or may be so required."[84]

The examination by the government's auditors was detailed and thorough. The fact that legislation in the University's interest was pending in the House, that statements regarding the use of the funds of the University had been made in hearings on this legislation and in the press, gave a special reason for an investigation at this time. Getting to work at once, Nelson B. Keyser and Sherrill Smith, special bank accountants for the Bureau of Investigation of the Department of Justice, were able to prepare for the Attorney General a preliminary report on the financial state of the University as of April 27, 1910, which was immediately transmitted to the Speaker of the House, to be supplemented by a later and more thorough report. The value of real estate and equipment was placed at $801,996.41 and the total indebtedness at $542,310.44. From this preliminary report it appeared that since December 31, 1899, expenses had exceeded income by $458,302.48, "which amount was partly provided out of the Corcoran endowment fund." This document, 124 pages in length, includes a historical account of certain trust funds, certain documents furnished by the University, an inventory of all the equipment, and a list of salaries.[85]

On December 6, 1910, the Attorney General submitted two further reports, one dated August 20 showing the history and present financial condition of the endowment, scholarship, prize, and other trusts; the other, dated November 15, stated the assets and liabilities of the University and enumerated recent acts of the Board of Trustees in untangling its affairs.[86]

The final report concluded with a statement of efforts being made to restore the institution to financial health. Attention was called to reduction in expenses and salary. Needham's successor, President Stockton, was serving without compensation. Interest, which in the previous year amounted to $22,273, had been practically eliminated, as was the cost of maintenance of the University and Law halls. The cost of maintenance of the buildings at 1528 to 1538 Eye Street was not expected to exceed that of the preceding year when these buildings were used as a "university annex." The Division of Architecture's use of 1532, and the women's dormitory at 1536 and 1538 which had been maintained at a loss, were discontinued. By utilizing these quarters and moving the chemical laboratories to the Medical building, room was found for the College of Arts and Sciences and the Graduate School. The College of the Political Sciences remained in the same rented quarters at 819 Fifteenth Street, but deficits in operation were expected to be covered by collection of the subscriptions obtained by Dr. Harlan. The Medical and Dental Schools and the hospital, which paid no rent for the use of buildings, were expected to be self-sustaining. Out of $5,000 paid by the Law School to the general treasury, rent of $2,300 to the Masonic Temple would be met.[87]

One important item remained. The investigations showed that, other than the Martin embezzlement, there was no evidence of any shortage. "All the money received either from tuitions or from the principal and income of endowment funds appears to have been expended in the conduct of the business of the University and its expenditure either authorized or ratified by the Board of Trustees."[88]

The investigations indicated that, while the money had been regularly appropriated by the Trustees, endowment and other trust funds had been impaired since 1821 on the order of $350,000 to defray operating and other expenses. It seems that up to this time universities had not always been too meticulous in protecting the integrity of their permanent funds. It can be hoped that the disclosure of the embarrassing situation of George Washington University helped improve the general tone of university financial administration. The device that was worked out to insure the repayment by the University to itself of the full amount of its impairment of its endowment and trust funds was rather complicated. The University executed a promissory note for $350,000 payable on or before ten years after date to the Washington Loan and Trust Company, fiscal agent of the University and trustee of endowment funds. The University then conveyed title to its property and its equipment on H Street between Thirteenth and Fourteenth Streets in trust to the National Savings and Trust Company, with the University's right to continued use and occupancy reserved. The trust provided that in default of payment of the note, at the request of the Attorney General the trustee would sell the property and first pay all costs, then pay $350,000 or as much as was then due to the Washington Loan and Trust Company, and any balance remaining to the University. In a simple but inaccurate statement, the endowment and trust funds, indirectly, held a mortgage on the Medical property, to insure that if that property were sold, the proceeds would go to restore the endowment and trust funds. The note was paid off in full during the Marvin administration, so there no longer existed any impairment of funds.[89]

Three weeks after Dr. Needham's resignation, Rear Admiral Charles Herbert Stockton, U.S.N. (ret.), was elected acting president, and Howard Lee McBain, Professor of Political Science, was designated as assistant to Admiral Stockton. President Needham continued to attend the meetings of the Board to the end of his term. Most of the arrangements for the radical reduction of expenses were approved during June, 1910. The sale of the property at Fifteenth and H Streets for $550,000 was approved on July 1, and a special committee was appointed to recommend on the allocation of the proceeds so as best to meet the commitments of the institution.[90]

In its physical appearance at least, the University which President

Needham's successor took over was greatly changed. The upper floors of the Masonic Temple housed the Law School. The Hospital, the Dispensary, and the Medical School remained. The Department of Arts and Sciences occupied a row of rented houses on Eye Street, and quarters for chemistry in the Medical Building. It was, to say the least, a startling change. Expenses had been cut to the bone; and in at least two departments members of the faculty had agreed to accept, for the time being, a reduction up to 50 per cent of their salary at the rate paid the preceding year. Some valuable members of the faculty resigned, readily finding posts in other institutions where many had distinguished careers. The essential core of the faculty remained, insuring instruction of the same high character as before, though in less convenient quarters. There was, miraculously, no break in educational continuity.

Sixteen years had elapsed since the close of the Welling administration. When Welling succeeded Samson, President Samson made a very wise observation. He welcomed his successor because Welling had gifts that he himself did not have. He said that he himself had gifts that his predecessor did not have, and they were as necessary for his times as were those special abilities of Welling for the days ahead. President Whitman's talents differed from those of his predecessors. He worked diligently to complete Welling's "University Plan," but he had no philanthropist and adviser like W. W. Corcoran on hand. He expanded the University organization, thus increasing its financial needs, but was unable to increase its endowment or its income. His experiment in denominational control was not only unproductive but damaging to the University's public posture. Dr. Needham had been connected with the University long enough and intimately enough as Trustee and dean to know the situation he inherited.

The Whitman–Needham period (1895-1910) was certainly not the best one in the economic history of the country for raising money. The Panic of 1893 not only was severe in itself but was followed by a very lengthy and severe depression that extended over almost the entire period of Whitman's administration. Whitman and General Coxey came to Washington within a year of each other. Needham also had a panic, the Panic of 1907, when it was said that the country experienced the most complete breakdown of its banking facilities it had known since the War of 1861-1865.

Due allowance being made for the national economic situation, would Needham's leadership have brought success under more favorable conditions? Frederick the Great is supposed to have said that when he offered

Maria Theresa the chance of participating in the partition of Poland, she cried but kept on taking. Needham warned his Board about incurring debts, but kept on spending. This he could rationalize by his unfortunate habit of mixing mathematics and optimistic imagination. No matter how heavy the mortgage on a property, he could always find a remaining equity. His statements of assets were always well padded with these estimated amounts. He was not always clear as to what productive investment was, but he was rarely at a loss when it came to showing that funds, potentially, or expectantly, or probably, were available.

President Needham was given to making recommendations quickly, as befitted his enthusiastic and optimistic nature, and then having the recommendation laid on the table or, if adopted, suspended. Each time there was a financial crisis, a campaign for funds was launched, the amount sought (up to $7,500,000) depending upon the apparent seriousness of the crisis. Subscriptions would be sought for a stated purpose. When circumstances indicated a shift in the objective—as, for example, a change in the site sought—subscribers would stand on their rights, literally, and refuse to pay. Perhaps because of his legal training, Needham tended toward overorganization and codification. There were ordinances galore. The plan for the separate incorporation of schools, carried through for Columbian College and the School of Engineering, was promptly forgotten because of the embarrassment caused by these separate corporations. The agreement with the George Washington Memorial Association, which involved large expenditures on the part of both parties, was entered into when the association had only $16,000 in cash.

Needham accepted Welling's dictum that the special mission of the University was in the area of professional and higher education, particularly in the fields of jurisprudence, politics, and diplomacy. The College of the Political Sciences enjoyed his special protection. To the Welling idea, Needham added emphasis on the College, dormitories, student activities, athletic teams, and all the fixings, feeling that such a college was owed to the youth of the District of Columbia. The part-time employed student was to a degree, in his way of thinking, a blot on the escutcheon, yet the part-time student paid fees and Needham was in no position to ignore fees. The legal mind solved the problem. All classes must end by six-thirty. There were no more "night" classes. This indicated a confusion as to the University's mission that had not been shared by Welling.

In happier times, President Needham's limitations would not have been so serious. Other presidents had had no more to offer, but circumstances favored them, and Needham had to deal with others' accumulated mistakes, as well as his own. General Maxwell Van Zandt Woodhull, who became an influential Trustee in the Stockton years and later, and who was largely responsible for bringing the University to its present location, frequently used to say that Needham's great sin was "rainbow-chasing." Needham's first statement to the Board was full of optimism, and so was his last statement eight years later. His loyalty to the University never wavered, and he carried his office with great dignity. The lessons learned from the Needham administration were perhaps a rich legacy: Never again would endowment funds be used for operating deficits.

CHAPTER THIRTEEN

Reorganization and Relocation

1910-1927

The task which faced the new president, Admiral Stockton, was colossal. The College and University had faced crisis before, but never of this magnitude. Here were a large and eager student body and a group of able teachers, the real ingredients of a great university; but all else seemed lacking. The endowment had all but disappeared. To restore a major portion of it (and that was the purpose of the mortgage the University held on its own medical property), the institution would have had to turn out the one branch of its educational organization which was still housed in University-owned structures. The administration and the Department of Arts and Sciences were located in a row of rented residences, the Law School in leased quarters in the Masonic Temple. There was even some difficulty in getting together the funds to pay for the moving and storage of equipment.

In a way, the outlook was more dismal than in earlier periods of economic stringency. There had been a lengthy effort to seek out and solicit every possible source of aid in a more systematic way than ever before. It had not yielded the necessary funds, or even a substantial part of them. In the early years of his administration, President Stockton served without salary, but he had no magic formula. What he did have was determination. His predecessors had more than once declared that expenditures must be brought into line with income, but they had gone on spending. Stockton made the same declaration and he carried it out. The cuts he made were radical, and in making them he restored public confidence in the University's credit and integrity.

The sale of the Law School building and of the University building at Fifteenth and H Streets and the removal of the units which had been housed in them to modest, cramped, rented quarters saved the institution heavy maintenance charges. There was a general reduction in salaries; and the teaching staff was reduced by the elimination of the office of dean of women, ten professors, three assistant professors, one instructor, three lecturers, and two assistants.[1] The Athletic Council was abolished, football was suspended, student activities and athletics were reorganized, and student indebtedness was assigned to a special committee for liquidation.[2]

With the sale of the property at Fifteenth and H Streets for $550,000—this was used as far as possible for paying off indebtedness—the Board canceled all subscriptions to the $400,000 Building Site and Expansion Fund and to the Alumni Hall Fund. Aside from a continuing effort that lasted three years more to get favorable action by Congress on the amendments to the Morrill Act, the decks had been cleared of all old projects. The way was open for a new beginning.

Tuition fees, being a principal source of income, were raised to a maximum annual charge of $150.[3]

On November 30, 1910, Acting President Stockton was elected president. A month before, Commissioner H. B. F. Macfarland had resigned as chairman of the Board and was succeeded by John Bell Larner, who held the post for twenty years.

Charles Herbert Stockton (1845-1923), who was called to the presidency at a most critical point in the University's life, was a native of Philadelphia and a graduate of the United States Naval Academy in the class of 1865. As a midshipman he saw active service in operations against ships of the Confederate States Navy. His distinguished career, begun thus early, brought him in time the command of the *U.S.S. Kentucky*, the presidency of the Naval War College, and appointment as naval attaché at London and as delegate plenipotentiary to the London Naval Conference of 1908-1909. Recognized as an outstanding authority on international law, he was the author of *The Laws and Usages of War at Sea*, of a manual of international law for the use of naval officers, and of *Outlines of International Law*, a highly regarded text in the field. Inclined to be short and rather stocky, but always military in carriage, President Stockton was dignified in both appearance and manner. As a college president he did not lay aside the habits of the admiral: punctuality, precision in speech, perfect frankness, a stern sense of duty. On his office door was printed "Office hours 9:30 to 12:30." This meant that he arrived at 9:30 and left at 12:30 precisely and without variation. Regularly his secretary made the uniform entries in his logbook as to weather and statements of important actions taken, and he signed his log before leaving for the day. Thought to be formal and aloof by those who did not know him, he was cordial to his associates and almost fatherly to the younger members of his official family. To an institution which had gone through a series of traumatic experiences, there was something positively tonic in the calm, dignified, and assured manner of this distinguished officer who gave up the leisure of retirement to serve, without compensation, an institution calling for strong administration and deep understanding.

At the beginning of his second year in office, President Stockton reported that, in spite of limited and largely improvised quarters, there was an increase in registration over the preceding year. He also reported the admission of a woman to the Medical School, the first since the practice had been discontinued twenty years before. After several attempts had been made, registration of women in the professional schools was authorized in June, 1911. In the fall of 1913, five women were admitted to the Law School.[4]

The financial reorganization of the University was formalized by the Board's acceptance of the findings of the Attorney General's report with reference to all the various funds of the University, with four exceptions. Since the Building Site and Expansion and the Alumni Hall subscription had been canceled, it was decided that all funds collected should be returned to the donors if they so desired. The Eleanor J. Cooper bequest, designated for the investigation of the "nature of the malarial poison arising from sewer gas and the antidote thereof," could not be carried out, but previous expenditures under this fund were considered sufficient to permit the omission of these amounts from the University's liabilities. A committee was set up to decide on the use of the Powell Fund. A deed of trust for $369,405.98 was placed on the Medical School and Hospital property to cover the impairment of endowment funds. The floating debt, once so formidable, had been reduced to $3,893.80.[5]

Serving as he was without compensation, Admiral Stockton was in a position to ask others to make sacrifices, and they were made readily. No salary with the exception of that of the dean of the Law School was to exceed $3,000 per annum. The exception was justified by the fact that Dean Lorenzen had accepted a call to Yale and Dean Charles Noble Gregory of Iowa State had just been appointed to succeed him. The

University was living frugally. Student pressure to resume a full program of activities, funded in part by a $3 activities fee, was resisted for four years. The first modest fund-raising effort of the new administration came to a successful close with the obtaining of the one-hundredth subscription to a $100 five-year fund, designed to ease immediate needs.[6]

At best, the situation as to quarters could not last. The top floors of the Masonic Temple could, and did with effort, house the Law School for many years. The Medical School and Hospital remained in the buildings they had held, but the Department of Arts and Sciences, jammed in a row of rented dwellings, did not have room for even essential equipment. The apparatus of the Department of Mechanical Engineering was put in storage and no students in that field were accepted. When notice came to vacate the Eye Street houses because the property had been sold and the new owner desired early possession, immediate action had to be taken. Desultory thought had been given to a new location for some months, but no decision had been reached.

Now, General Maxwell Van Zandt Woodhull, who lived at Twenty-first and G Streets and who had been elected to the Board of Trustees in the spring of 1911, brought his very considerable influence to bear in the selection of 2023 G Street as the new site. On June 6, 1912, the University closed its option for the purchase of this property which, five months before, it had agreed to rent for five years at an annual rental of not more than $2,000, with the privilege to buy within the first six months for $32,500. Lacking cash, the University bought 2023 G Street with borrowed money: a first mortgage of $22,500 taken by Riggs National Bank and a second mortgage of $10,000 taken by the seller. At the same time authorization was given to rent a house or houses in the same section for not over $900 per year. Under this authorization, 2024 G Street was rented. So, in 1912, the University came to what is, in contemporary affectation, called Foggy Bottom.

The name was never an official one, indicating fixed metes and bounds. For decades it was one of those popular terms of denigration which traditionally fix themselves to an area like Swampoodle, Bloodfield, Frog Island, Herring Hill. The inhabitants of the present University precincts would, to a man, have protested that they lived east of Foggy Bottom. Its great landmarks were two breweries, a large coal yard, extensive stables, the gas works, and a famous saloon. Time works a strange legerdemain. The development of a parkway along the Potomac, the contemporary craze for restoration of old dwellings, and the construction of great memorials, monumental government structures, high-rise office buildings, and luxurious apartments have given Foggy Bottom a distinct éclat and its name a place in the literature of politics, society, and the arts.

In the old days, there had been an appropriateness to the name, though Foggy Bottom had no official place in geographical nomenclature. It was bottom land and much of its lower fringe was swampy. The fogs which settled over the river bank were amplified by the smog from the gas works which emitted dirt-laden and malodorous clouds of smoke, day and night, touched up with violent spurts of flame that lit up the vicinity with an eerie glow. But the gas works are gone now, and in its present fine attire Foggy Bottom has taken on the ways of gentility.

If an ancient name is sought for the area which includes most of the University complex, that name would have to be Hamburg. Hamburg was an incorporated town consisting of 130 acres, purchased by a German, Jacob Funk, and laid out by him in 1768 in 287 building lots. In recent terms, the boundaries of the town would be approximately H Street on the north, Upper Water Street and B Street (now Constitution Avenue) on the south, Twenty-third Street on the west and a line midway between Eighteenth and Nineteenth Streets on the east. "Hamburg Wharf" at the foot of Twenty-first Street was an important river landing. Concordia Church, on the southeast corner of Twentieth and G Streets, is built on land dedicated by Jacob Funk for a German house of worship. The undeveloped land to the west of Hamburg became Foggy Bottom and, like the town, was embraced within the territory set aside for "the Federal City in the Territory of Columbia."[7]

Older Washingtonians still refer to the larger area in which the University is located as "the First Ward." This name is a survival from the nineteenth century when the city was divided into wards as political and fiscal units under the old city charter. The oldest arrangement (1801) included in the First Ward all of the city south of Pennsylvania Avenue and west of Sixth Street. This division into wards lasted as long as the old mayoralty government.[8]

The citizens' association into whose bailiwick the University now falls is called the West End Citizens' Association, thus contributing a new name to the area, really the western end of the old city which had extended to Florida Avenue on the north and the creek on the west.

What was to become the University's neighborhood had gone through many changes by 1912. Here were many houses which dated from the beginnings of the federal city. High officials of the government had lived here and many foreign legations were located here in the days of the early republic. In the period of the War of 1861-1865 and the decades that followed there was a great migration of admirals and generals into this part of the First Ward, due, no doubt, to the proximity of the State, War, and Navy Building and the many offices of the military along Seventeenth Street. By 1912 it had lost its exclusive character; and while a few of the old families remained, the area had become miscellaneous in character and gave a distinct impression of decadence.

The University's first purchase of land was 2023 G Street, in what is designated in the plat books of the District as Square 102. A quick look at the four sides of this square will indicate the general character of the neighborhood at the time. In the middle of the north side of G Street between Twentieth and Twenty-first Streets stood the old St. Rose's Industrial School which was vacant when bought by the University. To the west of it stood the two Easby Houses, three-story, flat-front, red brick structures; and, on the corner of Twenty-first Street, the Woodhull House, built in the 1850's, and in 1912 the home of General Maxwell Van Zandt Woodhull, his sister Miss Ellen Woodhull, and his brother, Mr. Charles H. Woodhull. To the east of 2023 on G Street were a large red brick three-story and basement house where Henry Adams had had rooms in 1869-1870; another red brick three-story and basement house with large bay windows which had been remodeled as an apartment house; a two-story and basement stuccoed house, which for a time housed the Faculty Club; a rather wide, light brick three-story house, showing a faint but ineffective Richardsonian influence in its architecture, used at the time as a tourist home; and a relatively modern red brick three-story building which for many years contained the offices of President Marvin and his staff. This south side was decidedly the most prepossessing face of Square 102.

On the west side, Twenty-first Street between G and H Streets, from the Woodhull property at the corner of G Street—this had a larger area than any other holding on the square—there were only small houses: three narrow brick structures squeezed into two lots; a larger brick residence with a Charleston-style porch along the north side; a small brick cottage, well back from the street, that was occupied by an aged Negro named George Washington and his wife; two more small two-story bricks, and a clapboard dwelling with a store front on the corner of H Street.

On the north side of the square, H Street between Twentieth and

Twenty-first Streets, after the little corner store there were two attractive two-story red brick houses; then some brick houses in sad disrepair, containing a shoemaker's shop, an upholsterer's shop, and a Chinese laundry. One of these structures, greatly changed, was tied in with the old gymnasium, the famous "Tin Tabernacle," which still defies the years. At the corner was the relatively large Marion Apartment, which, greatly remodeled, is known today as Bacon Hall.

On the eastern face of Square 102, south of the Marion, were two large brick dwellings and two small clapboard ones; a row of three bay-windowed red brick dwellings used for many years by the Department of Physical Education for Women; a single, detached, red brick house used as a tourist home; and the large three-story double house at the corner of G Street, later tied in with the attached house on G Street as a part of the president's office.

This attempt at the reconstruction of Square 102 will give a suggestion of the general character of the area—a mansion, dignified brick residences, tourists' homes, a laundry, a cottage, a cobbler's shop, a corner grocery, an upholsterer's shop, little brick and clapboard houses, and a small junk yard.[9]

For the neighborhood, as it was then, the old St. Rose's School was an impressive structure. Located somewhat back of the building line, it had a small front yard that was a few steps higher than the pavement from which it was separated by an iron fence and double gates. Large maple trees shaded the yard and the front of the building. Although a second entrance was made later (1917), there was at the time a single front entrance reached by a half-dozen brown stone steps. In front of the school was the traditional carriage block and gas lamp with a small letter-box fixed to the post. The building had three stories, a basement—half of which was above the pavement level—and a mansard. It was built of red brick with brown stone trimming. Antedating the use of steel in construction, it could hardly have been considered a good fire risk, although only one small fire (1918) is remembered during the quarter-century of the University's occupancy.

With the exception of the Department of Chemistry, all the departments of instruction in the arts and sciences were in 2023 G Street, as were all the offices of administration, with the single exception of the treasurer's office. The latter was situated in a rented residence of considerable size across the street at 2024. The staff of the financial office at that time consisted of the treasurer, a bookkeeper, and a secretary. There were offices on the first floor. The second floor contained three classrooms, and on the two top floors were the rooms of the sororities—Pi Beta Phi, Chi Omega, Sigma Kappa, and later Phi Mu. Aside from a small men's lounge in the basement of 2023 and an equally small women's lounge on the second floor, there was no provision for student comfort. Quigley's Pharmacy on the southeast corner of Twenty-first and G Streets, presided over by the kindly doctor himself (R. Lucien Quigley, Phar.D., 1890), was the real social center.[10]

The *arbiter elegantiarum* of the new campus was none other than the Trustee who lived in the mansion at the corner, through whose urging the University had moved to G Street. Maxwell Van Zandt Woodhull, brevetted Brigadier General in the Union Army at the age of twenty-two, and still, a half-century later, military in carriage and impeccable in attire, was a genial old martinet who loved to discuss religion and medieval history and hated Democrats. He kept a watchful eye on the University. Professors seen on the streets without hats were subject to reprimand, and unless the shades at the windows all over the building were pulled down an even length, an investigation would be started. In the General and his establishment alone the elegance and distinction of the old First Ward were still alive. But a new age was dawning.

Just as the University was moving, Dr. W. S. Hough, who had been dean of Teachers College since 1907, died and was succeeded by Professor W. C. Ruediger. In the years of Ruediger's deanship, it is said that more than half of the teachers in the public schools of the District were his students. Under him, a demonstration school for student teachers was maintained for years in St. John's Church Orphanage at Twentieth and F Streets.

At the end of the first year on G Street, the College of the Political Sciences, which in 1907 had taken over most of the nonprofessional courses formerly offered by the School of Jurisprudence and Diplomacy, was discontinued and its courses transferred to Columbian College. At the time of its discontinuance, Dr. C. W. A. Veditz was acting dean, Dean H. Parker Willis having resigned after unsuccessful attempts to get the College properly financed and strictly defined as to its course offerings.[11]

As the years of President Stockton's administration passed, anyone looking for the dramatic or the spectacular would have found instead the plain, the steady, and the prosaic. Therein was the president's greatness. He knew that the days of quick expansion, of "rainbow chasing," were over. His task was to establish more firmly than ever before the credit and the integrity of the institution. It had to be demonstrated that the University could live on its income. That meant rigid control of finances and cutting back wherever possible. President Stockton had the genius to direct retrenchment and growth at the same time, without lowering the quality of instruction. Contrasted with the budgets for today's University running into tens of millions of dollars, his budget for 1914-1915 showed a balance and was based on a total income of $162,945.[12] With little income from endowment, the problem resolved itself into operating on the funds paid in as tuition. Educationally, this is virtually impossible; but modest quarters, low maintenance, and double use of quarters and equipment by day and late-afternoon students for the time made possible the impossible.

The small surplus available each year was used in two ways: to reduce the debt on 2023 G Street and to acquire small parcels of property, immediately useful themselves or contiguous to other University holdings. A nurses' home at Thirteenth and L Streets was bought in 1913. Land adjacent to the north of the original holding at 2023 G Street was bought that same year to provide quarters for a mechanical engineering laboratory in a reconstructed building in the middle of the square. In 1914, the second mortgage for $10,000 on 2023 G Street was paid off in full, and the adjacent property on the west (2025 G Street) with a usable house was purchased. The following year, two more lots were acquired in Square 102 and also the property at 2017 G Street. In 1916, the property at 2027 G Street was acquired, and the noninterest-bearing mortgage on the Medical and Hospital property was reduced to $323,430.23. During the last year of President Stockton's administration, $3,000 more was applied to reduce the mortgage on 2023 G Street, and $2,000 from current income was used to establish an Endowment, Restoration, and Accretion Fund. This fund was designed to restore endowment funds used prior to August 31, 1910, for current expenses, with the Corcoran Fund to be the first restored. After the endowment funds were restored, this fund was to become a General Endowment Accretion Fund.[13]

The price of these parcels of land was generally between $4,000 and $8,000 each. Practically each one of them had been improved by a brick dwelling which, with slight modification, could be used for classrooms and offices. Half of the south side of Square 102, with much interior footage, was acquired during the Stockton regime of rigid economy. This was, in a way, Stockton's challenge to the future—slow expansion with economy in administration to insure permanence.

Although income from tuition was the very life blood of the institution, there was no radical increase in student fees. In 1917, tuition fees in the Medical School were increased from $150 to $175 per year, and in the Dental School from $125 to $150. In the following year, tuition fees in the Department of Arts and Sciences were increased from $150 to $180 for the year.[14]

After a lapse of many years, the University resumed summer school work in arts and sciences and in law, with the first summer session in 1916. This was the only major extension of academic offerings undertaken during the Stockton years. Dean W. C. Ruediger directed summer school work in the arts and sciences, and Professor W. C. Van Vleck that in the Law School. As first organized, this work involved no financial risk to the University; three-quarters of the fees were divided among the instructors, and the other quarter was assigned to maintenance and the director's salary. With a rapid gain in enrollment, the unsatisfactory fee system of compensation was soon abandoned and a regular salary schedule adopted.[15]

In a series of changes in nomenclature, the names of the College of Arts and Sciences and of the Departments of Medicine, Law, and Dentistry became, respectively, Columbian College (1912) and the Schools of Medicine, Law, and Dentistry (1914).

Operating an educational institution on tuition income was a dangerous practice, even though President Stockton had no choice when the institution was trying to raise itself by its own bootstraps. The situation was bound to be precarious and the first major jolt came just as the Stockton administration was coming to an end, when the Dental Council of America transferred the Dental School from Class A to Class C. As Dean Borden pointed out to the Trustees, if this classification were continued, the school would be taken off the approved list of the Surgeon General of the Army and the very considerable number of enlisted men then registered would be withdrawn, cutting down materially the income of the school. If the school discontinued night work, the major part of the normal clientele, because it was employed during the day, would be excluded. To improve the situation, Dean Borden presented to the Board for approval new ordinances for the governance of the Dental School.

The problem was not thus easily met. The Medical building housed the College Department of Chemistry and the Medical and Dental Schools, which made demands as to space and equipment far beyond the capacity of the building. If it had been feasible in terms of the dental students' commitments to move their classes to daytime hours, an impossible congestion would have been created. The only real solution would have been to build a Dental School. There were no funds for acquisition of site, building construction and equipment, and maintenance of the school on an independent basis. The hard answer to the question was indicated, but the decision would have to be made by the Admiral's successor.[16]

During the eight years of the Stockton administration, the ranks of senior members of the faculty showed practically no change. Younger men of the grade of instructor or assistant professor were added in sufficient numbers to bring the teaching staff back to its numerical strength before the period of retrenchment.

Student activities, especially athletics, had been a casualty of the economic stringency. By the spring of 1914, the President's Council felt called upon to deal the *coup de grâce*, and recommended a discontinuance of the few remaining intercollegiate and collegiate sports, with the University donating sufficient funds to pay off the athletic deficit and thus close the chapter. Student opinion was not inclined to acquiesce in such a move. A flood of petitions reached the Board of Trustees. Thirty student organizations and 700 out of 1,000 students canvassed pledged financial and moral support for athletics. A benefit performance held at the Columbia Theatre on May 4, 1914, realized more than sufficient funds to cancel the entire athletic debt. The Board acceded to the student demand. Leslie C. McNemar, Assistant Professor of Political Science, a warm advocate of athletics, was appointed Director of Athletics, and the continuance of track and basketball for one more year was authorized.

In spite of retrenchments, at no time had the practice of allowing full tuition to the editor and business manager of the *Hatchet* and the yearbook been discontinued.[17]

Under the sympathetic guidance of Dean Everett Fraser of the Law School, chairman of the Committee on Student Affairs, a further step of great importance was taken the following year, when the Trustees adopted comprehensive regulations for the governance of student activities. A voluntary student activities fee of $1 per month for the school year was instituted. This fee was collected from subscribers by the treasurer, along with other university charges. Interested members of both faculty and the student body could subscribe to and receive the *Hatchet* and the *Cherry Tree*, be admitted to all athletic contests except indoor track, and receive certain medical and hospital benefits. Intercollegiate indoor track and basketball were continued, football and outdoor track resumed, and interdepartmental athletics encouraged.[18] Funds received from the voluntary activities fee were apportioned as follows: medical benefits, 25 per cent; *Hatchet*, 7 per cent; *Cherry Tree*, 19 per cent; Student Council, 4 per cent; and athletics, 45 per cent. As a necessary officer for the administration of medical and hospital benefits, a university physician was appointed for the first time in 1916.[19]

At a student mass meeting held in the Law School in mid April, 1916, a set of resolutions prepared by Dean Fraser, providing for the election of a Student Council to supervise and encourage the development of student activities was adopted.[20] The new council fostered a complete resumption of athletics, including football. Undergraduate enthusiasm ran high. The student body, with police escort, marched over across the creek to attend the first of a new series of games with Georgetown on the Hilltop. When, by good fortune, a touchdown was scored in the first few minutes of play (the last in the game!), it seemed that glory shone all around. The new council resumed the custom of publishing an annual *Handbook*. It stood on its prerogatives, even to a sudden and serious brush with the faculty on the control of the *Hatchet*. But war, soon to involve the nation, suddenly made these matters of student concern tremendously unimportant.

World War I came to the United States slowly, but inevitably. The great American abhorrence of war acted as a deterrent to our quick entry as long as the conflict could be kept away from our doors. But complicating the whole question of America's stance was the fact that each of the belligerent nations involved or to be involved was represented by many of its sons and daughters who had found here a refuge from the political, social, and economic ills of the Old World. America was truly a melting pot of the nations, but the old ways and allegiances had in many cases not yet boiled down. Common origins and common cultures had a powerful cohesive force in maintaining national blocs of sympathy and understanding within the American composite. These ties were strong; they divided many people's feelings between the old home and the new. It was the age of the "hyphenates."

Aside from any general revulsion to war and the reluctance of national groups to be involved in war with their states of origin, the United States had been in the forefront of the movement for international peace. The American Peace Society had been in existence ever since 1828 and had published a magazine from the time of its organization. President

Theodore Roosevelt had won the Nobel Peace Prize.[21] Americans had made important contributions to the literature of the peace movement and many distinguished Americans were actively involved in considering ways and means of enforcing peace as the war got under way. President Woodrow Wilson, an academic liberal in straight descent from Jeremy Bentham, had all of the liberal's hatred for war and all of the liberal's aspiration for a world order which would know war no longer.

The result of the interplay of the forces shaping American policy was, for the first three years, neutrality. Within this framework the University moved slowly, but positively. At the beginning of the first academic year after the outbreak of the war in Europe, the Board of Trustees assigned the president $1,500 in tuition to be used, at his discretion, for European college students who, because of conditions at home, were unable to resume studies in their own colleges.[22] The University welcomed to its staff for the academic year 1915-1916, as a displaced scholar, the great Belgian, George Sarton, the most eminent historian of science of this century.[23]

Foreseeing the day when neutrality would be no longer possible, General Maxwell Van Zandt Woodhull in June, 1915, offered a resolution declaring that it was "the judgment of the Trustees that a Company or Battalion of Infantry or Coast Artillery, drilled as infantry, be organized from the student body and affiliated with the Militia of the District of Columbia." This resolution was passed. General Woodhull as chairman of the Trustees' Committee was given full power to act. Recruiting got under way at once.[24]

On November 3, 1915, announcement was made that Walter W. Burns, a student of the Law School and formerly Lieutenant (j.g.), D.C. Naval Militia, had been appointed Captain. The organization was designated as First Company, Coast Artillery Corps, National Guard, District of Columbia, with headquarters in the Armory at 230 First Street, N.W.

While the Coast Artillery unit was being organized, there was other evidence on the campus of approaching war. Lecture rooms, when not needed, were put at the service of the Potomac Division of Torpedo Control for purposes of instruction. Student participation in patriotic demonstrations for preparedness were enthusiastically undertaken. As soon as Liberty Bonds were issued, a campaign for their purchase was started. The proceeds of this bond drive were used a few years later to help pay the cost of the "Tin Tabernacle."

The days of neutrality came to a close. The overt act, which seems to be the necessary preliminary of any declaration of war, occurred. The House Memorandum of February 22, 1916, had indicated President Wilson's intention to propose a peace conference whenever England and France found the time favorable, and intimated American entry in the war against Germany if that power rejected the peace proposal. Still the American people, by and large, were not ready for war and Wilson was reelected in November, 1916, on a peace platform. The disclosure of a German project for an alliance with Mexico and Japan against this country and the beginning of unrestricted submarine warfare brought about a break in diplomatic relations, followed by a declaration of war two months later.

President Wilson's war message was delivered to the Senate on April 2, 1917. On the following day the Trustees adopted a resolution written by President Stockton. Citing "the humiliation and injury" suffered during the preceding two years, it declared, with a fine Palmerstonian ring, that "it is a primary and exclusive duty of a nation to protect its citizens and their property afloat and ashore." The Congress was called upon to take necessary steps "to further such objects and to protect our territory" by raising, equipping, and training "our land and sea forces in sufficient number and in a manner that will be equal and just to all." The President's message was endorsed and loyal support was pledged to him as Commander-in-Chief.

So successful had been the recruiting for the Coast Artillery Corps that a second company was formed and mustered in on July 26, 1917. As soon as they were federalized, the companies were assigned to Fort Washington, Maryland. First Lieutenant Howard W. Hodgkins, who had been an outstanding leader in student activities and was in later years to serve as an alumni trustee, was put in command of the Second Company. When, late in 1917, the 60th Regiment, Coast Artillery Corps, was formed, the companies were incorporated in that organization. In April, 1918, the regiment was sent to Brest aboard the *U.S.S. Siboney*. After brief intensive training in France, the regiment was moved to the Argonne front and fought throughout the Meuse-Argonne offensive. Used briefly in clean-up operations after the armistice, the 60th was landed in New York by the *Cedric* on February 4, 1919, and within a few days was demobilized at Forts Washington and Hunt.[25]

President Stockton was now in his seventy-third year. To a career of great distinction as a naval officer he had added one of equal distinction as a university president. He had announced his intention to resign well in advance. President Stockton could look back on eight years of service with complete satisfaction, for he had assured the continuation and growth of the University. He had restored it to solvency and laid the basis for the accumulation of both endowment and land. He had restored the faith of people in the integrity of the institution. He had supported the deans and faculty in raising and maintaining higher levels of academic excellence. There was never a year without increase in student registration, acquisition of at least a small addition to the property, reduction of debt, and increase in faculty. These additions were small but consistent, and there was no receding once an advance had been made. All of the divisive elements had been silenced, and there was an era of good feeling, appropriately symbolized by Professors Gore and Sterrett resuming their status as professors emeriti at the enthusiastic request of both Trustees and faculty.

The resolutions adopted by the Trustees at the time President Stockton's resignation was accepted, in 1918, are not the collection of rhetorical bombast too frequently found in such documents. There was no need for them; a solid achievement demanded a factual statement:

The University has been placed on a thoroughly sound financial basis, its teaching force strengthened, and student body greatly increased. Its steady and peaceful growth has been the result of conservative methods, maintained and promoted within the lines of constructive expansion.[26]

The Board's choice of a successor had fallen upon William Miller Collier, whose acceptance was communicated to the Board on January 9, 1918. President Stockton's term was to run until August 31, but because of the grave problems caused by the war, President-elect Collier was to take over the active duties of his office immediately after Commencement. The resignation of Professor Richard Cobb, Secretary of the University, took effect at the same time. The Board elected as his successor Elmer Louis Kayser, the last one to hold the title (1918-1929). In another major change, Professor Merton L. Ferson became Dean of the Law School, succeeding Dean Fraser.

Richard Cobb had served as Professor of English and Secretary of the University. He had been the loyal and efficient associate of the Admiral in reshaping the University. As secretary ex officio of the Board of Trustees, the President's Council, and the faculties, he had maintained and developed communication between all of those bodies in a critical period. The diploma used today is the one he designed, and the formula for conferring degrees is basically as he established it. A modest, self-effacing man, he spent his later years in retirement at his home in Barnstable, Massachusetts.

While the summer of 1918 fell formally within the administration of President Stockton, Mr. Collier was actively in charge, and his energetic policy in meeting the needs of the University in a wartime capital marked the beginning of a new era.[27]

William Miller Collier (1867-1956), tenth president of the University, found a crisis confronting him as he assumed the duties of his office. Fortunately, he was a man of great resourcefulness and energy. Like President Stockton, he was not a member of the Baptist denomination and, again like President Stockton, he too was the son of a clergyman. After graduating from Hamilton College in 1889, President Collier was called to the bar. Following a few years of private practice, he became a referee in bankruptcy, and then a member of the New York Civil Service Commission, of which he was chairman from 1901 to 1903. His first federal position was special Assistant Attorney General, engaged in the enforcement of antitrust regulations. In 1905, President Theodore Roosevelt appointed him Minister to Spain, a post which he held for four years. At the time of his election to the presidency of the University, he was practicing international law and lecturing on diplomacy and diplomatic usage at the University. After three years (1918-1921) he resigned his post to return to the foreign service as Ambassador to Chile (1921-1928).

The crisis which faced President Collier was not an internal one, but one imposed by the war with Germany. In terms of time, the better part of the war was over. President Stockton had met the earlier problems that had arisen as they appeared, but the passage of the so-called "man-power" bill opened up grave possibilities. Previously the draft had begun with the age of twenty-one. The new regulations required the registration of all males eighteen to forty-five years of age. If the war were at all protracted, this would practically wipe out the male student body.

By the time the new president met his Board at its first regular meeting, he, Treasurer Holmes, and the Secretary had been working around the clock for weeks on the major problem that had to be solved before the opening of the fall session. Recognizing the plight of the colleges, the government had created the Student Army Training Corps and a somewhat smaller but similar type of naval unit. College students in good standing could continue with their studies in college, subject to military need, by enlisting in one of the two units, where they would be housed, fed, and drilled as members of a military organization under the command of officers assigned for the purpose.

The need for space and facilities was immediate. There was no time for new construction, which, under war conditions, was virtually impossible anyway. The University was a strictly urban institution with meager facilities for instruction and none for feeding and housing military contingents. Other than a few government offices and the Powhatan (now the Roger Smith) Hotel, the area contained no large structures that might be adapted to the purpose. The president asked for authority to lease the Maury Apartments at Nineteenth and G Streets which the government then occupied but planned to leave, for an annual rental of $7,500, to acquire property at 1719 H Street and further property at an annual rental not to exceed $7,500. The government, unhappily, changed its plans and did not get out of the Maury as scheduled; but within the limits of the appropriations made by the Board, other facilities were found and quickly adapted for use as barracks. The Davidge house at Seventeenth and H Streets, 2027 G Street, 1719 Pennsylvania Avenue, and the Pharmacy building at 808 Eye Street, whose use had just been discontinued by the school, made up the living quarters. By the generous cooperation of the pastor and the trustees of Concordia Church at Twentieth and G Streets, the University installed there adequate equipment for food preparation and service; and the commodious basement of the church became the mess hall for the military units. After the war, continued hospitality on the part of the church made possible the use of the space for a lecture hall for many years. It was a mutually convenient arrangement.

Preparation of quarters was sufficiently far advanced to permit the formal induction of the military units on October 3, 1918. The scene of the ceremony was the University Yard, then much smaller than it is now. A wooden porch on the rear of the west wing of 2023 G Street, appropriately decorated with bunting, served as the speaker's stand. The United States Marine Band under the direction of Captain William H. Santelmann, U.S.M.C., Mus.D. (hon.), 1908, was in attendance. The oath was administered by Josephus Daniels, Secretary of the Navy, who was escorted to the ceremonies by Henry White, a Trustee of the University and a principal member of the United States delegation at the Paris peace conference.

The SATC unit consisted of 441 men with a staff of 13 officers under the command of Colonel Henry H. Ludlow, C.A., U.S.A. (ret.). The naval unit of 50 men was commanded by Rear Admiral Giles B. Harber, U.S.N. (ret.).[28]

Six weeks after the induction of the student soldiers and sailors, the armistice was signed. Demobilization got under way as the finishing touches were being put on the barracks. The abnormal expenditures for military purposes which the University had suddenly been forced to make required the raising of a considerable sum of money through loans. The sudden end of hostilities and the efficiency of the treasurer and his staff saved the University from any great burden. By April 25, 1919, all of the SATC claims against the government were settled and full reimbursement made. The SATC more than justified the effort and expense that it involved. It saved the male enrollment. These men, continuing their studies, together with returning veterans, created the first veterans' bulge, far smaller than the one to come a generation later.[29]

The returning veterans not only increased the size of the student body, but they changed its appearance. On account of the war, many men had been delayed a year or more in beginning college courses. Many in their late twenties and thirties found an opportunity to begin college work. For a time the student body was decidedly older. Because of the long tradition of late-afternoon classes, the average part-time student had tended to be older, so that this increase in age was not as noticeable as it would have been in many institutions. More conspicuous was the lower standard of male attire. The student body before the war had dressed well. Now many resumed study without any considerable civilian wardrobe or the means to acquire one. Military uniforms, the insignia (except the patches) removed, were seen in large numbers. Because the jackets with their high-standing tight collars were uncomfortable and could hardly be adapted to civilian wear, coats tended to be forgotten, as did ties on khaki shirts. A decided informality of dress was developing.

The problem of staffing the faculty and the administrative and maintenance forces was acute throughout the period. Secretarial and clerical help was in increasing demand from the government. Knowing the situation, President Collier persuaded two of his former secretaries in Auburn, New York, to join his staff in Washington. The difficulties in staffing which might have been expected in a wartime capital were tragically increased by a lengthy influenza epidemic. On October 9, 1918, the president reported to the Board that all civilian activity in the University had been suspended by order of the Health Department. Four weeks of instruction were lost and, in partial compensation, the academic year was extended to June 18, on which day the Commencement was held.[30]

The situation was particularly critical in the University Hospital at the height of the epidemic. The depleted staff, burdened with an impossible load of work and laboring day and night, fell easy victims to the disease. The press reported that Miss Mary Glasscock, Superintendent of Nurses, had died of it and that Dr. Thomas Miller, Jr., of the medical staff and twenty-four nurses were prostrated with it.

The new administration had a hectic beginning. As the second semester of 1918-1919 got under way, things brightened. In February, Abram Lisner, Trustee of the University, prominent merchant, and generous philanthropist, paid all outstanding indebtedness, amounting to $24,500, on the University's property on G Street. As an evidence of its gratitude, the building at 2023 G Street was named Lisner Hall.[31]

The problem of making a decision with reference to the Medical and Dental Schools had been inherited from the preceding administration. There was much consultation, investigation, and debate, and finally an appraisal of the whole problem. In essence it could be stated with bald simplicity as follows: If the Medical and Dental Schools continued to operate under the same roof, neither could retain its "A" rating. If the Medical School were to continue alone, it would require a substantial annual subsidy guaranteed over and beyond receipts from fees, a remodeling of the property, and a marked increase in the number of full-time faculty. The Dental School seemed doomed. But even in the light of this probability a final series of consultations was held with Dean Carl J. Mess and the dental faculty to try to find some ways and means. None was found.

The Board with great regret directed the closing of the Dental School at the end of the academic year 1919-1920. The entire Medical building, except the part temporarily occupied by the Chemistry Department of the College, was turned over to the Medical School, and $4,000 was made available for necessary remodeling. The Medical School was guaranteed $25,000 annually from the general funds of the University, over and above receipts from fees; and at least twelve full-time teachers were authorized. The Board directed that an attempt be made to sell the property and to affiliate with a good hospital. Dean W. C. Borden was to communicate, in person, these arrangements to the accrediting body and seek assurance that the "A" rating of the Medical School would be continued. He succeeded in his mission.

The Veterinary College, an affiliated school, was discontinued.[32]

With the return of peace and the marked increase in the size of the student body, there was naturally a demand for more room. It would have been easy to be led into a major building program, but resources for any large expansion were lacking. The administration moved slowly and cautiously. Some additional houses were bought, and the May house at 2022 G Street was rented to afford more classroom space for arts and sciences classes. The purchase of 1435 K Street, facing McPherson Square, in which at one time the Department of Justice had been located, was authorized for the Law School at a cost of $145,000, and $25,000 was made available for remodeling. A gift of $5,000 by Harry Wardman, later a Trustee, reduced the cost to $140,000. The building thus acquired, as remodeled, was a distinct improvement over the quarters on the top floors of the Masonic Temple which the Law School had occupied for a decade. Its location was particularly convenient for employed students; and in comparison with the old quarters its five large lecture halls, four moot court rooms, library, and lounging room were commodious.

Plans for an arts and sciences building on Twenty-first Street were drawn and laid before the Board, but action was postponed. The purchase of property by American University on F Street near Twentieth Street led anew to the consideration of a merger with that institution. Negotiations looking toward affiliation with an acceptable hospital continued, but neither the merger nor the affiliation was brought about.[33]

There was an important statement of policy embodied in the resolution authorizing the purchase of the McPherson Square property for the Law School. It was probably forgotten as in later years an unending debate went on as to the permanent location of the University. The circumstances that had brought about the purchase of 2023 G Street were entirely fortuitous. The rented buildings on Eye Street had been sold, the purchaser demanded possession, there was no place for the Department of Arts and Sciences and the administrative offices to go. Almost regardless of the location of St. Rose's, the result would have been the same. The building was large, vacant, and reasonable in price. There was one choice and the University made it; but would it stay in the First Ward? The purchase of valuable property on McPherson Square, a mile or more distant from 2023 G Street, might have been taken as an indication that the question of location was still open. In the mind of the Trustees, it was not. The property which they purchased, it was realized, was in an area where values were being rapidly enhanced. They were assured that the property was a sound investment, useful for the present as a Law School, but not to be held permanently. The Board, therefore, inserted in its resolution these very plain and positive words, "that the passage of this resolution does not change the permanent policy of the University to locate ultimately all of the activities [of the University] as far as practicable in the vicinity of the present buildings." The decision had been made.[34]

As this basic decision for the future was being declared thus formally, an interesting echo from the past was heard. A letter was received by President Collier from the chairman of a committee of the Southern Baptist Convention asking to confer with a committee from the University on the resumption of Baptist control of the institution. The receipt of the letter was noted in the *Minutes* of the Board of Trustees and acknowledged by the president with a general statement of the University's policy. A year later, in the fall of 1922, a second communication from the Southern Baptist Convention's officers with reference to the same question was addressed to the president and the chairman of the Board. Once again, the communication was noted in the *Minutes* and acknowledged by President Hodgkins. In the spring of 1924, correspondence was again initiated by representatives of the Baptist Convention, proposing increased endowment and the transfer of control to the convention. After full consideration, a special committee of Trustees reported adversely on the proposition. The Committee's report was approved, and President Lewis was directed to notify the officers of the Convention regarding the action taken.

As reasons for its decision the Board stated:

1. There should be at the capital an undenominational institution seeking general support.
2. The recent growth and prosperity of the University had been achieved since the severance of denominational ties.
3. Large resources were expected to become available for an appeal for an undenominational institution.
4. The recent campaign for funds had been based on an appeal for an undenominational institution.
5. Such an institution was best fitted for education in the modern world.[35]

There had, no doubt, been times in the past when such proposals might have received a favorable reception, if the surrender of control brought with it financial salvation. The historical record was plain. The Congress was unwilling to grant a charter to the Baptist denomination; in formulating the Charter that was given, it was careful to maintain the College's independence of everybody, in fact, except the Attorney General with his right of investigation and the Congress itself with its right to amend the Charter. Such practical control as the denomination did have came through the provision in the earliest Charter for the elections of Trustees by the contributors and to a lesser extent by the limitation imposed by the lease of property of the College. The change in the method of electing Trustees and the transfer of the property in fee simple closed those two channels of influence. It was true that temporarily, from 1898 to 1904, a change in the Charter did require that the Board be made up of a substantial number of Baptists. Hope for financial aid prompted the change, and failure to get the aid led to a speedy restoration of the old Charter provisions. In the view of the University, the question of sectarian control was answered forever. Denominational zeal had merely required a reiteration of that answer.

With the approach of the University's Centennial, it was felt that the time was ripe to make the first major appeal for the raising of a substantial endowment fund. A committee on subscriptions and endowments, appointed in the spring of 1920, recommended that a campaign for funds to celebrate the Centennial be started shortly after November 15. It recommended further the employment of a fund-raising firm to plan the campaign. Meanwhile the president was asked to visit major alumni centers to arouse interest and seek personal participation in obtaining a large sum to erect buildings for arts and sciences, law, and medicine, and to increase in a major fashion the size of the endowment.[36]

A happy augury for the success of any large effort was to be seen in the enthusiasm and spirit of the student body. This revived college spirit was obvious enough to lead to the adoption, for the first time in years, of a comprehensive system for the administration of student activities, proposed by the President's Council and heartily accepted by the Trustees.

A director of student activities, with faculty status, was to be appointed to administer a broad program supported by the funds paid into the treasury through a voluntary activities fee. The director would serve as chairman of a board of managers made up of faculty members appointed by the president of the University, alumni named by the president of the Alumni Association, and students elected by the Student Council. This board, superseding the old Faculty Committee and subject to the supervision and control of the President's Council, was given the direction of activities, the power to fix the amount of the voluntary fee and to appropriate funds from the activities' treasury, and the right to name coaches. The director was responsible for the academic status of members of teams, the protection of University property, and the arrangement of schedules, subject to the approval of the board of managers.[37]

President Collier enjoyed great popularity with the student body. He attended the major student parties and participated in them with obvious zest. He did not always enjoy the same unanimity of support in the faculty that his predecessors had had. There was at times vocal dissatisfaction, particularly over his budgetary arrangements and his interest in cultivating social and political contacts for the University. It was not so evident then in the rapid flux of affairs, but times had changed. President Stockton had assumed office at what was perhaps the nadir of the University's fortunes. He and his team of experienced and devoted deans and administrators were the institution's only hope. It was not humanly possible for a man to be more selfless in his administration than Charles Herbert Stockton. The confidence placed in him was justified in every way. He called for sacrifice, he accepted sacrifice, and men followed him. In eight years, he restored the University to solvency and reestablished its respect in the community. His problem was to hold the line, not too rigidly, but rigidly enough, and he did.

President Collier had to cope with the problems created by the war in its later phases. He showed an industry, an ingenuity, and a resourcefulness that were remarkable. But the war changed things. The student body grew rapidly and expansion was in the air. There was a sense of movement that could not be stilled. A new generation on the faculty was becoming vocal. The "Young Turks" did not always agree with the Old Guard, and at times one or both of them did not agree with the president. It was a wholesome sign, still no larger than a man's hand, but it betokened growth.

President Collier's great personal contribution was that he brought to the University a marked degree of social acceptance in areas where its influence had been limited. His object in these matters was not always appreciated by his colleagues. He did his best to bring the University to the favorable notice of the wide social, political, and diplomatic circles within which he moved and to involve them in an interest in the institution. He organized subscription series and public lectures by outstanding literary and public figures. Large formal dinners became characteristic events in the life of the institution.

A major feature of the president's policies was the formation of a

University Council made up of men and women of distinction who ordinarily might have been elected Trustees but who could not accept that responsiblity because of other commitments or distant residence. It was hoped that they might attend one meeting a year and give the University the benefit of their advice and support when called upon. The council consisted first of thirty members, ten of whom were elected each year by the Trustees for a three-year term.[38]

Elaborate academic ceremonies became an important part of the University's life, with large delegations from official, diplomatic, and social Washington always present. It was reminiscent of the early days of the College when the President of the United States, his Cabinet, and a generous representation from the Congress regularly attended Commencement. To receive honorary degrees there was a notable procession of great figures: soldiers like Leonard Wood and John J. Pershing; statesmen like Herbert Hoover, then head of Belgian Relief; representatives of the arts like Julia Marlowe (Mrs. E. H. Sothern), the actress, and Vicente Blasco-Ibáñez, author of *The Four Horsemen of the Apocalypse;* figures in the world of finance like Otto H. Kahn; public men like Albert, King of the Belgians.

The special convocation of October 30, 1919, in honor of the King of the Belgians was the first of the great convocations of the Collier administration, the Centennial Convocation the last. So great was the expertise developed in handling the numerous convocations that the Belgian Ambassador, Baron de Cartier de Marchienne, generously said that their precision compared favorably with that of the best court ceremonials he had seen.

The Centennial of the University was celebrated in February, 1921, by a series of events. In a simple cermony on February 19, Brigadier General L. Collardet in the name of the French government presented to the University a German cannon captured at Verdun. The cannon was placed on the grounds of Woodhull House (then 2100 G Street). On the same day the Centennial Dinner of the Arts and Sciences students was held at the Willard Hotel, with the late Michael A. Musmanno, A.B. 1921, A.M. 1922, later Justice of the Supreme Court of Pennsylvania, as toastmaster; and the Centennial Dinner of the Law School at the Franklin Square Hotel with L. Brooks Hays, LL.B. 1922, later Assistant to the President of the United States, as a student speaker, and Dean Roscoe Pound as the speaker of the evening. On Monday, February 21, 1921, the University Centennial Dinner was held at Rauscher's, with speeches delivered by representatives from each of the major regions of the United States. Julia Marlowe read some of the sonnets of Shakespeare. At the Centennial Convocation on February 22, President Charles A. Richmond of Union College gave the convocation address and William Bruce King of the Board of Trustees the commemorative address. Delegates from four foreign universities and 120 American institutions were in attendance. The days immediately following the convocation constituted the Centennial Junior Week, which included a reception at the Raleigh Hotel, a performance of Clyde Fitch's *The Truth*, and the Junior Prom at Rauscher's. Very significant were the elaborateness in planning and the enthusiastic participation of the student body in the programs of Centennial events.[39]

The celebration of the Centennial was basically social and uniformly festive in spirit; and the messages and greetings from the delegates of the universities, foreign and American, were highly laudatory. From a reading of the proceedings, it would appear that what was being celebrated was a chronological fact. But for those whose knowledge was more intimate, the commemorative address of William Bruce King alone suggested what was really being celebrated. A church-related college, in a century of striving, had thrown off all bonds of denominationalism, had struggled against lack of resources and, at the same time, against the clumsy handling of what it did have, had tardily recognized the error of its ways, and, chastened by experience, had had the courage and the leadership to overcome its difficulties and, in a new home, to lay a sound foundation for the great university of the future—this was what was being celebrated, even though protocol does not permit such frankness on occasions of high ceremony.

A few months after the Centennial celebration, two important figures departed from the University scene. On July 26, 1921, General Maxwell Van Zandt Woodhull died, and President Collier resigned as of August 31, 1921, to become Ambassador to Chile.

President Collier's administration was a brief one. In financial administration he followed generally the lines laid down by his predecessor. He continued to acquire parcels of real estate in the G Street area. The generosity of Mr. Lisner removed for the time all indebtedness from the purchase of 2023 G Street. By way of radical departure from the Stockton formula, a valuable property on K Street was acquired as a temporary home for the Law School, and the Medical School was guaranteed an annual subsidy of $25,000 above fees to insure the maintenance of required standards. The discontinuance of the Dental School, earlier foreshadowed, became a fact. There were consistent additions to and strengthening of the faculties. Finally, by his interest in politics and society, President Collier contributed in a signal way to the growing acceptance of the institution in the larger community.

General Woodhull's place in the history of the University will always be recalled by Woodhull House, which he left to the University by will, because around that house has grown the great University of the present which he brought to G Street to be his neighbor. The last years of his life were devoted entirely to the institution and its concerns. His name was on every subscription list. His last military service was the organization in the University of those elite companies of the Coast Artillery which fought with such distinction in the Meuse-Argonne campaign. He was wise in council and astute in business, and his best talents were at the service of the University. As a mother broods over her child, Maxwell Van Zandt Woodhull watched over the University he had adopted as his own.[40]

When President Collier's resignation became effective at the end of August, 1921, the Trustees naturally turned to Dean Howard Lincoln Hodgkins to be president *pro tempore.* Dr. Hodgkins had entered the Preparatory School in 1878, and had been associated with the University from that time. As a teacher of physics and mathematics, he had passed through all the academic grades—instructor to full professor—and had held, at the same time, various high administrative posts. For a generation he had been a principal adviser to the presidents of the University and, as the organization of the institution had evolved, had had as his bailiwick the schools and colleges included in the Department of Arts and Sciences—in a word, all but the Departments of Law and Medicine. At the same time, he had maintained close relations with the Alumni Association and with graduates throughout the world. A great teacher, a wise administrator, and a man of the highest integrity, he held the respect and esteem of his colleagues, students, graduates, members of the community, and the academic world at large. The interim of two years when he served as acting president was not devoted to a mere holding operation, but was one of marked progress.

The search for President Collier's successor began as soon as the vacancy occurred. The first choice of the Trustees fell upon an eminent scholar who had recently retired from a major post in a leading university. He was known to have definite ideas with reference to the development of the University and, with a group of associates of equal distinction, he prepared a detailed and well-matured statement of his concept and the means for its materialization. The booklet containing his statement was distributed confidentially to a small group. The project was an ambitious one, involving the acquisition of a new campus to the west of the G Street campus, with a frontage on or very near Potomac Park; emphasis on graduate work and research; and the immediate raising of adequate funds for endowment and construction. An earnest effort was made to see if the requirements of the plan could be met. Considerable real estate was acquired in the area indicated and later sold with profit. When insuperable difficulties were confronted—first, the inability to acquire adequate land, and second, the failure to get support from the larger foundations—the project was abandoned and its initiator asked to have his name withdrawn. The Board was therefore back again to its original policy, stated so positively just three years before, of locating all the activities of the University ultimately in the vicinity of the G Street buildings.[41]

Dr. Hodgkins did not let the pursuit of the new idea halt development along the lines laid down by Admiral Stockton and continued by Dr. Collier. In characteristic words, President Hodgkins told the Board, "As I understand it, we must prove ourselves before others will help us. We must grow, slowly, but safely and sanely before we can receive the aid we have asked."[42]

The Board had long discussed a campaign for funds in general terms, but specific to the extent that the campaign was to be tied in with the Centennial observance. Various fund-raising organizations had been consulted and the one to be employed had been chosen. A year after the Centennial, no drive was yet under way. At the president's urging the Board decided to start the campaign in January, 1922, but there was to be a delay of still another year.[43]

Dr. Hodgkins, as a long-time dean, knew better than anyone else how great the need was for classrooms, laboratories, and offices, and for a constant increase in the size of the faculty. His first major move was modest enough in itself, but major in what it implied. He was going to expand, but in the spirit of the Stockton formula. At the annual meeting in May, 1922, the Board authorized the purchase of 2014 H Street for $5,000 and the expenditure of $10,000 for alterations in the buildings of the G Street group.

Mr. Albert L. Harris presented a plan for the development of the whole square bounded by G, H, Twentieth, and Twenty-first Streets, half of which the University owned. The plan was worked out with the president. Eight units of similar construction and style, though with individual modifications, were to surround the square. It was recommended that the first unit be built on the northeast corner of Twenty-first and G Streets on a lot 125 feet square, made up of the Woodhull property and 2027 G Street.

The first unit would serve as a classroom building. If construction were not deemed wise at the time, the offices of the president, secretary, treasurer, and registrar were to be moved to Woodhull House. The third floor of 2101 G Street, used as a residence for three clerks, was to be vacated, and the second and third floors of the building were to be assigned to the Department of Architecture. The Department of Home Economics was to be moved into two University-owned buildings on Twentieth Street. A few months later the Committee on Buildings and Grounds was authorized to acquire as much property as possible on the east side of Twenty-first Street between G and H Streets. The effort was so successful that the Board decided to erect the building in the middle of the block instead of at the northeast corner of Twenty-first and G Streets; the cost was not to exceed $270,000. The new structure, named Corcoran Hall in honor of the great nineteenth-century patron of the institution, was the first building to be constructed after the reorganization of 1910.[44]

As President Hodgkins' interim tenure came to a close, he was able to describe in his Annual Report of 1923 the extent of the progress made since the reorganization of 1910. For nine years there had been no deficit. Real estate worth $450,000 had been acquired, in which the University's equity approached $350,000. In addition to $200,000 of the University's current funds, $80,000 in gifts had been invested in property, at the expense of faculty salaries. He protested against this. In 1910, the Arts and Sciences faculty, which had been his special responsibility, had 15 full-time and 17 part-time members. In 1922, the numbers were 41 full-time and 50 part-time. In 1910, Arts and Sciences had 681 students; in 1922, there were 3,243. The rest of the University showed proportionate growth.

President Hodgkins could report another substantial achievement. In 1920, the Commission on Higher Education of the Middle States had conducted its first inspection of the University. In two areas, there was trouble. The large number of part-time students, many of them listed as "special students," made the University suspect to those who did not know of the peculiar situation which had developed in Washington since the War of 1861-1865. Moreover, the University could not show the half-million dollars in productive endowment which the commission looked upon as a minimum requirement. When it came to accreditation, the commission demurred. The skillful presentation of the University's case by Dr. Hodgkins brought about the granting of the accreditation.[45]

The validity of what was called "night-school" work was not always as readily recognized as it is today. Frederick Rudolph in his history, *The*

The Law School, 1435 K Street, 1921-1925.

The Gymnasium, "The Tin Tabernacle," on the south side of H Street west of Twentieth, at the time of its completion in 1924.

North side of G Street, between Twentieth and Twenty-first Streets, *c.* 1932. *Left to right:* Woodhull House, Registrar's Office, the Easby houses, 2023 G Street (Lisner Hall).

Corner of Twentieth and G Streets, showing at the far left the Hall of Government, corner of Twenty-first and G Streets, Woodhull House, Alexander Graham Bell Hall, Lisner Library, Gilbert Stuart Hall and at the corner the office of the President; at right, residences used as offices and, at the extreme right, Stockton Hall, 1957.

Corcoran Hall, 1924. (R. W. Howard.)

The Jacob Burns Law Library, 1968, and Stockton Hall, 1925. (R. W. Howard.)

Convocation in honor of H.M. Albert, King of the Belgians, 1919. *Front row, from left to right:* the Rt. Rev. Alfred Harding, Bishop of Washington; Col. Archibald Hopkins, Vice Chairman of the Board of Trustees; John Bell Larner, Chairman of the Board of Trustees; Elmer Louis Kayser, Secretary of the University, standing with hood; Albert, King of the Belgians; Commissioner Henry B. Macfarland, Trustee; Col. Thomas Snell Hopkins, Trustee; President William Miller Collier, presenting diploma; the Duke of Brabant (later King Leopold III); Dr. Gilbert H. Grosvenor, President of the National Geographic Society, Trustee; Ernest L. Thurston, Superintendent of Schools, Trustee.

Delegates to the inauguration of University President William Mather Lewis at the White House, 1923, with President Calvin Coolidge. Chief Justice William Howard Taft was the delegate of Yale University.

Convocation in honor of the Rt. Hon. Ramsay MacDonald, Prime Minister of Great Britain, 1929. The British Ambassador, Sir Esme Howard, stands at the Prime Minister's left, President Cloyd Heck Marvin at his right; in the rear, between President Marvin and the Prime Minister is Dean William Allen Wilbur of Columbian College.

President Marvin receiving H.M. Prajadhipok, King of Siam, at the Convocation in his honor (1931). Dr. Leo S. Rowe, Director of the Pan American Union, stands at the extreme left.

University Hospital, at Washington Circle, Twenty-second, Twenty-third, Eye Streets and Pennsylvania Avenue, 1948.

Cloyd Heck Marvin, twelfth President, 1927-1959. (University Collection.)

Oswald Symister Colclough, Acting President, 1959-1961, 1964-1965. (University Collection.)

Thomas Henry Carroll, thirteenth
President, 1961-1964. (University
Collection.)

Lloyd Hartman Elliott, fourteenth
President, 1965-   . (University
Collection.)

Warwick Memorial, Washington Circle, 1954.

Lisner Auditorium, southwest corner of Twenty-first and H Streets, 1946.

American College and University, states that the City College of New York in 1909 inaugurated the first night-school course of study leading to a bachelor's degree.[46] As a matter of fact, Corcoran Scientific School, from its very beginning in 1884, offered courses leading to the baccalaureate degree for students taking late courses exclusively.

The Hodgkins interim was a productive one. Wise, sane leadership carried the University forward without any break in succession or any agonizing transition. Dr. Hodgkins had added to his already great stature. Returning to his office as dean of the University, he continued in his role as an active elder statesman during the administration of William Mather Lewis and the early part of Cloyd Heck Marvin's presidency. Howard Lincoln Hodgkins was perhaps the only one ever connected with the University who knew the institution in each of its three locations. He had been a student at College Hill and taught in the old Prep, a professor and dean when the University was located on H Street, and a mainstay of the institution as it regathered its forces in its third home and laid its sure foundation for the future.

The election of William Mather Lewis (1878-1945) as president of the University on May 31, 1923, brought to an end the interim tenure of Dr. Hodgkins. The new president had been headmaster of Lake Forest Academy and director of the savings division of the Treasury Department; at the time of his election, he was chief of educational service of the Chamber of Commerce of the United States.

Formal inaugural ceremonies were held in the late afternoon of November 7, 1923, in Memorial Continental Hall. Delegates from 161 foreign and American colleges and universities and from 21 learned and professional societies were present. Yale's representative was William Howard Taft, the Chief Justice of the United States. Preceding the inaugural luncheon, President Calvin Coolidge received the delegates at the White House. The academic procession formed in the Pan American Union building and moved across the street to the hall. After the invocation was given by the Right Reverend James E. Freeman, Bishop of Washington, John B. Larner, Chairman of the Board of Trustees of the University, delivered a brief introductory address. Greetings were then brought to President Lewis from the faculty by Dean Howard L. Hodgkins; from the alumni by Samuel Herrick; from the colleges by President William Wistar Comfort, of Haverford; from the universities by President Livingston Farrand, of Cornell; from the federal government by John J. Tigert, Commissioner of Education. President Lewis, being then inducted into office, delivered his inaugural address. The Reverend W. S. Abernethy, pastor of Calvary Baptist Church, pronounced the benediction. A large reception for the whole University community was held in the New Willard Hotel in the evening, with music by Meyer Davis.

The elaborateness of the inaugural ceremonies in no way indicated an intention to change policy and to strike out along entirely new lines. President Lewis in his brief administration of four years (1923-1927) followed the conservative and constructive policy of cautious expansion which had been the rule since the reorganization of 1910. The purchase of land in the square bounded by G, H, Twentieth, and Twenty-first Streets and in the immediate vicinity continued, but the University's interest in the area was reflected in the higher costs of real estate. The parcels which the University was now acquiring ran in price from $25,000 to $40,000. There was a healthy increase in gifts for endowment—moderate in size, it is true, but significant as a welcome sign of public interest. Work on Corcoran Hall went steadily forward in the early months of the new administration, and the building was dedicated on October 28, 1924, with John B. Larner, the Chairman of the Board, giving the dedicatory address.

The growth of athletics and the development of work in physical education pointed up dramatically the need for a gymnasium. The purchase of real estate on H Street, west of Twentieth Street, made available a modest-sized lot for the purpose. On the president's recommendation, $23,000 was appropriated for the construction of a building for temporary use. The gymnasium proper, 140 by 60 feet, was made of prefabricated materials, and a brick structure on the front of the site was remodeled for locker rooms and shower rooms in harmony with the new construction. In spite of strenuous efforts to achieve the utmost economy, when the appropriation was used up there were no funds for the flooring. A gift of $2,000 in Liberty Bonds, subscribed by the students during the World War, and a matching amount added by the Trustees paid for the flooring. Thus came into existence the noble structure, named by the secretary "The Tin Tabernacle," often maligned but still used.[47]

An offer from Harry Wardman to purchase the Law School property on McPherson Square for $250,000, subject to a mortgage of $70,000, and to erect a new building on Twentieth Street at a cost not to exceed $250,000, made it possible to bring another large unit into the university grouping. The new building, on the eastern face of the square opposite Corcoran Hall, was designed as the second unit in the Harris Plan for the development of the whole square. The cornerstone was laid on December 12, 1924, by the Grand Lodge of Masons of the District of Columbia, using the marble gavel which General Washington had used when he laid the southeast cornerstone of the Capitol on September 18, 1793. Not only was the University's patron saint a Mason, but Luther Rice, its founder, was also a member of the order. The new Law School building was named Stockton Hall after Admiral Charles H. Stockton, president of the University from 1910 to 1918.[48]

For a time it seemed that the announced plan to bring all the units of the University together was in jeopardy. The possibility of an affiliation with an existing hospital as desirable from the standpoint of both economy and improved facilities had long been in mind. Various soundings had been made without any real progress. In the last year of the Lewis administration, the possibility of an affiliation with Garfield Memorial Hospital, together with a working arrangement with the Washington Home for Foundlings, which administered the Warwick bequest for cancer research, brought about new and direct negotiations. Articles of agreement were adopted by the three institutions, looking toward their combination as a nucleus for a hospital center located at the Garfield site.

In essence, the agreement provided that each of the organizations would continue its corporate existence and control, but the University would have priority as far as all teaching rights were concerned. The University was to sell the Hospital, Dispensary, and Medical buildings on H Street as soon as practicable and with the proceeds erect a new medical building in the vicinity of Garfield. Garfield was to lease to the Washington Home for Foundlings, at an annual rental of $25,000, ground within its property for the erection of a building for the care and treatment of women with cancer, to be known as "The Helen L. and Mary E. Warwick Memorial." The University was to turn over to the new center all income from hospital endowment funds. The Nurses School at Garfield was to be continued as "The Washington Medical Center Nurses Training School." While the University did purchase lots on Sherman Avenue, near Garfield, the H Street buildings were not sold and the project never took form. In the course of time different arrangements were made by the three parties, and the University proceeded to develop its own Medical Center at Washington Circle with the Warwick Memorial related to it. The agreement was formally abrogated in 1929.[49]

Numerous changes in key personnel occurred during the early 1920's. Dean Charles E. Munroe, who had charted the course of the School of

Graduate Studies, was succeeded on his retirement by Professor George
N. Henning. Dean Merton L. Ferson of the Law School resigned, and
his place was taken by Professor William C. Van Vleck. When Dean
W. C. Ruediger retired as Director of the Summer School, he was suc-
ceeded in that post by Professor Elmer Louis Kayser. On Dean Henry
E. Kalusowski's death, Dr. Louis F. Bradley became Dean of the School
of Pharmacy; and on Dean Hugh Miller's resignation, Professor John R.
Lapham became Dean of the School of Engineering.

The sudden death of Profesor Hermann Schoenfeld (1861-1926) of
the Department of German, and the retirement, at an advanced age,
of Professor Charles Clinton Swisher (1846-1940) of the Department of
History—both men of great distinction who had served the University
since the time of President Whitman—underscored dramatically the fact
that the institution, hampered by meager finances and absorbed in its own
problems, had failed to set up any system of pensions for retired professors or their dependents. The Board adopted as a policy the retirement
of members of the faculty and university officers at the age of sixty-five
with a possibility of continuing in active service on annual tenure to the
age of seventy. The Board's committee recommended that the University
make an arrangement with the Teacher's Insurance and Annuity Association for pensions for its staff. Such an arrangement was not made until
eighteen years later, on July 30, 1945, when the Board passed the first of
several comprehensive and increasingly generous retirement resolutions.
In the interim, modest retirement allowances were granted as the occasion
arose on the retirement of full-time eligible staff members.[50]

By the time President Lewis' administration came to a close, the University was well over a hundred years old. It had celebrated its Centennial
with high ceremony under President Collier. Under President Lewis it
marked the one-hundredth anniversary of its first Commencement, with
M. J. J. Jusserand, the Ambassador of France and distinguished scholar
and warm friend of the University, delivering the commemorative address.

The period which began with the reorganization of 1910 under President Stockton and ended with the administration of President Lewis
constitutes a distinct epoch in the history of the University. There was
the definite and controlling conviction that the only policy which would
strengthen and renew the institution was one of slow and cautious expansion, always within the limited means of the University. There was
a steadily increasing flow of modest gifts, but no princely ones. The

major source of income was student fees. From what was at hand, the costs of instruction and maintenance were met, limited amounts were earmarked for the restoration of the endowment, and cautious expenditures were made for real estate and construction. This policy had seemed to pay off, even though it was a dubious one educationally. The administrators of the University were well indoctrinated in the policy and developed great expertise in its application. They maintained an institution that was financially stable, educationally decent, and, in its own view, outstanding. Its eminent roster of graduates, in terms of outcome, justified this point of view.

For the educational purist, however, there were some hard questions to answer. Was this uniqueness an asset or a liability? To be able to give an educational plant double use was, of course, a happy condition. But how could a student, employed for a full day's work, do a standard job in the classroom and laboratory after hours? The University's answer was that this was a unique condition that existed here. Hundreds of these employed students were in Washington through political patronage, quite deliberately bestowed so that young people, otherwise excluded financially, could obtain a college education. This was fixed policy with many members of the Congress. Speaker Cannon with his considerable patronage made college study possible for a large number, canceling the patronage as soon as a course was completed so that others could have a chance.

The purist was critical of the numbers of part-time teachers. This situation, however, had a dual base. It was a way to get teachers, often at a reasonable cost, but the teachers were frequently men of great scientific ability whose services could not otherwise be obtained. The University had no misgivings, but satisfaction with slow growth along familiar lines could breed inertia.

Any dangers on this score were minimized by the increasingly vocal activities of a faculty group outside the administration. They were unwilling that the University remain a closed corporation, meeting its own standards to its own satisfaction. They sought immediate and unquestioned acceptance in the larger college community. The members of the faculty were feeling a new sense of pride and achievement in the recognition that was coming to their colleagues in such forms as the award of the Pulitzer Prize in History to Professor Samuel Flagg Bemis in 1927 for his *Pinckney's Treaty* and the acclaim given Professor Robert F. Griggs for the scientific results of his explorations in the Katmai region in Alaska. "High Standards" was the battlecry. In the College and in the professional schools marked progress was made. The Medical School was challenged but won its "A" rating. The Middle States Association was at first reluctant but it then granted accreditation. It was the beginning of the movement which, in time, brought the highest accreditation to all of the University's departments and to its students full access to academic honors, such as Phi Beta Kappa. The going was slow at first. The American Association of University Women was dubious because there were so few women on the faculty. The Association of American Universities criticized the admission of special students, the number of part-time faculty members, deficiencies in library and laboratory equipment and housing, and the character of some degrees. The old protective dependence on uniqueness gave way to a desire to meet all comers on their own grounds, and to achieve in full whatever standard any accrediting agency required.[51] The troublesome question of inadequate endowment was to remain a standing challenge.

President Needham had felt the need of fuller student activities as a necessary step in humanizing the College and had used the full weight of his office to encourage such a development. Thanks to the leadership and industry of a small group of gifted students, considerable success had been achieved. The much more remarkable expansion of extracurricular activities in the decade following World War I was due entirely to the dynamism of a versatile group of undergraduate men and women who brought forth, with faculty support in many cases, an amazingly varied program. Through all the changes the *Hatchet* and the *Cherry Tree* maintained a schedule of regular publication and were a continuing feature of student life.

The reorganization of 1910 had brought about an almost complete cessation of all forms of competitive athletics. Student demand and the warm support of Dean Fraser of the Law School made possible a resumption of an athletic program, financed by a voluntary student activities tax. The entrance of the United States into World War I ended that effort very quickly. The post-World War renewal began in 1920 with the adoption of a comprehensive body of regulations for the control of student activities, supported by a voluntary fee and supervised by a director who was given faculty status. Four years later a student activities fee of $8 per year was made compulsory for all students taking more than six hours of work. On this firm financial base, a relatively elaborate system of activities began to take form. The construction of a gymnasium at this time was part of the evolving program.[52] The *Handbook* for 1925-1926 listed intercollegiate athletic competition in football, basketball, track, tennis, rifle, swimming, golf, wrestling, and baseball for men; in basketball, tennis, swimming, rifle, hockey, and fencing for women.

The rapidity with which the resumed program got under way is indicated by a statement in the *Handbook* for 1921-1922: "It is a matter of record that George Washington University maintained athletics on a larger scale and for a greater number of students than any other institution in the South Atlantic Division last year."[53]

During the preceding year, a third publication had been added to the weekly and the annual, a comic magazine of wit and satire called *The Ghost*. There were clubs galore: Men's Glee Club, Masonic Club, Women's Legal Club, Architectural Club, Art Society, Chemical Society, Engineering Society, Enosinian Society, El Círculo Español, Players, and many others. The Faculty Club dates also from this period. Organized in the fall of 1920, it maintained club rooms at 719 Twenty-first Street.

There were chapters of ten national fraternities, all maintaining houses and formed into an Interfraternity Association; four national sororities and four locals, represented on the Pan Hellenic Council; and numerous professional fraternities and sororities. The senior honor societies were Pyramid for men, Sphinx for women, and Sigma Tau for junior and senior engineers. The great formal social occasions were the Interfraternity Prom, the Junior Prom, and the Pan Hell Prom. Less formal major occasions were the Interfraternity Smokers, and the May Fête Carnival, a masked ball later superseded by the outdoor May Fiesta.

The growth in the number of student organizations was phenomenal. For example, in place of a single dramatic association four were formed, each emphasizing a different type of drama, and united in an overall association. Each spring a dramatic festival ran for a full week with crowded audiences. The versatile old gymnasium, fitted with stage, curtains, and apparatus for lighting and scenic effects, served as the theater.

The University's high standing in debate was maintained in contests with teams from the principal eastern universities and from Oxford and Cambridge.

It is hard to realize that the student body which maintained this elaborate program of activity was located in a university plant which covered only about two-thirds of the square bounded by G, H, Twentieth and Twenty-first Streets, and four houses facing the square.

When Harry W. ("Maud") Crum succeeded Bryan Morse as director of activities and football coach, the success of his teams led to increased mention in the press, with the University's athletes referred to as "Hatchetites" or "Crum-men." These names were particularly obnoxious to President Lewis because of their lack of any euphony. He asked the secretary to find a better name and try to get it accepted. The name suggested was "Colonials" and it has stuck.

The origin of the present extensive food service of today's University is to be found in the modest tearoom established during 1920-1921 by Beatrice Wilkins Tait, A.B. 1921 (Mrs. Charles P. Trussell), and her associate, the late Mrs. Lawrence Smoot (Mildred Duvall). With quarters in the basement of 2024 G Street, which had been properly equipped and tastefully furnished, this very popular spot, famed equally for its food and its sociability, was appropriately named "The Rabbit Hole." After a year Catherine Tonge, A.B. 1921 (the late Mrs. George L. Bowen) took over. Within a few years "The Rabbit Hole" was succeeded by the first University cafeteria in the first-floor rooms of 2022 G Street.[54]

By the time that President Lewis' administration came to a close, the ideas underlying the reorganization of 1910 had been brought to their conclusion. By their careful observance the reorganization had made possible, within a limited point of view, a stable University, solvent both financially and educationally and enjoying wide respect. Having an extensive acquaintance in the business community, President Lewis had involved many of its leaders in an intimate and helpful relationship with the University. A speaker of great ability and charm, eagerly sought after by many organizations, he had been able to carry the message of the institution far and wide. Within the accepted formula, he continued with great success and good will the policies of Presidents Stockton, Collier, and Hodgkins.

For seventeen years, the presidents had been putting down foundations. The question to be asked was, could those foundations support a larger structure than the limited one which extreme caution had built? President Lewis' successor gave an affirmative answer. As soon as President Lewis tendered his resignation, a Trustees' committee began the search for a successor. After a few months, two nominations were laid before the Board. A communication from a representative group of the teaching staff informed the Trustees that one of the nominees was not favored by the faculty. The other one was unanimously elected to take office on August 1, 1927. Thus began the thirty-two-year administration of Cloyd Heck Marvin.[55]

CHAPTER FOURTEEN

The Marvin Era

1927-1959

The new president's administration, the longest in the University's history, was to be a period of kaleidoscopic change in the relations of men and nations. It began while the great boom was still on, although the storm signals were beginning to go up. The Panic of 1929 was soon here. Then came the years of the Great Depression and, foreshadowed in the days of Hoover, the varied expedients in social and economic reform of the Rooseveltian New Deal. The old world order, whatever there was of it, collapsed. The idea of collective security became a mockery. Authoritarian philosophies took over governments and seated dictators. A new general war broke out, world wide in its extent and, thanks to modern technology, more intense than any war that had preceded it. Then a tardy and uncertain peace, that was no peace, prevented the reconciliation that peoples hoped for and demanded. The new United Nations began more and more to look like the old League of Nations as the Four Horsemen continued to ride over a disjointed world and threaten to extend their depredations even into outer space. In this age the directing of a university was no small task.

Cloyd Heck Marvin (1889-1969) at the time of his election as twelfth president of the University was only thirty-eight years old. He had already had a substantial background as a college teacher in the field of economics and as a university administrator as dean in the University of California at Los Angeles and president of the University of Arizona. None of his predecessors had brought to his task a fuller professional preparation, yet he was but slightly known to the members of the faculty and to a majority of the Board of Trustees who elected him with a confidence greatly strengthened by the recommendation of his friend Herbert Hoover, then Secretary of Commerce.

The new president immediately made his presence felt. Within a few weeks of his election he was in Washington, busily preparing office space for his occupancy and planning the reorganization of the University. By the time the Board met in the fall of 1927, he was ready to take the first steps. The formula which had governed the University's administration since 1910 was about to be laid aside. President Marvin was not particularly impressed by the abilities of his predecessors or by their achievements. There were two sides to the question, however. Descending suddenly on a new scene, he did not fully appreciate the way Stockton had saved the University, restored it to solvency, and reclaimed for it the respect of the community. He did not realize how opportunely Collier had reintroduced the institution to the official and social world, or how, by cultivating the business community, Lewis had brought into helpful relation with the University a new and larger group of civic leaders. He was not impressed by the loyal and unrelenting toil of Hodgkins and his profound understanding of the University's history and problems. The facts he granted; but their full significance, the essential nature of what they did, he did not grasp. "It may be," he wrote, "that the years of travail and marking time have served to keep and ready the University for this day and those yet to come."[1] In that spirit he went about his reorganization. As the years went on he became more and more convinced that the year 1927 marked the great divide.

There was also the other side to the question. The 1910 formula had been worked out almost to its logical conclusion. It had fulfilled its function, which was to reestablish the soundness of the institution. In a way, the Harris Plan for the development of Square 102 through the construction of eight large units enclosing the area graphically illustrated the 1910 formula. With two units—Corcoran and Stockton Halls—already built, Marvin rejected the Harris Plan, the architectural concept of a university idea compressed within a city block. He embarked on a program of physical expansion and centralized control.

Looking back more than a quarter of a century, he stated in 1954 "the basic problems that confronted the University in 1927." Briefly summarized, they were:

1. The establishment of an effective university organization;

2. The organization of the Board of Trustees so as to make for unity of administration;
3. Setting up a financial structure which would support the services of the University;
4. Determination of the location of the University in specific terms;
5. Setting up the objectives of the University;
6. Provision of adequate housing;
7. Development of academic responsibility of the personnel.[2]

The new president moved rapidly toward the reorganization of the University. At his first Board meeting he announced that the form of presenting minutes and reports had been changed. Up to this time, the form of minutes adopted by the Board at its first meeting in 1821 had been followed. At the same meeting a significant modification was made in the educational organization of the University. The Departments of Arts and Sciences, Law, and Medicine were dropped, and in their place the following were approved as units: Columbian College, the Graduate School, the School of Education, the School of Engineering, the Law School, the School of Medicine, the School of Pharmacy, the Summer Sessions, and the Division of Library Science. This was a great deal more than a change in nomenclature.

What had happened can be understood by borrowing feudal terms by way of illustration. The educational domain had consisted of three great fiefs: Arts and Sciences, Law, and Medicine, each presided over by a great feudatory (the dean) under a suzerain (the president), who, in effect, reigned but did not rule. Each of the great fiefs was now broken down into its component parts, presided over by a vassal, in the medieval sense, of the great feudatory. By the change, in terms of power, the great feudatories no longer existed, and their former vassals became directly answerable to the suzerain, who now moved into a sovereign position.

It is easy to account historically for the growth of this system which was changed by the reorganization of 1927. The Department of Arts and Sciences was essentially the old Columbian College in the District of Columbia in 1821. It was the trunk of the educational tree from which branches had grown from time to time as the widening concept of the liberal arts and sciences, as referred to in the Charter, had resulted in the creation of a more complex system. This Department of Arts and Sciences had come in time to include both graduate and undergraduate branches

in the liberal arts and sciences, education, engineering, and other specialized areas generally related to the liberal arts and sciences, their theory,
and their practice. As the president, in the language of the Charter, had
been "the Chief Master" of the College, so the dean of Arts and Sciences
had become "the Chief Master" of the educational organization that had
grown from the old College.

The right of the College to engage in educating youth outside of "the
English, learned, and foreign languages: the liberal arts and sciences, and
literature," as specified in the Charter, had been, in fact, strenuously
challenged by a group of citizens in a memorial to the Congress dated
February 20, 1826, although their position was not sustained. While the
Medical School was organized and began its work in 1825 as a department of the College, and there was some interchange of professors, financially the school was on its own for decades, the faculty finding its
quarters and financing its operation through student fees. The College
Trustees appointed the members of the medical faculty as nominated to
them and conferred the degree on candidates certified by the faculty. This
condition of financial autonomy and faculty independence was gradually
changed and the Medical Department was brought under University
control. The changing requirements of medical education, if no other
reason, made this necessary. Not only was self-support impossible for
a modern medical school, but a guaranteed annual subvention from the
University funds became a basic requirement.

The case of the Law School, when legal education was resumed in
1865, was somewhat similar. The large number of students who, unrestricted by exacting entrance requirements, crowded into the Law
School in its early years produced a revenue adequate at the time to
cover instructional costs and to produce a surplus. The increase in admission requirements, the growing need for added library materials
and adequate housing, and the addition of daytime courses, together with
other factors, changed the position of the Law School and made its
full integration into the University organization necessary.

Before the changes of 1927 the annual budget had been largely made
up of three parts, each prepared by one of the deans for the activities
under his supervision, combined by the treasurer, approved by the president, and submitted to the Board. Attempts on the part of the president
to modify it at times brought about clashes of authority in which the
presidents did not always prevail. As a result of the 1927 change, a true
University budget was initiated, brought together by the administration.[3]

Natural causes transpired to ease the transition. Illness forced the resignation of Dr. William Cline Borden (1857-1934) in 1930 after twenty-one years' service as Dean of the Medical School. On February 19, 1931, Dean Howard Lincoln Hodgkins died after a period of illness, and on December 10 of the same year John Bell Larner (1858-1931), Chairman of the Board of Trustees, passed away.

Dean Borden was a graduate of the Medical School in the class of 1883. Shortly thereafter he passed the examination of the Army Medical Board and reported for duty as an Acting Assistant Surgeon, pending the receipt of his commission as First Lieutenant and Assistant Surgeon, at the headquarters of the Department of The Platte at Omaha. Thus began a quarter of a century of distinguished service in the Army, which ended with his retirement in 1908 because of a heart condition. Not the least of his outstanding achievements were a successful campaign for the establishment of Walter Reed General Hospital, his selection of the site, and the planning and beginning of its actual construction. At a time of crisis in the University and the Medical School, Colonel Borden was elected Professor of Surgery, succeeding the late Dr. Ford Thompson, and Dean of the School. His persuasive power, his energy, and his resourcefulness gained and held a distinguished position for the school. His eminence as a surgeon and a teacher gave added luster to the record of a remarkable man.[4]

Howard Lincoln Hodgkins, Dean of the University, had as his special bailiwick the Department of Arts and Sciences. A graduate of the class of 1883 in the College, he had served the University in varied capacities from tutor in the Preparatory School while he was still a student, to president *ad interim* following the resignation of President Collier.[5]

John Bell Larner, LL.B. 1879, LL.D. (hon.) 1904, was for twenty-one years chairman of the Board of Trustees, the important post which had been held by such distinguished figures as the Reverend Obadiah B. Brown, Colonel James L. Edwards, Amos Kendall, and W. W. Corcoran. Prominent in civic affairs and in the banking community, Mr. Larner was for many years president of the Washington Loan and Trust Company. Elected a Trustee in 1899, and chairman of the Board in 1910, he served until his death in 1931. His official career covered a critical period in the life of the University.[6] Not only the old organization, but its major figures were disappearing.

Following closely on the discontinuance of the Departments of Arts and Sciences, Law, and Medicine, and the approval of the individual schools and colleges, the Trustees accepted the president's new listing of departments of instruction and created a Division of Fine Arts. Later these departments were grouped in divisions, each division having its own divisional organization and being charged with the overall educational supervision of its constituent departments of instruction. While the traditional independence of departments was strong enough to prevent any thoroughgoing application of the divisional idea, nevertheless a searching reappraisal of courses by divisional committees proved to be of great value.[7]

Attention was next given to the recodification of the bylaws of the Board of Trustees. In the new bylaws, the Board was authorized to designate a vice president, not at the time "a professor or tutor," and to accord him status as an ex officio member of the Board of Trustees. The officers of the Board were henceforth to be a chairman, a vice chairman, a secretary, and an assistant secretary elected annually by ballot. In the new bylaws there was no reference to the office and duties of the secretary of the University, or to the office and duties of the treasurer of the University. Section 9 dealing with the Committee on Finance referred to the University comptroller, the new designation of the principal financial officer of the University. The previous bylaws had provided only for an executive committee, a finance committee, and visiting committees. The new bylaws omitted the visiting committees from among the standing committees, listing the Executive Committee and the Committees on Educational Policy, University Libraries and Museums, Alumni Relations, Honors, Nomination of Trustees, Legal Affairs, Finance, Buildings and Lands, Endowment Funds, Personnel, Extracurricular Activities, and Public Relations. The multiplicity of standing committees indicated the broad front on which the president planned to operate with his Trustees.[8]

The duties originally assigned to the secretary of the University by the bylaws were distributed among other officers. As they related to the Board of Trustees, they had been transferred to the secretary of the Board of Trustees. The registrar became ex officio the secretary of all academic bodies and the keeper of the great seal of the University; the officer who was eventually designated as the administrative secretary took over most of the administrative functions. Article VI of the old bylaws had provided that the secretary "shall give to any meeting at which he is entitled to be present any information concerning University affairs which he may have and which may be proper to be brought before such meeting." Obviously this function of communication could no longer be discharged.[9]

The old educational ordinance was entirely recast. Details of organization and matters of educational policy were covered in special resolutions of the Board acting on recommendations of the faculties. A code governing academic personnel was established, including a system of sabbatical leave. The President's Council, which under the former ordinance had had charge of all administrative educational questions, was discontinued. A committee on educational policy partially took its place, but it was not until the institution of the present University Senate that a body was created with a similar composition and functions.[10]

In the course of the reorganization, a significant reassignment of areas was made by separating the freshman and sophomore years from the junior and senior years and assigning them to an autonomous Junior College. The junior and senior years in the College and the additional year leading to the Master of Arts degree were assigned to Columbian College, the departments of which were organized into four divisions: languages and literatures, mathematics and the physical sciences, the natural sciences, and the social sciences. An independent study plan was established to permit original work by students of demonstrated ability. Work in the Graduate Council leading to the degree of Doctor of Philosophy was organized on "a master–apprentice relation" which was conceived of as professional research training.[11]

Even as brief an account as this of the reorganization of 1927 and the years immediately following indicates the drive, vigor, and imagination of President Marvin. While the changes came about for the major part with the recommendation of the faculties, the initiative was invariably the president's, and he had cordial support. The Trustees received his statements with uniform appreciation and gratitude, and their *Minutes* record frequent resolutions of the most enthusiastic nature. In the fall of 1930, President Marvin was able to report, with great satisfaction, that in spite of the existing economic depression and general falling off of registrations elsewhere, there had been more than a 6 per cent increase in student charges for the semester. "With a full realization of the power that is beginning to manifest itself," he said, "the shifting political situations, that many times have been looked upon as a deterrent, may be thought of as adding strength to the University, for in the last analysis, it will be the stable element in the community."[12]

There were many tangible evidences of "the power that is beginning to manifest itself." Distinguished rulers and statesmen were officially received by the University and honored by the award of its doctorate, *honoris causa*. Among them in these first years were Ramsay MacDonald, Prime Minister of Great Britain; Prajadhipok, King of Siam; and Pascual Ortiz Rubio, President of Mexico. At the request of the Italian government, a special convocation addressed by Ambassador Giacomo de Martino and greeted by cable by Mussolini was held to celebrate the bimillennial of the birth of the poet Virgil.[13] At the February Convocation of 1929, honorary degrees were conferred upon President and Mrs. Coolidge.

In 1929, a circle of Omicron Delta Kappa was installed, and the same year the University was placed on the accredited list of the American Association of University Women.

On October 29, 1930, the University was placed on the approved list of the Association of American Universities, a most significant recognition of the institution's worth and academic standing.[14] In expressing its appreciation to the officers of the University for making this accreditation possible, the Board linked with the name of President Marvin that of Charles Riborg Mann (1869-1942), a Trustee. Dr. Mann was a distinguished physicist who during the First World War, particularly as chairman of the Citizens' Advisory Board of the War Department, played an outstanding role in dealing with educational problems of the armed forces. In the years following the war, he, more than any other, gave form and direction to the American Council on Education, following up on and enlarging the role that had been played by educational institutions during the war and developing an organization that spoke with increasing authority as the voice of American education not only to the lay world but among the institutions themselves. As President Marvin's principal adviser, he put his prestige and ability at the service of the University and made a signal contribution to its development and progress.

Another Trustee who at this time and for the remainder of her long and useful life served the University in a very special way was Jessie Fant Evans (Mrs. Joshua Evans, Jr.), A.B. 1913, Ed.D. (hon.) 1932. Coming to the Board in 1923 as an alumni Trustee, then elected a charter Trustee and finally an honorary Trustee, she served in a notable way as the link between the Board and the alumni, the faculty, and the students. A former teacher, a member of the press, civic leader, and officer in many women's organizations, her numerous contacts gave her information and a point of view that were of great service in the Board's human relations. It was through her hands that the frequent and generous contributions of the Columbian Women were brought to the Board; and through her loyal dedication of time, thought, and means, she prompted like dedication on the part of others.

Of the numerous transfers and changes in personnel that took place during the period of reorganization, none perhaps interested more people than the retirement of William Allen Wilbur (1864-1945) from the deanship of Columbian College to become provost of the University. An eminent Baptist layman who had written widely on the history of his denomination in the District, Dean Wilbur was to many the embodiment of the spirit of Columbian College. Coming to the University as the head of its Preparatory School, he became professor of English on the discontinuance of the Academy and, shortly thereafter, dean of Columbian College. He had no great interest in research. He was interested in the interpretation of literature, particularly the writings of Shakespeare and Browning, and, in his very personal course, freshman rhetoric. Thousands of freshmen have never forgotten the impression made upon them as the slightly stooped dean, his face in repose with just a faint suggestion of a smile, opened the door of his office and slowly came forward on the platform of the old chapel, which was dimly illuminated by the soft light from the long stained-glass windows, walked to the lectern, and announced that "rhetoric was self-expression through language." For years the course, even the list of topics for essays, was the same. The lectures found their way into print, were published first in fascicules, then bound into a volume which was treasured forever by those who probably in many cases had not read it but who looked upon it as an outward and visible reminder of an experience they had felt but never really understood. To the cynical, it was mysticism; to the believer, pure charisma; but they all felt it.

Wilbur's long tenure as dean of Columbian College (1904-1928) was almost equaled in length by that of Henry Grattan Doyle, who became dean of Columbian College six years after Wilbur's retirement and served for twenty-three years (1934-1957).

While changes were being made in existing units, new divisions and schools were being added to the University organization.

In 1930, Elmer Louis Kayser was appointed to organize the Division of University and Extension Students, which he served as director and later dean for thirty-two years. The basic idea underlying the creation of this new unit was simple and practical: to enable the University to meet more fully the special demands of an urban community. To make it clear, the new division was shortly separated into two parts: the Division of University Students, and the Division of Extension, for all students in off-campus courses. Then, excluding the extension students, all other students were put into two major categories: regular students, registered in degree-granting schools and colleges of the University, in full standing and active candidates for degrees; and University Students, not candidates for degrees from George Washington University, and registered in the Division of University Students. The term "special student" was no longer used. The Division of University Students, by definition, included a diverse group: mature individuals taking courses to increase vocational fitness or for personal enrichment; students officially registered in other institutions and taking courses for transfer with the approval of the home institution, or students taking courses to regularize their status before becoming candidates for degrees. In 1944, with the creation of the Division of Special Students under Dean W. R. West, the term "special student" again came into use, and students admitted within limited areas to regularize their status for degree candidacy were henceforth registered in the new division, rather than in the Division of University Students.

The most important of the new units was the School of Government, founded two years before the Division of University Students. In effect this was a revival of an older unit, rather than the creation of a new one. Its object, as announced in the catalogue of March, 1928, was to help men and women prepare for public service. In a way this was a logical and practical extension of the ideas so eloquently set forth in the will of George Washington. He had there expressed his "ardent wish to see a plan devised on a liberal scale which would have a tendency to spread systematic ideas through all parts of this rising Empire, thereby to do away local attachments and State prejudices, as far as the nature of things would, or indeed ought to admit, from our national councils." The School of Government was concerned in its earliest years with two courses of study—one a course in government, the other a foreign service course. They were undergraduate courses leading to the bachelor's degree. By 1931, interest and support had so increased that the school was also offering a master's degree, and six instead of the original two curricula: government, business administration, finance, domestic commerce, foreign commerce, and foreign service. The first administrative head of the school was Professor W. Reed West, who served as Chairman of the Executive

Committee from 1931 to 1934 and then as Assistant Dean from 1934 to 1945, when Professor Arthur E. Burns was appointed Dean.

The origin of the School of Government was to be found in the Department of Comparative Jurisprudence and Diplomacy, opened with great ceremony in 1898. This school had been planned by President Welling, who had looked upon it as the capstone of the educational structure. When, in President Whitman's administration, the school was opened, its distinguished faculty seemed to insure immediate success. Conceived as a graduate school, it offered the graduate degree in law (LL.M.) and the degrees of Master of Diplomacy and Doctor of Civil Law. Gradually the courses in law were pulled back into the Law School. From the beginning, the school was harassed by lack of adequate funds and became a marked financial drain on the whole institution. So impressed was he by its importance that President Needham continued to support the school even when other branches of the University were being forced to retrench. In 1905 its name was changed to the Department of Politics and Diplomacy and courses in law were reassigned to the Law School. There was a further abridgment two years later when the name was again changed to the College of the Political Sciences, which was assigned to the Department of Arts and Sciences. In the reorganization of 1910, the school, still hampered by lack of finances and by internal dissension, was discontinued and its courses transferred to Columbian College. In 1928, circumstances had happily changed.

For a number of years there had been a growing interest in the University among Masonic bodies. General Washington was a towering figure in the history of Masonry. Luther Rice, the founder of Columbian College, was a Mason. Dr. Marvin was a 33rd-degree Mason.[15]

Professor D. C. Croissant of the Department of English had been a leading figure in stimulating the practical interest of the League of Masonic Clubs. Becoming specifically interested in the need for a properly trained foreign service, the Masons were particularly aroused by the fact that the only institution formally offering such training through a School of Foreign Service was a church-related institution. Feeling that such training should be given in a nonsectarian institution, their Education Foundation was so sanguine as to its ability to raise substantial funds for endowment that its official publication announced the likely opening in September, 1926, of a School of Foreign Service in The George Washington University, two years before the University established its School

of Government.[16] While the league was never able to assist the University
in the massive way it had intended, its campaign throughout the Masonic
clubs of the country did bring some material assistance; but, more important, it brought the University and its sense of obligation to provide
training for governmental service to a large and hitherto uninformed
sector which resulted in various types of gifts from Masonic groups and
foundations.

An outstanding act of philanthropy came in the early months of the
Marvin administration, a happy augury for the success of the new
president. On December 28, 1927, the Board of Trustees accepted an
indenture between the University and the Supreme Council (Mother
Council of the World) of the Inspectors General, Knights Commanders
of the House of the Temple of Solomon of the 33rd degree of the
Ancient and Accepted Scottish Rite of Freemasonry of the Southern
Jurisdiction of the United States, whereby the University accepted a
gift of one million dollars with the understanding that the gift would
revert if at any time the institution ceased to be nonsectarian. The details
of the grant were the result of many conferences between President
Marvin and John Henry Cowles, then Sovereign Grand Commander of
the Scottish Rite.

This generous gift, a memorial to George Washington the Mason,
made possible the establishment of the School of Government. It was
"designed to perpetuate the principles of human freedom, the rights of
man and the sovereignty of the people, as these principles are enunciated
in the Constitution of the United States, and embodied in the system of
State and Federal Governments composing the United States of America;
granting to the University the fullest discretion in the choice of methods,
courses of instruction, selection of teachers and lectures and awards of degrees, certificates or diplomas as it may now possess or hereafter acquire by
virtue of its charter and the Acts of Congress aforesaid, or by the traditions of such institutions of learning, not inconsistent with or subversive
of the purpose of this donation as hereinabove outlined."[17]

The University now had a substantial fund for the support of a school
which had already a background in the institution's history and which
could carry out the objectives and meet the common aim of all the
Masonic groups by preparing students for leadership in the fields of
foreign service and of govermental theory and administration. Graduates
would be prepared for careers in either governmental service or a
related business or professional field. Other important grants from

Masonic groups for the support of fellows and scholars in the School of Government were to follow. Two were especially significant.

In 1954, Sovereign Grand Commander Luther Andrew Smith and President Marvin, with the consent and support of the Supreme Council, established the Scottish Rite Fellowships. These fellowships were to be granted to qualified students for one year of graduate study in the School of Government. Each carried a stipend to cover tuition and fees and an allowance for living expenses. In the period 1954-1968, 236 Scottish Rite Fellows completed their courses. Many of them are stationed in United States embassies all over the world.

A second highly important contribution from Masonic sources came in the same year with the foundation of the Wolcott Scholarships, sponsored by the High Twelve International and named for its founder, E. P. Wolcott. Wolcott Scholarships were to be granted for graduate study toward master's degrees in preparation for government service at federal, state, or local levels. They were to carry a stipend to cover tuition and fees and an allowance for living expenses. In the period 1954-1968, 52 Wolcott Scholars were graduated from the School of Government; most of them entered government service. In 1967, the Wolcott Foundation received a legacy of a million dollars, the income from which is to be used to maintain scholarships in the School of Government.[18]

The establishment of the school and the rallying to it of such massive Masonic and other support were a major achievement of the Marvin administration. Although a depression was in the offing at the time of the original Scottish Rite gift, the financial picture of the University was distinctly favorable in the early Marvin years. When the depression did hit the country with full force, its effects were delayed and minimized in the District of Columbia by the stabilizing power of the government payroll. In the fall of 1928 an administrative reserve fund of $100,000 was set up by the University, to be accumulated as funds became available, beginning with $25,441.29 saved from the operating fund during 1927-1928.[19] The acquisition of real estate in Square 102 was greatly expedited.

Expansion in a different direction was indicated when James E. Pixlee was appointed Professor of Physical Education for Men in the spring of 1929, forecasting the beginning of the most ambitious program of intercollegiate athletics that the University had ever known.

The creation of the Pairo Fund in 1931 raised prematurely the hopes of the athletically-minded that new and adequate physical facilities would soon be available. Richard E. Pairo (1852-1930), LL.B. 1875, left to the University a bequest, valued at something less than a half-million dollars, "for the use and benefit of the athletics of the University either by using the principal for the purchase of a campus or the building and equipping of a gymnasium, or investing the principal and devoting the income thereof in promoting athletic sports of the University as the Trustees or Faculty may deem best."

Significant also was the appointment of Dr. Earl Baldwin McKinley, with his well-known interest in developing research in the medical sciences, as Professor of Bacteriology and Dean of the Medical School. An addition to the Medical School to afford fuller facilities, which cost over $60,000, was authorized at the time of his appointment. In 1931, the School of Nursing was discontinued.[20]

When Dr. McKinley died seven years later, he was succeeded as dean by Dr. Walter Andrew Bloedorn, who held the post until his retirement in 1957. The years of Dean Bloedorn's leadership were highly significant in the development of the Medical School's program, work carried forward with equal vigor by his successor, Dr. John Parks. In addition to the usual duties of improving instruction and encouraging research, these deans were faced with the problem of undertaking major physical expansion. During its first forty years, the Medical School had many homes: first, for a brief period, rented quarters; then the building erected by the faculty on the northeast corner of Tenth and E Streets; next, the Washington Infirmary; again rented quarters; then the old Law School building on Fifth Street. Immediately after the close of the War of 1861-1865, the Medical Department moved to the building on H Street, the gift of W. W. Corcoran. That site has been occupied for more than a century. No other branch of the University has been located in the same place for as long a time. The construction and improvement of the new University Hospital, the addition of the Meyer Pavilion, the building of the Warwick Memorial, and the acquisition and adaptation of large and usable structures in the area immediately south of Washington Circle have been the approximating steps to the development of a vast Medical Center. The transfer of the activities carried on in the H Street buildings to new structures in the West End will again bring together in the same area all the branches of the University.

In a very personal way, as far as President Marvin was concerned, two relatively insignificant appropriations made toward the close of 1929 are interesting. They were the grant to the president of $1,200 for the improvement of the University Yard and an allowance of $1,750 for painting the buildings a light cream. While later there were many other and larger expenditures for the same purposes, these served not only as appropriations but as authorizations, or, at least, declarations of intent.[21]

The president had a deep interest in gardens and in buildings. With miscellaneous structures of varied styles and sizes being used for University purposes, he sought to give this bewildering diversity a measure of unity by painting all of the buildings (except Corcoran and Stockton) with a standard color of light paint. He wanted to give some interest to the interior area of Square 102 and the space around the buildings by planned landscaping. He found recreation and intense satisfaction in supervising these matters personally, usually early in the morning with Norris, his gardener, and his other groundsmen in attendance. As the holdings increased and the task became more complicated, a professional garden consultant, Mrs. Lilian Wright Smith, took over the major supervision of the work. The collection of roses in the Yard is a living reminder of the pioneering work of both the president and Mrs. Smith in improving the grounds. The president's predilection for white paint on the exterior and "Marvin green" on the interior remained a subject of conversation for years.

By the beginning of 1933, the effects of the depression were being keenly felt. With the approval of the Board, the president asked the deans and directors to make no recommendations for filling more posts vacated by resignation, unless the need was most urgent. At the same time, Dr. Marvin presented to the Trustees these resolutions which were unanimously approved:

Be it resolved, that the Board of Trustees of The George Washington University reaffirms its expression of appreciation of the proficient services of the members of the University staff during these later years and with special reference to the fine morale maintained during these difficult days of social and economic readjustments, and further

Be it resolved, that the Board as a means of expressing its appreciation to the staff announces at this time that it is making no salary changes during the current year unless emergencies arise that are now unknown.[22]

The best evidence of the president's ability in financial matters is shown by the fact that no cut in salaries was made during the entire period of the depression. As a matter of economic assistance to young men and women, unable financially to continue their education because of the depression, the University granted additional scholarships to twenty recent high school graduates in the metropolitan area.[23]

The University faculty seized upon the beginning of the president's eighth year as a proper occasion to review the achievements of the first seven years in a laudatory and appreciative resolution presented to Dr. Marvin and forwarded to the Board of Trustees for inclusion in its records. The faculty noted that, in difficult times, he had maintained the University's program without sacrifice of standards, that he had "simplified and coordinated" educational administration, that in the early years he had increased the faculty salary scale and held to it in spite of the depression, that he had introduced a general policy of sabbatical leave, and that he had scrupulously respected faculty prerogatives and tenure. In the furtherance of his policy, full cooperation and hearty support were pledged.[24]

The faculty's praise was warranted. The president had improved its economic status and respected its privileges in the classroom and its prerogatives as teachers. He had maintained the University's offerings and program. The full implication of his administrative changes the faculty did not see then. It appreciated the elimination of much that it considered archaic. It could not then appreciate the full extent of administrative centralization in the office of the president and its effects. If in its enumeration of Dr. Marvin's achievements the faculty had gone specifically into the financial phases of his activity, it would have pointed out that in the period between September, 1928, and September, 1934, the University had acquired nineteen pieces of property, increasing its holdings 26.44 per cent.[25]

If the first seven years had been a period of administrative and educational reorganization, of the improvement of faculty status, and of the beginning of large gifts and accelerated acquisition of property, the period to follow was, in the eyes of the public, to be an era of unprecedented building. Except for the large addition to the Medical School, building up to this time had been largely confined to the remodeling of existing structures for educational purposes, creating makeshifts which were usable but far from ideal.

The new movement got under way in December, 1934. In that month the Board authorized the construction of a building on G Street between Lisner Hall (2023) and Woodhull House to be used for laboratories, classrooms, and offices of the Departments of Biology and Zoology; and administrative offices for the registrar, the dean of Columbian College, and the dean of the Junior College; and to provide, in addition, six classrooms. The estimated cost was $75,000. In the same month Mrs. Henry Alvah Strong gave the University $200,000 "for a hall to house women."

The building for the Biological Sciences, Alexander Graham Bell Hall, was the first one to be built in Square 102 after the Harris Plan was abandoned. Strong Hall was the first major unit in the new dormitory system, a very important departure because it inaugurated the policy that changed the institution into a residential college within a few decades.[26]

While Strong Hall was being completed, work advanced rapidly on Gilbert Stuart Hall, located on G Street immediately east of Lisner Hall, so that this building was occupied at the beginning of the 1936-1937 academic year.

Alexander Graham Bell Hall and Gilbert Stuart Hall, originally designated unimaginatively as Buildings C and D respectively, were identical in appearance. They were, in a sense, depression buildings. At a time when many institutions were utilizing public funds of one sort or another to load their campuses with massive structures, President Marvin was pursuing a course of rugged individualism and expanding the University by its own resources. These two buildings, improvised by the president, and to an extent followed in later construction, were designed for the utmost economy in their original cost and in maintenance. Built of used brick, later painted white, they were essentially cubes, four stories and basement, with hollow-tile room partitions, and exposed pipes and wiring. Walls were unfinished and the ceiling design was derived from the cement forms of the floor above. Rooms could be changed in size, practically overnight, by moving the hollow tiles of the walls. Exposed pipes and wiring made repair easy. In this highly ingenious fashion, classrooms and laboratories were provided at an amazingly low cost. Later refinements and furnishing have done much to change the Spartan character of these buildings in their original form.

Strong Hall, on the southwest corner of Twenty-first and G Streets, was the first of the new buildings built outside the original Square 102 (G and H Streets, Twentieth and Twenty-first Streets). Contrary to the Marvin design, it was a red brick Colonial structure of six stories, topped by a solarium. In 1938, the Hall of Government, made possible by the generosity of Mrs. Henry Alvah Strong, was erected on the northwest corner of Twenty-first and G Streets, the second of the new buildings to be located facing the original Square 102. The cornerstone was laid by the Grand Lodge of the District of Columbia with full Masonic ceremony.

In general it matched in plan the earlier Marvin type of building, but it was constructed with outer walls of white stone instead of used brick, and made a dignified home for the School of Government.

As the Hall of Government was being completed, work got under way on Lisner Library, located on the site of old Lisner Hall, the building originally occupied by the University on G Street. The library was built by funds given by Abram Lisner as a memorial to his wife, the late Laura Hartmann Lisner. Opened in the fall of 1939, it was the first building that the institution had ever had devoted entirely to use as a library. It was of the Marvin type, six stories in height. With the two matching buildings, one on either side, it was designed to form an impressive group occupying practically the entire G Street side of Square 102.

These major structures and several smaller ones constituted the building activities of the 1930's. Never before in the history of the University had there been such tangible evidence of the institution's growth or of the energy of its president. There could be no possible doubt as to permanent location. Square 102 now contained an imposing group of buildings around an attractively landscaped University Yard. But construction had gone beyond the original square, and plans for other and larger structures were under way. The acquisition of property in the area was accelerated. The shape of things to come was apparent.

As the first decade of his administration came to a close, President Marvin was concluding successfully what had unexpectedly turned out to be a piece of unfinished business. On April 14, 1909, Mrs. Susan Whitney Dimock had informed President Needham that the George Washington Memorial Association had withdrawn from its agreement to raise a half-million dollars for erecting on the Van Ness site a building to be known as the George Washington Memorial. This structure was to belong to the University. It was to be used as an administration building and was to contain an auditorium for lectures and for international and scientific gatherings. As part of the arrangements, the University had taken the name of The George Washington University, in perpetuity.

After the termination of its agreement with the University, the association had continued to raise money, but had fallen far short of its original objectives. With the hope that new life could be given to the project, it was decided to link the spirit of 1776 with World War I patriotism and to build a George Washington Memorial Building and Victory Memorial. The government assigned a site for the purpose where the National Gallery now stands. The building, when completed, was to be under the control of the regents of the Smithsonian Institution. The cornerstone was laid November 14, 1921, and at the exercises an American flag to be flown over the building was presented in the name of the University by President Hodgkins.

The association was not able to proceed with the work of construction, and the gaunt masonry of the foundation lingered as a reminder of a noble object unattained until the site was desired for the projected National Gallery. Mrs. Dimock, who had carried the major burden of the project for a generation, was now advanced in years. It seemed proper at this time to liquidate the affairs of the association and in so doing to provide that the assets be used in a way consonant with the purposes of the George Washington Memorial Association. The National Gallery made noble use of the site.

On June 17, 1936, at a special meeting called for the purpose, a constitutional number of members of the George Washington Memorial Association directed that steps be taken to dissolve the association and to transfer its property to the University. The Board of Trustees accepted the gift for such purposes as it might deem best, "always having in mind the purposes of the George Washington Memorial Association."[27]

At the request of Mrs. Dimock, President Marvin became her successor as president of the George Washington Memorial Association to facilitate the transfer of the association's assets, which amounted to approximately $220,000 and were used to complete the University Auditorium. The desire for an auditorium, which had been a major feature in the association's project, was thus fulfilled.[28]

Mrs. Henry F. Dimock died on September 12, 1939. Her will, after making some small specific bequests, gave "all the rest, residue and remainder" to the University for its general purposes to perpetuate the memory of her daughter Susan.

It would be qualified praise to assess the achievement of a man or an institution on tangible things alone. Educational progress kept pace with the building program. Although well aware of the shortcomings and limitations of the University, President Marvin from the very beginning had been anxious that its essential value and worth be recognized by those formal acknowledgments by national organizations that are the visible signs of acceptance by the academic community. Improved physical facilities, the evidence of ability to finance the educational program, the quality and productiveness of the faculty, the tested performance of graduates, a healthy change in the role of the part-time student—all of these factors facilitated a sounder view of the University's position in the academic world.

In many ways, the effort to win recognition was climaxed by the granting of a charter to Alpha Chapter of the District of Columbia by Phi Beta Kappa. This chapter, formally installed on February 22, 1937, was the first to be established in the District of Columbia.[29]

Sigma Xi, Omicron Delta Kappa, Mortar Board, and many other honor societies were represented by chapters on the campus. Every branch of the University was accredited by the appropriate accrediting agency, a recognition of the energy of the president and the wholehearted cooperation of the faculties.

At the same time that the financial security of the teaching staff was being safeguarded against salary decreases in periods of unusual economic difficulty, attention was being given to other faculty benefits. A system of sabbatical leave was instituted, and special provision was made for extended leave for members of the faculty with lengthy service before the system was put into effect. As a matter of fixed policy, effort was made to provide every faculty member with a suitable office. A retirement system was established, providing for retirement at sixty-five, or earlier in cases of disability, with possible annual extension of active service until seventy, and a pension to be fixed in each case by the Trustees. A special committee's report on Faculty Privileges and Responsibilities was accepted by the Board of Trustees, with slight amendment, and adopted as policy.[30]

The educational organization was under constant scrutiny, and many changes were made. In 1927, fourteen departments were manned by part-time teachers exclusively. In his first two years, President Marvin reduced this number to four.[31] Several new departments were created, among them the Departments of Journalism, Slavonic Languages, Anthropology, Statistics, and, following the discontinuance of the Division of Architecture, of Fine Arts. The Department of Economics was divided into a Department of Business Organization and Administration and a Department of Economics. The School of Nursing was discontinued, and a Center of Inter-American Studies (later called the Inter-American Center) was established.[32]

Activity in scientific research received a new impetus. Among the outstanding scientists called to the University during this period were Vincent du Vigneaud in biochemistry (1932-1938), later to receive the Nobel Prize (1955), and the physicists Edward Teller (1935-1941) and the late George Gamow (1934-1956). A most fruitful and rewarding activity was the organization, in cooperation with the Carnegie Institution of Washington, of the Washington Conference on Theoretical Physics, which met annually at the University before World War II, with Gamow and Teller playing leading roles.

The first of the conferences held on April 19, 20, and 21, 1935, was attended by representatives from twenty universities and research organizations doing leading work in theoretical physics, including the National Bureau of Standards, the Naval Research Laboratory, the Carnegie Institution of Washington, and the following universities: Cambridge (England), Oxford (England), Queens (Canada), California, California Institute of Technology, Columbia, Cornell, George Washington, Harvard, Illinois, Kansas, North Carolina, Ohio State, Princeton, Purdue, and Wisconsin. This three-day conference, participated in by outstanding scientists in an informal fashion, with full opportunity for general discussion, proved so stimulating and so fruitful of results that arrangements were made for its continuation, year after year. For each conference, specific topics in the field were proposed in the invitation to participating physicists. At the sessions, the briefings to present the current state of research in the areas being considered were followed by general discussion that probed into the theoretical possibilities and the significance of this expanding field of knowledge. Each of the sessions was in a very real sense a working conference.[33]

While each of the conferences was of the greatest significance, the fifth conference, January 26, 27, and 28, 1939, is important in the history of our age.[34] The late George Gamow described this historic occasion very vividly:

In January, 1939, the Annual Conference on Theoretical Physics in Washington, D.C., organized jointly by The George Washington University (Edward Teller and the present reviewer at the wheel) and the Carnegie Institution of Washington (M. A. Tuve at the wheel) was to be honored by two distinguished guests: Niels Bohr, who was spending some time in the Institute for Advanced Study in Princeton, and Enrico Fermi, who a few years before had moved from Rome to Chicago.

The first day of the meeting followed the original schedule and was not very exciting, except that I got three flat tires driving the Bohrs to dinner at my home by running into a beer bottle somebody had left negligently on the street. The next day Bohr came to the meeting somewhat late, with a telegram in his hands. The telegram was from Lise Meitner in Stockholm and informed Bohr that she had just heard from her former colleague Otto Hahn in Berlin that uranium, being bombarded by neutrons, shows traces of radioactive elements of about one-half its weight. Meitner added that she and her nephew Otto Frisch believed that the uranium nucleus undergoes fission, i.e., splitting into two about equal fragments, as the result of the neutron impact.

The conference went off the originally planned track. Bohr and Fermi, both armed with chalk, started an animated discussion near the blackboard, and Tuve, recognizing that this discussion might be of paramount importance for war purposes, politely showed out two newspapermen covering the meeting. This was probably the first step toward atomic security. Nevertheless the word "fission" leaked into the press, and the next day Robert Oppenheimer telephoned to me from Berkeley to find out what it was all about.

Returning to Princeton, Bohr, in collaboration with John Wheeler, developed an elegant theory of nuclear fission that was published in the September issue of the *Physical Review*. This was the first and last extensive paper on that subject (in the U.S.A. at least) before the security curtain was tightly drawn around the subject.[35]

A tablet on the wall at the entrance to the room on the second floor of the Hall of Government where the session was held commemorates "the most exciting and important discussion" of the Fifth Washington Conference on Theoretical Physics.

The handful of scientists who were aware of the possibility that uranium research could lead the way to the production of powerful bombs of a new type, knew that research was going on at an accelerated pace in Germany following the splitting of the atom by two German scientists late in 1938. If the Nazis got the bomb first they would have a powerful weapon that others could not match in their drive for world domination. Only through massive assistance from the government could America get the means to quicken her nuclear research. Albert Einstein's direct approach to President Roosevelt obtained this aid. Two outstanding Hungarian-born physicists, Professors Wigner of Princeton and Szilard of Columbia, had been successful in enlisting Einstein's assistance. On Wednesday, August 2, 1939, Professor Teller drove Professor Szilard to Peconic Bay on Long Island, where Einstein was vacationing, to receive the signed letter to Roosevelt which had been drafted three days before. This letter was largely instrumental in getting the first assistance from the government in the form of a small appropriation of $6,000, the very modest beginning of appropriations that eventually expanded into billions.[36]

In the Marvin administration, student relations took on a new and more compelling form. The new breed of student was coming into existence, ready to condemn, agitate, and demonstrate, eager to adopt causes, and increasingly militant in tactics. Earlier efforts to stimulate such activity had not found massive support.

An effort to arouse a voice of student dissent was made in the twenties by the publication of *Sour Grapes* and *The Lash,* sheets that made their appearance suddenly throughout the University and at nearby newstands and were eagerly perused. *Sour Grapes* burst on the scene with Volume I Number 1 on December 12, 1923. Its banner head read "Bold Faculty Plot Exposed." It referred to an allegation, discussed at length, that a small group of professors had attempted to seize control of the University and seat a compliant dean as president. The story, totally unsubstantiated, went into great detail and mentioned individuals supposed to be in the plot. Other feature stories attacked *The Hatchet* and the Law School.

The Lash, underwritten by the same student, appeared three years later. Its first number ran into difficulty. Said the second number, "It offended the esthetic sense of some of our Mid-Victorians and drew from them such a shower of criticism that its distribution was impossible." *The Lash* took as its subjects for criticism all of the student politicians, the fraternities, most of the student activities, the Father of His Country, and the educational system in general. By the time it reached its third number, it was moving President Lewis in range to be its major target. "Caesar has his Brutus, Charles Stuart his Cromwell, George the Third his Washington, Harding his liquor, and Lewis his Lash."[37] The fourth number announced the reprinting of the suppressed *Sour Grapes* of 1923, available at a cost of 50 cents a copy.

The Lash and *Sour Grapes* were protests. They were well written, using sarcasm, irony, and touches of broad humor along with vitriolic attacks. They invited student revolt and called for the protection of the right to revolt "as the most sacred of our liberties." They found a handful of followers.[38] The student mind was not yet prepared for anything of this sort. Campus politics was practiced hot and heavy, but it was within the limits of student activities. The rather superior air of the radical sheets, skillfully poking fun at undergraduate naïveté, was not conducive to student support. In the development of the new type of student, *The Lash* and *Sour Grapes* came too early. Later in the thirties they might have found a considerable following. The crash and the depression created a new age.

Contrary to the views of many who would make the time a generation later, the new breed of college student, in George Washington University at least, was a product of the Great Depression and the New Deal. While the University had in the earlier days of the period eagerly refrained as an institution from dipping into the public till, it had cooperated with the Federal Educational Relief Organization and other agencies like the National Youth Administration to obtain available aid for students needing assistance to complete their education. The marked intervention of government into so many areas, traditionally reserved for the private sector, created an atmosphere in which the new breed was produced. Before this, organs of student government, particularly student councils, had been primarily concerned with the encouragement, development, and control of student organizations. While individual students and groups of students might petition for the redress of what they looked upon as a grievance, student bodies, even their extreme wings, had shown no desire or intent to take over the governance either of the nation or of the University. The change that was going on was implied when the Committee on Student Activities was renamed the Committee on Student Life.

In the preceding years when the University was struggling against great odds, the fraternities and sororities had played an essential role. When the Arts colleges, the Law School, and the Medical School were widely scattered in location, when a majority of the student body was employed and attended late-afternoon classes exclusively, it would have been natural for all sense of a student community, for all consciousness of a college spirit, to have disappeared completely. That it did not was due in large part to the fraternity system. Individual chapters brought together students from all departments, students who were full-time and students who were part-time. The Interfraternity and the Pan Hellenic Associations brought all of the chapters together on a University basis. Fraternity houses offered places of meeting when the University could not. The Greek letter societies kept social activities alive and they developed the leadership for student publications and athletics. Their interests were contained within the University and they kept its extracurricular life alive.

In the new age, the increasing dependence on government, as represented by the National Youth Administration, was felt by the new type of student, whose interest was no longer solely contained within the University. This new student looked to the government—what it was doing, and should be doing, for him. He was interested in transforming the University so that it would be in harmony with what he thought the new order of things would be.

This age was an age of ideologies. Students felt the urge to organize, line up ideologically: right, center, and left; and, by association, to show their solidarity with student bodies in general. They betrayed a not always latent desire to become a new estate in the educational power structure. The administration, realizing the tendencies of the time, was anxious to afford the student body opportunity and facilities for the freest possible expression and discussion of any views. Yet, in 1932, when a group petitioned for recognition as a unit of the National Student League, the Board of Trustees formally denied the petition. On the other hand, in January, 1935, a group of students began to plan, with the fullest official sanction, what became the George Washington Union. Describing itself as "the political voice of the student body of George Washington University," it was "a representative forum of 101 delegates elected annually" from the student body, serving as "a testing laboratory for social ideas and a mechanism for acquiring experience in politics, parliamentary procedure, and group leadership." Clearly its founders had the Oxford Union in mind. In its first election the Center got 55 seats, the Left 24, and the Right 22. When in the fall of 1935 the president of the National Student Federation, Thomas F. Neblett, asked the president of the University to inform him of his "attitude toward affiliation of your student governing board with the National Student Federation of America," Dr. Marvin's reply was very direct: "The George Washington University would not care to affiliate its student governing board at this time."[39]

What was the University's policy? By preventing affiliation with national organizations and favoring local ones, the administration sought to insure freedom of expression with freedom from coercion and involvement with larger pressure groups. The point of view was crystallized in the famous Rule 6. This rule, for decades the guide line in dealing with student organizations, read:

No student clubs or societies (except social fraternities, sororities, scholastic honor societies, religious or professional clubs or societies) organized as a branch or affiliate of a non-George Washington University organization will be recognized by the Student Life Committee.[40]

When a year later the George Washington Chapter of the American Student Union applied for recognition, the petition was denied by the Committee on Student Life on the basis of Rule 6, in spite of the protests of the Left party.[41]

The steady growth of fascism on the European continent, the threat of new war, and the increased tempo of military preparedness here, all conspired to arouse in youth a sense of concern of a very personal nature and to provoke demonstrations by groups within the colleges. Beginning noticeably in the middle 1930's, there was growing evidence of antiwar activity among high school and college students, particularly in the setting aside by the United Student Peace Committee of one day each year for an antiwar strike. What attitude should be taken by school authorities toward students who absented themselves for participation in such demonstrations? The president of the Teachers Union of the City of New York, in a letter to President Marvin and to other educators, obviously strongly opposed to any disciplinary action in such cases, asked if it was necessary to note information concerning participation in antiwar strikes on college application blanks.[42]

In a lengthy and thoughtful letter, the president, laying aside motives, addressed himself to the means employed:

I do not see how we can support students who, having signed up to abide by the laws of any university, see fit to take it into their hands, at the pronouncement of some outside body, to violate the integrity of the contract which they have signed as a member of the institution.[43]

Other inquiries received equally forthright answers.

When, a year and a half earlier, some students in the University had planned a peace meeting, and the Veterans of Foreign Wars, the Daughters of the American Revolution, and the Military Order of the World War demanded that the University call the meeting off, Dr. Marvin's answer was unequivocal: "No such action will be taken by the University." The University, he emphasized, was not giving official sanction to the views of the group. It was obeying its basic principle: to seek the truth.[44]

On November 8, 1935, a giant demonstration was planned by the student Strike Committee. The University declined to suspend classes for the demonstration. The *Evening Star* reported: "Plans for a gigantic demonstration at George Washington University failed to materialize."[45]

In 1936, Army Day, April 12, threatened to serve as the occasion for demonstrations both pro and con. The University in this case took the initiative by persuading all factions to join in a Peace Convocation on Monday, April 6. Three sessions were held: a general session at 11:10 A.M. and two afternoon sessions at 5:45 P.M., one in Stockton and the other in Corcoran Hall. All classes falling within the hours of the convocation were suspended. At each session two distinguished speakers were heard and a student panel of five carried on the discussion. All shades of opinion were represented in the list of speakers and in the student panels. The *Hatchet,* speaking editorially of the convocation, said: "Its success is sung by its proponents and admitted by its opponents. . . . Such was the success of the Convocation that all shades and grades of pacifists and militarists had their innings during the day's course."[46]

The following year, 1937, the George Washington University Strike Committee announced in the local press that 1,200 students would leave their classes at 11:00 A.M. and 6:00 P.M. on Wednesday, April 22, in a strike against war and fascism as part of a nation-wide protest.[47]

The national organizing group, the United Student Peace Committee, declared that the purpose of the strike was to dramatize the extent of student sentiment for peace and to signify to those who were resolved not to be drafted "a technique and preparation whereby to oppose mobilization."[48]

President Marvin, on the basis of Rule 6 and because of his fear of counterdemonstrations and resultant disorder, would not sanction the use of University buildings or grounds for the purpose of the meeting. A flood of unsigned and inflammatory printed and mimeographed material which had been circulated on the campus justified Dr. Marvin's position: "No demonstration or counter-demonstration on University property will be countenanced." Not all believed the president's position justified. An ominous-looking black-bordered sheet was distributed over the campus, headed: "DIED—Academic Freedom—Passed away, April 22, from a fatal blow struck below the belt by a reactionary administration. Never having enjoyed the best of health, the vicious onslaught proved too much for its delicate constitution."

While the liberal and left-of-center student groups that had sponsored demonstrations against war and fascism were somewhat silenced for a time, their resentment against the administration remained. They waited for a new occasion to make an even more vigorous attack. The occasion was offered by the Martha Gibbon case, when the same student groups —some of their members now spoke as alumni—with reinforcements, transformed their movement in support of Miss Gibbon to a broadside attack on President Marvin and the University establishment.

Miss Martha Gibbon was an Assistant Professor of English. She was a woman of deep convictions and liberal views. Highly articulate and dynamic in appeal, she was held in high regard by many students and by many of her colleagues. In her statement, circularized by the Student Committee on the Gibbon Case, she said that she was first apprehensive of her status when her promotion from instructor to assistant professor and appropriate salary adjustments were long delayed. When after the normal period for the assistant professorship, she was not promoted to an associate professorship with tenure, she renewed her efforts to get some clarification of her status. Finally, on the recommendation of a colleague, she submitted her resignation on March 9, 1940.

Her cause was immediately championed by the Student Committee; and under date of May 1, 1940, there appeared a pamphlet entitled *"A Preliminary Survey of the Administration of Dr. Cloyd Heck Marvin at The George Washington University.* Submitted by an Alumni Committee for the Investigation of Conditions at The George Washington University, this statement of facts is addressed to the students, alumni, faculty, and members of the Board of Trustees of The George Washington University, Vol. I, No. 1, 1940."

The committee noted that it was self-constituted and was in no way sponsored by the General Alumni Association. It began by listing several unfavorable comments on President Marvin's administration at the University of Arizona and then cited seventeen items, including thirteen cases —among them Miss Gibbon's—involving personnel in which the president's action was questioned. The matter then became one of notice in the press, in the form of rather full reports and "letters to the editor" pro and con. The student speaker in his valedictory at the Class Night Exercises on June 11 referred to the case: "Unhappy, too, is our Farewell to Martha Gibbon, who has resigned. Many of us in the class of 1940 feel an irreparable loss to the University in her resignation."[49] The name of no faculty member appeared in any of the profuse literature as a member of the sponsoring groups, although there was some faculty cooperation on the part of a few individuals.

In the flood of literature, there was one production not wholly without merit. A parody on the Gilbert and Sullivan classic, entitled *The Collegiate Mikado,* was written (anonymously) and distributed. The opening chorus gives a suggestion of the content:

> Here's a how-de-do
> This will never do
> Some professors *ought* to perish,
> But when the teachers whom you *cherish*
> Must be forced out too—
> Here's a how-de-do
> Here's a how-de-do!

Here's a pretty mess—
In three months or less
She must leave without a hearing—
Let the bitter tears we're tearing,
Witness our distress,
Here's a pretty mess,
Here's a pretty mess.

There's a state of things,
There's a state of things,
Meritorious promotion
Doesn't seem to fit his notion:—
Ph.D., he sings—
Here's a state of things,
Here's a state of things!

The president discussed the Gibbon case with the Board of Trustees, laying before them her letter of resignation, which was immediately accepted as voluntary. The Trustees next noted that a self-constituted group sponsoring her claim had made reference to the manner in which Dr. Marvin was elected in 1927. The president stated that when the office was tendered him he refused to accept unless a faculty committee reviewed his full record at the University of Arizona and, thus fully informed, announced that they were willing to accept his leadership. On the invitation of the Board of Trustees, he said, the President's Council elected a committee of three—Dean Borden, Dean Van Vleck, and Professor Croissant—the members of which, after a study of the record, declared that they had no objections to Dr. Marvin. After discussion the Board adopted a resolution expressing its complete confidence in his personal integrity, educational and administrative ability, and outstanding qualifications for his position.[50]

The characteristics of a new breed of students had now become quite fully manifest. To say what proportion of the whole student body belonged in this category is impossible. Undoubtedly it was a minority, but vocal beyond any other group, so vocal in fact that its voice came to be more and more considered by many as the typical student voice. These students, by the general color of their common convictions, could organize and, by their militancy, establish, as it were, a new form of student activity. There was still the major body of students, unorganized, and, by desire or inertia, going about the old activities in the old way. In fact, while the turn to this new militancy was occurring, the University was going through one of the most interesting phases of its athletic history. But while major athletics was to rise to its zenith and then fall, the militancy of the new breed did not disappear. The student body into which it found its way was just becoming conscious of politics, organized itself as a political party, struck out on the line of militancy against war and fascism, demanded its right to cooperate with national organizations and movements, injected itself into questions of faculty tenure, and attacked the president personally and so bitterly that the Trustees had to take cognizance of its charges and clear the president by a sweeping vote of confidence.

While the representatives of the new breed were trying their wings politically, the great mass of students went their way with the interests and enthusiasms that were traditional with the college undergraduate. During the first half of the Marvin administration renewed attention was given to intercollegiate athletics. Following World War I there was a revival of football when teams coached by Bryan Morse and William Quigley played full schedules with schools in the general area, but without conspicuous success. The difficulties they had to face were colossal: dearth of material, meagerness of support, and lack of facilities for training. To put teams into the field was itself an achievement. However, in spite of handicaps, football took fire in the five years 1924-1928. H. Watson (Maud) Crum was coach, with his famous "Iron Men," when the team was virtually his whole squad.

When President Marvin brought James E. Pixlee to the University, the picture changed. He was given what was, by comparison, massive support and well-organized publicity. From 1929 to 1937, his teams grew in caliber from the team in the first season which lost every game, to teams playing opponents of the character of Alabama, Auburn, Tennessee, Tulsa, West Virginia, Clemson, and others. In 1936, the record was: won 7, lost 1, tied 1. This was the period of Alphonse Emile (Tuffy) Leemans, B.S. 1937, perhaps the greatest name in the University's athletic history. After making a spectacular record at the University, he went on to win new laurels as a member of the New York Giants. Outstanding basketball teams were produced by William J. Reinhart, who began his long tenure as basketball coach with the team of 1935-1936, and continued until 1966. The record in basketball has been remarkable. For a period of twenty-four years (1929-1943, 1946-1956) the Colonials had no losing season. Such an impressive showing could not fail to inspire the typical college student. In George Washington it was the halcyon day of athletics, with tens of thousands at football games, elaborate between-the-halves entertainment, and expertly produced cheer leading. Professional teams had not yet become major competitors and television was not offering its rich programing of athletic events that was to come in a later day.

One area of nonathletic student activity experienced marked development during the Marvin administration. The Glee Club had been in continuous existence since its organization in 1920 by the late William Preston Haynes, A.B. 1921, M.D. 1924, with August King-Smith as director. In 1924, Robert Howe Harmon, M.D. 1929, was appointed director, and Grace Ruble (Mrs. R. H.) Harmon assistant director of the Men's and Women's Glee Clubs. Under the leadership of Dr. and Mrs. Harmon, the Glee Club became an outstanding musical organization, filling regular engagements in theaters in Washington and New York and singing as guest artists with the National Symphony Orchestra, then directed by Hans Kindler, Mus.D. (hon.) 1932, in annual concerts for nine years. Competing in the Intercollegiate Glee Club Contest in Carnegie Hall, New York, the Men's Club won first place in 1930, third place in 1931, and second place in 1935. In the postwar period, at the invitation of the Air Force, the Glee Clubs made fifteen military flights, most of them during the holiday season, to entertain military personnel at distant installations, many of them in the arctic region.

Cloyd Heck Marvin had been president of George Washington University for slightly more than fourteen years when the attack on Pearl Harbor occurred. In a way the outbreak of war ended the first period of his administration. It had been a time of marked and rapid change. The shape of things to come was clearly visible. The University in all its branches, administrative and educational, had been reorganized. The more restricted concept of a physical plant with its core in Square 102 had been discarded. Land acquisition and planned construction showed the intention to expand on all four sides of the original square. Substantial beginnings had been made for the establishment of a dormitory system. In some areas of extracurricular activity, the University had won national attention. Every branch of the University enjoyed full accreditation, and Phi Beta Kappa and other major honor societies had chapters in it.

The outbreak of World War II imposed a new series of exacting demands on the University. Contribution to the national defense became a major part of its mission. The student body underwent vast changes in composition and in interest. The recruiting of personnel to provide for increased demands and to replace staff members called to military service became increasingly difficult. Regular members of the staff who remained had to forget about normal loads and assume whatever additional burdens were necessary to carry on the work. President Marvin himself added to his university duties civilian assignments of great importance, particularly in connection with the scientific activities of the War Department. Because of the priority of the national interest and the shaping of the University so as to serve that interest, normal development was in abeyance during the war years. After the cessation of hostilities, another fourteen years was left in the Marvin administration. They were years particularly notable for physical growth.

On Monday, December 8, 1941, the day following the attack on Pearl Harbor, the faculty met in solemn conclave, under President Marvin's chairmanship, to hear one of its members give expression to the solemnity of the hour and to the sense of deep obligation resting on the University community for national service. The ranks of the faculty were rather quickly depleted as younger members entered the armed forces and specialists in fields related to the war effort took leave of absence for government service.

The Trustees authorized the use of the University-owned building at 2027 H Street as West End Civil Defense Headquarters and ordered the expenditure of as much as was necessary to protect the University property and its occupants. To enable students to compress as much as possible the time required for degrees, the work of the University was temporarily placed on a trimester basis. The faculties were authorized to encourage and develop accelerated programs wherever feasible educationally. An alumni defense council, called the Victory Council, was approved, with the development and sustaining of morale among the alumni throughout the country as its purpose. Under the resourceful and energetic chairmanship of Robert Elliott Freer, A.B. 1931, an alumni Trustee, the Council produced and widely distributed a publication, *Confidential from Washington*, during the entire period of the war.

A significant type of war effort (which was to continue after the war) was initiated when the Board authorized undertaking special research on behalf of the National Defense Council and the Department of the Navy. The University offered a site to the government as part of a plan for increasing hospital facilities in the District of Columbia should the government desire to erect temporary quarters which the University would maintain. The University came back to this idea in a more substantial form and with fruitful results a few years later.

Because the temporary removal of the Patent Office to Richmond interfered with the plans of many of its employees who were studying law at George Washington, a cooperative plan was put into effect for patent law being taught at the University of Richmond's T. C. Williams School of Law by regular members of the George Washington faculty.

These adjustments and arrangements, all authorized at the Trustees' meeting of February 18, 1942, suggest the variety and sweep of the University's wartime measures.[51]

But the great adjustments were those that had to be made in the lives of the students who went into the armed forces. As the war approached a close, President Marvin wrote that these numbered almost 7,000. Wartime conditions made difficult the continuance of extracurricular activities.[52] The question of participation in intercollegiate athletics was left in the hands of the Committee on Extra-Curricular Activities with the instruction that the committee use its own good judgment to the end of maintaining membership in the Southern Conference.[53]

While at the low point in the war period the student enrollment was down almost 20 per cent, what would have been a marked drop in income from tuition was made up by income from the University's charges for carrying out an ever-increasing number of contracts for war-related research. The National Defense Research Committee, through the Office of Scientific Research, asked the University to undertake the operation of a laboratory in Virginia and one in West Virginia. The Quartermaster General's Department requested the organization of a project to gather information to help in procurement problems. And so it went through scores of projects, some small, some large, some of brief duration, some lengthy.[54]

Writing just as the war closed, President Marvin pointed out that in the defense effort, "It was determined that we could carry on best through the maintenance and increase of our technical services. . . . So the University under contract did extensive work on items for ordnance, both in the development of new weapons and in the improvement of old ones." To do this required the recruiting of hundreds of skilled scientists, the development of extensive laboratories, and the accounting for millions of dollars in the execution of the work.[55]

A letter to President Marvin from Dr. Vannevar Bush, Director of the Office of Scientific Research and Development, referred to the University's contribution to the war effort:

> This letter gives me the pleasure of expressing to you my personal and official appreciation and commendation to the aid the George Washington University has given to the war effort through the work it has performed under contract with this Office. The University was called upon to do work on a far greater scale than ever contemplated as a peacetime activity of an educational institution. The work on rockets and related devices was in itself a task of major magnitude. It required building a large organization not only of scientists drawn from the staff of the University, but also of engineers and executives drawn from the fields of industry. On a smaller scale, but nonetheless important, was the work done by the special group concerned with the problems of tropical deterioration of military equipment and material. The University met the challenge with full credit to itself.[56]

In addition to the numerous research projects carried out with so much success, an equal contribution to the national effort was made in the training of students in areas of special importance. In this every branch of the University was actively involved. A single example will show the magnitude of the service performed. When the contract with the United States Office of Education for Engineering, Science, and Management War Training Courses was terminated at the end of the war, more than 12,750 students had been trained in 387 courses under this one contract alone.[57]

The institution's financial experience in the war years contrasts pleasantly with the economic uncertainties so characteristic of its early history. In the war years President Marvin had tried to maintain the University on the funds that came to it through regular channels, keeping the returns from government contracts in a reserve fund. The institution was out of debt except for some small amounts due on recently purchased property which was self-liquidating, and the mortgage for about a third of a million dollars placed on the Medical property at the time of the Attorney General's investigation in 1910 to insure restoration of all endowment funds which had been spent for operating expenses. This mortgage on the Medical property was paid off in 1944. With a fund that the University had accumulated and the proceeds of a loan to make up the remainder, the University paid to its endowment the sum of $323,430.33 and was thus able to certify to the Attorney General that there had been a complete restoration of the endowment.[58]

A significant change in the financial position of the University had taken place. Beginning with Admiral Stockton, every one of the presidents had sought consistently to establish faith in the financial soundness of the institution. Each year a budget was established within the limits of expected income and adhered to strictly. But the days when a university could be operated largely on a cash basis had ended. In carrying out expensive research projects during the war years and in making veterans' payments in the postwar years, large sums had to be advanced against later reimbursement by the government. Credit could thus be extended on a substantial scale if the University itself had a substantial credit which would enable it to obtain the funds. The sound financial record of the University over a period of thirty years, its extensive holdings of property, and confidence in the men directing its financial policy created a wider basis for an expanding credit. President Marvin and the University's principal financial officer, Henry W. Herzog, had demonstrated great ability. Robert V. Fleming (1890-1967) was a tower of strength. A charter Trustee from 1930 to 1966 and an Honorary Trustee from 1966 to the time of his death, he served as Chairman of the Board of Trustees for twenty-two years, the longest consecutive period of service in that office in the history of the institution. His great personal prestige and that of the influential financial institution which he headed, coupled with a total dedication to the University and its advancement, made him an outstanding figure in the history of George Washington University.

During the war period attention had been repeatedly drawn to the inadequacy of hospital facilities in the District of Columbia. A report on the hospital situation in the area was drawn up and sent to the Federal Works Administration. The need was obvious and it was apparent that a start should be made with the teaching hospitals. Howard University had a special relation to the government and could normally ask for aid for Freedmen's Hospital. George Washington and Georgetown had no such relationship and seemed to merit special attention.[59]

Inasmuch as a new hospital when built would involve problems of location in relation to a general plan of University development, such a plan was drawn up, approved February 10, 1944, presented to the Park and Planning Commission, and endorsed by them on April 20. It was decided to locate the projected hospital in Square 54, between Twenty-second and Twenty-third Streets, Eye Street and Pennsylvania Avenue. A hospital that provided five to six hundred beds was looked upon as the ideal size.

After preliminary consultation a formal application for federal assistance was made to the Federal Works Agency on May 2. The existing Medical School and Hospital property on H Street was to be deeded to the government in return for a 500-bed hospital in Square 54. As part of the planning, the possibility was discussed of removing the encumbrance on the H Street property by an appeal to the Attorney General. This possibility materialized and, as described above, the encumbrance was removed.

The University's application for federal assistance was approved by the Federal Works Agency and the President of the United States on September 8. Once made, the application received approval in record time. A lease agreement was drawn between the University and the agency effective for five years from the time the hospital was completed. This lease was modified five years later so that the Medical property on H Street, which was to be turned over to the government in return for the new hospital, could be retained by the University by the payment of $548,167.50, the estimated value of the property on H Street, credit being given toward this amount for the payments made previously under the lease agreement. In this way the University was able to retain ownership of the Medical and Hospital property and also to receive a quitclaim for Square 54 and all of its improvements.[60]

The University now had a magnificent hospital building on Washington Circle, thanks to the government's assistance, but the large sum needed for its equipment had to be raised from private sources. To undertake this important assignment and to deal with the manifold problems arising from the development of a great University plant within the capital city, Major General U. S. Grant, U.S.A., recently retired from active service, was chosen and was elected Vice President of the University. The choice was ideal. As a Trustee, General Grant knew the problems of the University; and as one long involved in public works and the planning of the city, he was peculiarly fitted for the post.[61]

To establish the University's eligibility for further assistance, the Trustees adopted a resolution citing the shortage of educational facilities for training under the Servicemen's Readjustment Act, thus permitting application to the government to provide facilities such as were needed to assure carrying out the government's purpose.[62]

While the hospital was being constructed, work was going on at the corner of Twenty-first and H Streets, which had finally been selected as the site for Lisner Auditorium. This building was made possible by the bequest of the late Abram Lisner, for many years a Trustee and a generous donor to the University, supplemented by other funds, particularly those from the George Washington Memorial Association and Mrs. Dimock's bequest. When it opened in the fall of 1946, Lisner Auditorium was immediately recognized as a distinct asset to the cultural life of the city and the University. The house was opened by a two-week engagement of *Joan of Lorraine*, with Ingrid Bergman in the leading role, and by a class in European Civilization which filled the auditorium three times a week—one of the evidences of the "veterans' bulge." Opera, symphony, ballet, drama, concerts by world-famous artists, lectures—all these have found dignified and efficient setting in Lisner Auditorium. It has been the scene of all large student and faculty meetings, of University convocations, and of student dramatic and musical productions. A battery of sound-proof rooms in Lisner houses much of the work of the Department of Speech, and the Dimock Gallery just off the large lower lounge has been devoted to the University's art exhibits.[63]

Five years after the completion of Lisner Auditorium, the next major structure was built. James Monroe Hall, on G Street, west of the Hall of Government, is a four-story classroom and office building.

There remained just one piece of major construction during the Marvin administration, though there was constant activity in assembling real estate, purchasing and remodeling large apartment houses as dormitories, building smaller structures, and adapting houses for office use. Although originally a combination of the Columbia Hotel and the Bender Building, the Student Union involved so much readaptation and new construction as to be practically a new building.

The last major building, though, was Tompkins Hall of Engineering, the gift of Mr. and Mrs. Charles H. Tompkins. Mr. Tompkins was for many years a Trustee of the University. Tompkins Hall houses the School of Engineering. An interesting feature of this building is "A Vault for the Future," to be opened in the year 2056. This underground vault, just below the main entrance, contains documents illustrative of the story of engineering in 1956, "and engineering hopes for the tomorrows as written in the records" of the University, the Board of Commissioners of the District, the National Academy of Sciences, the United States Atomic Energy Commission, the three branches of the armed forces, the National Advisory Committee for Aeronautics, local scientific groups, and Faulkner, Kingsbury, and Stenhouse, the architects, and the Charles

H. Tompkins Company, builders of Tompkins Hall of Engineering. On June 20, 1956, the vault was dedicated to Charles H. Tompkins, in recognition of his contributions as an engineer to the University, the city, and the nation.[64]

The rapid development of the University's physical plant and the increased tempo of construction of government buildings in the West End had for some time made evident the need for an overall plan for the University and the definite location of its area, in terms of specific metes and bounds, in relation to the total development of the capital city. Both President Marvin and Vice President Grant had long had these matters under consideration; furthermore, they had the assistance of outstanding consultants in the formulation of their plans.

Late in 1948 General Grant was able to lay before the Board a comprehensive report concerning the development of the campus. This plan, made with the assistance of Frederick Law Olmsted, had received favorable consideration by the National Park and Planning Commission. The Congress had recently created the Redevelopment Land Agency which had aided colleges in various parts of the country in their development of sites.

In 1955 the question of the definite location of the campus came up in a basic way in connection with the George Washington University Urban Renewal Project. In the summer of that year, Henry W. Herzog, the Treasurer of the University, had entered into conversations with the District of Columbia Land Development Agency to see whether that agency and the University could cooperate in the furtherance of the University's plan. That agency and the National Capital Planning Commission approved a George Washington University Renewal Project for the area bounded by Nineteenth Street, Twenty-third Street, Pennsylvania Avenue, E Street, and Virginia and New York Avenues. This was later changed to F, Nineteenth and Twenty-fourth Streets and Pennsylvania Avenue. It was next necessary to overcome some opposition in order to get the approval of the Commissioners of the District of Columbia. The setup, with the approval of the commission, would involve, on the part of the agency, financing, advice, general planning, and cost-estimating operations and also paying the cost of condemnation, assembly, and site development. On its side the University would pay for the preparation of the campus plan and would purchase the properties from the agency. Late in 1956 the treasurer was authorized to make preliminary application, under the College Housing Program of the

Housing and Home Finance Corporation, for $1,250,000 for the acquisition and remodeling of existing apartment houses to serve as dormitories, one for men and one for women, this sum to be amortized over a 40-year period at 2⅞ per cent interest.

New bases were thus being found for making possible the rapid development of the University's plant. A far different future opened up than would ever have been possible with the slow and piecemeal purchases of land and the hesitant ventures on new construction which had been the rule in the old days when modest operating surpluses had to finance expansion.[65]

During the same period, the number and size of gifts from foundations, corporations, and individuals increased notably, and permitted the University to accompany physical expansion with educational advance. By increases across the board, an effort was made to revise the levels of compensation for the staff. An important beginning to what was to become a comprehensive system of fringe benefits was made when, by signing a contract with the Teachers Insurance and Annuity Association, members of the faculty were assured a substantial income on retirement. The University added to the 5 per cent paid by the faculty members a contribution first of 5 per cent, then 8 per cent, and finally 10 per cent.[66]

An important new source of income to the University was opened up in 1953 when the president of the General Alumni Association, Elmer Louis Kayser, initiated the plan of annual alumni-giving which produced a constantly increasing fund yearly for general and specific purposes of the institution.[67]

At the termination of hostilities, the student body increased rapidly in size. At the beginning of the year 1947-1948, President Marvin announced that twice as many students were enrolled as in 1945. Of this student body of 12,000, 7,000 were veterans.[68] The return of the students meant the resumption of student activities after the enforced slowdown of the war period. There were more students living at the University than ever before. To supplement the permanent dormitory facilities, the University made available 200 housing units for single students and 60 units for married men. The University agreed to maintain these facilities for five years, the government contracting to pay the institution $165,000 for their installation.

The president was prepared to resume the athletic program without delay. C. M. Farrington, who had served as Director of Athletics before leaving for war service, was made Director of Activities for Men, beginning February 1, 1946. The resumption of intercollegiate competition was authorized but restricted to the Southern Conference. Because of a late start and limited facilities, difficulty was experienced in organizing a football team for 1946. President Marvin reported guardedly to the Trustees that "special consideration might have to be given to the scholastic status of a few of the prospective candidates for the football team." With all its difficulties, the 1946 team, coached by Neil Stahley, had a fair season of 4 games won and 3 lost. Arthur Zahn produced a great basketball team in 1947 that won 21 games and lost 7. Athletics had returned, not only in intercollegiate competition, but also in an expanded intramural program.[69]

The intramural program was initiated by directors elected each year by the Student Council and working under the sponsorship of the physical education and athletics department. By 1941, the program had expanded so rapidly that it was placed under the immediate direction of a member of the physical education department, with Professor Joseph H. Krupa as the first faculty director. With time out for the war years, Professor Krupa served until 1953 when he was succeeded by Professor V. J. DeAngelis, who had been the student council director of the program in 1938-1939, and then, as faculty director, developed the program from 1953 to 1966.

An equally comprehensive system of intramural sports for women was developed by Miss Ruth Atwell, who came to the University in 1929 and served for thirty-one years in the Department of Physical Education for Women. Under her guidance, and working through the Women's Athletic Association and its Intramural Board, emphasis was shifted "from the program of varsity competition to the broader and more inclusive program of inter-class and intramural competition." So that every undergraduate woman could meet her need for some physical activity as well as some recreational hobbies, a varied program was evolved, including the organization of a number of recreational sports clubs.

Another area of student life received attention. When Alexander Graham Bell Hall, then unceremoniously called Building C, was opened, the University established the Student Club in the basement of that building under a student manager, V. J. DeAngelis, who continued in that position after graduation from 1936 to 1942. The quarters were gradually expanded until the Student Club took in the entire basement level, serving drinks, hot and cold, sandwiches, hamburgers, and hot dogs, and carrying student supplies and a few books. As the only available place of the sort, it was a scene of teeming activity from morning to night during the war years. The development of the dormitory system required adequate provision for the central feeding of students and the provision of large areas for study and for recreation. This need was met by the purchase of the Columbia Hotel and the adjoining Bender Building which were connected and enlarged and completely remodeled to create the Student Union; it was opened in 1949. This structure provided complete facilities for food service, for study and recreation, and for offices for student activities. Immediately back of it on Mr. Joe Lane (named for Joseph Toomey, who had superintended construction of all the buildings of the Marvin period and had become a highly beloved campus figure) was the Student Store, with textbooks, supplies, and items of student demand.[70]

The war and postwar years witnessed many changes in the educational structure of the University. In 1942, the Extension Division was reorganized to bring under unified control the increasing number of off-campus courses that were constantly being organized to extend the University's educational facilities to special groups, in many cases located outside the city. In 1950, under the direction of Dean Mitchell Dreese, the Extension Division was given a larger mission and its name was changed to the College of General Studies. This new unit expanded on a very wide base. In theory it was absolutely distinct from the regular schools and colleges and yet its courses were all subject to approval as to instructor and content by the appropriate departments in the various schools and colleges. It offered credit and noncredit courses, had its own schedule of fees, and at first nominated, through the president, candidates to the Board of Trustees to receive its degrees. While its students could, under some circumstances, take on-campus courses, its work was given in special centers, many outside the city, and many of them taught by University-approved instructors who were not members of the regular faculty. It represented an effort to extend the educational outreach of the University. Its early growth was phenomenal.[71] Since 1968, all degrees received by students registered in the College of General Studies have been conferred on recommendation of a regular degree-granting college upon fulfillment of requirements prescribed by that college.

In the fall of 1949, planning began on the formation of a Patent Law Foundation. In the next year the Trustees approved a Declaration of Trust establishing a Patent Research and Educational Foundation in the

University, thus extending a field of legal activity in which the Law School had long played a distinguished role. The name of the foundation was changed in 1952 to the Patent, Trademark, and Copyright Foundation.[72]

The decision of the Carnegie Endowment for International Peace to move the activities of its Washington headquarters to New York City made available the very comprehensive library on international law and related subjects which it had maintained in Washington. This library was widely used not only by students but also by representatives of the State Department and other governmental agencies. The University purchased this library, which became a part of the institution's collection.[73]

In the summer of 1954, arrangements were made for a merger with National University. Over the years since 1869 this institution had offered professional and collegiate instruction in many fields, but particularly in law, where it had produced many distinguished members of the local bench and bar. At this time its efforts were centered entirely on legal education. The merger was agreed upon and effected under conditions that protected the interests of both institutions and provided that law students then at National could continue work for the degree sought.[74]

Early in 1951, the president reported to the Board that, noting the trends in enrollment, the University had, some months before, begun to undertake research for the government and had made available the necessary room in the University buildings.[75] The wisdom of this policy was soon apparent. In the difficult year 1951-1952, the University had an excess of more than $200,000 over expenses. Overhead on the research contracts, student fees, and endowment income were supporting the University's academic budget.[76]

The Office of the Coordinator of Scientific Activities had been established at the beginning of the fiscal year 1946-1947, just as the tidal wave of veteran students was approaching its height. Of the many projects of government-sponsored research, two of the older and major ones illustrate the magnitude and importance of the work carried on. The oldest of the projects, not an integral part of the departments of the University, was the Logistics Research Project, operated under a contract with the Department of the Navy. Its purpose was "to study problems of logistics planning and control in order to develop methodology permitting effective solutions." Its large-scale data-processing facility was based upon IBM 7080 and 360 computers.

The Human Resources Research Office (HumRRO) was originally established in 1951 to carry out an integrated program of human resources research for the Department of the Army. This project began doing work in training, motivation, morale, and leadership for the Army. At a later date its research was made available to other departments of the federal government, to state and local governments, and to organizations supporting training and educational research. Divisions of the office were located in Alexandria, Virginia; Fort Bliss, Texas; and Fort Rucker, Alabama. General James M. Gavin called HumRRO "the most outstandingly competent military training research institution in existence today." HumRRO was separated from the University in 1969.[77]

In 1952, Dr. Marvin completed a quarter of a century of service as president of the University. In length, his administration had already exceeded that of President Welling by two years. No one else had ever served so long. In responding to the congratulations of the Trustees on his achievements, he said, "An early reorganization of the Board, of administrative practice, of the fiscal structure, and of our academic procedure was the means by which these competent results were achieved." He pointed out, with justifiable pride, that salaries had been increased each year and that there had been no decrease or drops during the Depression. A comprehensive retirement plan had been adopted and all of the staff had been brought into the Social Security Program. Eighteen major buildings had been added and land holdings had increased 426 per cent in area, from 3.8 acres to 19.8 acres. A new type of functional architecture had been developed. There had never been an operating deficit, and $5.5 million had been saved from receipts. With reference to things tangible and financial, it was a brilliant record.[78]

At the close of the same year, Dr. Marvin added another item of accomplishment. At the end of the fiscal year 1926-1927, when his administration began, he pointed out that the University had accumulated $804,160 in endowments over 106 years. At the end of the year 1950-1951, the University's endowment had increased to $3,054,331.[79]

At various times the question of the admission of Negroes to the University had arisen. There was no regulation setting forth color or race as a criterion for admission. Negroes had been admitted to the Law School for a time after the War of 1861-1865, but the separate education of the races had become an established but unwritten practice. On the surface this seemed logical in a city where there were two parallel public school systems. The proximity of Howard University, with the education of Negro youth as a special but not exclusive mission and with substantial federal support, seemed to justify a dual college situation, analogous to the one existing in the public schools. The availability of certain types of graduate education at George Washington which were not provided at Howard seemed to justify the admission of Negroes who sought this graduate training. Admission of Negroes to all branches of the University and as residents in the dormitories soon followed in a transition that was entirely free of all friction.[80]

President Marvin was not as interested in high ceremonial as some of his predecessors had been. His natural preference was for the more informal and personal occasion. Yet, in spite of his democratic leanings, there were several notable convocations during his administration. Honorary degrees were conferred on many foreign heads of state: the kings of Morocco and of Siam, the presidents of Ecuador, Uruguay, Mexico, and Korea—the last, Syngman Rhee, was a graduate of the University. In a precedent-breaking ceremony both President and Mrs. Calvin Coolidge received the honorary doctorate on the same occasion. President Truman received the honorary doctorate and his daughter her A.B. at the same convocation. Among statesmen, Ramsay MacDonald, the British Prime Minister, and Cordell Hull, the Secretary of State, were honored. The granting of charters by Sigma Xi and Phi Beta Kappa, and the George Washington Bicentennial, were each the occasion for a convocation. When the honorary doctorate in music was conferred upon Hans Kindler, in lieu of a convocation address the National Symphony Orchestra played Haydn's Symphony in D Major (No. 104). Several convocations presented artists for programs of music, instead of convocation orators for speeches. Among these convocation artists were Gladys Swarthout, mezzo-soprano; John Charles Thomas, baritone; Efrem Zimbalist, violinist; Rose Bampton, soprano; and Bidu Sayao, soprano. A few weeks after his retirement, President Marvin received the degree of Doctor honoris causa of The George Washington University at the Winter Convocation of 1959.

As of May 15, 1952, President Marvin made effective a final piece of reorganization. His centralization of administration had been amazingly complete and, thanks to it, he had been able practically to remake the University with the loyal support of his Board of Trustees. But as his long administration progressed, the office of president had taken on a new aspect. The problems of war and depression, the new type of institutional financing, the growth of the University itself, greater activity in fund raising, the complexities of rapid land acquisition, and the new need for constant contact with government agencies and foundations— all of these together made an impossible load for one man, gifted and vigorous though he was, to carry. It is true that he was aided by a highly loyal, efficient, and intelligent administrative secretary of the University. Without Miss Myrna Sedgwick's firm grasp of details, his efforts would have been in vain. Something had to be left undone. The president's relation to the schools and colleges was tending to become purely fiscal. Committees like the one on educational policy rarely met. The opening faculty meetings became purely formal. The deans administered their units largely according to their own lights, with the budget as their guide. Centralization had broken down through the utter impossibility for one man to carry on his shoulders the whole burden of central administration. The president seemed to realize this when he proposed the creation of a new administrative level immediately under the president. O. S. Colclough, Dean of the Law School, was appointed Dean of Faculties and charged with the conduct and planning of academic units, the library, and other activities assigned to him. He was to serve as acting president in the absence of the president. Henry W. Herzog, the comptroller, was made comptroller and treasurer, his duties to include those normally carried by the business manager.[81]

In the fall of 1954, after a prolonged and systematic self-appraisal set forth in great detail in a series of volumes, the University was inspected by the Commission on Institutions of Higher Education of the Middle States Association of Colleges and Secondary Schools. As a result of its findings, this accrediting body extended full approval to the University. In the preliminary report of the Commission made in 1955, there is an interesting reference to the position of the president, courteous and laudatory but perceptive:

President Marvin was elected as the 12th President in 1927, at a time when there seemed to be great need of rather thorough reorganization, and his vigorous leadership during more than a quarter of a century is manifest in many points indeed. While there is ample evidence that the President himself desires and has inaugurated and strengthened what might well be termed democracy in administration through the participation of all in the making and carrying out of plans involving faculty appointments, curriculum studies, intra-university relationships, and similar significant areas of administration, it is still clearly evident that the President is the nerve center of the University; and that he looms so large in the pattern and practice of administration that he casts a long shadow indeed. The Committee would not wish the inference to be drawn that there is any element other than strength in such a relationship as exists; but it is clear that upon the Board of Trustees—at such time as it becomes necessary to find a worthy successor—there will rest a very significant and none too easily discharged responsibility. That the members of the various faculties at the present time have confidence in, and give loyal support to, the leadership of the President is unmistakable.[82]

President Marvin had been discussing his retirement for some time. In fact, in May, 1957, on the occasion of his reelection, the Trustees had fixed his retirement pay. In the spring of the following year, he expressed his conviction that the time had come for a change in leadership and suggested that the Board seek his successor. Toward the close of the year, he asked that his resignation be accepted at the end of the first semester, January 27, 1959. Acceding to his wish, the Board accepted his resignation and appointed Dean Colclough acting president *ad interim*. The longest administration in the University's history had come to an end.

Dr. Marvin died on April 28, 1969, and was buried in the University lot at Oak Hill Cemetery in Georgetown.

CLOYD HECK MARVIN will always have a large place in the history of George Washington University, but not solely on account of his lengthy tenure of office. He had a longer time to build than any of his predecessors, but by the same token he could have had a longer time to make mistakes. The University really knew three Marvins: a young man, a middle-aged man, and an older man.

He came to the University directly from a challenging experience at the University of Arizona, where he had had to deal with a state legislature that was not always friendly. He was young in years, but no novice in university administration. He knew what to do to achieve the results he sought, and he went after them. Nothing less than a complete reformation of the University, he felt, was necessary; and to accomplish that with relative ease, he centralized the administration so that he possessed power greater than that enjoyed by any previous president. He was the sole channel of approach, for all practical purposes, to the Board of Trustees; and in accordance with the bylaws he was Chairman of the Executive Committee of the Board. He had full cooperation from a working Board of Trustees. Men like Robert V. Fleming, the chairman of the Board; C. C. Glover, Jr., and Henry Parsons Erwin of the Finance Committee; Alfred Henry Lawson of the Building and Lands Committee; Harry C. Davis, the secretary of the Board, and others took vast segments of their time and ability away from other commitments to give constant and detailed attention to University business.

The youthful Marvin went about the task of reorganization with relish, vigor, and high determination and never hesitated until he had the new relationships of the University formulated and codified. In matters financial in those years he was exceedingly frugal, husbanding the modest surplus from operating expenses each year, holding to conservative faculty salaries, and buying land as rapidly as the meager surpluses would permit. As greater prosperity developed, he gave attention to faculty salaries and benefits. He then spent more because he had more to spend, but even to the end the old frugality had a way of reappearing. When after prolonged negotiation the price of the highly desirable property to the west owned by the Washington Gas Light Company was brought down to a realistic figure, the president resolutely refused to recommend purchase, because he thought the carrying charges would be too heavy. When federal funds first became available to colleges for plant expansion, he still held to a ruggedly individualistic policy, in spite of its retarding the improvement of facilities. Dr. Marvin showed great wisdom in his insistence on the growth of a full-time teaching staff and the purging of the program of course offerings by eliminating duplication and irrelevant or inadequately staffed courses. He was resourceful in finding new and helpful friends for the University, and in his early building program he evolved a type of construction agreeable to the limited means of the institution and the frugal ideas of its head. He rode though a depression without being diverted from his course or penalizing his staff by salary cuts. The achievements of the young Marvin were truly amazing.

The middle-aged Marvin had to cope with a world war and its aftermath. Already burdened with the mountain of detail imposed upon him by the high centralization of the administration, he had now to assume added problems in providing for war and defense needs and then for the education of the vast group of returned veterans. To it all he added large personal responsibilities as a citizen in the war and postwar efforts. Land acquisition quickened and there was new activity in planning buildings. Active partnership with the government had now become natural in research and the financing of plant expansion. As a period of great growth got under way and as student registration moved to a new and higher plateau, the president's attention was being drawn away more and more from the problems of instruction by the pressure of more tangible things.

The older Marvin had become a builder, a planner, a dreamer. He had passed from buildings of used bricks to buildings with white stone facing. With an Augustan sweep he was projecting a great University City in the heart of official Washington, a very tangible monument to the educational aspirations of the man for whom the University was named. The deans with their faculties were now running the schools and colleges as autonomous units. The student body was growing in numbers and in curiosity. The president prepared the budget and dreamed the dreams of a monumental university whose foundations he had laid.

What had he done in almost a third of a century? He had broken loose from the limited concept of a university occupying a restricted area and had laid out the metes and bounds of a great and expanded university. He had pointed out and demonstrated the way by which the development could be financed. He had laid a basis for the maintenance of a staff that could worthily people such an institution. There was much that was tangible to show; but that subtler thing, the integration of all levels of the University into a functioning democratic academic community, had as yet been barely explored.

CHAPTER FIFTEEN

Since 1959

Six years elapsed between the retirement of the twelfth president and the inauguration of the fourteenth. An acting president was in charge from 1959 to 1961 and again from 1964 to 1965. In the intervening years Thomas Henry Carroll served a brief term ended sadly by his death. Upon the shoulders of the chairman of the Board of Trustees, Newell Windom Ellison, fell the burden of selecting, with the advice of Trustees' and faculty committees, two heads of the University within a half dozen years.

Newell Windom Ellison, A.B. 1917, LL.B. 1921, LL.D. (hon.) 1957, had succeeded Robert V. Fleming as Chairman of the Board of Trustees. A distinguished member of the District bar, he had previously served for many years as a Trustee and as Secretary of the Board. As compared with that of his immediate predecessor, his own term of office was comparatively brief but unusually demanding.

The acting president before and after President Carroll's term was Oswald Symister Colclough, a graduate of the Naval Academy and of the Law School in the class of 1935. A former Judge Advocate General of the Navy, he retired with the rank of Vice-Admiral, U.S.N., and shortly after retirement joined the faculty of the Law School as dean and professor of law; he then became dean of faculties and, on the retirement of President Marvin, acting president.

In large degree, Admiral Colclough's efforts were directed to bringing to completion matters which had been initiated during the Marvin administration. In these efforts he was highly successful. The University had long felt the need to have the approval of the Commissioners of the District of Columbia of its plan for the expansion of the campus. Such approval was a necessary factor in securing the full cooperation of the federal government in granting funds. On July 19, 1959, after a long period of negotiation, Robert E. McLaughlin, Chairman of the Board of Commissioners, wrote to the University on behalf of the Board to "record the desire to be of whatever assistance we can in accomplishing this purpose [expansion of campus] consistent with our responsibilities to the community and our authority under law."[1]

A comprehensive plan for the organization and development of a Medical Center which had been a matter of lengthy and systematic research and consultation by a joint committee was presented and adopted.[2] Another important report was the University Faculty Organization Plan, adopted by the University faculty after long debate in May, 1960.[3]

This faculty organization report is often called the Tupper Report, after Professor Fred S. Tupper, who was chairman of the Academic Advisory Committee of Eighteen. Unlike the setup providing for a President's Council in the ordinances adopted in the 1910 reorganization and the provisions of the Fey Committee Report, carefully formulated but never presented for adoption by President Marvin, the plan provided for the establishment of two bodies: (1) the University Faculty Assembly, consisting of academic personnel in full-time service and certain administrative personnel; and (2) the University Senate, "a representative body acting for the University Faculty as a whole in legislative and advisory capacities." This area of competence was limited "to matters which are of concern to more than one college, school, or division, or to the University Faculty," as was the case with the earlier President's Council. This earlier council had consisted of administrative officers, deans, and elected members, each with the right to vote. In the new University Senate administrative officers and deans were members ex officiis, but they did not have the right to vote. The Tupper Plan, hence, was distinctly faculty-oriented.[4] Upon adoption by the Board, the plan was put into operation during the year 1960-1961.

On the basis of the findings of a select committee headed by Eugene M. Zuckert, later Secretary of the Air Force, a report of the faculty of the School of Government was adopted, changing the name of the school to the School of Government, Business, and International Affairs. Two sets of programs were offered, each under the supervision of an associate dean: programs in public and international affairs, and programs in business and public administration, with appropriate bachelor's and master's degrees. The changes reflected the lines of development taken by the School of Government in the first thirty years of its existence.

A final item of codification was the Articles of Association and the bylaws of the General Alumni Association, approved by the Board and put into effect immediately. By this action, any matriculated student who had left the University in good standing and any member of the staff or Board of Trustees was made eligible for membership in the Alumni Association.[5]

Some other changes were made in the schools and colleges. Although the plan had been authorized in 1951, Acting President Colclough was able to announce that the National Law Center had been established and Dr. Charles B. Nutting appointed Dean of the Center and Professor of Law. The Center included the Law School, the Graduate School of Public Law, and related educational, research, and publication activities.[6] Dean Nutting was succeeded in 1961 by Dean Robert Kramer as head of the National Law Center. The degree of Juris Doctor was discontinued as a first degree in law,[7] but its use was resumed a few years later.

The Junior College was discontinued, its work being assigned to Columbian College and the Associate in Arts degree made optional.[8] Calvin Darlington Linton continued as dean of Columbian College, but George Martin Koehl, who had been dean of the Junior College, became associate dean of Columbian College in charge of students in the lower division.

Particularly distressing was the case of a young scholar who was appointed an associate professor for a contractual period of two years, beginning September 1, 1959. Information was received that he was subpoenaed by the Committee on Un-American Activities of the House of Representatives and that at a hearing he pleaded the Fifth Amendment to all questions as to association with Communist activities. His department reconsidered and then withdrew its recommendation as to the young teacher's qualifications and suitability to join the faculty. He was then relieved of all duties. A lengthy period of hearings and representations in his behalf then ensued. The case was ended by the payment to the professor of the total salary he would have received during the whole contractual period of two years.[9]

Physical expansion proceeded at a steady pace. With the assistance of the College Housing Loan Program additional large apartment buildings were acquired and remodeled to become dormitories.[10] Aided by the Meyer Foundation, an official home for the president was purchased at 2330 Tracy Place."[11] Other generous gifts from the Meyer Foundation were granted for program improvements and expansion.[12] Of the many benevolences of the Meyer family before and during this period, the largest was one of $1,000,000 given by Mrs. Agnes E. Meyer in memory of Eugene Meyer, her husband, who died July 17, 1959. The addition to the University Hospital, for which this gift was given, was named the Eugene Meyer Pavilion.[13]

In financing the expansion and improvement of the hospital great credit was due Speaker John W. McCormack of the House of Representatives, who introduced personally a bill drafted by the Department of Health, Education, and Welfare to allow for the purpose federal funds not to exceed $2,500,000 on a matching basis.[14]

Although Dr. Thomas Henry Carroll was elected president on August 3, 1960, he did not take office until February 1, 1961, when Admiral Colclough relinquished the duties of acting president and became provost and dean of the faculties. The thirteenth president was of the new breed of college presidents, trained in business administration. He had been assistant dean of the Harvard School of Business Administration, dean and professor in the College of Business Administration at Syracuse, and then had held the same position at the University of North Carolina. He had next become associated with the Ford Foundation and at the time he was elected president of the University he was vice president of the Foundation.

On his induction into office, the new president was greeted with high ceremony by the various elements of the University community. President Carroll was introduced to the alumni at a gala dinner of the General Alumni Association. In an eloquent address he called for personal rededication, open-mindedness to new and different approaches to our common tasks, substantially increased financial support, and plain hard work. On the afternoon preceding the formal inauguration, President and Mrs. Carroll greeted more than two thousand faculty members and delegates from colleges, universities, and learned societies throughout the United States.

The inaugural ceremony, held in the University Yard, was honored by the presence of John Fitzgerald Kennedy, President of the United States. Dr. Carroll was formally installed by Newell W. Ellison, Chairman of the Board of Trustees, who presented him with the symbols of his office which he accepted "with both humility and confidence," pledging to the whole University community full devotion to duty. In his inaugural address, he referred to the "seemingly ever-present dualism in higher education. . . . We must worship neither the *status quo* nor change for the mere sake of change. We ourselves must develop and we must teach our students respect for progress. But we must not make the false assumption that change and progress are necessarily synonymous. We must cultivate and elevate creativity and must recognize that progress and growth do necessarily involve some change." Addressing himself particularly to George Washington University, he called for rededication to the principle of responsible academic freedom, for increasing acceptance of responsibilities in the field of international education, and for renewed acceptance of the central importance of the liberal arts college in the overall educational plan. In closing he emphasized that "the central interest of any great university faculty is students—both present and future, both at one's own university and elsewhere. We hope continuously to inculcate in our students a passion for learning, a respect for truth, a dedication to our nation's basic values and traditions, and a devotion to personal fulfillment." Messages of greeting were brought to the new president by President Clark Kerr of the University of California and former Dean McGeorge Bundy of Harvard University, representing institutions from which Dr. Carroll had received degrees, and by President-elect Logan Wilson of the American Council on Education.

The honorary degree of Doctor of Laws was conferred upon President Kennedy. In responding to President Carroll's citation he remarked in humorous vein that "my wife beat me to this honor by eight or nine years. It took her two years to get a degree, and it took me two minutes; but in any case we are both grateful."[15] He then referred to the obligations of the trained man. "Quite obviously," said the President, "the duty of the educated man and woman, the duty of the scholar, is to give his objective sense, his sense of liberty, to the maintenance of our society at a critical time. This is our opportunity as well as our responsibility." The distinguished guests of the University were honored at an Inaugural Luncheon following the ceremonies in the Yard.[16]

It was a tragic coincidence that the two young men who were the central figures at the inauguration were both to be cut down shortly, the President of the United States by an assassin's bullet, the president of the University by illness. Each had attained eminence early in life; and destiny ended their short careers at the summit, when great promise seemed the harbinger of large fulfillment.

As regretfully brief as it was, President Carroll's administration was in many ways a period of marked advance. The vice president and treasurer, Henry W. Herzog, even exceeded his own enviable past record in assembling and acquiring real estate in the University area. Alfred Henry Lawson, chairman of the Trustees' Committee on Buildings and Lands, and John Keown McKee, chairman of the Finance Committee, were the members of the Board who were particularly active in an unprecedented expansion of the University's holdings, facilitated by the very substantial assistance of the Federal Housing and Home Finance Agency. The dormitory system was expanded rapidly, the most spectacular single step being the acquisition of the large property on the southwest corner of Nineteenth and F Streets and the construction there, at a cost of over three million dollars, of Thurston Hall, a dormitory housing eleven hundred young women.[17] Negotiations were initiated which made possible the construction of the massive Joseph Henry Building at Twenty-first Street and Pennsylvania Avenue, with the National Academy of Sciences as the occupant on a twenty-year lease.[18]

The two major changes in the educational organization were the discontinuance of the School of Pharmacy as of June, 1964, and the division of the School of Government, Business, and International Affairs into a School of Government and Business and a School of International Affairs, each under its own dean.[19] The names were later changed to the School of Government and Business Administration and the School of Public and International Affairs. The Institute for Sino-Soviet Studies was organized to provide a program of specialized graduate study and research within the School of Public and International Affairs, giving an interdisciplinary approach to the study of the Soviet Union, Eastern Europe, the Far Eastern Communist states, and the World Communist movement.

In the spring of 1962, as a consultant for five universities in the District of Columbia Dr. Arthur Adams, then retiring as president of the American Council on Education, undertook a study of graduate work in the national capital. Although there had been earlier discussions, it was Dr. Adams' "Study of the possibilities of a coordinated plan of graduate study and research for the Metropolitan D.C. area" that led to the formation of the Joint Graduate Consortium and its incorporation in 1966 as "the Consortium of Universities of the Washington Metropolitan Area." A Board of Trustees was established, and an Administrative Committee composed of provosts or vice presidents (one from each university) assumed the overview function. The consortium immediately addressed itself to opening the courses of each institution to graduate students of all five. Most foreign language courses, covering over fifty languages, were opened to students at any level and plans were also made for general junior and senior participation. Particularly significant was the work of the consortium's Interuniversity Library Council in liberalizing the lending policy as related to the universities of the consortium, in sharing the facilities of member institutions, and in preparing a comprehensive plan of cooperation. The organization of the consortium was a tremendous step forward in the mobilization of the total university resources of the metropolitan area in the development of the District as an outstanding center of higher education.[20]

In the field of faculty relations, perhaps the most significant accomplishment was the redrafting and approval of the revised code governing academic personnel. The recent Fifth Amendment case, creating an unforeseen situation, had drawn attention to the need for a reworking of the code in the light of experience. With the active encouragement of the administration and the Trustees, the faculty formulated a code which was praised by the American Association of University Professors and accepted by it as adequate protection of academic tenure, removing completely any misgivings which might have existed over the initial handling of the recent case.[21]

Reference has been made to the appearance of a new type of student following World War I. In the 1920's there was a small but noisy group of critics of the University administration; in the 1930's the growth of European fascism suggested new wars and prompted peace demonstrations, much more vocal and of considerable size; in the 1940's youth was fighting in the war whose approach had been feared; in the late 1950's and early 1960's civil rights were beginning to cause general campus discussion. Alleged discrimination in fraternities and sororities was the peg on which the discussion was first hung. At a student referendum in April, 1964, propositions were submitted by the civil rights group, the Student Council, and the Interfraternity Council. The greatest number of votes was cast for the Interfraternity Council's proposal which imposed on the fraternities and sororities the responsibility for taking constructive steps to eliminate discrimination.

Speaking before the Faculty Assembly, President Carroll referred to the University's policy of nondiscrimination. He expressed the view that the matter "cannot be dealt with once and for all by an official broad-side, by a rule, by threats to ban fraternities and sororities which have constitutionally restrictive clauses." "It is," he said, "changed attitudes which accomplish the end of removing old prejudices. We must not lift the principal burden of the problem from the shoulders of the sororities and the fraternities where it belongs."[22]

In accordance with the administration's view and the vote of the student referendum, the Board of Trustees amended Title I, Article I, of the *Articles of Student Government* to read:

> There is hereby vested in the Student Council the jurisdiction and authority to regulate, supervise, and coordinate within the limitation of the Board of Trustees, all student activities except intercollegiate athletics, publications, Interfraternity, Pan Hellenic, and activities for which academic credit is given.[23]

The sudden death of President Carroll occurred on July 27, 1964, ending an administration that had hardly begun, with plans announced but fulfillment tragically denied. The talents of a man of great industry were lost to the University and another interregnum had to be faced. Admiral Colclough had planned to retire, but he was asked to return as acting president, and John Anthony Brown was made vice president and dean of the faculties. Declaring that in spite of a vacancy in the presidency "the work of the University must go forward," the Board asked its chairman to appoint a committee to select a new president and authorized him to ask the faculty also to appoint such a committee. The Faculty Committee was elected by the Faculty Assembly.[24]

Admiral Colclough's interim term of one year was a busy one. For 1964-1965, there were 12,000 students registered in the University, the largest registration since "the veterans' bulge" of twenty years previously. The increase was ascribed to the marked increase in dormitory accommodations through the acquisition of Thurston and Mitchell Halls.[25] The character of the student body, now so largely resident, made necessary attention to providing a new and comprehensive Student Center, and immediate planning was authorized. In a series of hearings Vice President Brown and a committee asked and were given opinions by all sectors of the student body as to what such a building should provide. The student areas in the vast University Center embody these numerous student suggestions.[26]

As a result of prolonged discussion, intercollegiate football was dis-

University Yard, Gilbert Stuart Hall, 1936; Lisner Library, 1939; Alexander Graham Bell Hall, 1935.

Hall of Government, northwest corner of Twenty-first and G Streets, 1938.

Hattie M. Strong Residence Hall for Women, southwest corner of Twenty-first and G Streets, 1936.

Meyer Pavilion, the University Hospital, Twenty-second Street between Eye Street and Pennsylvania Avenue, 1968.

James Monroe Hall, G Street, west of Twenty-first Street, 1951.

Thurston Hall, southwest corner of Nineteenth and F Streets, 1964. (R. W. Howard.)

Winter Convocation of 1929, at which President and Mrs. Calvin Coolidge received honorary degrees.

Commencement of 1946 at which President Harry S. Truman received an honorary degree and Margaret Truman (Mrs. Clifton Daniel) her degree in course.

Inauguration of Dr. Thomas Henry Carroll as thirteenth President of the University in 1962, at which President Kennedy was one of the speakers and received an honorary degree. *Left to right:* Judge Walter M. Bastian; President Clark Kerr, University of California at Berkeley; Robert V. Fleming, Chairman Emeritus of the Board of Trustees; President Emeritus Cloyd H. Marvin; President John F. Kennedy; Thomas H. Carroll, President of the University.

Syngman Rhee, A.B. 1907, President of Korea, at the special convocation in his honor, 1954.

Building C on G Street between Twenty-second and Twenty-third Streets, 1970. (R. W. Howard.)

Tompkins Hall, Twenty-third Street between G and H Streets, 1956.

Luther Rice Hall, Eye Street near Twenty-first (1968), and the Joseph Henry Building, Pennsylvania Avenue, Twenty-first and H Streets (1968). (R. W. Howard.)

The University Center on Twenty-first, H, and Eye Streets, 1970. (R. W. Howard.)

Equestrian statue of George Washington by Clark Mills, 1860. It is in Washington Circle, facing the northwest corner of the University area.

continued. Membership in the Southern Conference was maintained for the time, but at the Conference's spring meeting in 1969 the University's withdrawal was announced, effective June 30, 1970.

Dating from the revival of the Law School in 1865, the year 1965-1966 was designated Law School Centennial Year, and an elaborate program of observance was carried out. The new Law Library was authorized and construction was begun.[27] The Jacob Burns Law Library was opened in 1967.

The rapid acquisition of property in the University area continued; but particularly important were the conversations with the authorities of American University which led to the purchase and occupancy of its downtown plant, as arrangements for transfer to its Ward Circle Campus were completed. A contract was entered into with the National Academy of Sciences for a 20-year lease of the Joseph Henry Building.[28]

Admiral Colclough's year was not only a busy one; it became a troubled one. The trouble arose in connection with the election of President Carroll's successor. The Charter vests the power to elect the president in the hands of the Board of Trustees. A Trustees' committee and a faculty committee were appointed to make recommendations to the Board. Each of these committees went about its work quickly and thoroughly, exchanging information and points of view with reference to the more than one hundred possible nominees that each had considered, in the hope that both would decide on the same nomination. Unfortunately this was not to be the case. Whereas Admiral Colclough had asked not to be considered under any circumstances, another member of the administration was anxious to be elected. He managed to bring to his support several deans, many faculty members, and a number of students. Their views were aired in the public press and reflected in the faculty committee, which recommended that the search for a president be continued and withheld its approval of the man nominated by the Board's committee. Considering the reports of the two committees before it, the Board unanimously elected the nominee named by its own committee. There was an expression of continued belligerency in the University Assembly and on the campus in favor of the unsuccessful candidate. A new president and a new chairman of the Board of Trustees changed the picture almost miraculously, and a transition which in prospect had seemed so troubled occurred with ease and harmony.[29]

The new administration began not only with a new president, but with a new chairman of the Board of Trustees. Newell W. Ellison, a graduate of both the College and the Law School and a distinguished member of the bar, had served as chairman of the Board of Trustees for six rugged years. A man of intense loyalty and devotion to the University, he had given a major portion of his ability, time, and effort to his duties. His exertions had made inroads on his health and, following the election of Dr. Elliott, he found it necessary to say that he could not accept reelection to the chairmanship. The Trustees elected as Mr. Ellison's successor Edward Karrick Morris, a graduate of Williams College, a successful businessman, and one of Washington's outstanding civic leaders. His interest in the University was of long standing, dating back to the time when as a young man he had given it his services as baseball coach. He had consistently maintained friendly contact with many of the faculty and with students and student organizations. As a Trustee he was well known throughout the entire University community. Prepared to give practically his whole time to the institution, he was well equipped to undertake with President Elliott what came to be his special role.

Lloyd Hartman Elliott, fourteenth president of the University, was forty-seven years old at the time of his election. He had had wide experience in the field of education, as teacher in the public schools of his native state of West Virginia, as high school principal and assistant superintendent of the Boulder Public Schools, and as member of the faculty and administrator at Cornell and the University of Maine, which he served as president from 1958-1965. He was under no false illusions as to the difficulties as well as the opportunities of the position to which he had been elected. Immediately upon his election he began to make personal contacts with people on all levels in the University community. In three months, he was on the campus prepared to take charge, already possessed of considerable information, enough to make his impact felt from the very beginning. President Elliott and Chairman Morris were particularly gifted in their ability to meet people easily and informally, and they made use of that ability.

The president's problems were many. Most immediate, because it was necessary if a healthy atmosphere was to be restored, was the problem of reconciliation. Divisions in the faculty and student body brought about by the events preceding the election were deep and bitter. Dr. Elliott was as aware of the situation as anyone was. He merely accepted the past as prologue and looked to the future. The voices of opposition and protest which had been so strident quickly ceased to be heard. The president was easily available to a degree unusual with University heads. He practiced not only good communication, but personal communication.

The results of President Elliott's policy were quickly noticeable. Reporting to the Board in October, 1965, Chairman E. K. Morris pointed out that student "restlessness to a dangerous degree was prevalent last spring," but that the beginning of a changed attitude was seen in the reaction to the president's address at the freshmen orientation rally. There had been the same change in alumni sentiment. "It has now become imperative," he concluded, "for us to give evidence of performance if we are to maintain the favorable climate of enthusiastic cooperation of all the elements that make up our complex University society."[30]

The next problem was, in common parlance, to give the University a lift, to break up the inertia which had begun to settle down in the late years of the Marvin regime and which had not been basically changed during the period of two interregnums and a short administration, tragically ended before it could build up momentum. The new regime, stimulated by the optimism of the president, the activity of his Board and its chairman, the increasing involvement of faculty, students, and alumni, the tangible evidence of active planning, the beginning of new construction, and the improvement of the old plant, gave a sense of movement, of going forward, of getting off dead center. In the days of Lord Nelson, someone has said, Englishmen awakened each morning wondering what new victory had been won. So it was as the fourteenth president got his program under way.

Addressing the Board shortly after he assumed office, President Elliott had spoken of his intention to bring into sharper focus both short-range and long-range plans for the development of the University. This became a basic and continuing objective. At the same time, he called for a survey of the University's relations to the federal government so that the institution would not miss opportunities of value on the one hand, but on the other would not undertake obligations it did not want. Then there was the large problem of University organization.[31]

Forty years earlier, at the beginning of his administration, President Marvin had called for reorganization. With remarkable success he built up a system of unified control, by virtue of which practically all matters had to be processed through the president's office. With a much smaller institution to deal with, he was unusually successful in bringing about rapid change. But as the years passed and the concerns of the institution multiplied, the presidential grasp relaxed. Unity in fiscal control remained, but in other matters deans and administrators carved out for themselves autonomous control over their units. While for a time there was a vice president, charged primarily with a specialized function, and toward the end an upper echelon of dean of faculties and treasurer and comptroller, there was no comprehensive effort to take care of the situation when centralized control had begun to erode. In the Carroll regime, a vice president for development was created and there was some shifting of titles. The problem as a whole remained for the new president to meet.

The president's first proposal, warmly approved by the Trustees, was for the formation of a council for each school and college, made up of representative elements and concerned directly with matters pertaining to its constituency. These, in a way, resembled the old visiting committees of the Board set up in the 1910 reorganization, with the important difference that they were much more broadly based to insure ease in communication and wider stimulation of interest. Later councils of the same character were organized for each of the departments of instruction.

President Elliott moved toward a systematic grouping of functions, placing each group under an appropriate vice president. Five vice presidents were appointed: Vice President for Academic Affairs, Vice President and Treasurer, Vice President for Resources, Vice President for Advanced Policy Studies, and Vice President for Student Affairs.

The president's handling of the Academic Senate differed from the method of his predecessors. Instead of being a body engaged in hearing discussions and pronouncements from the chair, President Elliott used it more readily to receive information than to give it. Its sessions were more open. Nonmembers and students were invited to present points of view, so that resolutions coming out of the Senate were expected to be based on an informed consensus of the total community. Because of its size and the natural infrequency of meeting, the Faculty Assembly, broadly inclusive in its membership, remained a relatively formal body, receiving resolutions for its assent from the Senate, hearing statements from University officers, receiving reports, performing organizational chores, and welcoming new appointees into its membership. It was available as a forum, the extent to which it was thus used depending upon the disposition of its members at any given session.

The problem of student relations became more important and demanding than at any other period in the institution's history. The new breed of students did not suddenly appear in the middle 1960's. It had been in the making ever since the close of the First World War, but had never been as noisy and as aggressive. Every one of the issues that had been raised in earlier waves of student unrest was revived: the Establishment in government and in the University, war, discrimination, civil rights. These were the Bastilles they stormed. The selection of issues was entirely a matter of opportunism. If an issue would produce a confrontation it was used. If it did not, it was laid aside and others tried.

It must not be assumed that the total student body, or even a majority of it, was actively involved. Most students dressed according to the accepted mode, attended lectures, studied assignments, wrote reports, took and, in decent numbers, passed examinations. They naturally were present at demonstrations to see what was going on. Demonstrations in the late 1960's rivaled football as a spectator sport. Spectators were easily confused with participants, and sometimes paid dearly for their presence. The literary standards of demonstration oratory were not high. At best colloquial, they slipped too easily into the vulgar and obscene. The attendant results of such confrontation were often what could be expected from any large group fired by agitators: physical injury, wanton destruction and disfigurement of property, involvement with peace officers, and disruption of normal activity.

Why had these manifestations of student unrest become so violent? In part it was due to the increasingly urban character of our population. In classic accounts of the Industrial Revolution, the vast numbers who had come out of rural settings and had been poured into teeming industrial centers were often called the *déracinés*. Modern urban society had created a new *déraciné*. Roots were not easy to come by. A highly mobile society resulted, and millions of its members were students in the colleges. The old college had stood in *loco parentis*. It afforded a home away from home—food, lodging, medical services, organized recreation, and guidance. The new student did not reject facilities for his comfort; he demanded them, but not as a minor. Youths of eighteen were taken in the armed forces, and in some states had the suffrage. They were adults. In the mind of the new breed, the walls of the college were down. It was but a ward or a precinct in the local political unit, and they were involved in all the city's problems—in fact, all society's problems. It followed logically that they particularly must be involved in the governance of the University, a task for which the position of student gave them an especial aptitude. Such was their rationale, if they stopped to figure it out.

Events and situations had led students in large numbers into a militant expression of what they assumed their position in society to be. The civil rights struggle, the unpopular war in Vietnam, the alleged evidences of incipient fascism, the failure of Resurrection City, the assassination of popular leaders, liberal disappointments, cataclysms of destruction and violence—these were goads to action by the forces of unrest.

An element of picturesqueness to some and of repugnance to others was the omnipresence of the so-called hippies at all demonstrations and student meetings, and with them the professional agitator, moving rapidly from city to city, wherever the action was. The hippie was not a new creation; Greenwich Village had known his type for decades, and the Continent knew it before New York did. Whether he was a student or not was entirely irrelevant. He was there and even in an age of informal attire he stood out because of his costume and hirsute adornment; in the public mind student actionist and "hippie" became, incorrectly, synonymous to many people.

Assuming that in spite of liberal demands to take over a larger share of the governance of the University, chartered powers were bound to remain largely in the hands of Trustees and faculties, there were indications that a student's right to know would be granted, and that a responsible student request would be assured of a hearing. If there were concessions, they were primarily along the line of improved communications, presented in a way nowise disparaging to the student's claim to his own dignity and maturity or to the right to present his point of view before the decisions were taken.

This was the student body from which leadership for the next several decades was to be produced. Student demands, legitimate or otherwise, in no way reduced the obligations of the University, although they did increase its embarrassments at times. Under President Elliott's guidance, the plans for the development of the University were brought into sharp focus. "By establishing new, broad-based structures for participation," he wrote, "we hope to encourage the development of a true University community which can communicate its concerns within the University and then beyond; by cooperating with other institutions, and by using our talents and resources where most appropriate, we hope to make a real contribution toward ameliorating the urban problems of our time."[32] The necessary physical additions and changes over the next several years were outlined, and a financial plan for defraying the cost of needed plant changes and the proper funding of the University's mission was carefully worked out.[33] Although enormous in size, the task of raising this fund was accepted by the president and the Board of Trustees as a major task immediately ahead.

A five-year development plan adopted in 1967 called for the addition to University assets of nearly $90 million by 1972, including more than $54 million from private gifts. Looking confidently to the firmer basis which this would insure, the University prepared to move into the last half of its second century.

IT IS QUITE POSSIBLE, indeed highly probable, that in the future the effect of the city on the University will be much more complicated than it has been in the past. The city that we have known is being rapidly absorbed into the great eastern megalopolis. It has seen great demographic change. The decentralization of many government establishments and their removal outside the central city has had its effects. Vast shifts of population to neighboring counties of Maryland and Virginia and the movement into the city of new groups with a less favored economic status, particularly from the South, have transformed the character of the city's inhabitants. The frequent reference to the heart of the old city as "the inner city" suggests the social change which has occurred. Statistics of student enrollment indicate that already the University, with its students from every state in the Union and from eighty foreign countries, is a university of the eastern megalopolis, with its student body roughly proportional to the population of the states along the eastern seaboard. This poses new problems totally different from those with which the University had to contend during its first century and a half.

The strength of George Washington University today rests in its independence of any denominational or other control; its location, happily chosen in the heart of the capital city, and the utilization of the opportunities that that location offers; the loyalty and ability of its officers and faculty; the eminence of its graduates, particularly in the field of public service; the willingness of distinguished men and women to devote time and talents as Trustees; the faith of generous donors in its mission; and the inspiration of a worthy tradition and of a great name.

GENERAL BIBLIOGRAPHICAL NOTE
ON HISTORICAL MATERIALS
IN THE UNIVERSITY

The prime source for the history of the University is the *Minutes of the Board of Trustees*, preserved without a break from the organization meeting in 1821 to the present. The *Minutes* present the only continuing record of the University, or any of its parts, from the founding to the present. Fortunately the actions of the Executive Committee of the Board, whose minutes are available for scattered periods only, seem to have been regularly reported to the full Board and are recorded in its *Minutes*. The circulars of the early College and the annual catalogues form the next most important class of material. From the beginning to about 1850, there are many gaps in this material. For the earlier period, there were many years when no new circular was issued, due largely to the fact that a supply left over from a preceding year was used until exhausted. Some of them were even updated by hand.

Selected material from student files up to 1928 is available on microfilm. Since 1928 full student files have been preserved; they are being progressively microfilmed, and are in the custody of the registrar. As secretary ex officio of the University Senate and the faculties, the same officer has the more recent minutes of those bodies in his keeping. Faculty minutes for the first century have been preserved only in part. All the records of National University in its possession when merged in George Washington University in 1954 are arranged chronologically in bound volumes and are deposited in the Archives.

No student publications are available until the turn of the century except a few bound volumes of the records of the meetings and the compositions of the literary societies, of which the Enosinian was the most important and long-lived. The principal publications have been *Columbian Call*, 1895–1899; *Columbian Weekly*, 1903–1904; the *University Hatchet*, 1904–   , for many years a weekly, now issued twice a week; the annual, the *Columbiad*, 1898–1903; *The C*, 1904; the *Mall*, 1905–1907; and *The Cherry Tree*, 1908–   .

The George Washington University Bulletin has been published since 1901 and is the most important printed source for information during the most recent period of the University's history. The annual volumes of the *Bulletin* have varied in the numbers of parts issued during the year. The annual catalogue appears regularly as a number of the *Bulletin*. The content of the other numbers has not been consistent, including at various times the reports of the president and of the treasurer; accounts of important ceremonies such as centennial celebrations and inaugurals; announcements of new policies, schools, and curricula; and even, during one period, scientific and literary papers.

Student handbooks, manuals of information for undergraduates primarily, have been published with fair regularity since the Needham administration. Numerous periodicals have been published to acquaint alumni and the interested public with various aspects of University life and history. Both title and format of these periodicals changed frequently. The most useful have been *George Washington University Alumni Review*, 1936–1959; *Confidential from Washington*, 1942–1950; *George Washington University Federalist*, 1954–1963; *GW, The George Washington University Magazine*, 1964–   ; *George Washington University Newsletter*, 1958, 1961–   .

While many pieces of ephemera have been preserved, they represent a pitiful fraction of this very valuable material that has been produced. Much of it is undated, and its classification is impossible because its highly miscellaneous nature ranges from student manifestos, *sub rosa* publications of humor, satire, and protest, and even printed announcements of mass meetings, to official notices of changes in fees and regulations and new courses of study published and distributed by the University.

No recent general alumni catalogue has been published. The three most important are: *Historical Catalogue of the Officers and Graduates of the Columbian University, Washington, D.C., 1821–1891*, compiled by H. L. Hodgkins (Washington, 1891); *General Alumni Catalogue of George Washington University*, compiled by W. J. Maxwell (n.p.n.d.), extending from 1821 to 1916; and *The George Washington University Alumni Directory, 1824–1937* (Washington, 1938), edited by Marcelle Le Ménager Lane. A medical alumni directory and a law alumni directory were issued in 1965 and 1969 respectively.

While historical sketches galore have constantly appeared as introductory material in catalogues and other University publications, no full-length history has been previously attempted. Of the more lengthy publications devoted to University history over an extended period the most widely used have been the "Historical Sketch" in the Hodgkins catalogue and the "Historical Outline" in the Lane directory, both noted above, and the following: James C. Welling, *Brief Chronicles of the Columbian College from 1821 to 1873 and of the Columbian University from 1873 to 1889* (Washington, 1889); Charles Herbert Stockton, "Historical Sketch of George Washington University, Washington, D.C.—formerly known as Columbian University and Columbian College, accompanied by a sketch of the lives of the Presidents," *Records of the Columbia Historical Society*, Washington, D.C. (Washington, 1916), Vol. 19, pp. 99–139; Margaret Davis and Lester Smith, *A University in the Nation's Capital, 1821–1947* (Washington, 1947); Robert C. Willson, *A Chronological Outline of Some of the Major Steps in the Development of the George Washington University to 1954* (typescript, 1955); Elmer Louis Kayser, *The George Washington University, 1821–1966* (Washington, 1966).

Thirty-five years ago as an NYA project Professor Lowell Ragatz directed a team of students in making a full transcript of all references to the College during its first half-century which appeared in the Washington press and in certain denominational publications, particularly the *Columbian Star* and the *Latter Day Luminary*. Full use has been made of this material, which is now deposited in the University Collection.

The University has an important collection of Luther Rice documents, including one hundred thirty letters written by Rice 1821–1836, a major portion of his *Journal*, the logbook of his outward voyage to India in 1812, his register of letters written and received, notebooks, subscription books, accounts and checks, and many letters written to him. Of the letters of the first four presidents, very few remain in the possession of the University. The collection of President Samson, the fifth head of the college, is much fuller. The Welling material is largely in printed form, due to his custom of distributing printed communications to the Trustees for their information before Board meetings, some of them bearing dates for future release. Practically nothing remains of the correspondence of President Whitman during his brief administration. Beginning with the administration of President Needham in 1902, the correspondence of the presidents, now mainly in typewritten form, is basically fully preserved, subject always to the editorial zeal of the individual as to what he wants to leave in his files.

In the Bibliographical Comments which precede the Notes for each chapter, material of special value for the period covered is indicated.

CHAPTER ONE
Bibliographical Comments

In a chapter of such necessarily broad scope as an overview chapter, the range of bibliographical material is equally broad in scope. The chapters which follow each have Bibliographical Comments covering material pertinent to the particular chapter; therefore no such comments are included for this chapter.

Notes

1 Based on figures in *People and Land, a Portion of the Comprehensive Plan for the National Capital*, National Park & Planning Commission, Washington, D.C., Monograph No. 2 (June, 1950).

CHAPTER TWO
Bibliographical Comments

For the history of Washington, see Wilhelmus Bogart Bryan, *A History of the National Capital, from Its Foundation Through the Period of the Adoption of the Organic Act*, 2 vols. (New York, 1914, 1916); and Constance McLaughlin Green, *Washington, Village and Capital, 1800–1878* (Princeton, 1962), and *Washington, Capital City, 1878–1950* (Princeton, 1963). For the history of American colleges, see Frederick Rudolph, *The American College and University: A History* (New York, 1962); Donald G. Tewksbury, *The Founding of American Colleges and Universities Before the Civil War with Particular Reference to the Religious Influences Bearing upon the College Movement* (New York, 1932; Anchor, 1965).

For George Washington's bequest and its fate, see Elmer Louis Kayser, *Washington's Bequest to a National University* (Washington, 1965); Martin Paul Claussen, Jr., *The Fate of Washington's Bequest to a National University* (Washington, 1968); David L. Madsen, *The National University, Enduring Dream of the USA* (Detroit, 1966).

The sources for the development of the missionary movement, as it involved Rice, and for the life of Rice are: *First Ten Annual Reports of the American Board of Commissioners for Foreign Missions with Other Documents of the Board* (Boston, 1834); *Proceedings of Triennial Convention 1814–1846 and Annual Reports of the Board of Managers 1814–1846* (Ann Arbor, 1964); *Logbook of Rice on His Outward Journey to Asia in 1812*; Rice's *Journal; Letters* of Rice (1821–1836) and his contemporaries, business records, and miscellanea; Leonard Woods, *A Sermon Delivered at the Tabernacle in Salem, February 6, 1812* (Boston, 1812) at Rice's ordination; Stephen Chapin, *A Sermon Delivered in the First Baptist Church Before the Board of Trustees of the Columbian College, D.C., with an Obituary Notice of Its Principal*

Founder, the Rev. Luther Rice (Washington, 1837). The manuscript of Rice's *Journal*, a large portion of which is in the University Collection, has been microfilmed *in toto*. The other Rice manuscripts listed are in the University Collection.

Among the biographies of Luther Rice are: Saxon Rowe Carver, *Ropes to Burma: The Story of Luther Rice* (Nashville, 1961), "a fictionized biography for young readers"; Elmer Louis Kayser, *Luther Rice, Founder of Columbian College* (Washington, 1966); Edward Bagley Pollard, *Luther Rice, Pioneer in Missions and Education*, edited and completed by Daniel Gurden Stevens (Philadelphia, 1928); James Barnett Taylor, *Memoir of Rev. Luther Rice, One of the First American Missionaries to the East*, 2nd ed. (Nashville, 1937); Evelyn Wingo Thompson, *Luther Rice, Believer in Tomorrow* (Nashville, 1967).

For Adoniram Judson, see Edward Judson, *Life of Adoniram Judson* (New York, 1883); Francis Wayland, *A Memoir of the Life and Labors of the Rev. Adoniram Judson, D.D.*, 2 vols. (Boston, 1853); Courtney Anderson, *To the Golden Shore: The Life of Adoniram Judson* (Boston, 1956).

For the development of the Theological Institution of the Triennial Convention, the source is *Proceedings of the Triennial Convention (1814–1846) and Annual Reports of the Board of Managers (1814–1846)* (Ann Arbor, 1964).

Basic with reference to the Baptist relationships of the early college are *Baptist Missionary Magazine*, vols. 1–30, January, 1817–December, 1850 (Boston, J. Putnam); *Columbian Star*, vols. 1–4, February 2, 1822–December 31, 1825 (Washington, Anderson and Meehan); *Latter Day Luminary*, vols. 1–6, February, 1818–December, 1825 (Philadelphia, Anderson and Meehan). These are available in the *American Periodical Series, 1800–1850* (University Microfilms, Ann Arbor, Michigan).

Notes

[1] Frederick Rudolph, *The American College and University* (New York, 1962), p. 40.

[2] David L. Madsen, "The University of the United States," *Journal of Higher Education*, Vol. 23, No. 7 (October, 1962), pp. 354 ff.; Elmer Louis Kayser, *Washington's Bequest to a National University* (Washington, 1965); Martin Paul Claussen, Jr., *The Fate of Washington's Bequest to a National University* (Washington, 1968).

[3] Claussen, *op. cit.*, pp. 14–21.

[4] E. Richardson Holbrook, *General George Washington's Will, Records of Fairfax County, Virginia, Wherein He Lived and Died* (Fairfax, Va., 1904), p. 15.

[5] Luther Rice, *Journal*, September, 1804. No day stated.

[6] *Ibid.*, January 17, 1804.

[7] *Ibid.*, September 15, 1805.

[8] Quoted in Edward B. Pollard, *Luther Rice, Pioneer in Missions and Education*. Edited and completed by David Gurden Stevens (Philadelphia, 1928), p. 120. For a brief biography of Rice, see Elmer Louis Kayser, *Luther Rice, Founder of Columbian College* (Washington, 1966).

9 *First Ten Annual Reports of the American Board of Commissioners for Foreign Missions with Other Documents of the Board* (Boston, 1834), pp. 2, 10.

10 *Ibid.*, pp. 19–22.

11 Leonard Woods, *A Sermon Delivered at the Tabernacle in Salem, February 6, 1812* (Boston, 1812).

12 Rice, *op. cit.*, February 6, 1812.

13 *First Ten Annual Reports of the American Board of Commissioners*, pp. 55–62; Clifton Jackson Phillips, *Protestant America and the Pagan World: The First Half Century of the American Board of Commissioners for Foreign Missions, 1810–1860*, Harvard East Asian Monographs 32 (Cambridge, 1969), pp. 21, 23, 34–35, 37.

14 *Proceedings of the Baptist Convention for Missionary Purposes; Held in Philadelphia in May, 1814* (Philadelphia, 1814), pp. 3–12.

The numbering of the various sessions of the Triennial Convention is confusing. The sessions are described as follows:

First Session, 1814, is referred to as the Triennial Convention.

Second Session, 1817, as the First Triennial Meeting.

Third Session, 1820, as the Second Triennial Meeting.

Fourth Session, 1823, as the Fourth Triennial Meeting.

From the Fourth Triennial Meeting on, the number of the meeting and the number of the session are the same.

15 *First Annual Report of the Baptist Board of Foreign Missions for the United States* (Philadelphia, 1815), p. 10.

16 *Proceedings of the General Convention of the Baptist Denomination in the United States at Their First Triennial Meeting* (Philadelphia, 1817), pp. 131, 132.

17 *Proceedings of the Baptist Convention for Missionary Purposes*, pp. 25–42.

18 *Fourth Annual Report of the Baptist Board of Foreign Missions* (Philadelphia, 1818), pp. 193–203.

19 "First Annual Report of the Baptist Board of Foreign Missions for the United States," *Latter Day Luminary*, Vol. 1, No. 8 (May, 1819), p. 395.

20 "Proceedings of the General Convention at Their Second Triennial Meeting and the Sixth Annual Report of the Board," *ibid.*, Vol. 2, No. 13 (May, 1820), p. 124.

21 *Ibid.*, p. 128.

22 *Ibid.*, p. 129.

23 "General Education Plan," *ibid.*, pp. 153–155.

24 "Address of the General Convention of the Baptist Denomination Assembled at Philadelphia on the 26th of April, 1820," *ibid.*, p. 112.

25 "Seventh Annual Report of the Board," *ibid.*, Vol. 2, No. 18 (May, 1821), pp. 377–379.

CHAPTER THREE
Bibliographical Comments

For the purchase of College Hill, recourse must be had to the Land Records of the District of Columbia and to pertinent deeds in the Office of the Recorder of Deeds, to the *Proceedings of the Triennial Convention and Annual Reports of the Board of Managers*, as well as to Luther Rice's *Journal*.

The movement to obtain a charter can be traced through the *Annals of* the Congress of the United States and the Proceedings of the Triennial Convention and Annual Reports of the Board of Managers. The Charter (Stat. at Large, vol. 6, pp. 255–258, 16th Cong., 2d Sess., Chap. 10) is in the National Archives.

Notes

[1] H. Paul Caemmerer, Historic Washington, Capital of the Nation (Washington, 1948), p. 21.

[2] "Proceedings of the General Convention at Their Second Triennial Meeting and the Sixth Annual Report of the Board," Latter Day Luminary, Vol. 2, No. 13 (May, 1820), p. 129.

[3] Ibid., pp. 120, 146–150.

[4] Deed recorded March 10, 1821, in Liber WB2 at Folio 110, Office of Recorder of Deeds, District of Columbia.

[5] John Albert Tillema, "Church and State," Confidential from Washington, No. 37 (March, 1947).

When the attempt to obtain a charter from Congress failed, a committee of the Board consisting of the Reverend Dr. Staughton, the Reverend Mr. McLaughlin, and Professor Chase was appointed to seek a charter "through the channel of the Attorney General and Judges of the Supreme Court of the State of Pennsylvania." The committee succeeded in its efforts and "The General Convention of the Baptist Denomination in the United States for Foreign Missions, and other important Objects relating to the Redeemer's Kingdom" became a body politic and corporate in law, by the authority of the State of Pennsylvania. Latter Day Luminary, Vol. 2, No. 18 (May, 1821), p. 341.

[6] Annals of the Congress of the United States, 16th Cong., 2d Sess., pp. 27, 36, 40, 41.

[7] Ibid., pp. 117, 123, 149, 150, 802, 858, 865.

[8] Ibid., pp. 997–999.

[9] Tillema, op. cit.; Annals of the Congress, 16th Cong., 2d Sess., pp. 1792–1796; Report of an Investigation of the Financial and Educational Affairs of The George Washington University, Transmitted to the House of Representatives by the Attorney General, June 2, 1910, and Referred to the Committee on the District of Columbia (Washington, 1910), pp. 3, 4.

[10] "Seventh Annual Report of the Board," Latter Day Luminary, Vol. 2, No. 18 (May, 1821), p. 381.

[11] Minutes of the Board of Trustees, Vol. 1 (November 15, 1821), p. 25.

[12] Ibid., Vol. 1 (June 27, 1821), pp. 16–17.

[13] Ibid., Vol. 1 (November 24, 1821), pp. 26–27.

[14] "Seventh Annual Report of the Board," pp. 378–380.

[15] Ibid., p. 385.

[16] Eighth Annual Report of the Board of Managers of the General Convention of the Baptist Denomination in the United States, for Foreign Missions (Washington, 1822), p. 386.

[17] Indentures recorded December 11, 1821, in Liber WB4 at Folios 191–200, Office of the Recorder of Deeds, District of Columbia.

[18] "Seventh Annual Report of the Board," p. 382; Minutes of the Board of Trustees, Vol. 1 (April 19, 1821), p. 7.

CHAPTER FOUR
Bibliographical Comments

From the opening of the College, the *Minutes of the Board of Trustees* become the major source for the history of the institution. For its early history, the Trustees' *Minutes* are of greater value than would be expected, for two reasons. In the first place, the Board dealt with the widest range of matters, from questions of policy to details that would seem too minor to be brought up at faculty meetings. In the second place, all circulars of the early College, all matters concerning courses of instruction, fees, and student rules were incorporated in the *Minutes*. During this early period, the *Proceedings of the Triennial Convention and Annual Reports of the Board of Managers* remain an important source.

The *Laws of the Columbian College*, adopted January 13, 1824, was an elaborate piece of codification dealing with the whole question of governance of the institution. Included were the regulations for student conduct which remained virtually unchanged for decades. These were reprinted year after year, and students were required to read them and to declare their assent publicly. *The Laws* and many copies of the printed rules for students are in the University Archives.

For President Staughton, see William Staughton, *Address Delivered at the Opening of the Columbian College in the District of Columbia, January 9, 1822* (Washington, 1822); *Letters* of Rice (1821–1836) and his contemporaries, in the University Collection; S. W. Lynd, *Memoir of the Rev. William Staughton, D.D.* (Boston, 1834), in the University Collection.

The development of the Preparatory School and the professional departments can be followed through the *Minutes of the Board of Trustees*; but for the Medical Department, see also Thomas Sewall, *A Lecture Delivered at the Opening of the Medical Department of the Columbian College in the District of Columbia* (Washington, 1825); J. M. Toner, M.D., *Anniversary Oration Delivered Before the Medical Society of the District of Columbia, September 26, 1866* (Washington, Cunningham and McIntosh).

Interesting for a student's and a graduate's observations is John Calvin Stockbridge, *A Memoir of the Life and Correspondence of the Rev. Baron Stow, D.D., Late Pastor of the Rowe Street Baptist Church, Boston* (Boston, 1871). Stow was a graduate in the class of 1825.

Notes

[1] *Minutes of the Board of Trustees*, Vol. 1 (October 5, 1821), p. 20.

[2] *Eighth Annual Report of the Board of Managers of the General Convention of the Baptist Denomination in the United States, for Foreign Missions* (Washington, 1822), pp. 386, 387, 394.

[3] *Ibid.*, p. 386.

[4] William Staughton, *Address Delivered at the Opening of the Columbian College in*

the District of Columbia, January 9, 1822 (Washington, 1822), pp. 20, 24, 25, 26, 28, 29, 30, 31.

5 *Minutes of the Board of Trustees,* Vol. 1 (April 19, 1821), p. 9.

6 Elmer Louis Kayser, "Science in the Early College," *GW: The George Washington University Magazine,* Winter, 1968, pp. 27–29; *Minutes of the Board of Trustees,* Vol. 1 (April 19, 1821), p. 9.

7 *Minutes of the Board of Trustees,* Vol. 1 (April 20, 1822), pp. 37–38.

8 Laws of the Columbian College, adopted January 13, 1824.

9 *Minutes of the Board of Trustees,* Vol. 1 (April 19, 1821), p. 10.

10 *Ibid.,* Vol. 1 (June 30, 1821), pp. 18, 19.

11 *American Baptist Magazine,* 1823, p. 140.

12 S. W. Lynd, *Memoir of the Rev. William Staughton, D.D.* (Boston, 1834), pp. 251–257.

13 Deed of Trust recorded December 27, 1827, in Liber WB20 at Folio 294, Office of the Recorder of Deeds, District of Columbia.

14 Lynd, *op. cit.,* p. 203; James C. Welling, *Brief Chronicles of the Columbian College from 1821 to 1873, and of the Columbian University from 1873 to 1889* (Washington, 1889), pp. 7–8.

15 Lynd, *op. cit.,* p. 240.

16 *Minutes of the Board of Trustees,* Vol. 1 (April 20, 1822), p. 37.

17 *Ibid.,* Vol. 1 (November 24, 1821), pp. 27–29.

18 *Ibid.,* Vol. 1 (October 19, 1824), pp. 88–90; *Circular, The Medical Department of the Columbian College,* August, 1825.

19 Jonathan Elliot, *Historical Sketches of the Ten Miles Square Forming the District of Columbia* (Washington, J. Elliot, Jr., 1830), pp. 241–245; Wilhelmus Bogart Bryan, *A History of the National Capital* (New York, 1916), Vol. 2, pp. 200, 201; J. M. Toner, M.D., *Anniversary Oration Delivered Before the Medical Society of the District of Columbia, September 26, 1866* (Washington, Cunningham and McIntosh); Dean's Book, *Minutes of the Meetings of the Medical Professors of the Columbian College,* 1839–1880, pp. 4, 5, 7–9 (University Archives).

20 Thomas Sewall, *A Lecture Delivered at the Opening of the Medical Department of the Columbian College in the District of Columbia* (Washington, 1825).

21 *Minutes of the Board of Trustees,* Vol. 1 (February 3, 1826), p. 116.

22 *Ibid.,* Vol. 1 (February 24, 1826), pp. 117, 118; Helen Newman, "William Cranch, Judge, Law School Professor, Reporter," *Law Library Journal,* Vol. 26, No. 4 (October, 1933); Allen C. Clark, *Greenleaf and Law in the Federal City* (Washington, 1901), pp. 47–66; F. DeWolfe Miller, *Christopher Pearse Cranch* (Cambridge, 1951), pp. 6, 7.

23 Quoted in Newman, *op. cit.,* p. 14.

24 *Minutes of the Board of Trustees,* Vol. 1 (March 26, 1825), p. 100.

25 *General Catalogue of the Newton Theological Institution, 1826–43* (Newton Center, 1943), pp. xi, xii; *Andover Newton Quarterly,* January, 1966, inside front cover.

26 *Minutes of the Board of Trustees,* Vol. 1 (December 14, 1825), p. 111.

27 "Proposals for Publishing in Washington City *The Columbian Star,* Devoted to Religion and Science," *Eighth Annual Report of the Board of Managers* (Washington, 1822). This statement was printed on the cover.

28 *Columbian Star,* December 28, 1822, p. 3.

29 Bryan, *op. cit.,* vol. 2, p. 45.

30 *Columbian Star,* October 16, 1824, p. 3.

[31] *Daily National Intelligencer,* December 11, 1824, p. 3.
[32] *Ibid.,* December 15, 1824, p. 3.
[33] Frank E. and Helen B. Edgington, *History of New York Avenue Presbyterian Church* (Washington, 1962), p. 19.
[34] *Minutes of the Board of Trustees,* Vol. 1 (December 2, 1824), p. 93.
[35] *Columbian Star,* December 18, 1824, p. 2.
[36] *Daily National Journal,* December 17, 1824, p. 3; *Daily National Intelligencer,* December 18, 1824, p. 3.
[37] *Columbian Star,* December 18, 1824, p. 2; Lynd, *op. cit.,* p. 114.
[38] *Catalogue of the Enosinian Society, Columbian College, District of Columbia* (Washington, 1859), pp. 4–17.
[39] *Minutes of the Board of Trustees,* Vol. 1 (September 30, 1824), p. 87.
[40] *Ibid.,* Vol. 1 (December 20, 1824), p. 97.
[41] *American Baptist Magazine,* 1825, p. 217.

CHAPTER FIVE

Bibliographical Comments

The early financial crisis of the College can be followed through the *Minutes of the Board of Trustees,* the *Proceedings of the Triennial Convention and Annual Reports of the Board of Managers,* the *Letters* of Rice and his contemporaries in the University Collection, the *Columbian Star* and other Washington newspapers, and the *Annals of Congress* and the *Register of Debates in Congress.* See also Lynd, *Memoir of the Rev. William Staughton, D.D.,* and Stockbridge, *A Memoir of the Life and Correspondence of the Rev. Baron Stow.*

Notes

[1] *Latter Day Luminary,* Vol. 2, No. 18 (May, 1821), p. 384; *Eighth Annual Report of the Board of Managers of the General Convention of the Baptist Denomination in the United States, for Foreign Missions* (Washington, 1822), p. 386; *American Baptist Magazine,* 1823, p. 140; *ibid.,* 1824, p. 424; *ibid.,* 1825, p. 217.
[2] Luther Rice to O. B. Brown, September 5 and October 24, 1821 (University Collection).
[3] *Minutes of the Board of Trustees,* Vol. 1 (January 13, 1824), p. 76; James C. Welling, *Brief Chronicles of the Columbian College from 1821 to 1873, and of the Columbian University from 1873 to 1889* (Washington, 1889), pp. 9, 10.
[4] *Latter Day Luminary,* Vol. 2, No. 13 (May, 1820), pp. 122, 129; *Eighth Annual Report of the Board of Managers,* p. 380.
[5] Luther Rice to O. B. Brown, February 18, 1826 (University Collection).
[6] *Proceedings of the Baptist Convention for Missionary Purposes; Held in Philadelphia in May, 1814* (Philadelphia, 1814), p. 3.
[7] *Ibid.,* p. 42.
[8] *Latter Day Luminary,* Vol. 2, No. 13 (May, 1820), p. 124.
[9] *American Baptist Magazine,* 1825, p. 217.

[10] S. W. Lynd, *Memoir of the Rev. William Staughton, D.D.* (Boston, 1834), pp. 263, 264.

[11] *Proceedings of the Fifth Triennial Meeting of the Baptist General Convention, Held in New York, April, 1826* (Boston, 1826), pp. 14, 15.

[12] *Ibid.*, pp. 16, 24, 25.

[13] *Ibid.*, pp. 18, 29. See also pp. 76, 77.

[14] *Ibid.*, p. 18.

[15] *Ibid.*, pp. 18, 19; *Minutes of the Board of Trustees*, Vol. 1 (May 13, 1826), pp. 120, 121.

[16] *Proceedings of the Fifth Triennial Meeting*, p. 21.

[17] *Ibid.*, p. 42.

[18] Elon Galusha to William Ruggles, September 4, 1826 (University Collection).

[19] *Minutes of the Board of Trustees*, Vol. 1 (May 13 and 15, 1826), pp. 122–128.

[20] *Ibid.*, Vol. 1 (May 30, 1826), p. 130.

[21] *Ibid.*, Vol. 1 (September 18, October 2 and 18, 1826), pp. 153–157.

[22] *The Columbian College in the District of Columbia*, March 14, 1827 (four-page leaflet, University Collection).

[23] Luther Rice to O. B. Brown, August 21, 1826 (University Collection).

[24] *Minutes of the Board of Trustees*, Vol. 1 (February 23 and March 6, 1827), pp. 183–188.

[25] Luther Rice to O. B. Brown, August 21, 1826 (University Collection); *Minutes of First Baptist Church*, November 10, 20, and 24, 1826, quoted in Edward B. Pollard, *Luther Rice, Pioneer in Missions and Education*. Edited and completed by David Gurden Stevens (Philadelphia, 1928), pp. 96–99.

[26] Luther Rice to Iveson L. Brookes, November 23, 1826 (University Collection).

[27] Elmer Louis Kayser, "The 55-Year Professor," *The George Washington Faculty Newsletter*, Vol. 2, No. 1 (Spring, 1965); *Minutes of the Board of Trustees*, Vol. 1 (March 14 and 18, 1827), pp. 195–205.

[28] *Ibid.*, Vol. 1 (December 21, 1826), pp. 172, 173.

[29] *Ibid.*, Vol. 1 (March 26, 1827), p. 214.

[30] *Ibid.*, Vol. 1 (April 21 and 27, 1827), pp. 218, 219.

[31] *Ibid.*, Vol. 1 (April 30, 1827), pp. 219, 220.

[32] Assignment recorded April 12, 1827, in Liber WB17 at Folio 407, Office of the Recorder of Deeds, District of Columbia.

[33] *Minutes of the Board of Trustees*, Vol. 1 (May 9, 1827), p. 223.

[34] Lynd, *op. cit.*, pp. 263–271.

[35] *Minutes of the Board of Trustees*, Vol. 1 (April 11, 1827), p. 216.

[36] Quoted in Lynd, *op. cit.*, p. 291.

[37] *Minutes of the Board of Trustees*, Vol. 1 (December 15, 1827), p. 260.

[38] *Christian Secretary* (Hartford, Connecticut), May 10, 1828. See also pp. 64–65.

[39] *Minutes of the Board of Trustees*, Vol. 1 (May 9, 1828), pp. 273, 274.

[40] *Ibid.*, Vol. 1 (June 30, 1827), pp. 232, 233.

[41] *Ibid.*, Vol. 1 (August 30, 1827), p. 242.

[42] *Ibid.*, Vol. 1 (April 8, 1828), pp. 266, 267.

[43] *Columbian Star*, April 26, 1828.

[44] *Minutes of the Board of Trustees*, Vol. 1 (August 28, 1827), p. 218; *ibid.* (September 24, 1827), pp. 251, 252; *ibid.* (October 20, 1827), p. 254; *ibid.* (June 20, 1828), pp. 276, 277.

[45] *Records of the Columbia Historical Society* (Washington, D.C., 1916), Vol. 19, p. 130.

CHAPTER SIX
Bibliographical Comments

The various stages in the recovery of solvency can be traced in the *Minutes of the Board of Trustees*, the *Proceedings of the Triennial Convention and Annual Reports of the Board of Managers*, and the *Congressional Globe*. Information about gifts for endowment and scholarships during the period will be found in the report of the Attorney General on the financial condition of the University of December 6, 1910 (61st Cong., 3d Sess., H. Doc. 1060). On the transformation of the General Convention into the American Baptist Missionary Union and the transfer of the title to College Hill to the College, see *Baptist Missionary Magazine*, Vol. 26, and the deed in the Office of the Recorder of Deeds. Sessford's survey of the city lots granted by Congress is in the University Collection. For John Quincy Adams' relations with the College in reference to the use of the Smithsonian bequest and his loans to the College secured by mortgage, see Samuel Flagg Bemis, *John Quincy Adams and the Union* (New York, 1956) and George Brown Goode (ed.), *The Smithsonian Institution, 1846–1896: The History of its First Half Century* (Washington, 1897). The indenture and release can be found in the Office of the Recorder of Deeds. Letters with reference to the debt and Adams' receipt in full are in the University Collection.

Notes

[1] *Records of the Columbia Historical Society* (Washington, D.C.), vol. 19, p. 130; *Minutes of the Board of Trustees*, Vol. 1 (April 30, 1827), p. 221; *ibid.*, Vol. 1 (December 15, 1827), p. 260; *ibid.*, Vol. 2 (March 5, 1842), p.68.

[2] Quoted in Edward B. Pollard, *Luther Rice, Pioneer in Missions and Education.* Edited and completed by Daniel Gurden Stevens (Philadelphia, 1928), p. 69.

[3] *Minutes of the Board of Trustees*, Vol. 1 (September 10, 1828), p. 283.

[4] *Proceedings of the Sixth Triennial Meeting of the Baptist General Convention, Held in Philadelphia, 1829* (Boston, 1829), pp. 23–24.

[5] *Proceedings of the Seventh Triennial Meeting of the Baptist General Convention for Missionary Purposes, Held in New York, April, 1832* (Boston, 1832), p. 8.

[6] *Proceedings of the Eighth Triennial Meeting of the Baptist General Convention for Missionary Purposes, Held in Richmond, April, 1835* (Boston, 1835), pp. 7, 61, 62.

[7] *Baptist Missionary Magazine* (Boston), Vol. 18, No. 6 (June, 1838), pp. 124, 127.

[8] *Minutes of the Tenth Triennial Meeting of the Baptist General Convention for Foreign Missions, Together with the Twenty-seventh Annual Report of the Board of Managers, Baltimore, Maryland, April 28-May 4, 1841* (Boston, 1841), p. 8.

[9] *Baptist Missionary Magazine*, Vol. 24, No. 7 (July, 1844), pp. 156, 171, 226.

[10] *Ibid.*, Vol. 26, No. 1 (January, 1846), p. 9.

[11] *Ibid.*, Vol. 26, No. 7 (July, 1846), p. 219.

[12] Deed recorded November 10, 1851, in Liber JAS32 at Folio 170, Office of the Recorder of Deeds, District of Columbia.

[13] *Baptist Missionary Magazine,* Vol. 26, No. 1 (January, 1846), pp. 11, 12; *ibid.,* Vol. 26, No. 7 (July, 1846), pp. 165, 166, 224–228.

[14] See pp. 64, 65, 76, 77.

[15] Deed recorded May 6, 1834, in Liber WB50 at Folio 3, Office of the Recorder of Deeds, District of Columbia.

[16] 61st Cong., 3d Sess., H. Doc. 1060, pp. 5–7; *Minutes of the Board of Trustees,* Vol. 2 (January 23, 1839), p. 40.

[17] *Minutes of the Board of Trustees,* Vol. 2 (August 29, 1845), p. 90; *ibid.,* Vol. 2 (December 24, 1845), p. 93; *ibid.,* Vol. 2 (July 12, 1848), p. 124; *ibid.,* Vol. 2 (March 10, 1852), p. 147; *ibid.,* Vol. 2 (August 5, 1853), p. 224.

[18] *Ibid.,* Vol. 2 (May 3, 1852), p. 159; *ibid.,* Vol. 2 (June 1, 1852), p. 162; *ibid.,* Vol. 2 (May 12, 1853), p. 207.

[19] *Ibid.,* Vol. 2 (June 1, 1852), p. 162; *ibid.,* Vol. 2 (May 12, 1853), p. 207; *Historical Catalogue of the Officers and Graduates of the Columbian University, Washington, D.C., 1821–1891.* Compiled by H. L. Hodgkins (Washington, 1891), pp. 13, 33.

[20] Deed recorded June 6, 1829, in Liber WB25 at Folio 487, Office of the Recorder of Deeds, District of Columbia.

[21] Samuel Flagg Bemis, *John Quincy Adams and the Union* (New York, 1956), pp. 197*n.,* 506–509, 540, 541.

[22] *Minutes of the Board of Trustees,* Vol. 2 (May 25, 1839), pp. 41, 43; *ibid.,* Vol. 2 (October 12, 1840), p. 49; *ibid.,* Vol. 2 (April 23, 1841), p. 54; *ibid.,* Vol. 2 (May 21, 1841), p. 59; letter of J. Q. Adams to George Wood, October 20, 1837 (University Collection); Receipt of J. Q. Adams to Andrew Rothwell, May 5, 1842 (University Collection).

[23] Deed of Release recorded June 4, 1859, in Liber JAS176 at Folio 153, Office of the Recorder of Deeds, District of Columbia.

CHAPTER SEVEN

Bibliographical Comments

In the absence of other sources, the *Minutes of the Board of Trustees,* supplemented by James C. Welling, *Brief Chronicles of the Columbian College from 1821 to 1873 and of the Columbian University from 1873 to 1889,* and local newspapers, have been followed for the account of the administrations of Chapin, Binney, and Bacon. The correspondence in the Arnold case is in the University Collection.

Notes

[1] *Waterville Intelligencer,* quoted in the *Washington Chronicle,* October 18, 1828.

[2] *Washington Chronicle,* October 11 and November 29, 1828.

[3] *Minutes of the Board of Trustees,* Vol. 1 (December 20, 1824), p. 97.

There is a sheet inserted in the *Minutes,* written in Chapin's hand and dated March 7, 1842, recommending the sale of the walls of the West Wing, with a notation that the recommendations were adopted by a 4 to 1 vote.

4 *Minutes of the Board of Trustees,* Vol. 1 (January 10, 1827), p. 179; *ibid.,* Vol. 3 (November 16, 1860), p. 39.

5 *Ibid.,* Vol. 2 (September 27, 1841), pp. 61, 61½.

6 *Ibid.,* Vol. 2 (April 1, 1847), p. 104.

7 *Ibid.,* Vol. 2 (July 26, 1844), p. 82; *ibid.,* Vol. 2 (August 16, 1844), p. 84; *ibid.,* Vol. 2 (March 5, 1847), p. 100.

8 *Ibid.,* Vol. 2 (June 9, 1848), p. 121; *ibid.,* Vol. 2 (September 23, 1848), pp. 125, 126; *ibid.,* Vol. 2 (March 30, 1848), p. 128; *ibid.,* Vol. 2 (July 5, 1851), p. 142; *ibid.,* Vol. 2 (October 2, 1851), p. 144; *ibid.,* Vol. 2 (November 19, 1851), p. 145; *ibid.,* Vol. 2 (August 9, 1853), p. 229; *ibid.,* Vol. 2 (April 11, 1855), p. 280; *ibid.,* Vol. 3 (October 17, 1859), p. 7; *ibid.,* Vol. 2 (February 2, 1855), p. 274.

9 *Ibid.,* Vol. 2 (June 1, 1852), p. 160; *ibid.,* Vol. 2 (October 13, 1852), pp. 181, 186; *ibid.,* Vol. 2 (April 13, 1853), p. 201; *ibid.,* Vol. 2 (June 2, 1853), pp. 210 ff.; *ibid.,* Vol. 2 (July 13, 1853), pp. 220-224; *ibid.,* Vol. 2 (August 9, 1853), p. 228.

10 *Historical Catalogue of the Officers and Graduates of the Columbian University, Washington, D.C., 1821-1891.* Compiled by H. L. Hodgkins (Washington, 1891), pp. 16, 17; *Minutes of the Board of Trustees,* Vol. 2 (May 21, 1841), p. 58; *ibid.,* Vol. 2 (October 13, 1852), p. 181; *ibid.,* Vol. 2 (July 11, 1855), p. 284.

11 *Ibid.,* Vol. 2 (April 22, 1847), pp. 105, 106.

12 *Ibid.,* Vol. 2 (July 11, 1855), p. 288; *ibid.,* Vol. 2 (September 24, 1855), p. 298; *ibid.,* Vol. 3 (June 26, 1860), p. 17; *ibid.,* Vol. 3 (November 16, 1860), p. 39.

13 *Ibid.,* Vol. 2 (July 27, 1855), p. 290.

14 *Ibid.,* Vol. 2 (July 27, 1855), pp. 290 ff.; *ibid.,* Vol. 2 (February 23, 1859), p. 415; *ibid.,* Vol. 2 (April 13, 1859), pp. 425-430.

15 *Ibid.,* Vol. 3 (October 12, 1859), pp. 3, 4.

16 *The (Daily) Globe,* Vol. 2, No. 99 (October 6, 1832), p. 3.

17 *Minutes of the Board of Trustees,* Vol. 2 (October 10, 1855), pp. 304-306.

18 *Washington News,* October 14, 1848, p. 3.

19 *Minutes of the Board of Trustees,* Vol. 2 (March 1, 1847), p. 98.

20 Joel S. Bacon to S. S. Arnold, January 28, 1847; Joel S. Bacon to H. J. Arnold, February, 1847; Joel S. Bacon to Baron Stow, February, 1847; D. N. Sheldon to Joel S. Bacon, April 30, 1847; Joel S. Bacon to D. N. Sheldon, May 8, 1847 (University Collection).

21 *Minutes of the Board of Trustees,* Vol. 2 (September 1, 1858), p. 403.

22 *Ibid.,* Vol. 3 (June 26, 1860), p. 19.

CHAPTER EIGHT

Bibliographical Comments

In addition to what has been cited before, the Samson papers in the University Collection, the gift of the late Henry Whitefield Samson, are important. Also useful is Hodgkins (comp.), *Historical Catalogue.*

Notes

[1] Donald G. Tewksbury, *The Founding of American Colleges and Universities Before the Civil War* (Anchor, 1965), p. 28.

[2] *Washington News*, October 27, 1849, p. 3.

[3] Luther Rice to O. B. Brown, September 1, 1826, Petersburg, Virignia, and October 1, 1827, Richmond, Virginia (University Collection).

[4] *Minutes of the Board of Trustees*, Vol. 2 (August 14, 1841), p. 61½.

[5] *Minutes of the Tenth Triennial Meeting of the Baptist General Convention for Foreign Missions, Together with the Twenty-seventh Annual Report of the Board of Managers, Baltimore, Maryland, April 28-May 4, 1841* (Boston, 1841), p. 21.

[6] *Minutes of the Twenty-ninth Annual Meeting of the Board of Managers of the Baptist General Convention for Foreign Missions, Together with the Twenty-ninth Annual Report, Albany, April 26-27, 1843* (Boston, 1843), pp. 12, 49-51; *Minutes of the Tenth Triennial Meeting of the Baptist General Convention for Foreign Missions*, pp. 79-81.

[7] *Baptist Missionary Magazine* (Boston), Vol. 25, No. 7 (July, 1845), p. 146.

[8] Robert George Torbet, *A History of the Baptists* (Philadelphia, 1950), pp. 299-310; *Baptist Missionary Magazine*, Vol. 25, No. 7, pp. 150-151.

[9] Arthur Charles Cole, *The Irrepressible Conflict 1850-1865* (New York, 1934), p. 47.

[10] The County of Alexandria was retroceded to the State of Virginia in 1846.

[11] *Minutes of the Board of Trustees*, Vol. 2 (June 15, 1852), pp. 64 ff.

[12] *Ibid.*, Vol. 2 (February 23, 1859), p. 417.

[13] Rufus C. Burleson, *Statement with Reference to G. W. Samson*; George C. Samson *et al.*, *Samson Genealogy* (University Collection); William Allen Wilbur, *Temple Baptist Church, Washington, D.C., Through Ninety Years* (Washington, 1932), pp. 6-10.

[14] J. L. M. Curry, "Dr. Fuller and Dr. Samson During the War Between the States," *Religious Herald* (Richmond, Virginia), January 4, 1900.

[15] George Whitefield Samson, *Columbian University Realizing Washington's Mission*, p. 13. (Manuscript, no date, University Collection.)

[16] *Historical Catalogue of the Officers and Graduates of the Columbian University, Washington, D.C., 1821-1891*. Compiled by H. L. Hodgkins (Washington, 1891).

[17] *Ibid.*, pp. 13-14.

[18] 19th Cong., 1st Sess., Sen. Doc. 35, 36, 44, 48 (Gales and Seaton, Washington, 1826).

[19] *The Globe*, Vol. 10, No. 21 (July 8, 1840), p. 1.

[20] *Minutes of the Board of Trustees*, Vol. 2 (June 17, 1847), p. 113.

[21] *The Globe*, new series, Vol. 1 (July 27, 1844), p. 3.

[22] Sister Bernadette Arminger, R.N., Daughter of Charity of St. Vincent de Paul, *The History of the Hospital Work of the Daughters of Charity of Vincent de Paul in the Eastern Province of the United States, 1832-1860* (typescript, 1949); Robert Williams Prichard, M.D., *Historical Sketch of the Medical School, 1825-1947, The George Washington University* (Washington, 1947).

[23] Wilhelmus Bogart Bryan, *A History of the National Capital* (New York, 1916), Vol. 2, pp. 337-341; *Washington News*, November 13, 1853, p. 2; *ibid.*, January 21, 1854, p. 2; *The George Washington University Medical Alumni Directory 1826-1965* (Washington, 1965), p. vi.

CHAPTER NINE

Bibliographical Comments

For the War period (1861–1865), the Samson papers and the *Minutes of the Board of Trustees* have been followed. For Carver and Columbian College General Hospitals see, in addition, John Wells Bulkley, *The War Hospitals*, in the Washingtoniana Collection of the Public Library; Walt Whitman, *The Wound Dresser*, ed. by Richard M. Bucke (New York, 1949), and the records in the National Archives. The University Collection includes a large number of originals and copies of pictures of College Hill while it was being used for military purposes. A detailed account of conditions in Columbian College Hospital is given in Anna L. Boyden, *Echoes from Hospital and White House, A Record of Mrs. Rebecca R. Pomroy's Experiences in War-Times* (Boston, 1884).

Notes

1 "The Sessford Annals," *Records of the Columbia Historical Society, Washington, D.C.* (Washington, 1908), Vol. 11, pp. 272 ff.

2 Albert W. Atwood, ed., *Growing with Washington* (Washington, 1948), p. 36.

3 Wilhelmus Bogart Bryan, *A History of the National Capital* (New York, 1916), Vol. 2, pp. 451-462.

4 John Wells Bulkley, *The War Hospitals*, pp. 148-149 (Washingtoniana Collection, District of Columbia Public Library).

5 William D. Haley to Quartermaster General, U.S.A., June 10, 1861, with endorsements (National Archives).

6 *Minutes of the Board of Trustees*, Vol. 3 (June 15, 1861), pp. 51, 53; *ibid.*, Vol. 3 (October 26, 1862), p. 89.

7 George Whitefield Samson to Quartermaster General, U.S.A., August 12, 1861 (National Archives).

8 Bulkley, *op. cit.*, pp. 147, 148.

9 Walt Whitman, *The Wound Dresser*. Richard M. Bucke, ed. (New York, 1949), pp. xv, 31, 35, 36, 39, 182, 191.

10 George Whitefield Samson, "Religious Convictions of American Statesmen; Illustrated in President Lincoln," *Christian Inquirer*, April 13, 1893.

11 Theodore Calvin Pease and James C. Randall, eds., *The Diary of Orville Hickman Browning* (Springfield, Ill., State Historical Library, 1925), Vol. 50, 1850-1864, p. 546; Anna L. Boyden, *Echoes from Hospital and White House, A Record of Mrs. Rebecca R. Pomroy's Experience in War-Times* (Boston, 1884), pp. 93-98.

Mrs. Rebecca R. Pomroy, of Chelsea, Massachusetts, served for the greater part of the war as a nurse in Columbian College Hospital. Her activities covered a wide range. With direct personal access to Miss Dorothea Dix, the Superintendent of Women Nurses, and to President Lincoln, she was able to wield wide influence at the hospital and to get action on recommendations which otherwise would have been bogged down in official red tape. A record of her experiences has been preserved by Anna L. Boyden in the above title. From a highly personal point of view, this is probably the most circumstantial account of conditions at the hospital.

[12] George Whitefield Samson to C. A. Finley, Surgeon General, U.S.A., October 28, 1861.

[13] Captain C. J. H. Crowell to Brevet Major General D. H. Rucker, September 17, 1865.

[14] General Order No. 10, December 5, 1861, W. W. H. Davis, Commanding 1st Brigade, Casey's Division.

[15] *Minutes of the Board of Trustees,* Vol. 3 (April 24, 1861), pp. 47, 49; *ibid.,* Vol. 3 (June 24, 1862), p. 72; *ibid.,* Vol. 3 (June 23, 1863), pp. 97 ff.; *ibid.,* Vol. 3 (June 28, 1864), p. 116; *ibid.,* Vol. 3 (June 27, 1865), p. 142.

[16] *Ibid.,* Vol. 3 (June 24, 1862), p. 74.

[17] *Ibid.,* Vol. 3 (June 23, 1863), pp. 97-98; Dean's Book, *Minutes of the Meetings of the Medical Professors of the Columbian College* (University Archives); J. M. Toner, M.D., *Anniversary Oration Delivered Before the Medical Society of the District of Columbia, September 26, 1866* (Washington, Cunningham and McIntosh), pp. 47, 48.

[18] *Minutes of the Board of Trustees,* Vol. 3 (July 9, 1862), p. 79; *ibid.,* Vol. 3 (August 15, 1862), p. 87.

[19] *Ibid.,* Vol. 3 (June 28, 1864), p. 116; *ibid.,* Vol. 3 (June 27, 1865), p. 142.

[20] *Ibid.,* Vol. 3 (July 12, 1865), p. 150.

[21] *Historical Catalogue of the Officers and Graduates of the Columbian University, Washington, D.C., 1821-1891.* Compiled by H. L. Hodgkins (Washington, 1891), p. 107.

[22] Robert Williams Prichard, *Historical Sketch of the Medical School, 1825-1947, The George Washington University* (Washington, 1947), p. 7.

[23] John Frederick May, "The Mark of the Scalpel," *Records of the Columbia Historical Society, Washington, D.C.* (Washington, 1910), Vol. 13, pp. 51 ff.

CHAPTER TEN

Bibliographical Comments

The Minutes of the Board of Trustees and the Samson papers are the major sources for the concluding years of the administration of the fifth president.

Notes

[1] Wilhelmus Bogart Bryan, *A History of the National Capital* (New York, 1916), Vol. 2, pp. 472, 473, 489-491.

[2] *Minutes of the Board of Trustees,* Vol. 3 (May 10, 1865), p. 142.

[3] *Ibid.,* Vol. 3 (April 23, 1867), pp. 188 ff.; *ibid.,* Vol. 3 (June 25, 1867), pp. 191, 192.

[4] *Ibid.,* Vol. 3 (August 2, 1865), p. 158; *ibid.,* Vol. 3 (April 11, 1866), pp. 161, 162, 169; *ibid.,* Vol. 3 (June 25, 1867), pp. 191-192.

[5] *Ibid.,* Vol. 3 (July 27, 1865), p. 146.

[6] *Ibid.,* Vol. 3 (June 25, 1867), pp. 191, 192; *ibid.,* Vol. 3 (February 12, 1869), p. 236.

[7] *Ibid.,* Vol. 3 (April 23, 1865), p. 136.

[8] *Ibid.,* Vol. 3 (June 25, 1867), p. 194.

9 *Ibid.*, Vol. 3 (May 15, 1868), pp. 218, 219; *ibid.*, Vol. 3 (July 8, 1868), p. 232; *ibid.*, Vol. 3 (November 30, 1869), p. 256.

10 *In Memoriam* (Amos Kendall), Washington, 1869; Powrie Vaux Doctor, "Amos Kendall, Nineteenth Century Humanitarian," *Gallaudet College Bulletin*, Vol. 7, No. 1 (October, 1957); *Minutes of the Board of Trustees*, Vol. 3 (November 12, 1869), p. 249.

11 Elmer Louis Kayser, "The 55-Year Professor," *The George Washington University Faculty Newsletter*, Vol. 2, No. 1 (Spring, 1965).

12 *Historical Catalogue of the Officers and Graduates of the Columbian University*, *Washington, D.C., 1821-1891*. Compiled by H. L. Hodgkins (Washington, 1891), pp. 42-44.

13 Festus P. Summers, ed., *A Borderland Confederate* (Pittsburgh, 1962), pp. 1-6, 106-118.

14 George Crossette, *Founders of the Cosmos Club of Washington, 1878* (Washington, 1966), pp. 115-117.

15 *Minutes of the Board of Trustees*, Vol. 3 (April 13, 1870), pp. 265-266; *ibid.*, Vol. 3 (May 24, 1870), p. 270; *ibid.*, Vol. 3 (May 31, 1870), pp. 271-273; *ibid.*, Vol. 3 (June 27, 1870), pp. 262-265; *ibid.*, Vol. 3 (June 26, 1870), pp. 291-292; *ibid.*, Vol. 3 (July 12, 1871), p. 294; *ibid.*, Vol. 3 (July 22, 1871), p. 297; George Whitefield Samson, *Final Report as President of Columbian College* (Washington, D.C., June, 1871).

16 *Stat. at Large 50*, Vol. 6, Secs. 5, 6, pp. 255-258.

CHAPTER ELEVEN
Bibliographical Comments

For the Welling period the *Minutes of the Board of Trustees* must be supplemented by the pamphlets brought out at irregular intervals for the information of the Board. Some of these pamphlets lack titles, many of them lack dates. Some are drafts of resolutions recommended by the president and submitted for study before meetings of the Board, others are really reports or detailed recommendations. The texts of legislative enactments modifying the original Charter and the text of the Charter itself are given conveniently in 61st Cong., 3d Sess., H. Doc. 1060. Welling's *Brief Chronicles of the Columbian College from 1821 to 1873 and of the Columbian University from 1873 to 1889* and his *The Columbian University: Notes on Its Relations to the City of Washington Considered as the Seat of a National Baptist University* (Washington, 1889) are very valuable. Of the Welling pamphlets referred to above, the most important are *Plan of Columbian University (April 25, 1873)*; recommendations for graduate study, published without title, March 14, 1893; *The Columbian University, Extract from the Minutes of a Meeting of the Corporation, Held June 18, 1881*, all in the University Collection. For details on the administration of endowment and prize funds, see H. Doc. 1060, referred to above. The public occasions of the institution were fully reported in the Washington press of the period.

Notes

[1] *Laws of the District of Columbia, 1871–1872,* Pt. 2, pp. 21, 22; *Acts of the Legislative Assembly of the District of Columbia,* 1st Sess., Chap. 18.

[2] *Minutes of the Board of Trustees,* Vol. 3 (June 24, 1873), p. 366.

[3] *Ibid.,* Vol. 3 (July 22, 1871), p. 298; *ibid.,* Vol. 3 (August 11, 1871), p. 306; *ibid.,* Vol. 3 (October 11, 1871), pp. 314 ff.

[4] *Ibid.,* Vol. 3 (September 25, 1871), pp. 311-312.

[5] *Ibid.,* Vol. 3 (January 10, 1872), p. 317.

[6] *Ibid.,* Vol. 3 (March 5, 1872), p. 320; *ibid.,* Vol. 3 (April 10, 1872), pp. 321-322; *ibid.,* Vol. 3 (June 25, 1872), p. 336.

[7] *Ibid.,* Vol. 3 (August 11, 1871), pp. 308-309; *ibid.,* Vol. 3 (April 10, 1872), p. 323.

[8] *Ibid.,* Vol. 3 (September 18, 1872), pp. 341-348.

[9] Stat. 50, Vol. 17, p. 629, 42d Cong., 3d Sess., Chap. 328.

[10] James C. Welling, *Brief Chronicles of the Columbian College from 1821 to 1873 and of the Columbian University from 1873 to 1889* (Washington, 1889), p. 22.

[11] 61st Cong., 3d Sess., H. Doc. 1060, December 7, 1910.

[12] *Minutes of the Board of Trustees,* Vol. 3 (June 24, 1873), p. 361.

[13] *Ibid.,* Vol. 3 (December 17, 1873), p. 384.

[14] Welling, *op. cit.,* p. 23; Charles H. Stockton, "Historical Sketch of George Washington University," *Records of the Columbia Historical Society, Washington, D.C.* (Washington, D.C., 1908), Vol. 19, pp. 138-139.

[15] *Plan of Columbian University,* April 25, 1873 (4 pp., University Collection).

[16] *Minutes of the Board of Trustees,* Vol. 3 (April 10, 1872), p. 322.

[17] The report of the committee appears in a pamphlet of 9 pages printed by order of the Corporation for purposes of information, revision, and criticism, and headed *The Columbian University.* Extract from *Minutes of a Meeting of the Corporation,* held June 18, 1881 (University Collection).

[18] *Address by John W. Powell, LL.D., Delivered on the Inauguration of the Corcoran School of Science and Arts in the Columbian University, Washington, D.C., October 1, 1884* (Washington, 1884), 20 pp.

[19] *Minutes of the Board of Trustees,* Vol. 4 (June 15, 1885), pp. 122-125; *ibid.,* Vol. 4 (December 15, 1886), pp. 186-188; *ibid.,* Vol. 4 (June 13, 1887), pp. 199, 200.

[20] *Ibid.,* Vol. 4 (March 14, 1888), p. 225.

[21] *Ibid.,* Vol. 4 (June 17, 1889), p. 269; *ibid.,* Vol. 4 (October 22, 1890), p. 323; *ibid.,* Vol. 4 (September 28, 1892), pp. 407-410.

[22] *Ibid.,* Vol. 4 (June 6, 1888), pp. 227, 228; *ibid.,* Vol. 4 (December 21, 1892), pp 413-419.

[23] *Ibid.,* Vol. 4 (September 28, 1892), pp. 401, 404; *ibid.,* Vol. 4 (December 21 1892), p. 413.

[24] Recommendations for graduate study were published in a pamphlet, without title, for the information of the Board of Trustees, dated March 14, 1893 (University Collection).

[25] *Minutes of the Board of Trustees,* Vol. 4 (June 19, 1883), pp. 433, 455; *ibid.,* Vol. 4 (October 24, 1893), p. 517.

[26] *Ibid.,* Vol. 3 (June 29, 1875), p. 431.

[27] *Ibid.,* Vol. 3 (June 20, 1877), pp. 497-498.

[28] *Ibid.,* Vol. 3 (September 18, 1878), p. 548.

[29] *Ibid.,* Vol. 3 (December 15, 1880), pp. 584-587; *ibid.,* Vol. 3 (December 17, 1880), p. 589.

30 *Ibid.*, Vol. 3 (March 16, 1881), p. 589; *ibid.*, Vol. 3 (June 1, 1881), pp. 592-593.

31 *Ibid.*, Vol. 3 (June 8, 1881), pp. 594-596.

32 *Ibid.*, Vol. 3 (June 18, 1881), pp. 609-615.

33 *Ibid.*, Vol. 3 (November 22, 1881), pp. 615-618.

34 *Ibid.*, Vol. 3 (November 22, 1881), pp. 615-618; *ibid.*, Vol. 3 (January 11, 1882), pp. 621, 622; *ibid.*, Vol. 3 (March 11, 1882), pp. 621-622; *ibid.*, Vol. 3 (April 12, 1882), pp. 624-628.

35 *Ibid.*, Vol. 4 (June 14, 1882), pp. 1-3.

36 *Ibid.*, Vol. 4 (September 20, 1882), pp. 16, 17.

37 *Ibid.*, Vol. 4 (December 20, 1882), p. 18.

38 *Ibid.*, Vol. 4 (December 20, 1882), p. 22; *ibid.*, Vol. 4 (April 3, 1883), p. 25.

39 *Ibid.*, Vol. 4 (June 6, 1883), pp. 29, 30.

40 *Ibid.*, Vol. 4 (April 21, 1883), p. 26.

41 *Ibid.*, Vol. 4 (June 6, 1883), p. 30; *ibid.*, Vol. 4 (June 18, 1883), p. 36.

42 *Ibid.*, Vol. 4 (September 19, 1883), p. 67.

43 *Ibid.*, Vol. 4 (June 18, 1883), p. 37.

44 *Ibid.*, Vol. 4 (June 6, 1883), pp. 31, 32.

45 *Ibid.*, Vol. 4 (September 19, 1883), p. 61.

46 *Catalogue of the Officers and Students of the Columbian University, for the Academic Year 1883-1884* (Washington, 1884), p. 2.

47 *Minutes of the Board of Trustees*, Vol. 4 (June 15, 1885), p. 122.

48 *Ibid.*, Vol. 4 (April 25, 1884), p. 74; *ibid.*, Vol. 4 (September 17, 1884), p. 99.

49 *Ibid.*, Vol. 4 (June 16, 1884), pp. 80, 81; *ibid.*, Vol. 4 (December 17, 1884), pp. 106-110.

50 *Ibid.*, Vol. 4 (June 6, 1888), p. 227.

51 Stockton, *op. cit.*, p. 119; *Minutes of the Board of Trustees*, Vol. 4 (June 16, 1890), pp. 300, 301.

52 *Letter from the Attorney General Transmitting the Final Reports on the Financial Condition of The George Washington University*, 61st Cong., 3d Sess., H. Doc. 1060.

53 *Minutes of the Board of Trustees*, Vol. 4 (June 18, 1888), p. 231; William Wilson Corcoran, *A Grandfather's Legacy, Containing a Sketch of His Life, and Obituary Notices of Some Members of His Family, Together with Letters from His Friends* (Washington, 1879).

The work of art referred to was Henry Bacon's painting, "The Boston Boys."

54 *Minutes of the Board of Trustees*, Vol. 4 (June 18, 1888), p. 255.

55 *Ibid.*, Vol. 4 (March 20, 1889), p. 264; *ibid.*, Vol. 4 (June 5, 1889), p. 266; *ibid.*, Vol. 4 (June 17, 1889), p. 269; *ibid.*, Vol. 4 (October 9, 1889), pp. 290-292; *ibid.*, Vol. 4 (November 19, 1889), pp. 293-295.

56 *Ibid.*, Vol. 4 (January 25, 1894), pp. 530-538.

57 *Ibid.*, Vol. 4 (January 25, 1894), p. 523; *ibid.*, Vol. 4 (March 14, 1894), p. 541; *ibid.*, Vol. 4 (June 13, 1894), p. 552.

58 *Dictionary of American Biography* (New York, 1936), Vol. 19, pp. 633-634; *1871-1894 President James C. Welling, LL.D., Memorial Service Under the Joint Auspices of the Columbian University and the Societies and Organizations of Which He was a Member* (Washington, 1895); George Crossette, *Founders of the Cosmos Club of Washington, 1878* (Washington, 1966), pp. 168-170.

CHAPTER TWELVE
Bibliographical Comments

For the brief Whitman administration, the *Minutes of the Board of Trustees* is the only source available. For the Needham period, the material is quite ample. The proceedings of the Board are recorded with great fullness, many documents being quoted verbatim. The various numbers of *The George Washington University Bulletin* include much information, in addition to the annual educational offerings and lists of students. The presidential files, deposited in the Archives, begin with the Needham period—thanks, no doubt, to the use of the typewriter which had become general by that time. Important for the change of name and the affiliation with the George Washington Memorial Association is the correspondence with Mrs. Archibald Hopkins and Mrs. Susan Whitney Dimock; for the nation-wide campaign for funds for a new site, the correspondence with Mitchell Carroll and Richard Harlan. Recalling that the Attorney General's investigation was prompted by incidents that occurred in the Needham administration, we find in H. Doc. 1060, referred to frequently before, along with *A Report of an Investigation of the Financial and Educational Affairs of The George Washington University*, printed for the use of the House Committee of the District of Columbia (61st Cong., 2d Sess., 1910), a very detailed picture in quantitative terms of the University's funds, property, equipment, personnel, educational organization, and financial policies, fully documented. The attempt to have George Washington University designated as an institution to receive Morrill Act funds, which, in a way, prompted the Attorney General's investigation, is fairly well covered in the Needham correspondence.

Notes

[1] *Minutes of the Board of Trustees,* Vol. 5 (June 17, 1895), p. 43; Charles H. Stockton, "Historical Sketch of George Washington University," *Records of the Columbia Historical Society* (Washington, D.C., 1916), Vol. 19, p. 135.

[2] *Minutes of the Board of Trustees,* Vol. 5 (June 18, 1894), p. 19; *ibid.,* Vol. 5 (June 15, 1896), p. 107.

[3] *Ibid.,* Vol. 5 (December 4, 1895), p. 80; *ibid.,* Vol. 5 (March 11, 1896), p. 87.

[4] *Ibid.,* Vol. 5 (July 1, 1895), p. 74; *ibid.,* Vol. 5 (February 17, 1896), p. 81.

[5] *Ibid.,* Vol. 5 (April 29, 1897), p. 58.

[6] *Ibid.,* Vol. 5 (June 1, 1898), pp. 291 ff.; *ibid.,* Vol. 5 (July 16, 1898), p. 329.

[7] *Ibid.,* Vol. 5 (October 12, 1898), p. 331.

[8] *Ibid.,* Vol. 5 (May 31, 1899), pp. 364-365.

[9] *Ibid.,* Vol. 5 (May 31, 1899), p. 359.

[10] *Ibid.,* Vol. 5 (June 15, 1896), p. 138; *ibid.,* Vol. 5 (June 1, 1898), p. 284.

[11] *Ibid.,* Vol. 5 (June 1, 1898), p. 288; *ibid.,* Vol. 5 (May 31, 1899), p. 364.

[12] *Ibid.,* Vol. 5 (April 29, 1897), p. 159.

[13] *Ibid.,* Vol. 5 (April 13, 1898), pp. 266-269.

14 *Ibid.*, Vol. 5 (January 11, 1899), p. 341.

15 *Ibid.*, Vol. 5 (November 29, 1897), pp. 245-249; *ibid.*, Vol. 5 (June 1, 1898), pp. 279-280.

16 *Ibid.*, Vol. 5 (November 29, 1897), p. 244; *ibid.*, Vol. 5 (January 9, 1901), p. 478; *ibid.*, Vol. 5 (March 4 and March 8, 1902), pp. 533-535.

17 *Ibid.*, Vol. 5 (December 23, 1896), p. 142.

18 *Ibid.*, Vol. 5 (June 15, 1896), p. 104.

19 61st Cong., 3d Sess., H. Doc. 1060, pp. 72, 73.

20 *Minutes of the Board of Trustees*, Vol. 5 (April 6, 1898), pp. 261-263.

21 *Ibid.*, Vol. 5 (May 31, 1899), p. 373.

22 *Ibid.*, Vol. 5 (January 18, 1900), p. 449; *ibid.*, Vol. 5 (March 10, 1900), p. 450.

23 *Ibid.*, Vol. 5 (January 10, 1900), pp. 442, 443; *ibid.*, Vol. 5 (January 18, 1900), pp. 446-448.

24 *Ibid.*, Vol. 5 (March 12, 1897), p. 144; *ibid.*, Vol. 5 (April 14, 1897), pp. 146, 147; *Conversations with Charles Wendell Holmes*, 61st Cong., 3d Sess., H. Doc. 1060, p. 47.

25 *Minutes of the Board of Trustees*, Vol. 5 (June 1, 1898), pp. 275-276.

26 *Ibid.*, Vol. 5 (May 31, 1899), p. 351.

27 "Reverend George Whitefield Samson, D.D.," *The Evangelist*, September 24, 1896, p. 5.

28 Stockton, *op. cit.*, pp. 138-139; *Minutes of the Board of Trustees*, Vol. 5 (May 30, 1900), p. 470; *ibid.*, Vol. 5 (January 9, 1901), p. 474.

29 *Ibid.*, Vol. 5 (June 18, 1894), p. 17.

30 George Crossette, *Founders of the Cosmos Club of Washington, 1878* (Washington, 1966), pp. 115-117.

31 *Ibid.*, pp. 165-167.

32 *Minutes of the Board of Trustees*, Vol. 6 (June 18, 1902), p. 20.

33 *Ibid.*, Vol. 5 (March 10, 1900), p. 452.

34 *Ibid.*, Vol. 6 (October 13, 1902), pp. 25-29.

35 *Ibid.*, Vol. 6 (February 20, 1904), p. 168.

36 *Ibid.*, Vol. 6 (October 13, 1902), pp. 30-32; *ibid.*, Vol. 6 (January 14, 1903), p. 95; *ibid.*, Vol. 6 (May 26, 1903), p. 105.

37 *Ibid.*, Vol. 6 (January 14, 1903), pp. 84-86.

38 *The George Washington University Bulletin*, Vol. 8, No. 4 (December, 1909), p. 13.

39 *Minutes of the Board of Trustees*, Vol. 6 (October 14, 1903), pp. 123-137.

40 *Ibid.*, Vol. 6 (October 29, 1903), pp. 143-144.

41 Ethel M. B. Morganston, "Davy Burnes, His Ancestors and Their Descendants," *Records of the Columbia Historical Society, Washington, D.C., 1948-1950* (Washington, 1952), Vol. 50, pp. 116-119.

42 *Minutes of the Board of Trustees*, Vol. 6 (February 20, 1904), p. 183.

43 *Ibid.*, Vol. 6 (October 29, 1903), p. 140.

44 *Ibid.*, Vol. 6 (May 2, 1904), p. 188.

45 David L. Madsen, *The National University, Enduring Dream of the U.S.A.* (Detroit, 1966), pp. 67, 68, 107-110; *Minutes of the Board of Trustees*, Vol. 6 (May 26, 1903), p. 112; *ibid.*, Vol. 6 (May 2, 1904), p. 186.

46 *Ibid.*, Vol. 6 (February 20, 1904), pp. 183, 184.

47 *Ibid.*, Vol. 6 (May 2, 1904), pp. 188-191; *ibid.*, Vol. 6 (June 8, 1904), p. 199.

48 Elmer Louis Kayser, *The George Washington University 1821-1966* (Washington, 1966), pp. 18, 19.

[49] *Minutes of the Board of Trustees*, Vol. 6 (November 16, 1904), pp. 204-229.

[50] *Ibid.*, Vol. 6 (November 16, 1904), p. 230.

[51] *The George Washington University Bulletin*, Convocation Number, Vol. 4, No. 1 (Part 1, March, 1905).

[52] *Stat. at Large*, Vol. 33, Part 1, 58th Cong., 3d Sess., Chap. 1467, pp. 1036, 1037, approved March 3, 1905.

[53] *Minutes of the Board of Trustees*, Vol. 6 (May 2, 1905), pp. 250-254.

[54] *Ibid.*, Vol. 6 (November 22, 1905), pp. 268-271.

[55] *Ibid.*, Vol. 6 (May 2, 1905), p. 250; *ibid.*, Vol. 6 (May 23, 1905), p. 260.

[56] *The George Washington University Bulletin*, Alumni Number, Vol. 4, No. 2 (June, 1905), p. 6.

[57] "Carnegie Foundation for the Advancement of Teaching, a Notable Year," reprinted from the 1965-1966 *Annual Report*, pp. 3, 4.

[58] *Minutes of the Board of Trustees*, Vol. 6 (May 26, 1906), p. 286.

[59] *Ibid.*, Vol. 6 (November 14, 1906), pp. 297, 298.

[60] *Ibid.*, Vol. 6 (November 14, 1906), p. 295.

[61] *Ibid.*, Vol. 6 (November 14, 1906), pp. 296-299.

[62] *Ibid.*, Vol. 6 (November 14, 1906), p. 301.

[63] *Ibid.*, Vol. 6 (November 14, 1906), p. 298; *ibid.*, Vol. 6 (January 16, 1907), p. 305; *ibid.*, Vol. 6 (February 16, 1907), pp. 312-313.

[64] *Columbia Heights and The George Washington University of Washington D.C.*, The Columbia Heights Citizens' Association, 1907.

[65] *Minutes of the Board of Trustees*, Vol. 6 (April 29, 1907), p. 315; *ibid.*, Vol. 6 (January 8, 1908), p. 362.

[66] *Ibid.*, Vol. 6 (June 2, 1906), p. 292; *ibid.*, Vol. 6 (November 14, 1906), p. 300.

[67] *Ibid.*, Vol. 6 (January 16, 1907), p. 306; *ibid.*, Vol. 6 (February 16, 1907), p. 313; *ibid.*, Vol. 6 (May 27, 1907), p. 319.

[68] *Ibid.*, Vol. 6 (February 16, 1907), p. 310; *ibid.*, Vol. 6 (May 27, 1907), p. 319.

[69] *Ibid.*, Vol. 6 (January 8, 1908), pp. 359, 361.

[70] *The George Washington University Bulletin*, Alumni Number, Vol. 4, No. 2 (June, 1905), pp. 19-20; *ibid.*, Vol. 8, No. 4 (December, 1909), pp. 8, 11; *Minutes of the Board of Trustees*, Vol. 6 (May 7, 1908), pp. 284-285.

[71] *The George Washington University Bulletin*, Vol. 8, No. 4 (December, 1909), pp. 9-12; *ibid.*, Vol. 4, No. 2 (June 1905), pp. 21-24.

[72] *Minutes of the Board of Trustees*, Vol. 6 (March 17, 1908), p. 372.

[73] *Ibid.*, Vol. 6 (March 17, 1908), pp. 369-372; *ibid.*, Vol. 6 (May 7, 1908), pp. 375-383; *ibid.*, Vol. 6 (October 14, 1908), p. 413.

[74] *Ibid.*, Vol. 6 (November 10, 1908), pp. 421-422; *ibid.*, Vol. 6 (February 19, 1909), p. 437.

[75] *Ibid.*, Vol. 6 (March 8, 1909), pp. 440-445; *ibid.*, Vol. 6 (April 5, 1909), p. 454; *ibid.*, Vol. 6 (April 10, 1909), pp. 457-458.

[76] *Ibid.*, Vol. 6 (April 17, 1909), pp. 459-461.

[77] *Ibid.*, Vol. 6 (April 23, 1909), pp. 462-465; *ibid.*, Vol. 6 (May 6, 1909), pp. 470 ff.

[78] *Ibid.*, Vol. 6 (June 4, 1909), pp. 483-485.

[79] *Ibid.*, Vol. 6 (June 5, 1909), pp. 488-490.

[80] *Ibid.*, Vol. 6 (June 5, 1909), pp. 490, 492, 497; *ibid.*, Vol. 6 (June 9, 1909), p. 500.

[81] *Ibid.*, Vol. 6 (October 13, 1909), pp. 510-513; *The George Washington University Bulletin*, Vol. 8, No. 4 (December, 1909), pp. 7, 8.

[82] *Ibid.*, pp. 8, 11, 12; *Minutes of the Board of Trustees*, Vol. 6 (January 12, 1910), p. 533.

83 *Ibid.,* Vol. 6 (March 14, 1910), pp. 544-558.

84 *Ibid.,* Vol. 6 (April 27, 1910), pp. 574-575; *ibid.,* Vol. 6 (May 2, 1910), p. 577; *Stat. at Large,* Vol. 6, Chap. 10, Sec. 10, pp. 255-258.

85 *Report of an Investigation of the Financial and Educational Affairs of The George Washington University,* Transmitted to the House of Representatives by the Attorney General, June 2, 1910, and referred to the Committee on the District of Columbia (Washington, 1910).

86 61st Cong., 3d Sess., H. Doc. 1060.

87 *Ibid.,* pp. 86-87.

88 *Ibid.,* p. 87.

89 *Ibid.,* pp. 169-170.

90 *Minutes of the Board of Trustees,* Vol. 6 (May 26, 1910), p. 590; *ibid.,* Vol. 7 (June 10, 1910), p. 19; *ibid.,* Vol. 7 (June 15, 1910), pp. 25-28; *ibid.,* Vol. 7 (June 20, 1910), p. 33; *ibid.,* Vol. 7 (June 27, 1910), p. 36; *ibid.,* Vol. 7 (July 1, 1910), p. 40.

CHAPTER THIRTEEN

Bibliographical Comments

For the seventeen-year period following the misfortunes of 1910, the principal sources of information are the *Minutes of the Board of Trustees;* the various issues of the *University Bulletin;* the student publications, the *Hatchet* and *The Cherry Tree;* the presidential correspondence in the Archives; and much ephemeral material, most of it of student origin.

Notes

1 *Minutes of the Board of Trustees,* Vol. 7 (January 11, 1911), pp. 84-90.

2 *Ibid.,* Vol. 7 (December 22, 1910), p. 74.

3 *Ibid.,* Vol. 7 (October 24, 1910), p. 62.

4 *Ibid.,* Vol. 7 (June 1, 1911), p. 118; *ibid.,* Vol. 7 (June 16, 1911), p. 125; *ibid.,* Vol. 7 (October 11, 1911), pp. 128, 129; *ibid.,* Vol. 7 (October 8, 1913), p. 245.

5 *Ibid.,* Vol. 7 (October 11, 1911), p. 130.

6 *Ibid.,* Vol. 7 (January 10, 1912), p. 147; *ibid.,* Vol. 7 (May 31, 1911), p. 118; *ibid.,* Vol. 7 (February 13, 1912), pp. 152, 153.

7 Jessie Fant Evans, *Hamburg, the Colonial Town That Became the Seat of The George Washington University* (Washington, 1935), pp. 1-5.

8 Wilhelmus Bogart Bryan, *A History of the National Capital* (New York, 1916), Vol. 1, pp. 468-469; *ibid.,* Vol. 2, pp. 286-289.

9 For details on the neighborhood, see Evans, *op. cit.*
This reconstruction of Square 102 is from memory, aided by the city directories of the time.

10 Elmer Louis Kayser, "2023 G Street," *The George Washington Alumni Review,* Summer, 1962, pp. 19-24; Elmer Louis Kayser, "Professors Everybody Knew," *GW: The George Washington University Magazine,* Spring, 1967, pp. 30-34.

[11] *Minutes of the Board of Trustees*, Vol. 7 (January 8, 1913), p. 209.

[12] *Ibid.*, Vol. 7 (June 3, 1914), p. 278.

[13] *Ibid.*, Vol. 7 (October 10, 1917), p. 449.

[14] *Ibid.*, Vol. 7 (February 19, 1917), p. 425; *ibid.*, Vol. 7 (January 9, 1918), p. 463.

[15] *Ibid.*, Vol. 7 (October 13, 1915), p. 346; *ibid.*, Vol. 7 (February 18, 1916), p. 354.

[16] *Ibid.*, Vol. 7 (April 30, 1918), p. 483.

[17] *Ibid.*, Vol. 7 (May 5, 1914), pp. 272-276; *ibid.*, Vol. 7 (June 3, 1914), p. 278.

[18] *Ibid.*, Vol. 7 (February 18, 1916), pp. 356, 357.

[19] *Ibid.*, Vol. 7 (October 11, 1916), p. 393.

[20] The members of the first Student Council were: Chairman, Rhesa M. Norris (Law); Secretary-Treasurer, Elmer L. Kayser (T.C.); Martha McGrew (C.C.); Theodosia D. Seibold (C.C.); John S. Bixler (C.C.); Z. Alvin Briggs (Eng.); Bertram Groesbeck (Med.); John H. Lyons (Med.); M. Q. Cannon (Dent.); Leon Frost (Dent.); William H. Stayton, Jr. (Law); P. M. Johnson (Phar.); James Patterson (Vet.).

[21] Elson L. Whitney, *The American Peace Society: A Centennial History* (Washington, 1929), pp. 17-23.

[22] *Minutes of the Board of Trustees*, Vol. 7 (October 14, 1914), p. 305.

[23] *Ibid.*, Vol. 7 (June 2, 1915), p. 323.

[24] *Ibid.*, Vol. 7 (June 2, 1915), p. 328.

[25] *The District of Columbia Coast Artillery, National Guard 1915-1919* (The Collegiate Press, Menasha, Wisconsin, 1921), pp. 5-38.

[26] *Minutes of the Board of Trustees*, Vol. 7 (May 29, 1918), pp. 500-508.

[27] *Ibid.*, Vol. 7 (December 4, 1917), p. 460; *Ibid.*, Vol. 7 (January 9, 1918), p. 461; *ibid.*, Vol. 7 (April 5, 1918), p. 476; *ibid.*, Vol. 7 (April 30, 1918), p. 479; *ibid.*, Vol. 7 (May 29, 1918), p. 494.

[28] For a complete roster of officers and men, see *The George Washington University Bulletin*, Vol. 18, No. 2 (June, 1919), pp. 306-318.

[29] Elmer Louis Kayser, "World War I at the University," *GW: The George Washington University Magazine*, Fall, 1964, pp. 28-31.

[30] *Minutes of the Board of Trustees*, Vol. 7 (October 9, 1918), p. 511; *ibid.*, Vol. 7 (February 15, 1919), p. 529.

[31] *Ibid.*, Vol. 7 (February 15, 1919), p. 532; *ibid.*, Vol. 8 (January 20, 1920), p. 2.

[32] *Ibid.*, Vol. 8 (March 19, 1920), p. 11; *ibid.*, Vol. 8 (April 3, 1920), pp. 18-20.

[33] *Ibid.*, Vol. 8 (April 17, 1920), p. 25; *ibid.*, Vol. 8 (May 26, 1920), p. 33; *ibid.*, Vol. 8 (November 10, 1920), p. 62; *ibid.*, Vol. 8 (January 12, 1921), pp. 66, 69, 70.

[34] *Ibid.*, Vol. 8 (April 17, 1920), p. 25.

[35] *Ibid.*, Vol. 8 (February 12, 1921), p. 74; *ibid.*, Vol. 8 (October 18, 1922), p. 160; *ibid.*, Vol. 8 (April 9, 1924), p. 261; *ibid.*, Vol. 8 (April 29, 1924), pp. 265-268.

[36] *Ibid.*, Vol. 8 (April 3, 1920), pp. 23-24; *ibid.*, Vol. 8 (May 26, 1920), pp. 30, 31.

[37] *Ibid.*, Vol. 8 (April 3, 1920), pp. 21-23.

[38] *Ibid.*, Vol. 7 (January 8, 1919), pp. 526, 527.

[39] *The George Washington University Bulletin*, Vol. 18, No. 5 (December, 1919), pp. 1-7; *ibid.*, Vol. 20, No. 1 (March, 1921), pp. 1-72.

[40] *Minutes of the Board of Trustees*, Vol. 8 (October 12, 1921), pp. 113-115.

[41] *Ibid.*, Vol. 8 (October 12, 1921), pp. 116-117; *ibid.*, Vol. 8 (February 13, 1922), p. 130; *ibid.*, Vol. 8 (May 31, 1922), p. 133; *ibid.*, Vol. 8 (May 31, 1923), p. 187.

[42] *Ibid.*, Vol. 8 (January 11, 1923), p. 173.

[43] *Ibid.*, Vol. 8 (May 25, 1921), p. 88; *ibid.*, Vol. 8 (October 12, 1921), p. 122; *ibid.*, Vol. 8 (January 11, 1923), p. 170.

44 *Ibid.*, Vol. 8 (May 31, 1922), p. 136; *ibid.*, Vol. 8 (December 12, 1922), p. 169; *ibid.*, Vol. 8 (January 11, 1923), pp. 170-171; *ibid.*, Vol. 8 (January 29, 1923), p. 177; *ibid.*, Vol. 8 (October 10, 1923), p. 218.

45 *Ibid.*, Vol. 8 (January 11, 1923), pp. 173-175.

46 Frederick Rudolph, *The American College and University* (New York, 1962), p. 344.

47 *Minutes of the Board of Trustees*, Vol. 8 (January 16, 1924), p. 246; *ibid.*, Vol. 8 (March 12, 1924), p. 257; *ibid.*, Vol. 8 (April 9, 1924), p. 260; *ibid.*, Vol. 8 (October 8, 1924), pp. 288-289.

48 *Ibid.*, Vol. 8 (May 24, 1924), p. 271; *ibid.*, Vol. 8 (November 12, 1924), pp. 295, 297; *ibid.*, Vol. 8 (December 10, 1924), p. 298; Elmer Louis Kayser, *Luther Rice, Founder of Columbian College* (Washington, 1966), p. 11; Elmer Louis Kayser, "Homes of the Law School," *GW: The George Washington University Magazine*, Fall, 1965, pp. 24-25.

49 *Minutes of the Board of Trustees*, Vol. 8 (October 27, 1926), p. 382; *ibid.*, Vol. 8 (January 19, 1927), pp. 391-394; *ibid.*, Vol. 8 (December 26, 1929), p. 529.

50 *Ibid.*, Vol. 8 (May 18, 1927), p. 416.

51 *Ibid.*, Vol. 8 (December 8, 1926), pp. 386-387; *ibid.*, Vol. 8 (May 9, 1927), pp. 405 ff.

52 *Ibid.*, Vol. 8 (June 4, 1924), pp. 273-274.

53 *GWU Handbook*, 1921-1922, p. 10.

54 Letter of Mrs. Charles P. Trussell to Elmer L. Kayser, July 30, 1968.

55 *Minutes of the Board of Trustees*, Vol. 8 (June 1, 1927), p. 419; *ibid.*, Vol. 8 (June 6, 1927), p. 420; *ibid.*, Vol. 8 (June 13, 1927), p. 422; *ibid.*, Vol. 8 (July 7, 1927), p. 424.

CHAPTER FOURTEEN
Bibliographical Comments

For the Marvin period material will be found in the *Minutes of the Board of Trustees;* the *University Bulletin; Confidential from Washington,* published by the University during the war years; the University student newspaper, the *Hatchet; George Washington University, Self-Evaluation of the University 1954,* an elaborate, multi-volume report on the University prepared for the Association of Colleges and Secondary Schools of the Middle States and Maryland; presidential letters in the Archives; and a great mass of informal publications, much of them critical of the administration.

Notes

1 *Self-Evaluation Study of the University,* The George Washington University (Washington, 1954), Introduction, pp. 24, 25.

2 *Ibid.*, pp. 27-32.

3 *Minutes of the Board of Trustees,* Vol. 8 (October 12, 1927), p. 436.

4 Daniel L. Borden, "William Cline Borden 1858-1934," *Medical Annals of the District of Columbia,* Vol. 5 (September and October, 1936), pp. 1-15.

[5] *Minutes of the Board of Trustees*, Vol. 8 (October 11, 1930), p. 585.

[6] *Ibid.*, Vol. 9 (December 10, 1931), p. 24.

[7] *Ibid.*, Vol. 8 (November 14, 1927), pp. 444-445.

[8] *The Charter and Acts Supplementary Thereto and the By-Laws of the Board of Trustees of The George Washington University* (Washington, D.C., n.d.), pp. 29-41.

[9] *Minutes of the Board of Trustees*, Vol. 8 (December 3, 1923), p. 244; *ibid.*, Vol. 8 (January 16, 1924), p. 245; *ibid.*, Vol. 8 (June 7, 1929), p. 521; *The George Washington University Bulletin*, March, 1917, p. 22.

[10] *Ibid.*, pp. 25-27; *Self-Evaluation Study of the University*, Sec. 2, pp. 47, 73-79.

[11] *Minutes of the Board of Trustees*, Vol. 8 (June 4, 1930), p. 566.

[12] *Ibid.*, Vol. 8 (October 9, 1930), p. 577.

[13] J. Ramsay MacDonald, *American Speeches* (Boston, 1930), pp. 36-39.

[14] *Minutes of the Board of Trustees*, Vol. 8 (December 11, 1930), p. 586.

[15] Elmer Louis Kayser, *Luther Rice, Founder of Columbian College* (Washington, 1966), p. 11.

[16] *The Kraftsman* (Washington), Vol. 6, No. 4 (October, 1925), p. 6.

[17] *Minutes of the Board of Trustees*, Vol. 8 (December 22, 1927), p. 448; *ibid.*, Vol. 8 (December 28, 1927), p. 450.

[18] Memo, Max Farrington to Elmer Louis Kayser, September 10, 1968.

[19] *Minutes of the Board of Trustees*, Vol. 8 (October 4, 1928), p. 483.

[20] *Ibid.*, Vol. 8 (March 27, 1929), p. 499; *ibid.*, Vol. 9 (October 8, 1931), pp. 17, 20; *ibid.*, Vol. 9 (December 10, 1931), p. 38; *ibid.*, Vol. 9 (December 10, 1931), p. 25.

[21] *Ibid.*, Vol. 8 (December 26, 1929), pp. 533, 540.

[22] *Ibid.*, Vol. 9 (February 9, 1933), pp. 68, 69, 73

[23] *Ibid.*, Vol. 9 (December 14, 1933), p. 119.

[24] *Ibid.*, Vol. 9 (October 11, 1934), pp. 153-154.

[25] *Ibid.*, Vol. 9 (October 11, 1934), p. 154.

[26] *Ibid.*, Vol. 9 (December 6, 1934), p. 157; *ibid.*, Vol. 9 (December 12, 1934), p. 162.

[27] *Ibid.*, Vol. 9 (July 16, 1937), p. 317.

[28] Cloyd Heck Marvin to Henry Phelps Gage, December 22, 1955.

[29] *Minutes of the Board of Trustees*, Vol. 9 (October 20, 1937), p. 236.

[30] *Ibid.*, Vol. 9 (June 3, 1937), p. 282.

[31] *Ibid.*, Vol. 8 (March 26, 1930), p. 555.

[32] *Ibid.*, Vol. 9 (February 14, 1935), pp. 172, 173; *ibid.*, Vol. 9 (March 11, 1937), p. 273; *ibid.*, Vol. 9 (February 10, 1938), p. 362; *ibid.*, Vol. 9 (March 11, 1937), p. 271.

[33] John A. Fleming to John C. Merriam, May 10, 1935.

[34] John A. Fleming, "The Fifth Washington Conference of Theoretical Physics," *Science*, Vol. 89, No. 2304 (February 24, 1939), pp. 180-182.

[35] George Gamow, "The Great Dane," *New York Times Book Review*, October 23, 1966, p. 6. © 1966 by The New York Times Company. Reprinted by permission of the *New York Times* and the estate of George Gamow.

[36] Ralph E. Lapp, "The Einstein Letter That Started It All," *New York Times Magazine*, August 2, 1964, pp. 13 ff.

[37] *The Lash* (Washington, D.C.), Vol. 1, No. 3 (February 2, 1926), p. 2.

[38] *Ibid.*, p. 4.

[39] *Minutes of the Board of Trustees*, Vol. 9 (October 13, 1932), p. 57; *The George Washington Union* (Washington, D.C.), 1936, p. 2; Thomas F. Neblett to Cloyd Heck Marvin, October 23, 1935; Cloyd Heck Marvin to Thomas F. Neblett, November 2, 1935.

[40] *Minutes of the Board of Trustees*, Vol. 9 (June 4, 1936), p. 236.

41 Everett H. Bellows to Cloyd Heck Marvin, November 30, 1937.

42 Charles J. Hendley to Cloyd Heck Marvin, April 6, 1936.

43 Cloyd Heck Marvin to Charles J. Hendley, April 17, 1936.

44 Statement of Cloyd Heck Marvin, December 12, 1934.

45 *Evening Star*, November 8, 1935.

46 *University Hatchet*, April 7, 1936, p. 2.

47 *Washington Post*, April 21, 1937, p. 11.

48 Helen Morton to the president, no date.

49 *Washington Daily News*, March 13, 1940; *ibid.*, June 12, 1940, p. 18.

50 *Minutes of the Board of Trustees*, Vol. 9 (March 14, 1940), pp. 571-572, 588-592.

51 *Ibid.*, Vol. 10 (February 18, 1942), pp. 68-82.

52 *Confidential from Washington*, No. 26 (April, 1945).

53 *Minutes of the Board of Trustees*, Vol. 10 (December 10, 1942), p. 115.

54 *Ibid.*, Vol. 10 (February 10, 1944), p. 167; *ibid.*, Vol. 10 (March 9, 1944), p. 169; *ibid.*, Vol. 10 (April 25, 1944), p. 175.

55 *Confidential from Washington*, No. 26 (April, 1945), p. 3.

56 Vannevar Bush to Cloyd Heck Marvin, April 14, 1946, in *Minutes of the Board of Trustees*, Vol. 10 (May 23, 1946), p. 301.

57 *Minutes of the Board of Trustees*, Vol. 10 (May 24, 1945), p. 230.

58 *Ibid.*, Vol. 10 (December 14, 1944), pp. 195, 196.

59 *Ibid.*, Vol. 10 (April 24, 1944), pp. 176-179.

60 *Ibid.*, Vol. 10 (May 25, 1944), pp. 176-179; *ibid.*, Vol. 10 (December 14, 1944), pp. 195 ff., 209; *ibid.*, Vol. 10 (February 10, 1949), pp. 471-474.

61 *Ibid.*, Vol. 10 (July 30, 1946), p. 304; *The Golden Book of the George Washington University Hospital* (Washington), March, 1949; U. S. Grant III, "The New Hospital," *The George Washington University Alumni Review*, Fall, 1946, pp. 1, 3.

62 *Minutes of the Board of Trustees*, Vol. 10 (December 12, 1946), p. 326.

63 *Ibid.*, Vol. 10 (November 12, 1941), p. 73.

64 *Ibid.*, Vol. 11 (March 22, 1956), p. 491; *ibid.*, Vol. 12 (December 13, 1956), p. 16.

65 *Ibid.*, Vol. 10 (December 9, 1948), p. 465; *ibid.*, Vol. 11 (March 8, 1951), p. 138; *ibid.*, Vol. 11 (October 13, 1955), pp. 445-448; *ibid.*, Vol. 11 (December 1, 1955), p. 454; *ibid.*, Vol. 12 (December 13, 1956), p. 2.

66 *Ibid.*, Vol. 10 (July 30, 1945), p. 34; *ibid.*, Vol. 12 (March 14, 1957), p. 47.

67 *Ibid.*, Vol. 12 (October 9, 1958), p. 163.

68 *Ibid.*, Vol. 10 (October 9, 1947), p. 384.

69 *Ibid.*, Vol. 10 (February 14, 1946), p. 267; *ibid.*, Vol. 10 (August 13, 1946), p. 307.

70 *Ibid.*, Vol. 11 (October 13, 1949), p. 37.

71 *Ibid.*, Vol. 10 (March 10, 1949), p. 485; *ibid.*, Vol. 11 (October 12, 1950), p. 111.

72 *Ibid.*, Vol. 11 (October 13, 1949), p. 30; *ibid.*, Vol. 11 (May 18, 1950), p. 72; *ibid.*, Vol. 11 (December 11, 1952), p. 243.

73 *Ibid.*, Vol. 11 (May 18, 1950), p. 72.

74 *Ibid.*, Vol. 11 (June 30, 1954), p. 242.

75 *Ibid.*, Vol. 11 (February 14, 1951), p. 203.

76 *Ibid.*, Vol. 11 (October 9, 1952), p. 241.

77 *Annual Report of the Dean for Sponsored Research*, 1957, p. 2; *ibid.*, 1959, p. 2; *The George Washington University Bulletin*, Vol. 67, No. 9 (March, 1968), pp. 163-169; *University Hatchet*, Vol. 65, No. 44 (April 10, 1969).

78 *Minutes of the Board of Trustees*, Vol. 11 (October 9, 1952), p. 240.

79 *Ibid.*, Vol. 11 (December 11, 1952), p. 247.

80 *Ibid.*, Vol. 12 (July 1, 1957), p. 90.

[81] *Ibid.*, Vol. 11 (February 12, 1953), p. 260.

[82] *Ibid.*, Vol. 11 (March 31, 1955), pp. 412-414; *ibid.*, Vol. 11 (May 19, 1955), pp. 430-431.

CHAPTER FIFTEEN

Bibliographical Comments

For the years since 1959, the Trustees' *Minutes* are still the indispensable guide. *GW*, the University's quarterly magazine; the *Hatchet*; the Washington newspapers; and the presidential letters in the Archives are important. A considerable number of printed and mimeographed student pamphlets and broadsides in the University's collection deal with such matters as the Gibbon Case, the pacifism of the 1930's, Vietnam, student participation in University governance and decision making.

Notes

[1] *Minutes of the Board of Trustees*, Vol. 12 (October 8, 1959), p. 285.

[2] *Ibid.*, Vol. 12 (May 12, 1960), pp. 347-350.

[3] *Ibid.*, Vol. 12 (October 13, 1960), p. 372.

[4] *Ibid.*, Vol. 12 (May 12, 1960), pp. 347, 354-358.

[5] *Ibid.*, Vol. 12 (October 13, 1960), p. 374.

[6] *Ibid.*, Vol. 12 (December 12, 1959), pp. 291-292.

[7] *Ibid.*, Vol. 12 (October 13, 1960), p. 262.

[8] *Ibid.*, Vol. 12 (May 11, 1961), p. 413.

[9] *Ibid.*, Vol. 12 (December 12, 1959), pp. 295-297; *ibid.*, Vol. 12 (February 11, 1960), p. 308; *ibid.*, Vol. 12 (May 11, 1961), p. 416.

[10] *Ibid.*, Vol. 12 (May 11, 1961), p. 414; *ibid.*, Vol. 12 (March 15, 1962), p. 487.

[11] *Ibid.*, Vol. 12 (October 13, 1960), p. 361; *ibid.*, Vol. 12 (December 8, 1960), p. 379.

[12] *Ibid.*, Vol. 12 (December 12, 1961), p. 460.

[13] *Ibid.*, Vol. 12 (October 13, 1960), p. 360.

[14] *Ibid.*, Vol. 12 (February 8, 1962), p. 484.

[15] Jacqueline Bouvier Kennedy Onassis, A.B. 1951, George Washington University.

[16] *The George Washington University Alumni Review*, President's Issue, Summer, 1961, pp. 16-18; Elmer Louis Keyser, "The Presidents and the University," *GW: The George Washington University Magazine*, Spring, 1964, pp. 14-16.

[17] *Minutes of the Board of Trustees*, Vol. 13 (May 9, 1963), p. 44.

[18] *Ibid.*, p. 99.

[19] *Ibid.*, Vol. 13 (October 17, 1963), pp. 125, 126.

[20] Elmer D. West, "The Joint Graduate Consortium," *Journal of Higher Education*, Vol. 36, No. 7 (October 1965), pp. 366-372; Articles of Incorporation of Consortium of Universities of the Washington Metropolitan Area, December, 1967; "Charter for the Establishment of Procedure for the Coordination of Graduate Study and Research Among the Five Universities of the District of Columbia," *NCEA Bulletin*, February, 1964.

21 *Minutes of the Board of Trustees,* Vol. 13 (October 17, 1963), p. 127; *ibid.,* Vol. 13 (March 19, 1964), p. 175.

22 *GW: The George Washington University Magazine,* Spring, 1964, inside back cover.

23 *Minutes of the Board of Trustees,* Vol. 13 (June 6, 1964), pp. 220 ff.

24 *Ibid.,* Vol. 13 (July 29, 1964), pp. 234-236.

25 *Ibid.,* Vol. 13 (October 15, 1964), pp. 238-239.

26 *Ibid.,* Vol. 13 (March 18, 1965), p. 304.

27 *Ibid.,* Vol. 13 (January 22, 1965), p. 256.

28 *Ibid.,* Vol. 13 (June 5, 1965), p. 342; *ibid.,* Vol. 13 (January 22, 1965), p. 257.

29 *Ibid.,* Vol. 13 (June 5, 1965), p. 344; "Faculty Revolt," *New York Times,* June 13, 1965, p. E8; "Unrest Stirs G.W. as Board Meets," *Washington Post,* June 5, 1965, p. B 1; "Synthetic Crisis at G.W.U.," *ibid.,* June 9, 1965; "Faculty Furor," *Evening Star,* June 10, 1965, p. A 12; *Minutes of a Special Committee of the Faculty Assembly on June 7, 1965,* with supplemental statement.

30 *Minutes of the Board of Trustees,* Vol. 13 (October 13, 1965), p. 364.

31 *Ibid.,* Vol. 13 (October 13, 1965), p. 366.

32 *Annual Report of the President,* The George Washington University, October, 1968, p. 15.

33 *Ibid.,* October, 1967, p. 19.

Presidents of the University

1821–1827	William Staughton
1828–1841	Stephen Chapin
1843–1854	Joel Smith Bacon
1855–1858	Joseph Getchell Binney
1859–1871	George Whitefield Samson
1871–1894	James Clarke Welling
1894–1895	Samuel Harrison Greene, Acting
1895–1900	Benaiah L. Whitman
1900–1902	Samuel Harrison Greene, Acting
1902–1910	Charles Willis Needham
1910–1918	Charles Herbert Stockton
1918–1921	William Miller Collier
1921–1923	Howard L. Hodgkins, *ad interim*
1923–1927	William Mather Lewis
1927–1959	Cloyd Heck Marvin
1959–1961	Oswald Symister Colclough, Acting
1961–1964	Thomas Henry Carroll
1964–1965	Oswald Symister Colclough, Acting
1965–	Lloyd Hartman Elliott

INDEX

New Jersey Regt

Ca...
Meridia...